D1084991

Love's Civil War

ALSO BY VICTORIA GLENDINNING

NON-FICTION

Trollope

Rebecca West: A Life

Vita: The Life of Vita Sackville West

Edith Sitwell: A Unicorn Among Lions

Elizabeth Bowen: Portrait of a Writer

Jonathan Swift

A Suppressed Cry

Hertfordshire

Sons and Mothers (ed., with Matthew Glendinning)

Leonard Woolf: A Biography

FICTION

Flight

The Grown-Ups

Electricity

Love's Civil War

ELIZABETH BOWEN AND CHARLES RITCHIE

Letters and Diaries

1941-1973

Edited by

VICTORIA GLENDINNING

with

JUDITH ROBERTSON

McClelland & Stewart

Library and Archives Canada Cataloguing in Publication

Bowen, Elizabeth, 1899-1973.
Love's civil war : Elizabeth Bowen and Charles Ritchie, letters and diaries 1941-1973 / edited by Victoria Glendinning ; with Judith Robertson.

ISBN 978-0-7710-3566-1

1. Bowen, Elizabeth, 1899-1973. – Correspondence. 2. Ritchie, Charles 1906-1995. – Diaries. 3. Bowen, Elizabeth, 1899-1973. 4. Ritchie, Charles, 1906-1995. 5. Novelists, English – 20th century – Correspondence. 6. Diplomats – Canada – Diaries. I. Glendinning, Victoria II. Ritchie, Charles, 1906-1995. III. Robertson, Judith IV. Title.

PR6003.O6757Z48 2008 823'.912 C2008-901275-5

We acknowledge the financial support of the Government of Canada through the Book Publishing Industry Development Program and that of the Government of Ontario through the Ontario Media Development Corporation's Ontario Book Initiative. We further acknowledge the support of the Canada Council for the Arts and the Ontario Arts Council for our publishing program.

Typeset in New Baskerville by M&S, Toronto
Printed and bound in the United States of America

McClelland & Stewart Ltd.
75 Sherbourne Street
Toronto, Ontario
M5A 2P9
www.mcclelland.com

1 2 3 4 5 12 11 10 09 08

Contents

Editor's Introduction

Elizabeth Bowen is increasingly recognized as one of the most important and best-loved British women novelists of the first half of the twentieth century. In life she was charming, and perhaps a little formidable. In this book the private Elizabeth Bowen is revealed: passionate, vulnerable, fierce, and brave. Above all, she was loving – of her friends and family and of the man she loved more than any other, Charles Ritchie.

Born in 1899, she was, as she liked to say, almost the same age as the century. When she met the young Canadian diplomat Charles Ritchie during World War II, she had been married for eighteen years and was an established and successful author, having published six novels – among them the best-selling *The Death of the Heart* (1938) – and four books of short stories. Another collection of stories, *Look at All Those Roses*, appeared in 1941, the year that she and Ritchie met.

For Charles Ritchie – unmarried, something of a philanderer, and seven years younger than she – it was, at first, just a particularly intriguing and flattering affair, and one that he might well have put an end to. For Elizabeth Bowen, it was a matter of life and death from the beginning. Their love fuelled both her creative energy and what Ritchie called her 'life-illusion' – as he shrewdly observed early on, if their love had failed she might not then have found another.

But gradually Elizabeth Bowen became essential to Charles Ritchie, and to his sense of himself. Their world of love, and her idea of him and of his qualities, were the very opposite of the conventional social and diplomatic life he wanted, and needed, to lead. She became the secret sharer of his imaginative, subversive, inner self, and represented the poetry of life. While their relationship was sometimes problematic to him, his greatest dread was that she would stop loving him. If she did, that inner self would shrivel.

There is a particular poignancy in the fact that Charles's private diaries have survived, but not his letters to Elizabeth; while her letters to him have survived, but no diaries. What he was feeling, and what she was feeling (or told him she was feeling), do not always tally. That imbalance is one of the painful but generally undiscoverable truths of love.

Charles's diary documents the beginning of their love story, which lasted until Elizabeth's death twenty-eight years later. In all those years they were never parted emotionally, even though they were never under the same roof for more than a week at a time. In my own mind, this book is unofficially dedicated to all those unofficial couples who are caught up, long-term, in what Charles called 'love's civil war.'

Elizabeth Bowen was Anglo-Irish, from Protestant Ascendancy families on both her father's and her mother's side. Her family home, Bowen's Court in Co Cork, Ireland, was a late eighteenth-century 'big house' in the Anglo-Irish tradition, built by an ancestor on lands granted by Oliver Cromwell. In Elizabeth's girlhood, all Ireland was part of the United Kingdom. She grew up into the 'Troubles' which followed the Easter Rebellion of 1916, when many Anglo-Irish mansions were burnt by Sinn Fein, as happens in her novel *The Last September* (1929). Bowen's Court, however, survived.

When the Irish Free State was proclaimed in 1922, with the six counties of what became Northern Ireland remaining under British rule, there was civil war in the Free State between those nationalists who accepted partition and republicans under de Valera who did not. In the 1930s de Valera's party, Fianna Fail, prevailed in the polls and a new constitution in 1937 established Eire as a sovereign state, in which the Roman Catholic church had a special position. Eire remained part of the British Commonwealth for another twelve years, becoming the Republic of Ireland in 1949.

These cataclysmic events form the background to the Ireland that Elizabeth Bowen writes about so eloquently in her letters to Charles. The Anglo-Irish who stayed on, like the Bowens, always in some sense 'settlers' after hundreds of years – but with their feudal position diminished in the new dispensation – maintained their beautiful, often uncomfortable houses 'under the strong rule of the family myth' (as Elizabeth wrote in *Bowen's Court,* 1942). There was in the Anglo-Irish psyche a mystical, dreamy streak, connected with a heightened sense of the past and the magic of place, which Elizabeth inherited in full. There was also a hearty, horsey, streak; she always enjoyed the hospitable, vital, showy side of Irish life. In any society, she enjoyed being with people who liked to gossip and be comfortable and have a good time. She liked, too, the company of sophisticated intellectuals but, although many of her friends were writers, the purely literary world did not stimulate her.

An only child, she spent her first seven winters in Dublin where her lawyer father, Robert Cole Bowen, practised at the Irish bar, and the summers at Bowen's Court. Then her father, always a little odd, succumbed to severe mental illness. It was thought inadvisable for his wife and daughter to remain with him, so Elizabeth and her mother moved to England, where there were aunts and cousins. They perched on the Kent coast, in Hythe and Sandgate, in a series of rented rose-covered seaside villas which seemed to Elizabeth far more romantic and exciting than the fine houses of her relations in Ireland. The Kent coast always retained its allure for her. She recreated its atmosphere in her fiction, notably in her late novel *The Little Girls* (1964), and it was in Hythe that she made her last home.

In September 1912, when Elizabeth was thirteen, her mother died of cancer at home in Hythe. Elizabeth's upbringing was taken over by 'a committee of aunts,' between whose homes in England and Ireland she shuttled. Her troubled childhood left her with a stammer, and a policy of 'not noticing.' A characteristic Bowen phrase is 'life with the lid on.' What fascinated her as a writer was the moment when the surface of life cracks, revealing agonizing truths beneath. In spite of her sociable nature, she thought of herself as solitary and '*farouche*,' 'unrelatable,' always adjusting to other people's expectations – except with Charles Ritchie.

Elizabeth's father recovered, and remarried. There were summer holidays again at Bowen's Court during her teens. The British Army presence in Ireland was increased in the aftermath of 1916, providing dancing-partners for the daughters of the 'big houses,' and Elizabeth refers in these letters to her brief and mistaken early engagement to a young officer. Most of the time she remained in England, flitting between aunts. She wrote her first story, 'Breakfast,' which was also the first story in her first published book, in the attic of her Aunt Laura's house in Hertfordshire. Aunt Gertrude, the mother of Elizabeth's favourite cousin Audrey, lived in Oxfordshire. It was while staying with Aunt Gertrude that Elizabeth met Alan Charles Cameron, the man she would marry in 1923 – the same year as that first book of stories, *Encounters*, was published.

Alan Cameron was six years older than Elizabeth. Conscientious, intelligent, and a born administrator, he was Assistant Secretary for Education for the county of Northamptonshire. He was quite good-looking, with a high, mannered voice which contrasted oddly with his military bluffness. At first, he was the dominant partner. He had an Oxford degree and had fought in the Great War (he won the Military Cross). Elizabeth was not university educated, and was a little gauche. She had big hands and feet, a strong physique, and features which were more striking than pretty. But she was definitely attractive, to both men and women. (Her looks came into their own in maturity, around the time she met Charles Ritchie.) Alan, with his feminine streak, taught her how to present herself, and how to dress smartly in ways that suited her. Always, Alan looked after her.

In 1925 Alan got a new job as Secretary for Education for the city of Oxford, and they moved to Old Headington, up the hill on the outskirts of the city. Elizabeth blossomed in Oxford. Her next book of stories came out the following year, and her first novel *The Hotel* the year after that, 1927. Two years later *The Last September* was published . . . and so on, in a fertile stream. Praised by the critics, popular with a general readership, she was of great interest to the clever, sociable young academics she met in Oxford such as David Cecil and Isaiah Berlin, who became lifelong friends.

When in 1935 she and Alan moved to London – he was appointed Secretary to the Central Council of School Broadcasting at the BBC – the Oxford friends were supplemented by London friends. Elizabeth Bowen became the centre of a coterie, and the Camerons' house in Clarence Terrace, Regent's Park, a rendezvous for the gifted and talented, both literary and otherwise. This is the Elizabeth Bowen whom Charles Ritchie met in 1941.

From that point on, the story tells itself. In this book, you will hear the lovers' voices. Circumstances and geography were against them, but listening to their voices one understands what they had in common. Both 'passed' in upper-class English society, and yet, because of their respective hinterlands in colonial Canada and Ireland, each came at it from an oblique angle, which made them unusually observant; Elizabeth felt that they were both in some sense 'spies.' They shared a deep sense of family, a fascination with all social relationships, acute aesthetic sensibility and an appetite for life; each aspired to live and work at the highest and most intense level, and both possessed an undogmatic belief in 'another world than this.' And, one cannot help remarking, a frank dependence on alcohol.

But two important people in the story are voiceless, even though their words are sometimes reported. They are Charles's wife, Sylvia Smellie, and Elizabeth's husband, Alan Cameron.

Alan was an able and a cultivated man, but he was not amusing or sophisticated like his wife's literary, academic and social friends. They did not see the point of him. He went straight to his study when he came home from the office hearing, from the drawing-room the animated voices of those he called the 'Black Hats.' (Visitors left their hats in the hall.) He was not overawed by the success of his wife. He knew the 'displaced' Elizabeth he had married, and that their marriage was her anchor and her security. He also knew that he was not enough for her, sexually or otherwise. He did not see through her, he saw through *to* her.

Elizabeth was loyal to the institution of marriage. She believed in social convention, good manners, and the Anglican Church. Divorce was never on the cards. The Camerons' alliance was always close – but companionate, not sexual. There were no children. Elizabeth had had affairs before Charles Ritchie: with the Irish writer Sean O'Faolain, and with a young lecturer at Wadham College, Oxford, Humphry House, which had ended much as her affair with Charles could have ended, but did not. Elizabeth, high-handed and ambitious in love, had seen House's marriage as no bar to continuing their liaison. Nor did she when Charles, in 1948, married Sylvia. Elizabeth strove to see Sylvia, and subtly to make Charles see Sylvia, as an irrelevance – which she was not.

But while Charles and Elizabeth were both married, essentially nothing did change. It was when Alan Cameron died in 1952 that a cruel imbalance became apparent. Elizabeth was a middle-aged woman on her own, having difficulty in maintaining Bowen's Court, which she thought of as 'their' house – hers and Charles's – even though he could so seldom be there with her.

Charles was by now outstandingly successful in his absorbing international career, a public man with a devoted wife. In her letters Elizabeth presents herself, not inaccurately, as busy, sociable, filling her life with her writing, travel and friends, remaining the brilliantly life-enhancing and vital person whom Charles loved and could not do without. As she wrote to him, 'The moment one is sad one is ordinary.' Only occasionally does she lose her grip. The surface of life cracks. Her awful loneliness, and her bitter resentment of Sylvia, break through. Her loyalty to the institution of marriage does not include Charles's. For him, the meetings and partings and subterfuges which make Elizabeth so unhappy are part of the established pattern of his life. From early on, he was physically unfaithful to her.

For Elizabeth, whose fiction hinges on arrivals and departures, their fractured life provided the intensity she needed, the sense of living life at its highest. She was an artist even in love, fighting for love's survival. She said to her former lover Humphry House that she was 'a writer before she was a woman.' It is in Charles's absence, writing to him about his remembered presence, pouring out with instinctive artistry the words and phrases about himself and their unbreakable love which would bind him to her, that she is most brilliantly Elizabeth Bowen. She thought she wanted more than anything to live with him all the time. But if they had married, might theirs not have become just like the 'ordinary' marriages which she so despised, and which in his own case he made tolerable by his physical infidelities?

The letters to Charles are Elizabeth Bowen's 'writing' in almost the same way as her books and stories are. Even though her commitment to her work is patently paramount, she has a modest reticence, saying little to Charles about her books and their success – until, late in life, she starts writing *The Little Girls*, when she shares the process of creation with him as she had not before. The other exception to this is *The Heat of the Day* (1949), which is 'his' book and dedicated to him.

These are love letters, but if that were all, they would not be so valuable. Elizabeth Bowen's narrative and graphic talent unfolds for Charles the intimate texture of social and domestic life in Ireland, and of literary and social life in England. Opinionated and prejudiced, she can say anything, however outrageous, to him. American campuses, cities and landscapes in Italy, Spain, the Middle East, all leap into focus in the brilliant light of her perception, whether loved or loathed. She sends him her uniquely candid pen sketches of obscure eccentrics, and of eminent friends and acquaintances whose fame lives on and who figure in the memoirs and biographies of her times – writers, statesmen, scholars, socialites, English, American and Canadian – not just well-known names with labels, but real men and women with voices and smells and annoying or delightful mannerisms. We bemoan with her the exhausted postwar austerity of the 1950s with no sense of perspective on what is to come – and then share her delighted astonishment at London in what came to be called the Swinging Sixties. In short, to read her letters to Charles is to experience history in real time.

Elizabeth Bowen believed there was an affinity between writing and witchcraft. Charles too thinks of her as a witch – 'a good witch,' 'an immensely potent witch.' Their personalities had different weights. Her constancy is heartbreaking, her strength of will formidable. It was by the power of her will that their love survived all difficulties, as Charles acknowledges – just as he acknowledges that it is by the power of Sylvia's will that his marriage was a happy one.

Their love, and the life of the heart, are the mainsprings of Elizabeth Bowen's life. She binds Charles to her with her artistry, her love, her appreciation and praise, showing him as in a golden mirror his ideal self, and making that ideal self real to him. In the course of reading this book, one is inevitably left with mysteries and unanswered questions. We cannot know, to take just one example of many, exactly what happened between Elizabeth, Charles and Sylvia in Bonn, which nearly put an end to the relationship. I have preferred not to make editorial guesses, but to stand back and leave it to the reader to speculate intuitively. That is all that any of us can do. You may feel sometimes that Elizabeth is too strenuous, and that she is making most of the running. But Charles's diaries tell their own complex story. Do not look at the last sentence now. But when you reach it, I do believe you will feel that what he says there is accurate.

In the two decades between Elizabeth Bowen's death and his own, Charles Ritchie constantly fretted about what he should do with her letters to him and proposed destroying them – just as he had destroyed his to her when they were finally returned to him, He said he could not bear anyone else ever to read them. Yet since, undoubtedly, they were remarkable letters by an important author, some of his friends, including myself, urged him to bequeath them, with an embargo, to a university library. This did not appeal to him.

He did not, in the end, destroy her letters. But he culled them, removing the most intimate material by cutting or tearing, by taking out whole pages or, sometimes, whole batches of letters covering consecutive weeks or months,. There is nothing here, for example, about the death of her husband Alan Cameron, nor about her last farewell to Bowen's Court; nor, one may be sure, about the worst of her resentment and hatred of Charles's married state.

He bequeathed the surviving letters, with his diaries, to his niece Elizabeth Ritchie, of whom Elizabeth Bowen had been fond and who figures in these pages. She died in 2001, leaving the letters and diaries to her friend and contemporary Judith Robertson, the daughter of Charles's senior colleague and longtime friend Norman Robertson. Judith Robertson provides the following biographical introduction to Charles Ritchie.

VICTORIA GLENDINNING,
Bruton 2008

Charles Stewart Almon Ritchie, diplomat and diarist, was born in Halifax, Nova Scotia, on 23 September 1906. He was educated at Trinity College School, Port Hope, Ontario; King's College University, Halifax; Pembroke College, Oxford; Harvard University, Cambridge, Massachusetts; and École Libre des Sciences Politiques, Paris. His professional life with the Canadian government began in 1934 when, as he said, 'the Victorian Gothic portals of the Department of External Affairs opened' and he entered as third secretary. His was a brilliant career, the most important jobs were to be his, but he may well be best remembered as a diarist.

The Halifax society into which Charles Ritchie was born was, as he wrote, one 'in which everything British was Best and "Upper Canada" was a remote and unloved abstraction.' His family had been in Canada for four or five generations and they considered themselves 'Nova Scotians first. Canadians second. They were North Americans with a difference and they clung tenaciously to the difference.' When Charles was ten his father died, and from then on his mother shuttled Charles and his younger brother Roland back and forth across the Atlantic until 'England began to seem the other half of one's life.' It was while Charles was on the Canadian side of the Atlantic and a student at 'an Anglican concentration camp of a boarding school in Ontario' that a letter came to him from the then Prime Minister of Canada, Sir Robert Borden. Sir Robert, a law partner and lifelong friend of Charles's father, had been told by Mrs Ritchie of her son's interest in international affairs, and suggested that Charles should consider a career in the soon-to-be established Canadian Foreign Service. As was so well put in a foreword to *The Siren Years*, 'Thus was planted the germ of an ambition.'

As a young man Charles tried journalism (a stint with the *Evening Standard* in London) and teaching (a year at Pickering College, Ontario). Neither proved satisfactory and, in search of a 'settled profession,' he sought out my father, Norman Robertson, with a letter of introduction, to ask his advice on applying to the Department of External Affairs. My father, who had been with the department since 1929, was encouraging. Charles was taken on, and became the colleague and friend of 'a handful of unusually gifted men who shared the belief that Canada had its own role to play in the world and a conception of what that role should be.' This group of Canadian nationalists included Mike Pearson (later to become Prime Minister), Norman Robertson, and Hume Wrong; these three, with their families, became Charles's lifelong friends. The period has since been described as the golden age of Canadian diplomacy, and Charles Ritchie was part of it.

His professional career, which began in Ottawa in 1934, took Charles to Washington as Third Secretary in 1936, to London in 1939, Ottawa in 1945, Paris as Counsellor in 1947, and back to Ottawa as Assistant Under-Secretary of State for External Affairs in 1950. In 1954 he went to the Federal Republic of Germany as Ambassador; in 1958 to New York as Canada's Ambassador and Permanent Representative to the United Nations, and in 1962 was appointed Ambassador to the United States of America. His last two posts were Canadian Permanent Representative and Ambassador to NATO and to the office of the European Economic Council in 1966 and Canadian High Commissioner to the United Kingdom in 1967.

Charles was posted to London in 1939 as Private Secretary to the High Commissioner, Vincent Massey (later Canadian Governor General), and remained there in various capacities until 1945. It was this period that he captured in *The Siren Years*, a selection from his diaries considered one of the best books about London in the Second World War, and it was during this time that he met and fell in love with Elizabeth Bowen.

When he returned to Ottawa from London in 1945, Charles tried, as he wrote, 'to adapt myself to be a success here, to find a wife, to get full marks as an efficient higher civil servant.' He had realized that 'what I feel for E[lizabeth] with all its imperfections (on my side) is the "Love of my Life" and that I must never hope to find that again. Any other love will have to be of a different kind.' He found that 'different kind' of love with his cousin Sylvia Smellie, whom he married in 1948. Their grandfathers were brothers and they had known each other for many years. Their marriage, unconventional though it may have been, was an alliance based on companionship, love, and a slowly developing dependency, particularly Charles's dependence on Sylvia.

Over the years, as Charles battled the forces of convention and domesticity, he found in Sylvia a deep loyalty and, though not always an acceptance, an understanding of him. She was an ideal partner through their years of diplomatic life, devoting herself to the demands of her position as his wife. A sadness of the marriage was that they were unable to have the children they both wanted so much. It was not, as Charles said, a brand of married happiness that showed up in a diary, but it allowed Sylvia to reply, when complimented by him on looking twenty-eight when she was in fact fifty-six, 'It's happy, happy marriage.' In his diary entry that day Charles wrote, 'and it is a happy marriage, partly because she has willed it to be so.'

Despite the impression sometimes given by Charles's diaries, his work as a diplomat and civil servant was of great interest and importance to him, and there were periods when the demands and excitement of his work for the Canadian government absorbed him completely. This was particularly true of times he worked in Ottawa, the centre of policy-making, and when he was Ambassador and Permanent Representative to the United Nations 1958-62. He felt at home in England, and his years as High Commissioner in London (1967-71) were ones he enjoyed fully. He had maintained his connections with the literary and political worlds, begun at Oxford and developed in part through his relationship with Elizabeth Bowen. The names of the Sitwell and Buchan families, Lady Diana Cooper, Eric Duncannon (later the Earl of

Bessborough), Miriam Rothschild, Isaiah Berlin, Nancy Mitford and Lord David Cecil, among many others, appear and reappear in his diary entries.

Charles had less satisfaction from his work as Canadian Ambassador to the United States. He did not find the Washington of the Kennedy years to be a replay of Camelot. The issue of nuclear weapons, with John Diefenbaker, the Canadian Prime Minister, opposed to the arming of Canada's Bomarc missiles with nuclear warheads, was a test of Canadian/U.S. relations seldom equalled. During the Johnson presidency, Canadian and American relations were also strained, this time by differences over the Vietnam War. As Ambassador to the Federal Republic of Germany, a post he had accepted in part to be closer to Elizabeth Bowen, Charles found both his imagination and energy exhausted. He was twice posted to Paris, where he had been a student and where he would always be haunted by his affair with Anne Maher, his first love; and by times spent there with Elizabeth Bowen.

Charles, because he hated 'being exterior to what is going on around me and always fear[ed] the easy path of just seeing the other diplomats . . . and living in an artificial enclosure' found his way under the carapace of national stereotypes wherever he was posted. He learned the language, he read the literature, he worked at understanding the people. As Elizabeth wrote to him on 1 January 1958, 'You have so much more fibre and self-command than I have – indeed than most people have. You see, along with the effective, operative side of yourself, you carry the burden of an imaginative nature – for it is a burden, as well as a gift, the equivalent of genius.'

In a diary entry of 1938, Charles, staying at the Vanderbilts' Newport home, writes: 'On my breakfast tray was a gardenia in a glass of water. Anxious to miss nothing, I was sniffing it when the footman appeared.' It is the 'anxious to miss nothing' that crystallizes Charles for me. He may have thought 'appetite for life' an overworked phrase, but it very much applied to him. It was this quality that made him so attractive, particularly to women. He was an unlikely-looking Lothario; there was a thin beakiness about him, but his loves saw him otherwise. He had many love affairs, and many long-standing and important friendships with both sexes. It was the intellectual cast of mind of those he met that was often the catalyst for his attention and friendship. He had a fascination for human relations, and could divine the kernel of interest in people seemingly without any. He was the man everyone wanted to have at their party – the most amusing man you could meet. His reputation must have imposed a strain, but he lived up to it.

When Charles retired from his last posting as High Commissioner to London in 1971, he returned to Ottawa. Though he continued in retirement as a special advisor to the Privy Council, he had time to turn to publishing selections from his diaries. Between 1974 and 1982 he published *The Siren Years: Undiplomatic Diaries 1937-1945* [subtitled *An Appetite for Life* in Canada]; *Diplomatic Passport: More Undiplomatic Diaries 1946-1962*; and *Storm Signals*, covering the following decade. The published diaries constitute about one tenth of the surviving original diaries. It is from the original diaries that passages are selected for this book. *My Grandfather's House* (1987), his final book, is a series of portraits of family and friends. Charles recognized that he gave his relatives a particular status. He was infinitely forgiving, and found many of them fascinating in ways not always apparent to those outside the charmed circle. He travelled with family portraits of dubious authenticity, and had them hung in each new residence.

After Elizabeth Bowen died in 1973, Charles wrote to Anne Maher: 'I feel as though I were all the time carrying a very full glass. I mean I have to walk carefully or all this grief will overflow. You see I never lost anyone except my mother and that was a long time ago and "in another country". I never knew this pain before. She was buried in the small church at Bowen's Court – it snowed that day. How can I write about it?'

Despite feeling that the poetry in his life had died with Elizabeth, he and Sylvia continued the pattern of dividing life between Ottawa, London, and his beloved Chester, Nova Scotia. Charles, as always, kept his social contacts alive: the Press Club in Ottawa, the old friends in London, the family and friends in Nova Scotia. In the later years Charles, incompetent domestically and never able to drive, was increasingly dependent on Sylvia for the practicalities of life. The diaries from this time show an acceptance of domestic happiness and he writes more of his appreciation and love for Sylvia. Elizabeth Ritchie, Charles's beloved niece, came to be the one who made a social life and travel possible. Despite illness and frailty, Charles could write to Anne Maher, 'We are the lucky ones – you and I – just when zest seems dead – it comes rushing back . . . like a gust of wind.' He also escaped what he most feared as he grew older – 'the drying-up of feeling,' which Elizabeth Bowen had called 'the Arctic Circle of Old Age.'

Charles Ritchie died in Ottawa, Ontario on 7 June 1995. Sylvia's death followed five months later, on 14 November 1995.

JUDITH ROBERTSON,
Toronto 2008

Editor's Note on the Text

Editorial cuts are represented by '. . .'. Elizabeth Bowen and Charles Ritchie's own suspension marks are represented by '. . .'.

Book titles are italicised where they are given correctly, otherwise they are as they wrote them. Occasional small liberties have been taken with punctuation in the interest of clarity. This includes standardisation of dates and addresses in headings to both letters and diaries. Some sentences, both in the letters and diaries, do not make grammatical sense but that is how they were written.

The text has been cut, but never for reasons of taste or discretion. Some of Elizabeth's attitudes and prejudices will give offence. Some are entirely idiosyncratic, others typical of her class and period.

The beginnings of Elizabeth's letters, as of most people's love letters, tend to be similar: frantic flurries about whether Charles's expected letter has come or not come, whether he has received her last letter, where he should post his next one, when she may next see him, when and where this will be, and so on. After samples of this, the preliminaries have generally been cut, as have some details, throughout the letters, of the practical arrangements of their semi-shared lives.

Some dozen letters have been omitted entirely, either because they referred forward to events or persons described more fully in the next one, or because, written to maintain continuity and contact rather than because Elizabeth had anything of particular interest to say, they were inconsequential, repetitive or rambling. The narrow predictability of her social life in her last years at Bowen's Court has also occasioned some cutting.

Chiefly for reasons of space, a certain amount of 'diary-letter' travelogue, and some anecdotes and descriptions, have also been omitted. Care has been taken to omit nothing important, and nothing strikingly funny, sad, or particularly characteristic. Readers of Elizabeth Bowen's fiction know how tellingly she wrote about landscape and weather, but in these letters she sometimes wrote just too much about the weather for present purposes.

Elizabeth almost always dated her letters with the day of the week and the date of the month, but not with the year. Charles Ritchie cannot have kept them in a very organized way, and when he went through them he wrote the year – or what he thought was the year – on each one. Elizabeth Ritchie, afterwards, did the same where she did not agree with his decision. Some changes in the final ordering for publication have been made according to internal evidence, to known chronology, and to common sense. I could not swear in a court of law that the result is wholly accurate, but I hope that it is.

V.G.

Acknowledgements

For the use of Elizabeth Bowen's copyright material, I thank Finlay Colley and Curtis Brown Ltd. For the use of Charles Ritchie's copyright material, and for permission to reproduce the words of both Bowen and Ritchie, I thank Judith Robertson, as also for her labour in transcribing the letters and diaries, and for her invaluable input and patient responses to my many queries about matters Canadian.

I would also like to thank Francesca Main and Allison Moore at Simon & Schuster UK; Dinah Forbes at McClelland & Stewart, Toronto; my agent Bruce Hunter; and Robyn Karney, for her editorial skills.

Special thanks, too, to Jane Urquhart, Charles Ritchie's friend and mine, for her encouragement and support at the inception of the project, and to Ramsay Derry, Charles Ritchie's editor and literary advisor. I am also grateful to those who responded to queries, unanswerable even by the resources of the London Library or by Google, on a wildly varied range of topics: Roy Foster, Colin Franklin, Henry Hardy, Nicholas Lander, Hermione Lee, Tim Moreton (at the National Portrait Gallery), John Julius Norwich.

VG

part

one

1941-1952

1941

Charles Ritchie's diary entries throughout are instantly recognisable for the reader by their dated headings in bold type. From time to time, where helpful to indicate his whereabouts, the place from where Charles is writing is given in [ ].

Elizabeth Bowen's letters (and her whereabouts) are obvious from their italicised addresses and dates.

Charles Ritchie did not keep Elizabeth Bowen's early letters to him. The first four years of their relationship can be traced only from his point of view, through his diaries.

He was thirty-five when they met, unmarried, and working in London as Second Secretary at the Canadian High Commission (promoted to First Secretary from 1942). She was forty-one, an established and successful author of novels and short stories, living with her husband Alan Cameron at 2 Clarence Terrace, Regent's Park, London.

These selections do not reflect the busy working lives both were leading, the large numbers of friends they saw together and separately, or the overwhelming fact of the war – with deaths of friends in the services, the threat of German invasion, and the heightened and heady atmosphere of a London blacked-out by night and under the constant onslaught of air raids and bombings.

10 February [London]

Weekend at Oxford. Motored down with Alistair Buchan and went first to Elsfield[1] to the christening of Bill B's child. . . . Met Elizabeth Bowen, well-dressed middle-aged with the air of being the somewhat worldly wife of a don, a narrow intelligent face, watching eyes and a cruel, witty mouth. I had expected something more Irish, more silent and brooding, and at the same time more irresponsible. I was slightly put off by her being so much 'on the spot'. She told me that the early part of *The House in Paris*,[2] that part about the two children, had 'come to her' without her being conscious of inventing or thinking it out.

2 September

She says it began when she saw me standing outside the church after the christening, but I find that hard to believe. It smells to me of literary artifice. But then with her I never know what to believe. She croons away at me in that sympathetic, sensitive young voice of hers, with its stutter of shyness. She seems all romance and girlish seriousness. It can't all be a bluff – and yet . . . She is as acute as a razor blade and about as merciful. . . . She is a witch, that's what it is. In the first place how can a woman of forty with gold bangles and the face of a woman of forty and the air of a don's wife, how can such a woman have such a body – like Donatello's David I told

---

[1] Elsfield Manor, the house five miles from Oxford of the late John Buchan (1st Baron Tweedsmuir, 1875-1940) and his widow Susan (née Grosvenor), a close friend of EB's. Buchan had combined successful novel-writing with a career in public life, and died in office as Governor General of Canada.

Johnnie, William and [*sic*] Alastair were the Buchans' sons, and friends of CR. They also had an elder sister, Alice. William (Billy) Buchan had lodged with EB and Alan Cameron at Clarence Terrace when he first worked in London, and EB had a special fondness for him. In 1942 both EB and CR were at Alastair Buchan's wedding to Hope Gilmour, where CR was best man.

[2] EB's novel *The House in Paris* was published in 1935.

her when I first saw what it was like. Those small firm breasts, that modelled neck set with such beauty on her shoulders, that magnificent back. . . . Would I ever have fallen for her if it hadn't been for her books? I very much doubt it. But now I can't separate her from her literary self. It's as if the woman I 'love' were always accompanied by a companion spirit infinitely more exciting and more poetic and more profound than E herself. . . . When it comes to writing, well I had a letter from her the other day so blunderingly expressed, so repetitive, that the least of the characters in one of her books would never have been guilty of it.

6 September

I tried to tell her some of this the other day at lunch, but I didn't get far. The trouble is I now believe that she is in love with me . . . Like all women she fears that because she has become my mistress I shall think she is a 'light woman'. It's a waste of time trying to discuss character, personal behaviour etc with a woman who is in love with one; it always comes back to a few simple variations on the one theme.

I told her how bewildering it was being in love with a genius. She says she has no genius, only talent and great concentration.

29 September

'Take it from one of the best living novelists that people's personalities are not interesting,' she said in a dry voice unlike the voice she uses with me as a rule. 'Except,' she added, 'when you are in love with them.' She is in love with me and she talks about me to me; she describes my smiles, when I am smiling; my gestures when I touch her. Everything is put into words in that faintly sing-song Anglo-Irish voice of hers. She says in a novel which describes one of her other lovers that his body and his gestures were 'losing their naiveté'. I don't wonder if she did the same thing to him. I am perpetually showing off to her, like a male coquette. . . . She treats me as though I were a boy. I resent this, but at the same time I know that she has fastened on to something adolescent in my nature. . . .

It is graceless of me to think like this. I suppose I get the kind of love I deserve. The contrast between her face and body seems symbolic. . . . It is a face with a strong family resemblance to Virginia Woolf, and even to George Eliot. It is a powerful, mature, rather handsome face. But the body is that of a young woman. The most beautiful body I have seen. It is pure in line and contour, lovely long legs and arms and small almost immature firm breasts. Naked she becomes poetic, ruthless and young. . . .

Our first few days and nights were like one of her intensely poetic short stories. But the affair threatens to develop into one of her long psychological novels in which I see myself being smothered in love and then dissected at leisure.

If I am not cruel now, she will be later. . . .

The truth is that I am sick of the whole thing and wish it was over.

Every now and then I recapture for an hour or so the charm of the first few days. For instance that afternoon when we went to see the roses in Regents Park. For days we had been talking of those roses, but I could not get away from the office before nightfall and it seemed as if we should never go together to see them. Then on one perfect September afternoon she telephoned to say that if we did not go today it would be too late, they were almost over. So I put away the FO boxes in the safe, locked up the files and took a taxi to Regents Park. As we walked together I seemed to see the flowers through the lens of her sensibility. The whole scene, the misty river, the Regency villas with their walled gardens and damp lawns, and the late September afternoon weather blended into a dream of our love . . .

She holds me by the imagination. My daylight feelings, solid affections and passions are on another plane and go on untouched.

Yet I am getting very fond of her in a mistrustful way.

18 October

My bed smells of her over-sweet violet scent. It is queer that she uses such an obvious scent – the perfume that goes with blondes and floating veils and sentiment . . .

I am reading *The Death of the Heart*[3] in her special edition. It is an exact description of her house and of her husband. The position of the sofa in the drawing-room, the electric fire in his 'study' are all described exactly as they are. What is alarming is the husband is an unsparing portrait of A. I read this novel with most curious feelings as 'a work of the imagination'; it has been destroyed for me by my knowledge of the particular circumstances. . . . She took that from here, she copied that turn of speech, that must be so-and-so, these thoughts go through my mind as I am reading. It is like eating an elaborate dish after seeing the materials of which it is made up lying about in the kitchen, or being so near the ballet that you can see the make-up.

26 October

E has gone to Ireland.[4] I ought to be writing her a letter now instead of doing this diary.

3 December

E has been telling me how she goes about writing a novel. She told me about *Death of the Heart.* She thought first of the Eddie-Portia

---

[3] EB, *The Death of the Heart*, 1938.

[4] To Bowen's Court, her family house in County Cork, and to Dublin. As a contribution to the Allied cause, she travelled frequently to neutral Ireland during the war to collect intelligence from her professional and political friends in Dublin, without their knowledge, and reported back to the Ministry of Information in London. Of particular concern were Irish attitudes to Britain having access to the 'Treaty Ports' in the south and west of the island, which was denied. EB reported that attempted coercion would reinforce German propaganda.

relationship (why? Because she was brooding over her own love-affair with GR?[5] And the essential character of that love was Eddie-Portia despite the reversal of age and circumstance in the novel). I see the two women in *Death of the Heart* as the two halves of E. Portia has the naiveté of childhood – or genius. She is the hidden E who I have got to know through love. The other woman (whose name in the novel I have forgotten[6]) is E as an outside hostile person might see her. . . . But all this is surmise and not what E told me. She said that besides this Eddie-Portia theme, there was a second situation, that of the poor unworldly girl who comes lonely with her pathetic trunk containing all the things she owns to live in the house of grand relations. E says this is a well-worn favourite with Maria Edgeworth[7] etc. Portia is in the position of the governess in *Jane Eyre*. . . . The visit to the seaside and the life in the bungalow there comes from her memories of the time when she and her mother lived in such places and knew such people when she was a child. . . . She is going to a psychoanalyst to be cured of her stammer which is so much part of her.[8]

21 December

E came to tea. I should hate to lose her friendship. It would be shattering to quarrel with her. I have so much more respect for her than I have for myself.

---

[5] Goronwy Rees, journalist and spy, 10 years younger than EB who had a brief affair with him in 1936. At a house party at Bowen's Court in September 1936 Rees fell precipitately in love with a fellow guest, the novelist Rosamond Lehmann. This episode caused EB much suffering and contributed to the plot of *The Death of the Heart*, as CR surmised, though EB's friendship with Lehmann survived and was lifelong.

[6] It is Anna Quayne.

[7] Maria Edgeworth (1767-1849), Anglo-Irish novelist. Her *Castle Rackrent* was published in 1800.

[8] She was never cured of her stammer.

1942

11 January

E came to see me in the a.m. and brought me a cyclamen. . . . E is sad because she loves me more than I love her. It is sad for me too in another way.

12 January

I was so depressed by my interview today with E that I came home and meditated suicide over my electric fire. She sees through me more and more and still loves me, which is a most painful situation for me. She has now reached the stage of letting her disillusionment become visible – loving me for myself and not for my 'act'. If she makes me sincere, I just can't manage the thing any longer.

M[9] said tonight, 'So you don't have the guts to break it off.' That's it.

---

[9] Miriam Rothschild (1908-2005), distinguished entomologist and world expert on fleas, sister of Victor, 3rd Baron Rothschild. A good friend of CR, she married Captain George Lane MC in 1943 and had six children.

20 January
E and I dined at Claridges Causerie. She was in a very easy and cheerful mood. She said, I would like to put you in a novel, looking at me through half closed eyes in a suddenly detached way like a painter looking at a model. 'You probably wouldn't recognise yourself.' 'I am sure I wouldn't,' I lied.

22 January
Dined with E at her house. She always manages to have unheard of quantities of smoked salmon. The house was so cold that we put the electric heater on a chair close to us so as to have it on a level with our bodies. E was wearing a necklace and bracelet of gold and red of the kind of glass that Christmas tree decorations are made of. . . . She had on a white silk jacket over a black dress. We sat on the sofa and talked as she had the curse. She is either educating me or corrupting me; I cannot quite make out which.

26 January
A rather sad and painful evening with E. She suddenly said in that cool voice of hers, 'One interesting thing my psychoanalyst got out of me, that I have a hidden wish that all my acquaintances should die, should be eliminated or at least disappear to South America.' . . . Her disillusionment goes so many layers deeper than mine. She also said, 'I might some day like to kill you, but that would be different. I suppose it would give me some sort of voluptuous pleasure.' I know that that is and always has been one of her phantasies about me. The first time she saw my revolver she said, 'You are the sort of young man some woman might shoot.'

5 February
E has gone to Ireland. Miss her more than last time. She has just telephoned. Am getting dependent on her.

28 February

E has gone away to an Aunt's funeral. I feel even fonder of her than usual at the moment when I am planning to be unfaithful to her. . . .

I asked E the other night if she thought I had a weak character. 'You drift in things that you don't think important, but you have a will of india rubber.'

3 March

E was discussing her method of writing the other night. She says that when she is writing a scene the first time, she always throws in all the descriptive words that come to her mind. . . . Like, as she said, someone doing clay-modelling who will smack on handfuls of clay before beginning to cut away and do the fine modelling. Then afterwards she cuts down and discards and whittles away. The neurotic part of writing, she says, is the temptation to stop for the exact word or the most deliberate analysis of a situation. . . .

Dined with E last night. . . . I was not in a good mood. Rather struggling in the toils, grudging and thinking how nice it would be if we were 'just friends'. . . . If I was really ruthless I wouldn't get into these fits of panic which are so unattractive and silly. Any woman who kept me in a state of anxiety could keep me permanently. It's so simple but they none of them will.

14 March

I am writing a separate war-diary. (Posterity please note.)

All my love affairs have been floated on alcohol. If the rationing of wines and spirits becomes effective I shall become considerably less interesting as a lover. These reflections are bred of my first entirely non-alcoholic evening with E. We dined quietly (too quietly) at a cheap little Russian restaurant. She paid for her share of the dinner. We talked, not of our complex temperaments, childish memories or mutual passion, but of my overdraft. Quite a married evening in every way.

9 April

I told her the other evening that I was a crook, which was a guarded way of saying that I had been and would continue to be unfaithful to her. She said my 'being a crook' was the use I made of my surplus cleverness – like her writing.

20 April

In the afternoon went with E to Hampstead. (I think but am not sure that she knows what is happening and has decided to close her eyes to it – if so I admire her all the more.) We had tea with Elizabeth Jenkins[10]. . . .

On the way back. . . . E talked of Virginia Woolf who must certainly have been a great influence in her life. An influence I can still feel alive in her. She told me how she looked, tall and graceful and wearing some flowing dress of mauve or grey and of her incomparable conversation. She had, E said, a sort of 'fairy cruelty' and could be sadistic. 'But she did not know how much she could hurt.' There were many forms of being hurt about which she knew nothing. She had never been humiliated herself although she used to half jokingly talk of how shy she was, of how she could never go into a room full of strange people without feeling that they thought her odd. In fact, said E, she had always lived in a sort of Chinese world of intelligent complicated people who made a cult of her. From that world she never issued, she led a guarded life. 'How I wish,' she said, that you had known her, that you had not just missed her.'[11] . . .

E met a female admirer last night at dinner who said to her, 'To me meeting you is like meeting Christ.'

---

[10] Elizabeth Jenkins (1905-), novelist and biographer. She lived in Downshire Hill, Hampstead.

[11] Virginia Woolf had drowned herself on 28 March 1941

21 April

The day has been overhung by a desolating evening with E. I was tired and so was she. After dinner we got into one of those stupid, brutishly serious conversations about our feelings. What I was trying to convey, and did in fact convey, was that I did not love her. But eventually we went sadly to bed and that was a fiasco. How painfully one learns. . . . Yet I always feel it would be so simple. All they would need to do is use a light hand – a little indifference goes such a long way with me – indeed my system requires it, like the need for salt.

25 April

If E was not so much in love with me, she would be bored beyond bearing by my conversation. But she encourages me to talk about myself. . . . Of course I enjoy it, but would have thrown myself much more wholeheartedly into the game when I was ten years younger. I would have been a shameless Cheri.[12] She would have been my *femme de trente ans.* Now I am her 'last' and she must know it. That is what she means when she calls me her 'Destiny'.

2 May

E seems to be regaining her hold on me. After having, as I thought, almost lost it.

10 May

Something of the panic of middle-age is coming upon me. It's the bald spot beginning on the back of my head. . . . Perhaps this is the last spring in which I shall not be entirely inappropriate. My fancy turns more and more to marrying and settling to a routine life of small pleasures. I seem surrounded by nice but ugly girls –

---

[12] Eponymous character in the novel by Colette (1920) about an affair between a young man and an older woman.

if one of them was pretty, I'd be engaged by now. . . . E is beginning to wear that distracted unhappy look which cannot be concealed. I have been through all this before. It is better for me to love more than I am loved.

24 May

E and I went to Kew. It is hardly worth my while to describe the scene, or to dwell upon the dreamlike state in which we drifted among the towering ravines of rhododendrons and azaleas as I am sure that it will all be found in her next novel. It was a day like a page from one of her books, the involved relationship between the two lovers who are wandering among the flower beds. . . . One of the luxuries of this love affair is the giddy feeling of being carried along on the tide of her imagination, being transmuted into literature; sitting for my portrait, or being swallowed alive? It was a Feast Day in our calendar. But all this vanity of interchange, these shared delicacies and dreams must be fed from desire. And in me desire is dead.

25 May

I am in love with E imaginatively. She even has a strange beauty like a woman in a tapestry.

2 June

Woke up feeling baffled by E's behaviour last night and unable to decide at what point in the evening she won her complete victory. She made me feel childish and rather humiliated at my own silliness and immaturity. I went to see her this afternoon. She was standing on the balcony that looks over Regent's Park in a summery dress, the tall cool room with its regency mirrors and flowers and books looked pretty. She wants to dedicate her next novel to me. I hope she will and that it will be her best.

4 June

I am in one of the two most important posts in our service at the crisis of the greatest war in history and I am filling in time. Glorious hot June day. I had a 'workman's lunch' of smoked sausage and a bottle of red wine in Regent's Park with E. We sat on the river's bank and watched the swans go by in slow indignation. . . . We are happiest in this dreamlike state, watching, talking, drifting, and when we are happy it always seems as though we were figures in a tapestry.

13 June

Dined with E. . . . We drank a lot of red wine. She is domesticating me, although I fight every inch of the way. Who could help becoming attached to her? She is the most remarkable woman I have ever known; and when she has finished with me, I may be grown-up instead of a permanent adolescent.

In July 1942 Charles went to Ireland and stayed with Elizabeth at Bowen's Court. She stayed on when he returned to London.

15 August

E is back again. We dined together. She brought me some flowers. She seemed somehow less remarkable, to have 'lost height'. I wonder if the spell is broken or if it just happened to be an off night. . . .

All the same my existence has come to life again since she came back.

19 August

It is only now that I am out of love with E that I realize how much I have been in love all this time – and yet that is not a safe thing for me to say. This may be just one of those doldrums in which I am temporarily becalmed.

25 August

It was in this kind of weather last year that our affair started. The magic has evaporated; we are friends. It is almost incredible to me that she still loves me with any degree of excitement. . . . We sat in her cool, tall, pale drawing-room in Clarence Terrace drinking Alan's whiskeys. Breezes blow through from Regent's Park. This was the house of the D of the H[13]. . . . It says in an article that so many love affairs go wrong because people have their heads full of ideas out of novels. Some would never start if it were not for the novels.

30 August

Spent most of the day with E. She was wearing her black witch's hat, a black dress with white necklace and looked strange and elegant. I said to her the other night, 'You sometimes look younger but however tired you never look older.' She is certainly the most delightful companion in the world. She has never bored me, and how often I must have bored her. . . . We talked books in the morning.

3 September

It began by being a perfect autumn day and E and I planned to go to Kew. When E came we went for a walk in Hyde Park. It blew from the east and she had to hold her hat on with one hand while we walked past the AA[14] guns to the river and by the cylindrical tin huts behind their barbed wire where the soldiers have made neat little streets and gardens like a fairy tale illustration.

4 September

The only way to continue to live with a woman you no longer love is to be unfaithful. You then have an overflow of sensual good nature to help oil the wheels.

---

[13] *The Death of the Heart*

[14] Anti-aircraft.

7 September

Lunch with E. We lay on the grass in Regents Park, watched the sky and the swans and she talked about her novels. That was the best part of the day.

19 September

Long talk with E who is just on the point of beginning a new novel of our Present Discontents.[15] She says that she has ideas, situations, mise-en-scène in her head, but as yet no characters and that she can only think on paper. London she says looks like 'a worn out carpet'. And Alan C is like a character in a Chekhov play who always repeats the same lines at his entrances and exits.

12 November

E came to see me for a few minutes. I was rather at a loss with her. Where will it end? I never seem to say to her what I want to say.

And marriage is an idea that I am always playing with in my mind now. I might do more than play with the idea but for the complete absence of eligible girls in my life at present. Went back after the film and drank a bottle of claret with E in front of the electrical fire in her upstairs drawing-room with my photo on the mantelpiece. . . . Her new novel too opens in Regent's Park. . . . After the second glass of claret we began to talk about our feelings in love and how our love affair had changed us. . . . She said she thought that if we had married we would have been perfectly happy together.

---

[15] This was to be *The Heat of the Day*, not published until 1949, and dedicated 'To Charles Ritchie.'

1943

1 January
This is a queer sort of New Year. The war has caught up with me at last and I am thinking of joining the army.

3 January
It has taken an artist to put a little commonsense into me. My yearnings to play-act my life, my bookish conception of what love should be like, E has borne with all that. . . . Without ever making me feel a fool, she has shown me up to myself. It is for her a triumph of character. . . . To her I owe Growth.

30 January
I said to E last night that I wondered if it was possible to regard oneself not with violent self-disgust but with a steady cold distaste, as one might an unattractive acquaintance whose character one knew all too well. She thought, 'Yes, if he had been over-praised for the wrong reasons.'

I want to say to her that I have taken a mortal risk in becoming and remaining her lover. I knew from the first that she was a witch who had put a spell on me.

6 February

E has become the centre of my life. As usual I struggle with my own love for her and with a lamentable but characteristic panic. I insist in my own mind that I do not love her, because I am not 'in love' with her; that however is true in a narrow sense in that I do not desire her. Yet what I feel for her is quite different from friendship. . . .

Of course with E I have found the perfect companion and intelligence and above all a power of expression incomparably superior to my own. . . . She and A[nne Maher[16]] talk the same language – that of the aesthete of the '20s – but A distracted, embarrassed and maddened me, and satisfied my desire for drama. . . . I was more 'in love' with her. E has her own spell, and insensibly she has put at a distance not only all rivals, but all rival memories. I grasp at the thought of A like a drowning man. I am being absorbed by a love which wishes to penetrate and to possess.

6 November

E came round in the morning in a new hat. Very elegant if only she can be bothered taking the trouble to put it on at just the right angle each time she wears it.

25 December

In the morning E and I went to the Abbey. It was crowded as it always should be. . . . We came back to lunch with Alan off cold duck and a white Corton 1924.

---

[16] Anne Payne was with CR in Paris when he was studying there 1929-30. This was probably his first real love affair. She married John Maher, in the Colonial Office, and CR was godfather to one of their daughters. She and CR kept in touch and sustained a loving relationship.

1944

20 January

E is on fire-watching duty. She came in for a drink today. I kept on interrupting her stories till she said plaintively, 'Many people would be interested to hear EB give a description of an experience like this one!' I felt thoroughly ashamed of myself, as well I might. I feel morally and intellectually inferior to E.

30 January

Night and day at Richmond with E. Happy – but there is no need to describe it. I shall recognize it later in one of her books. It was a day out of an EB book. She said, 'I haven't been so happy since we were in Ireland,' which meant, 'We have reached a pedestrian level – this was a peak above it.'

18 February

We had lunch at Claridges Causerie. Agreed that the attraction which the Great World had for us when we were young now attaches to Provincial Life. Wolfville for me, Hythe[17] for her. . . .

---

[17] Wolfville is the small town in Nova Scotia where the Ritchie family had a holiday house. Hythe is the small town on the coast of Kent where EB and her mother lived in her childhood, and where her mother died (1912).

I like to think that the atmosphere of wartime London will be preserved in E's new novel, and that things we have seen and felt together will be preserved there. Of course what I would like best would be to find a romanticized portrait of myself but I shall be lucky, I daresay, not to be mentioned. . . . She said of someone today that he was too interested in the psychology of people ever to be in love. Is that true of her? Of all writers? Of myself who am not a writer?

27 February

E came in in the morning wearing her black witch's hat which always makes me see her as a distinguished woman writer, the *marraine*[18] of Bloomsbury, the successor of Virginia Woolf. What she has been to me I can never express without sounding as if I were writing an obituary letter to The Times. Through her I have grown up. . . . If only I had known her ten years ago, for both our sakes.

13 March

Is it possible that I am slightly, just slightly in love with that 'little number'. That would be silly. At the same time my happiness with her has made me appreciate E much more.

7 May

I lunched with E in the downstairs grill in the Ritz. There were pink tulips on the tables and a pinkish light. . . . The unreality suited my mood and we talked as we used to when we first knew each other. It was one of those times which we shall both remember afterwards and say to each other, 'That fine windy Sunday in Spring when we lunched underground in the Ritz.' Our queer kind of love came alive.

---

[18] 'Marraine' means godmother. EB was never part of Bloomsbury, though she had close friends who were.

20 July

E's house 2 Clarence Terrace hit by blast for the third time. She has at last decided to move out now that all the ceilings are down and all the windows broken and they only escaped being killed by a chance. I hate the disappearance of Clarence Terrace, so will her other friends. . . . I feel E is without her background. I do not like the idea of her living about in hotels. A dignified retreat to B Court seems indicated. She is shattered really. Her nerves have been under a terrible strain. But she is resilient, if she can get away and get some rest she will be all right. And in the midst of it all she is still trying frantically to write her novel.

12 August

E was saying the other day that she thought there was a danger that my office life, my ambitions would get the upper hand of me and drive the 'poetry' out of my life. That may happen, but success will never satisfy me. . . .

E had moved to Clarissa Churchill's[19] as their house has been blasted once too often. I went to see her there last night. It is high up in a monstrous new block of flats overlooking Regent's Park – rather lovely up there. . . . She is writing a short story 'The Happy Autumn Fields'[20] and told me about it in an excited way while I lay on the sofa looking out at the sky. I like it when she talks to me about her writing. I caught her out last night in a lie to me for the first time since I have known her. Talking of dining with Cyril,[21] herself,

---

[19] Clarissa Churchill, niece of Winston Churchill, married the Conservative MP Anthony Eden (later Lord Avon), who resigned over Munich, subsequently became Prime Minister, and would be brought down by the Suez crisis. EB and Alan moved back to Clarence Terrace two months later.

[20] Included in her collection of short stories *The Demon Lover* (1945).

[21] Cyril Connolly (1903-1974), author, critic, and editor of *Horizon*, the most significant British literary periodical 1940-1950. His wife at this time was Jean Bakewell, who was American.

and Alan in the Mayfair Ballroom she said to me, 'As you can imagine we did not dance.' Alan came in and described how they 'had taken the floor together for the first time after so many years'.

Ten months before he met EB, in April 1940, Charles had written to his mother: 'I agree with what you say about my false idea of love. I think it would be a mistake for me to marry anyone I was in love with anyway. Too much love gives me claustrophobia. . . . I should think the best thing for me would be someone companionable of whom I am fond like Sylvia.'

Sylvia Smellie was his second cousin. The idea of marrying her came again to the fore as he prepared to leave London for Ottawa, having been promoted to Assistant Under-Secretary for External Affairs. Sylvia came over from Canada for his farewell party in London. Charles spoke to Elizabeth about her.

3 December

E says she would not mind me marrying S so much, it would be like 'marrying myself'.

19 December

Today I bought a necklace for E, large white amethysts – or almost white – they have mauve lights in them, alternating with small purple amethysts. I was going to buy topazes but fortunately heard just in time that they are unlucky. I wouldn't want to give her an unlucky present – our future looks unlucky enough without that.

1945

Charles left for Canada in January 1945. This was the first time that Elizabeth had been separated from him for more than a few weeks since their affair began. From now on, he kept most of her letters, including this last one she wrote to him before his departure:

2 *Clarence Terrace, Wednesday, 17th January 1945*
Beloved, I can't believe any human being can ever have made another as purely wholly unchangeably and yet increasingly happy as you have made me. We are so close to each other in understanding, closer than words could make us that I think you must know this. You are in all ways and all parts of your being, and of my being, my joy.

You know too, don't you, that you take with you my real life, my only life, everything that is meant by my heart. I am in your keeping. And you are in mine.

It's hopeless to try to say anything to you or to myself to make this parting better. It's sheer injury, and such pain that one does not know where to turn. There's only this: what we have between us is timeless and unchangeable. We must suffer. But I don't believe that our love need – or will, in the sense of deteriorating.

I shall do all I can – mostly in the most prosaic, childish and trivial ways – to bridge the geographical distance. We must stand up as best we can against their losses – the loss of presence and voice and touch. I don't believe that these losses will be forever.

I am so proud of you – of your mind and energy and good judgement, your fairness to people and to ideas, your sweetness of nature, your adorable looks and person. I shall be turning, you can imagine, to other people left in London who know you and love you and see what I see, if not so much.

This last is probably the most unnecessary thing of all to say – you know that I shall not change. It's not a case of will not so much as of cannot. For me, you are the ultimate of something. Till I met you, I did not even imagine that such an ultimate could be reached. Now I rest in it, and cannot go beyond.

A good journey, my darling.

Elizabeth

The following three fragments of letters from Elizabeth are not among those Charles left to his niece Elizabeth Ritchie on his death. They are from the heavily edited typed extracts which he gave to Victoria Glendinning for her biography, Elizabeth Bowen: Portrait of a Writer *(1977). He probably never put the originals back with the rest of her correspondence, and they got lost:*

2 *Clarence Terrace, [?] March 1945*

. . . Any novel I have ever written has been difficult to write and this[22] is being far the most difficult of all. . . . The thing revolves round and round in my brain like what you're at work at does in your brain. Almost anything that happens around me contributes to it.

---

[22] *The Heat of the Day.*

Sometimes I think this novel may be a point-blank failure but I shall still be glad to have tried. I would not in the least mind if this were my last shot, if I never wrote anything else again.

It presents every possible problem in the world. In some parts of it, even, it seems right to give an effect of garrulity or carelessness. A good deal is written already, much of what is still to be written must be point-blank melodrama. . . .

In a way the novel seems to have the same difficulties as making a film, if one were an ambitious director; continuity, the to and fro between different themes. . . . Some of it is quite funny. I don't mind, rather like, broad Dickens-type burlesque funniness but I do loathe and want to avoid a particular kind of pursey irony – coterie irony. . . .

2 Clarence Terrace, 7/8th May 1945
. . . On a monster scale it [*VE day – the end of the war in Europe*] was like an experience in love. Everything, physically – beginning and ending with the smell of sweat, so strong and so everywhere that it travelled all through this house by the open windows – was against exultation and yet it happened.

. . . [*The previous night*] I switched off the wireless and said to Alan, 'Well, the war's over', and he said, 'Yes I know', and we went into the dining-room and sat on the window-sill for about an hour, quite unable to rally, he furious because he hadn't made any arrangements about his office, and I furious because I hadn't got any flags. The park looked as dark as a photograph and was quite empty; and I thought, well, I knew one would feel like this.

[*They walked to Westminster Abbey*]

Almost everyone wore a curious limpidity of expression, like newborn babies or souls just after death. Dazed but curiously dignified. As you know, I do in general loathe Demos:[23] I don't think

---

[23] Common people *en masse*

anyone has less warm feelings or fewer illusions than I have. But after a crise (which happened quite early on) of hysterical revulsion and tiredness, I passed beyond, and became entered by a rather sublime feeling.

. . . I suppose that everyone, in those two days, found one thing that was in their own language, and seemed to be speaking to them, specially. The searchlights were mine. For me they were the music of the occasion.

Elizabeth was alone in Ireland for a week or two before her husband Alan Cameron joined her.

Bowen's Court[24] *[early June 1945]*
. . . The stillness and the silence of the first few hours are like something dripping on one's nerves, almost uncanny. And the strong, strange, indoor smell of the house. At first it never seems anything to do with me. More like something arrived at in the middle of a bois dormant. I should never be surprised as I first walk in to find ferns growing on the staircase or a mythical animal crouching outside my bedroom door. Considering how frightened I am in general of the supernatural, it's extraordinary that I am not very frightened; in fact never frightened here.

Bowen's Court, Sunday, 17th June 1945
Charles, angel, none of your letters have reached me since I have been in Ireland: I have had nothing to live on but my beautiful thoughts. Lack of letters (yours) leaves an awful hole in my life. The last I've had was the one dated May 22nd, which I shall go on

---

[24] Bowen's Court in north Co Cork was a large, plain, intractable country house – a 'Big House' as Anglo-Irish houses were called in Ireland – built by EB's ancestor in the 1770s. An only child, EB inherited it on the death of her father in 1930. She immortalised the house and her forebears in her book *Bowen's Court* (1942).

re-reading till I get any others. I know this is not your fault; I am simply cursing the posts and, presumably, censors between England and Eire. I rang up Alan 2 days ago, Friday, and asked him not to forward any more letters, as everything seems to be taking about a week, and I am due back at Clarence Terrace on Friday next, 22nd.

No, being without letters from you for a fortnight all the more makes me realise how I love them; how my week, really, focuses internally on what you say, how you are and what you tell me you're doing. I also do realise how angelic you've been about making and seizing time to write, through thick and thin – and the thick has been thick – under all circumstances, such as measles and height of conference pressure, and in all places, such as hotels. The week before last, when I wrote you that incoherent little scribble from the Shelbourne,[25] I was on the point of saying, 'You know how impossible it is to write anything in a hotel.' And then I realised you'd been living in one for weeks . . .

I have been as happy as the day is long here by myself. In fact I should be happier if the days were longer. The weather hasn't really been very nice – a few bursts of sun and colour, otherwise a queer rather soporific grey-green, sleepy and rather cold. The birds sing beautifully round the house, in the evenings and in the early mornings. Unfortunately I've had to do rather a lot of work – articles and things that have to be in by a fixed date. This produces conflict; as the whole tempo and temperature of this place suggests slow motion, reflectiveness, ease. Especially when one's by oneself. And I have been entirely by myself. Jim Gates[26] comes crawling down Kildorrery hill at intervals in his large blue lorry; I went out

---

[25] Shelbourne Hotel, a Dublin hub, on St Stephen's Green. EB would chronicle its history in *The Shelbourne*, published as *The Shelbourne Hotel* in the USA (1951).

[26] The Gates family lived in a modern bungalow in Kildorrery, the nearest village to Bowen's Court, apart from the hamlet of Farahy. EB had known Jim since childhood. He was genial and unintellectual, a close friend providing local support. He managed the Kildorrery creamery, which became part of the Cow & Gate empire.

to dinner one night with Sylvia Cooke-Collis[27] and her husband, nine miles away in a house overlooking the river, who have the most marvellous food; Hilda Annesley drove over in a pony and trap to tea yesterday; and the Rector is coming to lunch tomorrow. That has been my social life. My nice friend Dorothy Bucknal at Creagh Castle (do you remember our going over there one evening?) has been most appallingly ill, almost dying, with dry pleurisy in both lungs and pneumonia. She has been too ill to see anyone, but I have been telephoning every day. She has now, I am very glad to say, turned the corner. I should have been miserable, selfishly, if anything had happened to her, as she is an angel, really an awfully nice woman, and much my greatest ally round here.

Today is lovely. The sun's come right out – though I cannot say there are no clouds – and it's a proper June country Sunday, bumbling with insects, and with the bronze uncut hay outside the windows rippling in a very slight breeze. I have been to church, and come back. The Gospel for this Sunday was the Good Shepherd. For lunch I shall eat cold meat and salad, and probably rather unripe strawberries, but with cream. In the afternoon I shall read, and in the evening I am going to a great carnival-fair in Kildorrery, in aid of the RC church. Merry-go-rounds, shooting galleries and all sorts of things, culminating in a fancy dress procession. As the RC's always come to Protestant church fêtes here, I tell myself that I ought to return the compliment – actually, of course, I am dying to go anyhow . . .

Oh yes, and I went to Cork (city) on Friday, in the Gates' lorry. What a fascinating city it is – I long to show it to you next time you're here. It's about thirty-five miles away from this house; and when I had my motor car it used to take about one and a half hours to drive there. Now, I hadn't been there for about 2 years. It's very

[27] Irish painter. The Cooke-Collis family house was Castle Cooke, County Cork.

Continental; or rather, it's so un-English (much more un-English than Dublin) that there's nothing to call it but Continental. It has a long and highly animated river front, lined with puce and pistachio-coloured buildings. Several small steamers, with guns still mounted, along the docks. A long wide serpentine main street, which used to have beautiful buildings, but they were all burned down by the Black-and-Tans, or the IRA, during the troubles, and have now been replaced by vast modern stores, Burton the fifty-shilling tailor, Woolworth's, etc. However, most of the older part of the town's intact; it is criss-crossed through with canals and small hump-backed bridges. The houses have steep roofs, and many of them are painted. There's a very dashing Opera House, overlooking the river. Across the river from the main part of the house is a very sheer, steep hill, rather beautifully clustered over with houses (some of them elegant) terraces and trees. The whole place has a sultry, sweetish smell, which I'm afraid arises from its being imperfectly clean – a slightly Italian smell, except for the absence of garlic. One can smell the incense out of the many churches, and the slight saltiness of the tidal river. In the shops were quite a lot of luxury cosmetics which have run out in London, so I laid in a store. . . .

I've been re-reading *Pride and Prejudice*, which is the JA novel I know least well. I adore these love-hate passages between Elizabeth and Darcy. And E's reflections on Darcy, when she thinks the affair has come to an end: 'If he is satisfied with only regretting me . . . I shall cease to regret him at all.' And her advice to him: 'Think only of the past as its remembrance gives you pleasure.'

What a lot of books there are in this house. When I have finished my novel, I should like to stop writing for two years and just simply read.

Hilda Annesley and I had a fascinating conversation about artificial insemination (human). Subject introduced by her. The Mothers' Union in which she is a moving spirit, are much exercised about it, and do not know what line to take up. I could only say that it always sounded to me rather dreary. . . . I keep on making plans, seeing pictures, building castles in the air. About you and me, I mean, notably. This country is conducive to dreams. There are such lovely places round here – river valleys, woods, sides of mountains, that you and I never had time to see. I long to wander about them.

Dearest dear. The next letter I shall be writing you will be, I suppose, from London. I look round and see the corduroy arm-chair, near the fire, that you sat in; and can almost see you in it.

You are well aren't you? I'm so particularly glad, as things have turned out, that I got that cable you sent to Dublin. I shall be cabling you from there.

All my love, Elizabeth

2 *Clarence Terrace, Tuesday, 26th June 1945*

Darling. . . .

I found your long and lovely letter, about the 12-hour séance. Really. I don't wonder people are cracking up. . . . And so, yesterday (25th) you had that enormous do in the Opera House ('brightly lighted', I read, and remembered your description of the glare at the Opening and today you sign.)[28]

As for you, my love

'Lord of lords!
Oh infinite virtue! Com'st thou smiling from
The world's great snare uncaught?'

Antony and Cleopatra,[29] which I was reading at Bowen's Court. What a play – and I am surprised at any man, even Shakespeare, knowing so much about any one woman. Why do all these great fat actresses of about 50 always want to go on playing Juliet and none apparently want to play Cleopatra? Please read it again, when

---

[28] CR, as an adviser to the Canadian delegation, was attending the San Francisco Conference to set up the machinery of the United Nations. This was an exciting time for him, as recorded in diary entries excerpted in *The Siren Years* (1974). The plenary sessions and receptions were held in the Opera House.

[29] *Antony and Cleopatra*, Act IV, Scene 8.

you have time. I expect you know it better than I do, anyway. Now I know what she means about 'Roman Thoughts'.[30]

Anyway, oh infinite virtue, I am glad your angelic temper is as angelic as ever. I do think really that says a lot. I sometimes wonder if you are a saint, or something. How else given the fact that you are highly organised, can you have, or at least command, such angelic calm? I mean, I haven't got a bad nature, really, but you have seen the frenzies I can get into, over quite small things. In this way I regard myself as inferior.

Well, I had a very pleasant 3 warm, sunny days in Dublin on my way back. Spent a long afternoon in the Dail,[31] listening as closely as possible to the proceedings, but unfortunately they are almost inaudible. I should be prepared to bet that, as to length, longue haleine,[32] the TD's[33] outdo South Americans. But no baroque eloquence there. As a matter of fact, the virtue of most speakers, there, is that though flat-footed, long-winded, styleless, and absolutely without apprehensions as to boring their fellows – which they palpably do – they are admirably concrete.

Our new President, Sean T. O'Kelly,[34] is apparently rather a lamb: just every bit as much of a comic as he looks, and immensely bonhomous. No fool, and bon viveur (rare in middle-class Ireland). He sounds rather like Dulanty.[35] His wife 'was one of the clever Ryans'. Sir J. Maffey,[36] sensitive in these matters, says she lacks feminine charm.

---

[30] *Antony and Cleopatra*, Act I, Scene 2: 'He was dispos'd to mirth, but on the sudden/ A Roman Thought hath strook him' (i.e. thoughts of duty).

[31] Dail Eireann, the Irish Parliament.

[32] French: EB means 'long-winded.'

[33] Members of the Dail.

[34] Sean T. O'Kelly (1882-1966), founder of Fianna Fail (political party), elected second President of Ireland 1945.

[35] John Whelan Dulanty (1883-1955), then High Commissioner in London for the Irish Free State.

[36] Sir John Maffey (1877-1969), from 1947 the first Baron Rugby, Britain's first High Commissioner to the Irish Free State 1939-1949.

Dear George O'Brien[37] – do you remember him, and his house – you and I went to a party there? – had a very nice little dinner party of 5 the evening before I came away. There is something very idyllic about those Dublin houses, surrounded by green, tree-shaded roads and gardens glittering in the evening sunshine. Old furniture, roses on the dinner table, excellent servants and marvellous wine. The decorum of Dublin is very pleasing to me: it appeals to all my back-to-the-wombishness. London, returned to, seems rude, lewd and untidy.

All the roses are out and blazing away in the middle of Regent's Park. In the late evenings, since I have come back, they are so lovely I can hardly bear to look at them. Regent's Park is also now enriched by Cyril,[38] who has moved into 25 Sussex Place (the crescent-shaped terrace next to this, with the domes). His existence is rather skeleton still poor thing as he has got no windows, no electric light, no telephone, no bath water, and dry rot has been discovered all down the front of the house, which necessitates its being picked to pieces. However the rooms he has got straight are lovely. The effect – windowless windows looking out on to a hot white column, dead white walls, and all his classical Empire candlesticks, couches, etc. is rather Greek, or Roman. And Cyril is in a very bland epicurean Greek or Roman mood. 3 little girls in slacks – Lys, Gianetta, and Sonia B,[39] scurry round like mice, doing all the work. Really he looks rather like a Sultan in a harem. He comes in here for baths: what the poor little girls do, I don't know.

I have only been back about 4 days – so far, have done nothing but write and help the Connollys move, and walk about the park

---

[37] George O'Brien (1892-1973), professor of economics at University College, Dublin. Literary and sociable, a member of many Irish government committees and an influential figure in internal politics and policies.

[38] Cyril Connolly.

[39] Lys Lubbock, Janetta Woolley and Sonia Brownell (who became George Orwell's second wife).

wishing for you. Electioneering seems to be getting more and more idiotic on all sides: at intervals loud-speaker vans dash round the park. I have rather had my bluff called by a Liberal candidate for S[outh] Marylebone having cropped up at the last moment. I suppose I shall have to support this lost cause. I always have gone about blowing off and saying I was a Liberal. . . . Alan says he is going to vote Labour because the Labour candidate is a woman. (His 1912 feminism.) I ask him whether he wants this country run by Jews and Welshmen? I am afraid these are only election angles I am able to give you.[40] Oh
[Ends][41]

8 July [Wolfville, Nova Scotia]
And I miss E. I more and more realize how when I am working I can banish her daily from my conscious mind by thinking always of something that has to be thought of first . . . But now that I am idle thoughts of her besiege me. She from whom All Blessings Flow – all but one.

Elsfield, Sunday, 29th July 1945
Darling Charles – I cannot resist writing to you from here. I say 'cannot resist' as I feel rather a cad – Susan [Tweedsmuir] has arranged me all beautifully at the John Buchan writing table, in his

---

[40] The General Election of 1945, following the end of World War II, resulted in the ousting of Churchill and the Conservatives, with the first Labour government ever to have a clear majority coming to power under the premiership of Clement Attlee. Jewish intellectuals have tended to be Labour supporters, and several (such as Maurice Edelman, Ian Mikardo) entered Parliament as new MPs in 1945. Aneurin Bevan, Attlee's Minister of Health, was a Welshman. Usually EB was romantic about Wales and the Welsh, and about her own Welsh roots (see letter 14 May 1950).
[41] Here and throughout, '[Ends]' signifies that the final page or pages of a letter are missing, whether lost or, as in many cases, destroyed by CR as being too personal to preserve.

upstairs study, and I am all set to be doing creative work. This is the walnut table with the model of the 39 Steps[42]; and there is also a slab of some sort of quartz rock, 'product of La Bine Point, NWT'[43] inscribed to him. It's a cloudy but pleasant day, and the Oxon plain extends from under the windows as far as the eye can see; criss-crossed by smoky-looking dark blue trees. A <u>very</u> good room to write in.

Alan was kept in London by a conference, so I came alone . . .

I must say, the results[44] were a terrific psychic shock to me: for the first few hours (in fact while I was writing to you) I felt sick, and shortly afterwards was. I don't think I minded the Socialist walkover: it was the complete collapse and failure and ignominy of the people who represent the ideas I support that got me down. In a flash I saw so many things that I had been trying to hide from myself.

The most awful chasm-like views of complacency and blindness, misinformation and misjudgement, have opened during the last few days. One could feel, <u>at</u> the time, that the Tory campaign was being conducted with, apart from everything else, a <u>tactlessness</u>, a sheer psychological ineptitude, that was shattering. Keeping on telling the people Churchill had won the war for them. Of course he <u>had</u>, but it was not the thing to say. <u>His</u> moment of genius was the "This is <u>your</u> victory", from the balcony. Nothing should have been allowed to expunge that. The people are firmly convinced that they won the war, Ma by standing in the fish queues, little Herbert by helping with the fire-watching. It now seems clear that their voting was a reflex of indignation at being told anything to the contrary. At least, a percentage of votes went the way they did for that reason.

---

[42] John Buchan's novel *The Thirty-Nine Steps* (1915). Filmed by Hitchcock in 1935.

[43] North West Territory

[44] Of the General Election.

There were some fine scenes, as you may imagine, in the Dorchester. The new Lady Rothermere[45] gave a ticker-tape party, drinks from 12 noon, and everybody gathered in high spirits. Soon, it began to be like tumbril after tumbril arriving. Lady Cunard[46] retired to bed. Another lot who are put out are those who for some years have been mildly pink. They are now in a great (and I imagine for some time unnecessary) fuss about their investments. Also they are faced by the fact that their political ideas are no longer daring. How I wish Proust were here.

Personally, selfishly, I am feeling what a terrific advantage it is to be Anglo-Irish. I mean, to belong to a class, that potted at by the Irish and sold out by the British, has made an art of maintaining its position in vacuo. . . . What has happened may of course make a class of Anglo-English. But I feel, don't you, that they would rot. People can't just be passengers without going to pieces. . . .

David Cecil[47] was saying (he was here at tea at Elsfield yesterday) that an equally sweeping conservative victory, with the Conservative Party as it at present is would have made him feel horribly uneasy. Not merely out of apprehension, but because he would have felt the situation was false and squalid. Which is just what I have felt. Obviously, from the point of the good Conservative, the Party needs a terrific purge.

---

[45] Lady Rothermere (1913-1981), née Anne Charteris, whose first husband Lord O'Neill was killed in the war. She became the second wife of Tory MP and newspaper magnate Esmond Harmsworth, 2nd Lord Rothermere, after the war, while sustaining an affair with Ian Fleming, creator of James Bond, whom she married as her third husband in 1952.

[46] Lady Cunard (1872-1948) lived on the sixth floor of the Dorchester Hotel, with a dining room where she entertained indefatigably. An American heiress, nee Maude Burke, she renamed herself 'Emerald,' married Sir Bache Cunard (1851-1925) of the shipping line, and parted from him in 1911.

[47] Lord David Cecil (1902-1986), academic, literary critic, biographer, and Goldsmith Professor of English at Oxford 1948-1969. He was one of EB's dearest friends, from the time when she and her husband Alan lived at Old Headington, on the outskirts of Oxford, 1925-1935.

I am all in favour of Labour doing some heavy bulldozing work within the next two years or so – aren't you? Surely it will be admirable if they break Big Business? I had always had a hope, or a pipe dream, that the aristocratic Tories would round on, and repudiate, Big Business. Which shows how hopelessly unrealistic I am. . . .

The Sunday papers have not come in yet – or, if they have, I haven't seen them. So we don't yet know who's at the Dominions Office. Charles, how will this affect Dominions relations?

This letter has been interrupted by a chat with Susan, who angelically came in bringing morning coffee. I do feel a fake, posing as a worker. . . .

I am going to send you, darling, 2 of my short stories.

If there is any aspect of Red England you are particularly interested in, do ask me, and I'll employ my well-known faculties for espionage.[48] I have woken up from my melancholia, to a degree, at any rate; and am feeling more ginned up and observant.

Ought you not to come over and observe the changed face of England for yourself? Nobody could give Ottawa a more valuable report than you.

Sweetness and light goodbye for the present –
All my love, E.

Bowen's Court, Friday, 24 August 1945
My darling – your letter of Aug. 15th. – the first addressed to Bowen's Court – has just, this morning, come. Post here arrives very late: I came in to lunch from weeding in the garden, and found it on the hall table. I couldn't have been happier. . . . And attacks on weeds in the walled garden and groves of nettles about the grounds are an excellent outlet for my aggressive instinct.

---

[48] See footnote 4.

Because really do you know I have been feeling desperately aggressive and disaffected. . . . I can't dis-obsess myself from the feeling that democracy has celebrated its victory by being had for a mutt in a big way. The smug blah being talked in England, inside and outside Parliament, was beginning to make me quite ill. I know that at least 20% of these people[49] are All Right – I mean that they have principles etc that one may not share but can admire. (And really, I enjoy admiring anything.) But the few good ones have this awful entourage of the sissy, the half-baked, the manqués, the people with the chips on their shoulder, the people who've never made any grade and are convinced that it must be the grade's fault.

VJ Day[50] meant nothing. You know how I felt about VE Day. But that sort of thing can't happen twice. The days were listless and a flop, the nights orgiastic and unpleasant. (Violent anti-Yank demonstrations in Piccadilly, etc: a lot of fights all over the West End and people beaten up.) The most enjoyable human touch was that the poor Queen's hat – powder-blue – fell to pieces on her during the return drive from the opening of Parliament, owing to being saturated with rain. The crowd would not permit her to put up an umbrella.

I don't think anybody felt much – I mean about VJ day. Feeling was exhausted. And there was a majority guilt-feeling (wrong, I think) about the atomic bomb.[51]

So you see it was high time to be here. I stare at the outside of this house and think my ancestors didn't care a damn about English politics, and how right they were. This country, come back to, seems very amiable and good and sweet (in the sense one speaks of air being sweet). Quite illicitly – I mean, in view of their having been

---

49 Left-wing people and the new Labour government.

50 Victory in Japan – 15 Aug 1945

51 The nuclear bomb was dropped on Hiroshima on 6 August 1945, and on Nagasaki on 9 August.

neutrals – everybody is enjoying peace madly; going about with shining and beaming faces. In fact the Irish are the only people I have met so far who really are getting 100% kick out of world peace. They also remark with justifiable smugness that they always knew this war would end up in Bolshevism, and they are gladder than ever they kept out of it.

In fact it's a small, cheerful, concrete world. I have just engaged 2 divine maids, both aged 17, and both called Mary Hannon (they are first cousins). The one who is to be parlourmaid is tall, slender, beautiful and intelligent. . . . The other is rather runty, but seems to be tough and gay. I am setting them to work to scrub the fly-marks off the white paint all over the house.

Arriving straight into the south of Ireland (instead of going round by Dublin) is great fun. We steamed up the estuary of the river Suir and landed at Waterford – which is rather like a French river-port town. Rows of great high decaying beautiful buildings along the quay, and a smell of wood smoke in the damp morning air. We disembarked at about 9.30 a.m. without fuss and went and ate a large breakfast in the decaying Georgian glories of the Imperial Hotel. Then motored here, about 90 miles, arriving in time for lunch – with, of course, that inevitable stop for drinks at the Gateses.

This house was built by that long-ago, unconscious Bowen[52] for you and me to be happy in. That July when you and I were here it reached its height. It will again when you're back. I often wonder what time of year that will be. The only time when it's out-and-out impossible here is mid-winter.

It is a drowsy late-August afternoon. I am writing in the library with the windows open. One large blue bottle fly is bumbling about the ceiling: outdoors there is a hum of unspecified insects in the trees. The sky is overcast, but there is a sort of sheen of obstructed

---

[52] EB's great-great-great grandfather Henry Cole Bowen.

sunshine on the heavy dark-green trees and the grass. An ass-cart with orange wheels has just rattled across the field in front of the house, between the haystacks. It is now about 4.15, and tea will be coming in shortly: after that I think I will go and cut down some nettles. Except for my Tatler reviews,[53] I have decided not to do any more writing for at least 3 weeks.

Goodbye for now, my darling love. E.

Bowen's Court, Sunday, 2nd September 1945

Beloved, your letter of August 22nd came on Friday. I couldn't bear your not having got one from me. . . . I don't know how I should live if it were not for letters. Things are bad enough as they are. How people whom war and distance cut off from one another for months together get through at all, I don't know. How would one not (as you say), without the beloved evidence of a letter, come to torment oneself with the fear that love and the entire world of life that surrounds it was an illusion, subjective, brain-spun. As it is, the unfolding of a letter from you, the whole cast and shape of the handwriting on the paper, even before I have begun to read what is written, gives me a sort of rush of nearness. The hour – day or evening – in which you write, the things round you, the Ottawa bells ringing (like when you wrote last) envelops me. Partly, of course, it stirs up an agonising restlessness. But the happiness, the whole sense and aura of you, is worth that.

I felt a particular nostalgia (the kind one can feel for something one's never actually known) for the early autumn Ottawa weather – the crystal clearness, the colours beginning, the queer electric stimulus to the senses and brain. . . . Here, all seasons come late: it is still late summer, dark, fatigued but beautiful foliage on the trees, insect-droning, the corn still stooked in the fields. I am

---

53 EB had been reviewing books for *Tatler* (and other periodicals) since the early 1930s.

longing for autumn now – the first light frost, the crisping and crystallising of everything; mists in the early mornings and evenings, the trees beginning to turn. This summer has been too long. And except for the 3 weeks when I was in Ireland in June it is a summer that I shall always remember with repugnance. Like when one's inside is upset, everything has disagreed with me. I have desired nothing (that I could have) and enjoyed nothing. To recollect London, as it has been for me since last January, is to recollect a nightmare.

. . . The fact is, I've been living in the vague hope (I mean, a hope I never openly formulated, but clung to) that this autumn or early winter might, would, somehow bring you back to Europe even for a few weeks. I expect really I'd better be realistic, write that off, and pull strings to try and get in some capacity across the Atlantic? Hadn't I? . . .

Everything here goes on being very nice. 3 days of divine weather, followed by 2 days uninterrupted downpour. The downpour coincided with a woman coming to stay for this weekend. I must say, she asked herself – which does not mean I'm not very pleased to see her, but does mean it's not my fault if she is bored. . . . However, we must not become inhuman. Perhaps I'm reverting to type – gaunt and solitary Protestant land-owner.

Today it is, thank God, again fine and sunny. Deck chairs on the steps.

. . . Oh darling, my collection of short stories *The Demon Lover* comes out this month: I've told the publisher to send you a copy, via Canada House.[54] I hate its going off all bleakly like that, I mean without your name in it, but if it were sent here first and then off from here I have a feeling it would never arrive. No parcel sent off by me personally ever, somehow, seems quite real.

---

[54] Canada House in Trafalgar Square is the office of the Canadian High Commissioner to the UK.

I had hoped your lovely-sounding parcel of soap would have reached Clarence Terrace before I left. The soap here's bad and poor, so I'll ask Alan to bring your soap back – he goes over on a business trip of 6 days on September 18th. . . . One is short of the oddest things here – though of cream, peaches, eggs, meat, lobsters (due to kindness of friends) and (most unofficially) butter, there are plenty. The sense of profusion, ease, courtesy, leisure, space drips like warm honey over one's nerves. Actually that only exists if one stays quietly in a country house. If one tries to travel, or to go to Dublin, everything (I'm told) is as bad as England.

Oh Charles, I must stop. I cannot live through another autumn and winter without seeing you. Somehow, I know I shall. Take care of yourself, dear dearest. To one person you are an entire world.

Love. Your E.

When you told me you'd re-read the first chapter of *Bowen's Court,* I re-read it.

6 September [Ottawa]

Conditions for remaining in Ottawa: a conference every six months; work of real importance; promotion, and a wife???

Bowen's Court, Sunday, 9th September 1945

Dearest. . . .

Oh darling – have you been away for any more week-ends on lakes,[55] and is the early autumn and colour and crispness lovelier than ever? I still think, keep thinking, about you and me in New York. It is one of those absorbing phases of 'pretend' life one used to have as a child; a life lived to the last detail, so real one could hear curtains rustle in imaginary rooms, and street-sounds in a city one was not in.

---

55 CR had spent a weekend with the Southams at the Rideau Lakes south of Ottawa. Harry Southam was a wealthy newspaper proprietor.

There has been a week of perfect weather here – sun and crispness; the most literally heavenly evenings in which everything looked transparent, like painted glass, and white cows in the fields, gold with sunset, positively celestial. Do you remember that story I wrote, 'The Happy Autumn Fields'?[56] This was the time of year that I had in mind, and I was thinking about the fields round here, which are all now blonde and crisp with stubble, crisscrossed with belts of bronze-brown beeches.

The weather began on Monday (the day after I wrote to you).... I went into Mallow to put our week-end guest into the Dublin train, then walked about Mallow, sent off that cable to you and did some shopping. It was beautifully grillingly hot and sunny; Mallow (which consists of one crabbed ex-18th century main street) felt like a small French town, when one used to be touring in summer. So beautifully overpowering was the glare that I was glad of the dark musty and normally rather dank interior of the hotel bar. In Ireland it's hardly ever as hot as it was that Monday: I felt exotic and rather happy.

This week (I mean this past week) has been divided between going out to lunch, tea or dinner with neighbours, and extremely hard outdoor work. The second is a good correction to the first, as the food in all Co Cork houses (other than mine where it is rather haphazard) is simply marvellous – swimming in cream and eggs. Tea-tables groan with the most delectable cakes and hot scones running with melted butter. I suppose, strictly, Irish country house life is the last form of comfortable, old-fashioned existence left anywhere in Europe. How absolutely furious it would make the British. On the other hand, all these poor good Anglo-Irish have been furiously patriotic; all sons and younger husbands are away at the war – only too many, even from this small neighbourhood,

---

[56] This story was published in the collection *The Demon Lover* (1945), which includes EB's stories written during and about the war.

killed. There is no coal and no petrol and no forms of transport (except expensive hired cars) without chaotic discomfort.

Right or wrong, I cannot tell you how well all this agrees with me. I really was getting into a most odd state in London, Charles. I don't know what would have happened if I had stayed there much longer. I used, for instance, to wake up nearly every morning in floods of tears; and at intervals during the days I used to catch myself groaning aloud with exasperation.

... As I told you, I've developed a passion for forestry. At least I suppose one would call it that: it is too violent to be called gardening. Having begun by slashing acres of nettles, I now spend whole days (literally, from after breakfast to dinner time) sawing down small superfluous trees – elders, sapling of all kinds, which had been beginning to choke up the proper woods round the house. By hacking and slashing I have cleared, or rather restored, the most lovely vistas.

I now want to get John Summerson[57] or John Piper[58] or someone to design me a small temple, to be built at the corner of the lawn. But perhaps that would be rather ambitious?

This work in the woods has a most reducing effect, like a Turkish bath.

[Ends]

Bowen's Court, Monday, 17th September 1945

My darling – Your letter of Sept. 4th, about, among other things, the weekend at the Massey's fascinating-sounding house, came last Wednesday, and made me very happy. I could quite see the oddness, and in its way charm, of this curious imposed English-type country

---

57 John Summerson (1904-1992), architectural historian specializing in the Georgian period.

58 John Piper (1903-1992), painter and printmaker, chiefly of architectural and topographical subjects, and during the war one of a group of government-sponsored 'war artists.'

house with its formal gardens, etc, on an Ontario landscape. Flowers, wall-papers, glossy magazines. What, I wonder, becomes of it all the time they are away in London? I wonder if they don't sometimes feel homesick for it, specially in the Dorchester. They must have loved having you – Mr M does palpably love you. How long, I wonder, are they over for, and what did they think of everything – both in Canada and the British political scene?[59]

Did you talk to Mr Massey about your life – your future? I wonder what he said. *He* would be, I imagine, for 'abroad'?

The conflicts, the fors and againsts of your being in Ottawa or in Europe are complex and in one aspect frenzying. It is so hard for me, darling, as you can imagine, to be dispassionate or sensible. I suppose many men are dual men: you are certainly. I can't see happiness or wholeness or satisfaction for you at the cost of the starvation of *either* part of you. I know you wouldn't be happy if you were not going all out, executive, effective, using your whole power of brain *and* whatever the psychic drive behind the brain (that makes one's work part of oneself) is. All that, I can see, goes with the work in Ottawa. . . . On the other hand I can't bear the thought of the inanition or suppression of all your imaginative and sensuous part, and of your power to live through feeling and apprehension which makes you in nature more an artist or a poet than any orthodox artist or poet I have known. I don't see how one can live without an irrational delight, even if it is sometimes a melancholy delight, in existence for its own sake. It seems to me that for even the brain to breathe (if one can separate the brain from the rest of oneself) there needs to be something congenial about the

---

[59] The Masseys' house, with its 'English' décor and garden, was Batterwood. Vincent Massey (1887-1967) was High Commissioner for Canada in the UK 1935-1946, during which period CR was at Canada House as second and first secretary, and they became friends. Massey was to be Canada's first Canadian-born Governor General 1952-1959, and in the course of an illustrious career was variously academic, business-man, politician, diplomat, and champion of the arts.

surrounding air. And, how can you or I live without love? Without that, one feels an exile any place that one is.

I feel melancholy and exiled even here.

If only the new Europe would crystallise – if its new stresses (in the architectural sense) and power-centres would begin to appear. I suppose that will take years. . . . War brutalised physical life; post-war seems to dissipate, in a way that is almost brutalising, psychic life. To me, for me, it does not raise concrete problems. But everything I live for and by is involved in the problems it raises for you.

I suppose that's why I find all the little concrete problems of 'a place' so engrossing and soothing. Re-allocation of garden space – clearing and cleaning woods – where to get the best price for the apples. . . .

The Butlers, Gilbert and Noreen,[60] are here for the week-end: they leave after lunch today. I'm devoted to Noreen (who is a beautiful, affectionate, malignant and funny creature) and fond of Gilbert; and the weekend passed, I am bound to say, in a haze of drink, with a few tottering walks through the dripping woods, and a Sunday afternoon visit to Annesgrove. They had to make the most awful cross-country country bus journey, from Co Kilkenny, to get here. A 3-hour wait, for instance, in Clonmel, which apart from being Sterne's[61] birth place and a genial, fly-blown small city, is of little interest. Noreen bought up half the Clonmel Woolworth's, and arrived here with it in paper bags. It is thought that private cars in <u>this</u> country may be allowed on the roads again by Christmas. That would be very nice.

---

[60] Noreen Colley was EB's first cousin, the daughter of Aunt Edie Colley who played a large part in bringing up EB. Noreen was younger than EB, but they were always close. She married Gilbert Butler, and their home was Scatorish, at Bennettsbridge in Co Kilkenny.

[61] Laurence Sterne (1713-68), author of *Tristram Shandy*.

Alan goes to London for a week tomorrow, for a British Institute of Adult Education annual conference. His morale is low – can one wonder? He will have to camp in great discomfort at Clarence Terrace as Nancy's[62] away on her holiday. . . . I really do rather like being on my own here.

The only inducement to go back to London is that you could ring up. Oh my beautiful, I can't tell you what that would mean! Literally 3 minutes, even, of your beloved voice. I'm glad I didn't know of the possibility of your ringing up here, as I should have been so terribly disappointed when it went wrong . . .

It's curious how often I do hear your voice. It wakes me up, sometimes, in the night when I'm asleep.

I think I ought to stop now and go down and talk to the Butlers, as it's almost lunch-time and they are leaving directly after lunch. . . . I have felt particularly near you all this last week – so much so that sometimes I can't bear to be spoken to; as though someone else had come into the room when we were together.

Take care of yourself, my darling darling love.

Your E.

17 September

I don't think of E as much as I did. I don't even think about myself. How long can I stand this midday light of commonplace common sense which is the light of middle age? How long can I stand the neatness and emptiness of my life? And in a way I am quite content. I am not even at all sure that if I could go back to England and begin that life again, I should want to do it. Something has happened to me – a sort of brisk indifference has come over me – at least on the surface.

---

[62] Nancy was the maid at 2 Clarence Terrace. She had previously been employed by the Buchans.

Bowen's Court, Sunday, 30th September 1945

Darling – no letter from you this week, consequently I have fallen into a panic that your cold (which you had last time you wrote) got worse, and that you're now ill. You're not, are you? These last 3 days I have been uncannily conscious of you, seeing you by me as I walked along lanes, etc, which is itself a happy state, but it also made me afraid you might be dead. I expect it's one of those periodic thinning of the atmospheres – like when in the extreme distance (specially in this country) there is an extraordinary crystal clearness, a spot of startling visibility to which the miles make no distance at all.

... Alan came back from London on Wednesday, bringing with him the contents of 2 of your beloved parcels, and the soap. You will never know, I'm afraid, what a joy the soap is; those large curved mauve-pink cakes are completely voluptuous. And of all the things out of the parcels, the packets of to-drink chocolate most brought a lump to my throat. From their being the same as the packets you used to have in Grosvenor St[63] . . . I thought of the Sunday mornings and times late at night when we used to make cups of chocolate with the electric kettle.

The other things cheese, sardines, etc., are just as welcome here as they'd be in London, as they are what is missing in this country.

Constantia Maxwell[64] is here and is being most trying, poor dear, as she developed a chill or bilious attack or something, and crawls about saying how bad she feels most of the time. It's awful, but people being 'nervous' about themselves has the most anaphrodisiac effect on me. I should be much sorrier for the poor old dear

---

[63] In London, CR had had a service flat at 32 Grosvenor Street.

[64] Constantia Maxwell (1886-1962), historian, and first woman ever on the academic staff of Trinity College, Dublin, where in 1946 she was appointed Lecky Professor of Modern History.

if she weren't so sorry for herself. When she is not fussing about her health she is fussing about mine, which I also loathe, telling me I look tired (which is the last thing I feel, except when she has that effect on me) or that she is certain I have a sore throat. . . . You can imagine, this has a dire effect on Alan. However, she is going back to Dublin tomorrow – half of her visit, fortunately, was over when he returned from England. . . .
[Ends]

Bowen's Court, Sunday, 14th October 1945
Dear love. . . .

I am trying to imagine you in the pale shell-rimmed glasses. I am madly conservative, and in principle don't like to contemplate any change in your appearance. But on the other hand I expect you do look adorable in them; and that I shall be reconciled the moment (or after the first moment) I see you. Oh beloved, if I could only see you I wouldn't mind if you wore a jazz-shaped rectangular, bright pink pair! At any rate, I'm glad you're keeping the dark-framed ones . . . I am still trying to imagine the pale-rimmed ones. Actually, you don't make blunders about appearance, so I expect you're right.

I think you're right about not writing any more plans until things take form. I won't ask anything more until I hear – I know when there is anything to be known, or even liable to be known, you'll tell me. I am in a continuous state of inside concentration on that one hope and wish; but I promise I won't let that develop into 'a state'.

2 days ago there was a complete – but complete – cigarette famine and literally not one in any shop in village or town in a 30 mile radius. Not even definite hopes of when there would be any. A rumour must have gone round that I was in danger of madness, because the most unexpected people suddenly turned up trumps and handed me across their private supplies – the blacksmith, the

rector, the chemist, the MFH[65] – small mysterious parcels of 3 or 4 battered musty cigarettes arrived, as it were, carried by ravens – And even some complete 20 packets. I felt really unscrupulous and degraded, preying on everyone's feeling and robbing them. But I really did feel awful – I was alarmed to find what a grip smoking has got on me. Supplies, however, reached Kildorrery late yesterday evening.

Which put me in a more appropriate mood for the Harvest Thanksgiving in church today. During the height of my cigarette-less neurosis, yesterday morning, I decorated the church – which was probably rather a good thing to do, as I couldn't have smoked in church anyhow. So our small rather musty church looked much engayé this morning, with beets, dahlias, turnips, carrots, michaelmas daisy. No sheaves of corn could be got, as all the corn has been threshed. I also badgered Jim Gates into playing 2 hymns on the organ – we had 'Come ye thankful people, come' and 'Shall we gather by the river?' – a favourite childhood hymn of Farahy church.[66] It was really rather a moving little service – all the congregation are farmers and farmers' wives, and all has safely been gathered in, so the thanksgiving really had some point.

Jim's playing is rather of the bar-piano type; and Ava Gates and I were the only choir – have you ever heard me sing? I hope not. However, much heart went into it.

Oh, I do want to talk to you so. Still more, so much to hear you talk: there are so many things, so much, I want to hear. And my mind, my being, has become very silent, with you away.

By now, I expect you guess by the degree of illegibility of my letters where they are written from. I mean, in what part of the house, and in what attitude. You are right (probably) this one is

---

65 Master of Fox Hounds

66 The tiny Farahy church (Church of Ireland) is at the gates of the avenue to Bowen's Court.

again written on the library sofa in front of the fire, me curled up and the writing-pad propped on my thigh. It's 6.30 Sunday evening, the rooks are beginning to cross the sky cawing, the dusk is falling – and the point is wearing right off my pencil. I have no pen-knife; so, darling, I'd better stop.

Oh my beloved Charles –

Your E.

The Demon Lover is to be published on Oct. 22nd. So I expect the copy I ordered will soon be making its way to you.

Bowen's Court, Monday, 22nd October 1945

Dearest – I've had your beloved October 10th letter. I won't breathe a premature thing – breath, hope, exclamation – but I can't turn away from the thought that you <u>may</u> be in London at the (end) of November, or beginning of December. When and if there is anything definite, will you send me a cable to here – as cryptic a cable as you like. On the possibility of seeing you, I'm planning to go back to London in the 3rd week of November. If anything goes wrong and you don't come over, I shall probably stay <u>here</u> till the other side of Christmas. That is that. It is only possible to write shortly and bleakly about anything that matters so much.

All the same, how can I get the joy of this possibility out of my mind? I'm glad you've told me of it, even if there should be a disappointment. It's worth a lot to feel – to have felt – as happy as I feel now. Oh Charles.

<u>Angel</u> to be sending me those cosmetics – beautiful and imaginative angel. Whatever the duty may be it will be worth it: there are so few glamorous objects, or what we might call commodities, left in the Old World. Every time I use that mauve-pink soap of yours I experience pleasure. I reluctantly put one cake of it in the guest room, but rushed upstairs and reclaimed it (wonderfully little diminished) before the departing guest's car had turned the first bend of the avenue. How mean one gets.

I make myself cups of chocolate out of those packets you sent. Especially on Sunday mornings when I get back from church. Church here (I mean the service) is at 10.15 a.m. and the building, shut up during the week, is decidedly cold and musty. So I always come home rather goose-fleshy, though gay – I must say I do like going to church – and at once light the primus[67] in the pantry, there being no electric kettle in the house as the current isn't strong enough to carry one, and make my cup of chocolate. Which to my mind is a Sunday-morningish thing, connected with those Sunday mornings at Grosvenor Street. In fact drinking that chocolate does to me what the madeleine did to Proust[68] – I see your Grosvenor St sitting room, the grain of that light wood furniture, the off-white damask coverings of the chairs, the thick net curtains over the window, the folds of the green curtains, and the beloved ridiculous artificial palpitations of the electric fire. There is a slight smell of soap coming out of the bathroom where you have just done shaving. Please darling send me some more packets of chocolate.

My advance copy of *The Demon Lover* has arrived – a rather mousy-looking slim volume. Yours is I hope on the way to you. But oh how I wish that it were the novel. . . .

Did I tell you we are having an auction here? I decided to sell a whole lot of repellent non-indigenous furniture that has long been mouldering in unused rooms of the house. It is mostly stuff that my grandfather, whose fine mind decayed into a passion for auction-going, brought back from auctions all over the country. I am told that now is the time to sell. Auctions are madly popular functions in this country – at all times, and especially now – second

---

67 Primus stoves, developed in the late 19th century, vaporised kerosene into a gas for cooking.

68 A trigger to memory and reminiscence.

only to funerals and race-meetings. The whole countryside is humming about this auction, which is to be the day after tomorrow, Wed Oct 24th. If I only make twenty or thirty pounds, I shall be content, if that awful furniture goes. Other people are also sending things to be auctioned – the most fantastic objects keep arriving on carts. The auctioneer Denis Murphy, who is a great snob, is only accepting outside goods he considers high class. Some madly recherché Regency clocks and candlesticks, which would sell for large sums in those Grosvenor and Davies and Albemarle St shops[69] we used to look into, have arrived; I don't know from where. . . . I am rather looking forward to the auction; I expect it will be awfully entertaining. But for the present it has rather upset the peace of the house – straws blow about outside, chaos reigns within. And the smell when it is all over will I expect be like that the morning after a hunt ball only worse because more proletarian. The auction is only taking place in 3 rooms of the house: A and I are barricaded into the other part.

It has been the most heavenly beautiful week – sun all day, full moon all night, and mists, filtering sunshine and moonlight equally. Glittering dew and cobwebs in the early mornings. Such a week for you to be here, if you were here. Oh most beloved.

Love. Your E.

Have you read – I've just read – Le Fanu's Carmilla,[70] the first vampire story? It's most exquisite, delicate, beautiful; an amitié amoureuse between 2 young girls, one of whom turns out to be a vampire. It had the most erotic effect on me – more so than any book I have read for a long time. Do you think I have got a vampire complex?

---

[69] In Mayfair, London.

[70] 'Carmilla' (1872), a novella about a lesbian vampire by Anglo-Irish writer of ghostly and mystery stories Sheridan Le Fanu (1814-1873).

Creagh Castle,[71] *12th November 1945*
Dear beloved – I got your letter of Nov. 1st this morning. Till January, then – oh darling it does seem terribly far away. I've got into an inner habit of saying 'next month . . .' I pray God nothing may go wrong about January. I love you so much. I don't think I can go on living much longer without you. . . .

Charles, how have we lived through this last year?

Yes, I have been and am (as you have felt) infinitely happier here than I am in London. I do hope my letters from London weren't getting to sound awfully cantankerous and scatty? I enjoy life here like one enjoys a book – it's like an Edwardian novel though also with curious veins of poetry and spirituality.

At the same time it's a life that must have something in its core – something not it. You and my love for you are in the core, or are the core. If you were dead or lost, or if I were confronted by having no prospect of seeing you again, I could not bear life here. The possibility of suffering here could be endless, more than anywhere else: one's heart and imagination and nerves and senses are so exposed. If anything died in the inner part of my life, which is you, I should leave B Court, part with the house and never come back again. . . . Beloved, I am so idiotically in love with you – I mean it takes such naïve idiotic forms. I suddenly think of something about you, and break into smiles all over my face. Not only when I am alone, but sometimes when I am with other people, or walking down the middle of a street.

As things are, I shall stay here till January 2nd, then cross back to London that day. Alan returns from London at the end of this month, and we might just as well spend December at B Court, as it gives him heaps to do and he's much happier.

---

[71] Creagh Castle, six miles from Bowen's Court in north Co Cork, was the home of EB's friend Dorothy Bucknal.

. . . I am writing this in bed at Creagh Castle. It's now 11.15 p.m. A very bright new moon has been gleaming through a crack of the curtains, and I can hear the sound of the river weir in the valley below the house. I am here just for the night. . . .

The people I was staying with – Bobby and Molly Keane[72] have the most heavenly child called Sally; you would have loved her: I did. In fact all that week-end I wished particularly that you were there. Sally is six or seven, with dark red hair and very dark eyes, under that kind of high white prominent forehead that is curiously touching and beautiful in a child. She made a set at me and I lost my heart to her. The Keanes have this last summer had another baby – also a girl, and to be called Virginia – they say they did not particularly want one, but that Sally bullied them into it by her disparaging remarks. She said that all her friends' parents seemed able to have other babies, and that it seemed funny to her that her own couldn't. . . .

Talking of little girls, how is your niece Elizabeth?[73] And talking of relations, I had a letter the other day from Dor.[74] She says *The Gazebo* is just out. I have written to The Tatler asking them not to fail to send it to me in the next batch of books. . . . If only I were in London I'd push it round – I mean, push it a bit on my fellow reviewers. But I hope it may do extremely well under its own steam any way. In fact – as I always did say to you – I wouldn't a bit wonder if it had a spanking success.

---

[72] Molly Keane (1904-1996), playwright and novelist, a witty chronicler of Anglo-Ireland.

[73] Elizabeth Ritchie (1941-2001) was the daughter of CR's younger brother Roland (Roley) Ritchie (1910-1988), a lawyer and later Supreme Court Justice, and his wife Mary (Bunny).

[74] Doris Almon Ponsonby (1907-1993), a cousin of CR's, who went on to become a prolific author of historical fiction under the name D.A. Ponsonby. Her first husband was the 1st Baron Ponsonby. She also published under the names Doris Rybot (her subsequent married name) and Sarah Tempest.

No, I've never read the Paston Letters:[75] I've always meant to and wanted to, and you make me want to more, now. As a family book, I'm sending you Tony Butts' book (which is completely mad but I think very fascinating) about his family. I expect you remember me talking about him often? He was that great friend of William Plomer's and mine who committed suicide in 1941. He left the MSS of this book, in a most awful mess, and William has edited it – inevitably he has had to cut the more outrageous passages, but it is pretty off as it stands. It is called *Curious Relations*, and William[76] has had to say on the cover that it's by 'William d'Arfey', as all Tony's relations, especially his step-relations, the Colville Hydes (whom he has called 'the Montfaucons') are furious and are threatening to take actions. Actually the stories in the book are funnier the way Tony used to tell them (as I remember) than they are written down.

It's past midnight now: I've already blunted the points off 3 beautifully-sharpened pencils. I wish – to put it mildly – that you were here in this room, with the sound of the river outside the windows.

Oh beloved – good night. Love E.

Bowen's Court, Sunday, 18th November 1945

Beloved dear Charles – I came back here on Tuesday evening after a day in Cork to find a cable from you on the hall table, which made me very happy. . . .

Also, that same Tuesday evening when I got back from Cork I found, oh you angel, that cosmetic parcel of yours from Ottawa. A whole world of Ardens.[77] I don't think anything concrete short

---

75 A collection of letters of three generations of a fifteenth-century Norfolk family. In 1945, CR must have been reading them in a nineteenth or early twentieth-century (1904) edition.

76 The poet and novelist William Plomer (1903-1973), who also wrote an elegy in memory of Anthony Butts, whom he had loved.

77 High-class cosmetics by Elizabeth Arden.

of actually you could have made me happier. And as far as I know (and as doubtless you did know) these particular Ardens are all new numbers; at any rate where the Old World is concerned: I had certainly never even heard of the 'fluffy' vanishing cream. I can't tell you what heaven it is to put on the face, it makes one feel masked in velvet, and one's skin feels like velvet after it. The day cream, hand cream and powder are also a mad success. Living alone in this house, painted and creamed and blooming up to the nines, I'm developing a positive narcissism, like darling Stephen T[78] (who is very well; I've had several long letters from him) and am always rushing to look at myself in the glass. I also épater my neighbours when I go out. I'd bought in Cork, where there's one not bad shop, a rather bright green-blue (they call it petrol blue) tweed suit – strictly, dress and short coat. It's a brighter colour than I normally wear, but the effect plus Arden (including the Winged Victory lipstick) is extremely dashing – if slightly what used to be called fast.

I can see what would happen to my clothes if I lived in Ireland: my eye would get slightly out. There's nothing here between the out-and-out dowdy and the bad style – rather large checks, rather bright colours. Acclimatised to the Irish dress atmosphere, when one gets back to London one will look distinctly odd. But then, I am a born, to-the-bone provincial; and I suppose, like my ancestors, in a twisted and haughty way rather proud of it. Like all provincials, I expect London, or any capital city, to be something terrific: hence my depression and irritation and neurosis which you must have felt in my letters all those months after the official finish of the war – when London in any way breaks down, when the illusion fails.

---

[78] Stephen Tennant (1906-1987), an extravagantly camp, aristocratic aesthete with dyed golden hair. In 1942 EB introduced him to CR who described him in his diary as 'a high spirited and amusing pansy.' They spent a 'dreamlike, unrepeatable' weekend with him at Wilsford Manor in Wiltshire.

By that same Tuesday post – or rather, discovered here that same Tuesday evening – I found the enclosed extraordinary letter from Shaya.[79] I suppose that – in view of his 'burn this, burn this, destroy this' – I ought not to be sending it on. But really I cannot see that it is in any way dangerous or compromising. Is it? You, having greater background of knowledge, may see more in it than I do. I don't find that any of the facts are other than I had dimly imagined: what is interesting – and to me fascinating – is their effect on him. Though one never forgets that Shaya is a Jew, I suppose I had rather forgotten that Shaya is a Russian Jew and that, until he was 9, Russian, his native language, was his only language. I shall very much like to know what you think of this letter. I suppose you had better either burn it; or better, keep it locked up and give it back to me some day. And, as you will feel, don't quote it. There certainly would be a breach if he knew that I'd sent it on. Though I can't see the point of all this mystery. . . .

Reading the letter nearly sent me mad – not, obviously, with boredom or unsympathy, but with a mixture of communicated fever and frustration owing to Shaya's difficult writing and the fact that he'd crammed the pages into the envelope in the wrong order and upside down. I have numbered them, so you won't have to go through the same thing. I also feel guilty because his whole letter is inspired by a misapprehension – I know I never said, in any way that Pravda could have got hold of, that I wanted more Russian works to be translated.[80]

Here, it's passed over from autumn into early winter. . . . I've started having a log fire in my bedroom: I love going to sleep by its light. With the beginning of the hunting, Co Cork has woken

---

[79] The Oxford don and political philosopher Isaiah Berlin (1909-1997) was 'Shaya' to his friends. EB and he became close friends during the decade when she and Alan lived in Old Headington, Oxford. CR met him with EB at 2 Clarence Terrace in 1942.

[80] Berlin's letter has not survived, and it has proved impossible (so far) to discover what it was about.

up from its long summer sleep, houses that were empty are being opened, and men just out of the army are rushing about doing things about their horses. It's like scenes out of *War and Peace* – they might really be coming back after the Napoleonic wars – pretty women in 1938 evening dresses sitting round them in groups in lamplit drawing-rooms, hanging on their words. It's being like that in your country, I hope and expect. And, of course, both the Anglo-Irish and the Canadians have the distinction of being voluntary fighters, with the old gallant surround. Certainly, they are both luckier, now, than the young men coming back to England – to tired women, long tales of civilian suffering and, in so many cases, no homes at all. It's desperate for the English. I'm beginning – anyhow at this safe distance – to have a renewed, emergency, 1940 fondness for them.

... I think of you night and day

All my love

E.

Bowen's Court, Monday, 26th November 1945

My dearest. ... I am very glad you told me about the projected possibilities, the plans – always subject, as you say, to so many things – for the United Nations meetings. January, London – all being well. Then the next full one, after the interval, some time in spring, not yet known where. Oh, may it be in Europe, even if it can't be London! ...

I think of you so much and love you so much and am so proud of you. I'm so very glad and happy that I know you – which sounds a naïve and anti-climaxic thing to say – doesn't it. ... How queer: we parted in the cold weather, the short days. A whole round of seasons has gone round since then – spring, summer, autumn. In a way, this past year has been rather like a year on the screen (if such a thing were possible) or a year in a vivid but cold book to me. A year of terrific happenings but with no inner meaning for me. One week differentiated from another by your letters. No, really I haven't been as unmoved as all that by what's happening outside: who could be? I suppose millions of people in the world are feeling, for different reasons (some interior love or hope or even obsession that the convulsions round them have only driven in deeper) pretty much the same.

. . . What do you think of this new pen, the one I'm writing with? I bought it in Dublin and it's called a 'Biro'. Perhaps this is no novelty to you: it is to me. It is, its makers claim, not a mere pen but 'a precision writing instrument'. It's got ball-bearings inside it, or something. Anyway, it does run very smoothly; so much so that it's like being run away with on roller-skates. . . .

Dublin was very enjoyable. I saw a lot of people, was shown a beautiful private collection of old Irish silver belonging to a German Jew, went to the museum to look at more silver (while I was in the vein) and bought some clothes – black suede and other gloves – much nicer than they now have in London – some oddments, and a black wool dress which I do hope my darling that you will like. I can't tell you what it feels like to be buying clothes that you may possibly see.

The dear Shelbourne was very much the same: I had a nice room looking out at the back (I mean, the reverse direction from Stephen's Green) over low roofs toward the dome and clock of the Government buildings. The latter was very useful as I have no watch. A tremendous blinding white fog – more completely dense than any London fog I remember and only less bad in not leaving that foul taste on the tongue – came on in the middle of the day on Thursday. This completely dislocated Dublin's business and social life. In the middle of it I picked my way along the Merrion Square railings to 50 Upper Mount Street, as I was going to meet Sir John Maffey there and drive with him out to his house (some miles outside Dublin) for lunch. The British Representative's office was in the grip of a diplomatic crisis because of the fog. Sir John buoyantly determined to drive out to Dundrum, come what might, and his two detectives (who look the most awful thugs) dissuading him. . . . So we filed to the club through the blind fog, preceded by the detectives who attempted by fanning movements to disperse the fog ahead of Sir John. They also when we had to cross streets uttered foghorn-like noises. Certainly if British Representatives had been knocked into by a bicycle it would have looked like an incident.

George O'Brien had another of his nice mellow little dinner parties.

The last night, Friday, I stayed at Corkagh.[81] Reggie Ross Williamson[82] having a car, kindly picked me up somewhere else and drove me out there, which simplified matters. As we drove down the avenue from that upper gate he said, 'How do you feel, coming back here?' I said, 'Why?' and he said that, though he loved Corkagh he thought it was the most melancholy house in Ireland. I must say it has never struck me like that. Peculiar, yes. . . . I had a hornet in my bedroom which got into my hair, and at dinner I swallowed a fish bone, which got wedged in my throat and made me feel quite feverish the whole evening. It is so like darling Corkagh to have a bone the size of a whale's vertebra inside an apparent fillet of plaice. The idea, apart from the feeling, of anything stuck in my throat rattles me and fills me with animal fear. I felt my eyes glazing, as the evening went on, and my manner becoming madder and madder. The family all took it rather calmly, saying that the fish bone would in the course of time, they were sure, dissolve into glue. . . .

I've just been reviewing Dor's novel for the Tatler. . . . Talking of books, *The Demon Lover* has had some very nice reviews. I wonder

---

[81] Corkagh Park, Clondalkin, Co Dublin, a large property where EB had spent much time as a child, was the home of her Aunt Edie and Uncle George Colley.

[82] Reginald Ross Williamson, attached to the British Representative's office.

whether you saw the New Statesman one. If you do see the NS, I hope you haven't missed the sharp little rap Raymond[83] delivered to Existentialism in general, Sartre in particular. I asked Cyril, who has been flirting with it for some time, exactly what Existentialism was, and he said 'Something to do with picking one's nose.' All the same, I do want to read *Huis Clos*[84]. . . .

I live to see you.

Good night. All my love

E.

23 December [Ottawa]

This Ottawa part of my life may be over. When I come back it and I will be different. Already it is beginning to take on the first blush of nostalgic charm, when only a week ago it seemed unendurable. Sylvia [Smellie] had become a symbol of obligations, and this was stripping her of all charms in my eyes. Now that I am leaving her, I begin to love her. What can I do with my shifting irresolute nature which spoils other people's lives and my own.

25 December

Nothing gloomier than this Christmas has ever happened to me. . . . I suppose someday this Death of the Heart, this paralysis of the mind, this dreary vacuum will end – in fact it should end very shortly with my departure for England. The situation with S is so sad and so familiar. It has so many echoes both of the past and of the future in it. How dare we be so silly as to imagine that we have free will? I have been frozen in the same trance of indecision

---

[83] Raymond Mortimer (1895-1980), a good friend of EB, was a literary critic, literary editor of the *New Statesman* and later lead reviewer of *The Sunday Times*.

[84] Existentialist play (1944) by Jean-Paul Sartre, translated as *No Exit*, in which occurs the famous remark 'Hell is other people.'

between love and doubt for twenty years. The face of love has changed, but the pain goes on. . . .

Christmas lunch with the Smellies. Somehow with gallant bravura we kept the conversation going. S and I were both hag-ridden with melancholia. . . . Poor S last night saying 'Tout va bien', that broke me. Oh damn this stupid diary.

1946

Charles was in London for most of January and February 1946 for meetings of the General Assembly of the United Nations Organization. The agenda included the first elections to the Security Council, which Canada was expected to win, but did not. Elizabeth was in London, at 2 Clarence Terrace.

23 February

Back in Ottawa busily engaged in routine. My present way of life is very much like it used to be at boarding-school. Then I lived in a state of suspended animation waiting for the holidays. . . . I lived more in an hour in London than in a month here. But there is a difference between my feelings now and before I went away. Before I was trying, honestly trying, to adapt myself, to be a success here, to find a wife, to get full marks as an efficient higher civil servant, and I was deeply concerned at my failure to do all these things. Now I feel a blissful indifference. . . . I doubt if I shall ever make the kind of charming, domestic, conventional marriage that I once longed for. And at last, at long long last I have stopped caring – much. . . . Then I believe again in love. I see now that what I feel for E with all its imperfections (on my side) is the 'Love of my Life' and that I must never hope to find that again. Any other love will have to be of a different kind.

2 Clarence Terrace, Tuesday, 26th February 1946
My darling. . . . 'Back to letters again', as you say. How little they are, for two people like us – and yet how much, everything, when one has nothing else. Today, as things are, the one thing that could have made me happy was a letter from you. And one came. But we mustn't again for months and years on end have to live on a substitute for being alive, together. . . .

I have in the practical sense no news, not having since I last wrote risen from my bed, except to potter about, or left my room. Really jaundice is fantastic. I keep remembering things you told me about when you had it. I've disconnected the telephone by my bed, and feel so remote from London that I might almost be miles away in some queer hut-hospital on a stretch of wind-blasted heath, like you were. Dr B came again yesterday and said I could start getting up in a day or two, and could probably go out (tottering round the park) towards the end of the week. . . .

When I feel slightly more energetic and get my brain back, this will be or at any rate should be an excellent opportunity to get on with work. One night, in bed, if you have got a Coleridge, will you read The Ancient Mariner, again, and Kubla Khan, for my sake? I have read and brooded over those poems, this last week, so that I seem to have absorbed them into my system forever. And they are all merged into, and dyed by, the thoughts and feelings and memories I have had of you.

I'm all the more determined to snap out of this illness because I see how insidious it could be: I know perfectly well how much I dread going out again, back to life, round about London, in the already brightening spring air with sweetness in it, and your not being there. What extraordinary spring brightness there was, for instance, that last Sunday afternoon when we were standing in that nice sluttish gin-gutted Mayfair queue outside the Curzon [Cinema]. Such unearthly brightness not only in the sun but in the shadow; really for a moment I felt as though we were standing in a Sunday-afternoon street in some modern part of Rome. . . .

William Plomer wrote today, asking me to lunch and asking if you could come too – or rather, asking for your address in order that he might write to you. Writing back, I had to tell him that your present address was Ottawa. Peter Q[85] wrote suggesting he and I soon have our projected vingt-et-un party and ask Anne Rothermere, as anybody, he says, can make 4 or 5 pounds out of her, at that game, any night. What sharks our men of letters are becoming. . . .

Yes, certainly you <u>are</u> my life. I have felt and still feel as though I were not here – in this room, in this house, in London – at all; but as though I had crossed the air over the Atlantic with you, and were now following you round Ottawa, from place to place.

Goodbye for now, sweet. I'll write again towards the end of the week. I love you.

Elizabeth

2 Clarence Terrace, Friday, 1st March 1946

Darling. . . .

I am now up and tottering round the house; the jaundice is evaporating from my system but I feel weak and cross. Not, so far, particularly depressed – except about, and by, my appearance. When in bed I simply lie on my back and forget that I <u>am</u>, or, at any rate, that I look like anything. But the necessity of dressing, looking at oneself in the glass, is awful. Truly, I look like something just out of Belsen, or an aged she-wolf. However I suppose I shall improve. Not seeing anybody, as I'm firmly not doing, is at any rate a great

---

85 Peter Quennell (1905-1993), poet, historian, biographer and editor, and a notable aficionado of women.

pleasure. Before I return to the world I shall take a taxi across to E Arden's and have a terrifically expensive, I hope efficient, face-do. Another thing that worries me is that I really seem to be suffering from softening of the brain; I can't remember anything or find anything; and when I pick up anything I tend to drop it.

One thing, it's a tremendous time to read; one's imagination sucks everything into its own cloudy hinterland, like damp blotting-paper. Poetry, and Victorian novels, and even our brilliant younger critics like George Orwell – his *Critical Essays* are rather fascinating. And John Summerson's *Georgian London*, which I've been waiting for for ages, has come today. If it's as good as I hope and have reason to hope, I'll send you a copy.

Oh and darling, I must be completely mad; several days ago (in fact, I've written to you at least once since) a Canada House car delivered a beautifully packed parcel with your card, containing those 2 superb bottles of rye. My darling, it was angelic and good of you! It's futile to say, 'You shouldn't have!' because obviously nothing could have given more pleasure to this household. But it just was, like many things you have done, superhumanly imaginative and sweet. I passed one bottle to Alan for immediate consumption: the other he has locked away for me as soon as I am able to drink again. . . .

One Victorian writer I simply cannot take is Charlotte M. Yonge.[86] I detested any books of hers that I tried to read when young, and I find I react in exactly the same way, only more strongly, now. So many people I know have got a thing about her. Hester[87] has felt it her mission to make me read and like Miss Yonge for years; and now, with the kindest, sweetest intentions and profiting

---

[86] Charlotte M. Yonge (1823-1901), devout High Anglican, novelist, schoolteacher and philanthropist. Her most famous novel is *The Heir of Redclyffe* (1853).

[87] Hester Chapman (1899-1976), author of historical biographies and romantic fiction.

by my jaundice, has sent me *The Pillars of the House* (2 vols).[88] It seems to me charnel and dreary to a degree; and in passages positively disgusting. The grinding ghastly poverty, the High Anglican atmosphere, the muffishness of everybody; the awful pale stew with rice in it they are always eating, the neurosis, the absence of sex-appeal. Her awful way of referring to Holy Communion, which everybody is always going to, as 'The Feast'. Even the incest is dull. No the fact is, I can't bear books, novels, which are not either elegant or cosy, ideally both. 'Elegant' may include of course the highest aesthetic quality – I mean, I'd call *Wuthering Heights*[89] elegant. And cosiness may crop up in the oddest places: I'd call Proust, for instance, a cosy writer. Jane Austen is my ideal woman writer because she is one hundred percent both. Poor repellent Miss Yonge is neither: she couldn't possibly be elegant if she tried, but it's her lack of cosiness that is unpardonable. . . .

I'm down in the front room, on the sofa, looking out at the park. Snow is lying, and there's a light glare from it which is rather nice. It's the early afternoon. I think I'm going across the room to the telephone, to send you a cable. Oh Charles, you are the only one in the world that I really care if I look beautiful for. And yet, if I could only see you for a moment, now, I wouldn't mind your seeing me like this. I do long for you so constantly. I've had several odd, semi-delirious dreams about you: they've all been happy ones. You have the most adorable glowing face.

Goodbye for now, sweetness. I shall be writing again soon.

Elizabeth

2 *Clarence Terrace, Wednesday, 6th March 1946*

My darling, I'm upright and at the typewriter, so today I'll write you a more legible letter. I am longing for another from you – the

---

[88] Published 1873

[89] By Emily Brontë

concentrated happiness of seeing your handwriting is extraordinary. I haven't been outside the house yet; it seems idiotic, but we're having a spell of the most gripping cold, sleety snow at intervals, with all the time the most icelike winds. . . . I literally haven't been outside this house since the Sunday evening of the day you left, the evening I came in after saying goodbye to you.

I must go out tomorrow, as far as Cyril's – one block up the Park – because at half-past six he has got Lord Gorell of the Committee coming – that terrible committee that's 'sitting' on the future of the Regent's Park terraces. The most nightmarish reports of the probable findings of the committee are coming in – it seems more and more likely that they will pull all these terraces down. That they should do so exceeds one's most horrific imaginations of the brave new world. . . . So really I must see Lord Gorell. The committee, I hear, is from time to time asking people to give evidence, and I should rather like to do so.[90]

. . . Alan has taken that job with the Gramophone Company,[91] and now he has got started seems quite happy – he went through the most awful (and trying for all) crisis about having turned down the other thing – the Ministry of Education and UNESCO liaison job – he thinks it would have been more public-spirited to have done that. . . . Your rye, arriving at the height of this crisis, really was a godsend, my darling. I was feeling stupefied with jaundice misery, and the poor tortured creature, ramping round and round my room at intervals having regrets and conscience-storms, was

---

[90] The Gorell Committee, appointed in 1946 to advise on the war-damaged Regent's Park terraces, of which Clarence Terrace was one, recommended in 1947 that they should be preserved and repaired.

[91] Alan Cameron had retired early from his post as Secretary to the Central Council of School Broadcasting at the BBC, due to failing eyesight. For the next seven years he worked as educational adviser for EMI, carrying through a scheme for educational gramophone records. His health was poor. He was overweight, and drank heavily.

driving me crazy. The bottle of rye I passed over had a cheering, calming and equanimity-making effect on him. . . .

How lovely that time was, in April, when you stayed here when you were semi-convalescent. I think you still felt awful, really, and I know you felt weak, but you were so sweet and it was lovely having you under this roof. It was April; we used to walk round the park – I remember going for a long walk in the rain one morning, to explore those two Regency 'villages' along the canal, on the far side.[92] Not the best thing for you, probably, but it was lovely. I remember you talking about Halifax [Nova Scotia], describing it. Oh Charles, you are such a sweetness. I can't bear being without your companionship. Every place, every part of London I have been in with you has a touch of heaven about it for me – does that sound a silly thing to say? But no, I can't be indifferent to any place I have walked in with you, or walked past with you, or looked at with you. I wish I had been in Ottawa; I wish you could also connect me with things and places there. . . .

You will send me your mother's address, won't you.

My cousin Audrey Fiennes[93] is in London today and is coming to see me this evening; which I shall enjoy very much. Except for one girl friend, B. Horton,[94] I haven't so far seen anyone; because I haven't wanted to. However, I go back to social life next week.

I'm back into, and at, my novel again, which is agitating but makes me very absorbed, and in one kind of way happy. I could

---

[92] In April 1943 CR, recovering from flu, had convalesced at 2 Clarence Terrace. The two Regency 'villages' are Park Village East and Park Village West. CR often fondly recalled that walk in his diary.

[93] Audrey Fiennes (properly Twistleton-Wykeham-Fiennes) was the daughter of EB's maternal Aunt Gertrude, and the cousins were bosom friends from childhood. Audrey knew Alan Cameron before EB did. Though never engaged to be married, they had been a 'couple,' and remained fond of one another. After Alan and EB married in 1923, the three took holidays or stayed at Bowen's Court together.

[94] Beatrice Horton was the sister of EB's literary agent Spencer Curtis Brown.

not have chosen to write a more difficult book; I seem to have set myself every kind of problem, technical and psychological.[95]

I live for your letters – which doesn't mean you must have a compulsion about writing. But loving you so much and missing you so horribly and feeling so dejected and bewildered with you away, I suppose it's inevitable for me to feel like this.

Goodbye for now, beloved,

Elizabeth

7 April [New York]

Sex Excesses

Symptoms. 12 hours after – rapid heart action, sense of guilt, feverish erotic spasms. . . . fits of irritability and cruelty, indifference to invitations and unanswered letters, coarsening of sympathy, aversion to old people, loose tongue, muddled brain, carelessness about appearance. 24 hours after. 'In my bosom a full sun', moving on oiled wheels, a new good-natured insolence, 'in the groove'. Illusions as to one's possibilities and attractions, an innocent eye when cashing a bum cheque, good timing in dancing.

19 May

Things are beginning to catch up with me. Turn and twist as I may, marriage looms ahead. It is not so much marriage that frightens me as the necessity for a decision at a given moment at a given date. Panic seizes me and to escape from panic I turn to reading over and over the poems which T.S. Eliot has written since the war: 'East Coker', 'Little Gidding' and the others.[96] They have the soothing effect of barbitual.

---

95 She was working on *The Heat of the Day*

96 T.S. Eliot's *Four Quartets*, in which these poems first appeared in book form, was published in 1944.

Bowen's Court, Kildorrery, Monday, 20th May 1946

My darling. . . . Oh Charles when shall I see you? I feel so lonely sometimes that I feel almost dotty. Failing anything else you couldn't simply take a holiday could you, and come over here? . . . I keep dreaming, I mean day-dreaming, that you are arriving at Rineanna airport[97] (only about 45 miles from here) and that I am driving there to pick you up in the car. Why shouldn't one be able to be happy. Really love does matter more than anything else in the world. If more people were as right-minded and as happy as you and I are capable of being, the world would be a very different place.

My car is rattling along, falling to pieces round me as I drive. I do hope it will last. I must say that romantic as this old ruin of a Morris tourer is, I do like having something to drive again so much that I long for something more banal and bourgeois but more dependable and less decomposing, like an Austin. Also the side-curtains of the car have got lost and it is very very cold. It is so odd here, like an uncanny tropical January, all the beauty of colour and frozen sunshine. Rather like everything is when you're not with me. We had one icy storm from the mountains and I found a drift of snow in the garden just where the roses are beginning to come out.

I've finished reading with passionate enjoyment *Thérèse Desqueroux* and I am now going on to another Mauriac[98] I've got here, *Les Chemins de la Mer.* I'm also half way through an absolutely heavenly book Gerald gave me, *Le Grand Meaulnes.*[99] Have you read it? If not, I shall send it when I've finished it; I feel certain you would love it.

---

97 The airport at Rineanna in Co Clare was already in 1946 renamed Shannon Airport, now Shannon International Airport.

98 François Mauriac (1885-1970), French author and Nobel prize-winner.

99 *Le Grand Meaulnes* (1913) by Alain-Fournier, who was called up into the French army in 1914 and killed a month later, aged 27. The 'Gerald' who lent it to EB was Lord Berners (1883-1950), composer, novelist, painter and aesthete. It was a book which meant a lot to CR.

It's about a truant schoolboy getting lost in the woods in the middle of December and coming to a lonely mysterious chateau, among pools and reeds, where an enormous party, consisting principally of children, is going on, night after night, day after day. Pianos playing, candles burning, little girls chasing each other along passages, pony races, parties boating on the lake in the winter sunshine. Everybody is waiting for the arrival of a bridal couple, who never come. I am still only half way through it – it is a romantic and magic book, which I feel you'd love. Please let me know if you've read it. It's by Alain Fournier, who was killed, quite young, in the 1914 war.

The world of letters has followed me here in the person of Henry Reed, one of those young men who write for the New Statesman. He was staying in Dublin and asked if he could come here. He is one of these rather fascinating homosexual characters, and a very good poet – has just published a book of poems called *Map of Verona.*[100] He comes from Birmingham and is of lower-middle-class origin, but has romantic aristocratic views. His boy friend, a gentle creature whom I met in London, is lurking in some other part of Ireland, waiting about for him, so I said he had better come here too: they had had some notion of a tryst in Killarney, but Henry did not seem very enthusiastic about that, and as he evidently prefers to stop here I think he had better have his friend with him. He is very good company (I mean Henry) and does not interfere with me, as he regards it as essential that I should get on with my novel. So if the boy friend, who is at present preserving a moody silence, can be traced, they are to forgather here. I wish I had Anne-Marie's[101] passion for intervening in masculine love affairs, but I haven't.

---

[100] Henry Reed (1914-1986), poet and radio dramatist. *A Map of Verona* included his war poems, among them the well-known 'Naming of Parts.'

[101] Anne-Marie, Princess Callimachi, a Romanian exile and a friend of CR.

I am in the middle of a most cryptic part of my novel – heavens, it is difficult to write. I discard every page, rewrite it and throw discarded sheets of conversation about the floor. Is everything you do as difficult as that? I imagine so. From rubbing my forehead I have worn an enormous hole in it, which bleeds.

Oh darling what it will mean to be able to have a definite day to look forward to; a day on which I can say – this time next week, I shall see Charles. I hope I don't sound very hysterical: I am not only I do so terribly want and miss you. But I'm sure that before the end of the summer I shall see you. I went to the Wishing Well yesterday. . . .

It must have been fun, that weekend with your mother, drinking tea, smoking, talking in her room. I could imagine you. . . . Oh Charles darling.

Love from E.

Bowen's Court, Tuesday, 18th June 1946
My darling. . . . I sort through the letters, when the postman brings them up the steps to the glass door at about 10 o'clock in the mornings, with shaking hands. It's funny, letters from you almost always seem to come on sunny mornings. . . .

I am so fond of my bed here, that large green fourposter. I like its being high, so that I lie on a level with the sills of the 4 windows. I read the last letter I've had from you over again in that bed, sometimes at nights, sometimes in the early mornings, until the next comes. Of course, there's extraordinary happiness in the fact of being in love – however much the sufferings of separation are. I hope it makes you happy to love me. Of course, like all people in love, I like best (when I can't be with you) being alone and at leisure. One of the reasons I hate leaving here is, leaving behind all the vague happy hours in which I think about you in this place.

In London I feel frayed and pin-pricked so much of the time: its expense of spirit is a waste not even of shame, of nothing in particular.

I hope I haven't been making things more difficult while you're working so hard and not all the time feeling too good yourself, by my frenzies and frettings at not seeing you. I often do try hard to behave, though you might not think so, like a good soldier's (or diplomat's) wife. I tell myself how much our wonderful women had to put up with during the war years (those years inside which I was so happy). I can only feel that it must be slightly easier to be wonderful if you're married – that is, to the beloved.

Beloved, tell me that knowing me makes you happy, more not less so. You have changed me so much and given me so much.

All the roses are beginning to come out in the garden here, particularly the dark-red and the cream climbing ones. I have a large pie of them in a silver tureen in the middle of the hall table at which one eats meals. The strawberries are by way of ripening: some of them have been brought into the house, but they are still rather turnipy – they need more sun. This hasn't been a sunny June, on the whole, though there's a lovely silvery rushing of leaves round the house all day which is most consoling.

I've been alone here since I last wrote – except that last night Sylvia Cooke-Collis (my painter girl friend) stayed the night, as she is painting some scenes in the garden and woods here.

Last Sunday Jim Gates put some extra petrol into my car and we went off for a romantic, though highly respectable, day out. We drove over a mountain road to a seaside hotel (former country house) called Monatrea,[102] which stands on one side of the Blackwater river estuary just where the estuary debouches into the sea. We had an excellent lunch (the hotel proprietor learned his business at the Savoy or somewhere) went for a walk on top of the cliffs then returned and took part in a Sunday tea-dance at the hotel. A very animated little swing band in brown tweed coats

[102] Near Youghal in Co Cork.

played Strauss waltzes by request beautifully, and I in the intervals of dancing, sat luxuriously weeping into my strong tea. Darling old Jim (who is partly Austrian on his mother's side) became quite the flashing Austrian for the occasion. . . .

Well, on Friday next I go back to London. So I shall next be writing to you, oh my beautiful creature, from Clarence Terrace.

I love you so much, Charles. Elizabeth

2 Clarence Terrace, Sunday, 30th June 1946
Charles darling. . . .

Yes, yesterday I was lying flat on the long blue sofa here, in a state of Saturday afternoon torpor, looking out of the window ahead of me at the flickering-about branches of a tree in the terrace, when I heard the letters of the afternoon post being dropped by the postman on to the mat. I thought, 'There could be one from my darling,' did not allow myself to hope too much, but heaved myself off the sofa and went to look and there was. I came back to the sofa with it and read it through 3 times. . . .

I had a most uncanny moment the other day, in daylight; I was coming down the last flight of stairs into the hall and thought I saw the outlines of someone standing (as though on the step, having rung the bell and now waiting for the door to open) on the other side of those awful painted glass panels of the front door. I felt certain it would be you – saw, in anticipation, the clothes you would be wearing, your attitude, the expression of your face. I opened the door, but of course there was no one there. . . .

This is a stuffy, warm day, with puffs of wind. I am wearing a frock I always associate with summers while you were here, that white and cochineal-pink diamond-patterned one. It is very old now – 1942, I think I bought it – and fit only for a Sunday afternoon at home, but I do for associative reasons love it.

Hot, empty Ottawa (I mean empty of most of the people you know) must be queer: not unpleasant. By the way, how do you get enough whisky? Oh, one improvement in London is that there's quite a lot of wine – not too bad in price.

All my love,
Elizabeth

In August 1946 Charles Ritchie was appointed as an advisor to the Canadian Delegation to the Paris Peace Conference, convened to formulate the peace treaties between the wartime Allies and Italy and the Balkan States. The Canadian delegates stayed at the Hotel Crillon, and the conference sessions took place in the Palais du Luxembourg. Elizabeth went over to visit Charles. None of her letters to him survive from his time at the Peace Conference.

21 August [Paris]

The Manchester Guardian compares the Peace Conference to the situation described in Sartre's play Huis Clos. Like the characters in Sartre's Hell the nations are trapped by their own past actions and cannot escape. The situation is frozen. The delegates can only repeat endlessly the same arguments and the same gestures. . . .

Having these afternoons off has made all the difference to me. Instead of the Conference life being a fatiguing grind it is just pleasantly interesting. . . . Now I am coming alive again and with everything in me that attaches to life I am determined not ever again to get into that state of joyless overwork. . . .

But to avoid that I must avoid Ottawa. Once in Ottawa there's no escaping my fate. Not a word about E. How much is she the cause of my happiness? I had hardened, now I am sliding back towards her. As she stood waiting for me outside the Meurice Hotel I saw her bent head and the line of her neck and shoulders through the window. She looked noble and sad and she touched me. I cannot bear to write about myself and her.

For his Diplomatic Passport: More Undiplomatic Diaries 1946-1962 *(1981), Charles composed a nostalgic and not undiplomatic entry:*

15 October
Elizabeth Bowen is here. She has got herself accredited to the Conference as a journalist. We meet every day in the fenced-off area of the gravelled terrace outside the Palais de Luxembourg, where the press are permitted to mingle with the diplomats. We sit talking and drinking coffee at one of the small tables set up there and sometimes afterwards have time for a stroll along the tree-lined walks on the shady side of the gardens, past the statues of dead poets. She is staying around the corner at the Hotel Condé, still unchanged as I remember it in the twenties, with its narrow stone stairways leading up to the garret bedrooms. We often dine together in one of the small restaurants on the Left Bank. Her being here is the reality which shows up for me the unreality of this sad charade of a conference.

When the conference ended, Charles went for a short stay with Elizabeth at Bowen's Court, and returned with her to London before sailing for New York on his way back to Ottawa.

2 Clarence Terrace, Wednesday, 6th November 1946
Beloved – this time yesterday (it's the late afternoon) I was waiting to hear you ring at the bell, and now you are forging, with every minute, further and further away in the QE[103] I feel torn in pieces as though I were being drawn after you. How happy we have been – and more than happy: I feel welded together with you forever. I don't want at the moment to write about feeling, and I won't: the joy and love goes too deep, and the pain of your being gone away is too raw.

---

[103] The *Queen Elizabeth*, transatlantic liner.

Yes, inevitably I do feel in my being, when I can't be with you, like a tree dropping its leaves or a plant going out of flower. I think we both of us only do live fully when we're together.

Your beloved flowers – as I wirelessed you today – came this morning. They are beautiful, I mean even apart from their having come from you. Their colour and their lovely delicate shape – full and open at the same time. They made me weep. You'll laugh, but I shot out of the house and bought a special vase to put them in. I didn't seem to have one that was either beautiful enough or the right style, size and shape. I'd seen a rather beautiful antique vase in the window of one of the little shops in the road back-to-back with this house, so I bought that. I wish you could, now, see them. . . .

I feel, as I always do when I've been much with you, the unfamiliarity of letter-writing. Soon, again, I'll get into it. I expect I'll write again at the end of the week. If I can't live through the small things of life with you I like, in fact I need, to tell you about them: anything I don't tell you about seems to go down the drain and be quite unreal. I must try and shake off the feeling of unreality about all these things I do when you're not here. As for you, I long to know about every minute of your life. Sweetest love, your life is so very precious to me.

Be happy, and keep me inside yourself as I keep you inside myself. I suppose eventually we'll grow old together: I think at present we're growing up together, don't you?

I cannot forget the very slightest thing about your person or mind or nature. I see you at so many moments, at every moment. This is something more powerful and of the present than just 'remembering'.

Bless you, dear love.

Elizabeth

2 Clarence Terrace, Sunday, 10th November 1946

My darling. . . . All this last week, I've been re-living our days at Bowen's Court – thinking 'this time last week' – Also, at the same time, I've been imagining you on that fantastic great ship, wondering what you were doing at every moment. I wonder how soon a letter from you will come, or a cable to say you're back in Ottawa. Your lovely yellow flowers are still in full bloom. I shall be sad when they die, as they are such a lovely living link, still, between you and me: you saw them and chose them.

It's Sunday evening, about 6.30. It was sunny and pretty but very cold today. Alan and I walked up the park due north, along the edge of the lake, then into St John's Wood to tea with a woman called Veronica Wedgwood.[104] She belongs to the Wedgwood china family, which gives her charm for me. . . . Inevitably, all the end part of this last week, since you left on Tuesday, has felt pretty ghastly. I have what is called thrown myself into my work (I have started another chapter of the novel) and drunk anything that there was to hand. I should have liked to have gone to a lot of movies, but there has not been time. I went to dinner with Cyril Connolly one evening – Cyril is shortly going to America and had hoped to sail with you, on the Q.E. . . . Another evening I went to dinner with Gerald Berners which was amusing as he is staying in that ducal boarding house in Hamilton Terrace, St. John's Wood. I must say he is in clover there – marvellous suite of rooms and superb food. If you ask me, I hold that money can buy almost everything that is worth having. We dined with his landlord and landlady, the Duke and Duchess of Leinster, in their part of the house – a basement made over in Mayfair Baroque style. I must say it made me sad to see Ireland's premier duke, with that terrific Fitzgerald family history behind him, ending his days in a baroqued-over St John's Wood kitchen. Still, they were rather sweet. He is a gentle, soft-voiced, weak, pink-lidded, courteous little Irishman, who seems

[104] Historian, chiefly of the seventeenth century, C.V. (Veronica) Wedgwood (1910-1997) was to become a DBE (Dame of the British Empire) in 1968 and a member of the Order of Merit (OM) in 1969.

to spend most of his time popping out to the movies at their local, the Swiss Cottage Odeon. She, as you no doubt know, used to be an Edwardian musical comedy star, Denise Orme[105]. . . .

On Friday I lunched with Billy Buchan to meet his bride-to-be, Barbara Ensor. She is, as he says, a pet: seems very young indeed, I should think about 21 or 22. She is dark, bright-eyed, what older people approvingly call 'fresh', and has pretty and prettily-kept hands. She obviously absolutely adores him, and he I thought very happy and at his best. At intervals they clasped hands, very sweetly and naively, across the table. It is really rather nice being with 2 people who are completely happy, isn't it. Also, it gave me the oddest feeling: I am easily old enough to be this girl's mother, and yet I am as much in love as she is – and, I don't think, really, even in a more sophisticated or hardened way than she is . . .

I am living, now, till your first letter comes. Dear and beloved joy of my life, there is so much I want to hear and know.

Goodbye for now

Your Elizabeth

2 Clarence Terrace, Monday, 18th November 1946

My darling. . . . All this last week I've been in a state of submerged sadness, that frightens me. It's nothing my mind can explain so it's nothing my mind can cope with. It's like something supernatural. It goes on underneath whatever is happening in the day, and at nights I have dreams I can't remember but which leave me when I wake up with a feeling of loss and fear. I think you feel like this more often than I do: with me till now sadness has always been something definite and explicable that I could fight against. It makes me wonder whether it's true that when two people have been as much and as close together as you and I have lately, their

[105] Denise Orme had been a musical-hall singer and actress. Edward Fitzgerald, the 7th Duke of Leinster, was her third husband.

blood-streams really do get mixed up, so that the nature of one begins to circulate through the nature of the other. I know this sounds a fantastical thing to say, and I am not usually fantastical, am I. But do you think it can be true? If this sadness really were part of you I should not mind it. Particularly if I thought you were having it any less – because it is a most terrible feeling: one does not know which way to turn.

Please answer this – I mean, this part of this letter – some day when you can. I don't think I go deeper into experience than you do: I think experience goes deeper than we both realise into us both.

Yes, how happy we have been, in Paris and at Bowen's Court. That goes on still – in fact I do feel ungrateful, I suppose to God, in being unhappy now.

I have been doing several nice things: for instance, that Covent Garden first night of Gerald's[106] ballet Les Sirènes was lovely. The ballet divinely pretty and funny; and a great success – the house rocked with applause. Loelia Westminster[107] was of the party, and we walked about and talked in the intervals, and she said in a very heart-warming manner 'And how is our darling Charles?' She was looking very handsome indeed (as indeed she should) in a 2nd Empire black net dress, white ermine wrap and black lace gloves. What a curious duality there is about her looks – and with it, I suppose, personality, isn't there? I also talked, on the way in, to Anne-Marie [Callimachi], who looked stunning: diamonds in the hair and black gloves up to the shoulder. It was a very full-dress, and therefore very enjoyable, occasion. I had got a new dress, which I hope you will like. I must say, trying to buy an evening dress in London is heart-breaking. Mine is a sort of Renaissance effect:

---

106 Berners

107 Loelia Ponsonby became the third of the four wives of the 2nd Duke of Westminster in 1930. He divorced her in 1947.

gold, silver and black. After the ballet was over there was a supper party in the royal box, overlooking the huge empty theatre, which remained lit up. When we came to leave, all the staircases were pitch dark and we found we were locked in and looked like becoming phantoms of the opera. Gerald and Lady Cunard, who were the last to leave, said they ended by being let out through a cellar trapdoor by somebody in a nightgown.

On Friday night the Connollys, Clarissa C[hurchill] and Alan Pryce-Jones[108] came to dinner here: it was a nice evening. . . . On Saturday Alan and I went down to Barnet (Herts,[109] a fantastic place) to spend the day with my uncle Mervyn Bowen and his son Charles. Charles took me for a walk through that queer sad London forest, Hadley Wood – all cut across by gasworks and railway lines and with a derelict fun fair. The trees were oaks, still yellow, and it was a misty day. On a plateau on the tip of the hill we came to a Georgian village called Monken Hadley, with a very old beautiful flint church. What a curious country England is, really: more uncanny than France and more deceptive, because of its apparent prosaicness, than Ireland. . . .

I need not say, I love you

Your

E.

Clarence Terrace, Saturday, 23rd November 1946

Well my dearest, how are you and what are you doing? You do not mind my writing often to you like this, do you. It makes you feel so near, or rather you do feel so near that I can't help doing it. I have got so much in the way, at Paris and at Bowen's Court, of living with you, in the sense of talking about everything. . . .

---

[108] Alan Pryce-Jones (1908-2000) writer and critic, editor of *The Times Literary Supplement* 1948-59, after which he moved to the USA.

[109] Hertfordshire, just north of London.

King Lear was wonderful. You know I think Aristotle was quite right in saying tragedy is a purgation by pity and terror: I came out feeling dead tired but pure. I went alone, which sounds rather an intense thing to do, but there was nobody I wanted to go with and I did want to go. The effect of *Lear* on me or rather on some part of my sorrow was that of a hot compress on a boil – it 'drew' something to the surface and made it burst. The funny thing about *Lear* is that no one scene makes a profound impression on one (several, especially the first, are irritating or ludicrous or simply tedious) the effect is cumulative. It isn't a play that hits one between the eyes, it's a play that gets under one's skin. Olivier as Lear was marvellous – he made him so fidgety, vain, such an old player-up – tremendous or noble only malgré soi.[110] What a terrifying view of age, really – that inside every old man there's a desperate young man crying to be let out.

I'm sorry this is in pencil – I left that peculiar pen of mine at B Court, and I am writing on the sofa in the front room. I hope you'll be able to read it. Your yellow chrysanthemums are still alive. . . .

One thing I have done is buy, or rather order, what I think ought to be a really beautiful new hat. At that Mrs. Ritcher's, where I have got other hats you have said you liked. It is to be black (as usual) with 2 feathers of a curious blue-green curling against the cheek. The context of the hat was Billy Buchan's wedding on December 5th, but I have now said I will go to a party of Loelia's on next Wednesday, so I expect I shall be glad of the hat there. . . .

Charles, I don't want you to think I am going to take your marriage au grand tragique. I can take it how you want me to, and I will.[111]

---

[110] French: 'in spite of himself.'

[111] 'Au grand tragique' – 'as a big tragedy.' This is the first reference in EB's surviving letters to CR's marriage to Sylvia Smellie. They were not married until more than a year later, and it is probable that he had now simply indicated his intention to EB. He proposed to Sylvia in Ottawa by telephone from Paris.

I keep thinking about our days in France. When I say France, I suppose I mean Sundays – Fontainebleau, Senlis, Chartres. You will always remember them as clearly as I do, won't you?

Good night for now beloved.

Your Elizabeth

Bowen's Court, Thursday, 12th December 1946

Darling Charles. . . . I do miss you so terribly here. Existence in this house seems all lopsided without you. At the same time, you seem to inhabit this house, and will do so always. It is beautiful here now – the trees bare, of course, and the weather cold, but at intervals floods of pale brilliant December sunshine indoors and out.

The evening I got here it was full moon: the moon rose during the last part of the drive from Limerick to Kildorrery; it was shining brilliantly on the outside of the house when I arrived, about 6.30 pm; and the library fire roaring away indoors. It is a nice time of the evening to get home. That first night I did not sleep much, partly because of over-excitement, partly because my bed was very cold – I felt as though I were lying between 2 slabs of ice. I lay awake watching the firelight edging down on the ceiling, and listening to the rooks, who were also kept awake by the cold and moonlight, rustling and muttering in the trees outside. I was also very much haunted by thoughts of you; kept dozing off then waking up with a start thinking I heard the intonations of your voice, though I could never remember what you'd said. . . .

They are having a meet (the Duhallows[112]) here, at the house, next Saturday; so I shall be having a very horsey morning. I wish you were going to be here. Also how I do wish I had a horse – I know I shall melt into tears, as I always do, seeing them all move off.

Charles, shall I really be seeing you in about 4 weeks time? You

[112] The Duhallow Hunt

sail from Halifax on Jan. 7th don't you? That is what I am living for.

I went to William Buchan's wedding just before I left London. . . . Owing to the church being bomb-ruined, the former drawing-room of St. Columba's[113] manse has been converted into a small chapel: we were all packed in very tight. What a queer, almost mystic tie one has with the Buchans – it came over me in the middle of the service – they are so much more like relations than friends. On this occasion they were all running very true to form – Johnnie on his way to the House of Lords in a paper collar; darling Alistair (usher, but his activities cramped by the small space) looking incredibly seedy, pouchy and not-at-all-the-thing: even the white carnation in his buttonhole looked as though it had been spending a night out . . . Susan[114] handsome and quite her best in almost bridal oyster brocade. Bill himself looked sweet,[115] and on this occasion less odd than either of his brothers. Bride also very sweet in a Victor Stiebel Picasso-blue suit and red toque and veil. Aunt Anna Buchan ('O. Douglas'[116]) and Uncle Walter[117] were down from Peebles – she rather touchingly clutched my arm during the reception and said, 'Oh dear I do hope he will be happy this time!'

How nice you looked writing at this writing table (in the library).

Today I am going in to Cork to shop.

All my love E.

---

113 St Columba's in Pont Street, London SW1 (Church of Scotland).

114 Lady Buchan

115 EB was particularly fond of William (Bill or Billy) Buchan. This was William's second marriage, to Barbara Ensor. It was dissolved in 1960. William succeeded his brother John as 3rd Baron Tweedsmuir in 1996.

116 Anna Buchan, sister of John Buchan, was under the pseudonym O. Douglas a successful novelist and a biographer of the Buchan family.

117 Walter Buchan, lawyer, scholar and philanthropist. Neither he nor his sister Anna married, and remained in the Buchan family hometown of Peebles, in Scotland.

1947

From January 1947 Charles was in Paris for three years as Counsellor to the Canadian Embassy. The Embassy was a mansion on the Avenue Foch, and Charles had a small flat up one flight of stairs at 218 Boulevard St Germain. No letters to him from Elizabeth survive from the first months of this period. She went to Paris several times to spend time with him, and he went to Ireland to visit her at Bowen's Court.

The diary entries that follow were all written in Paris unless indicated otherwise.

3 January

On my way to Paris to go as counsellor to the Embassy there – second day out on the Aquitania. A slight fog and a slight swell, fucking providentially 'laid on', my only regret that I have finished my Somerset Maugham novel, *The Narrow Corner.* Perfect novel for my present mood[118]. . . .

[118] *The Narrow Corner* (1932) is an ironic tale about three differently problematic men marooned on a tropical island and involved in the fate of a beautiful and tragic young woman.

18 January

Walking in the Champs Elysées I feel as alien as an American GI. Why had I come here? . . . I ought to be in Canada playing my part in the affairs of my own country. And the sooner I get back the better. . . . But I thought the life would be amusing! I can't imagine why I thought so. I am really only interested in people. And there isn't a person here who interests me. The politics I see only from the outside after seeing our own politics from the inside. As for the women – well I am not at all tempted to sit round at café tables on the chance of picking up a girl. It is quite unsuitable in fact ridiculous for me 'at the peak of my career' to have exiled myself to this dreary, expensive city.

That is what I feel now – let's hang on till July and if I still feel the same way I'll give up the experiment – go home, get married and call it a day.

20 February

V happy with E. We have spent the weekend huddled over the weak radiator and the whiskey bottle or on the enormous 'made for love' bed. It's like life on board ship, we sally out on the windswept deck-like boulevards for a 'blow' and are glad to be back in this cabin-like flat – which more than anything else is like a suite on a luxury liner.

9 March

I did not very much want to sleep with her.[119] She is too old – nearly as old as I am. I can't believe it when I see these women who are my contemporaries and sometimes younger with hardened and raddled faces. Yet I don't feel young. I feel floating *entre les deux ages.* I feel about 36. I suffer from about 5 years arrested development –

---

[119] Unidentified Swede.

the years I spent adhering to my youthful programme. My obstinacy kept me young.

1 April

E has gone and I am alone in the flat. It puts me in a panic to be left alone now. I see myself always alone, moving down a long corridor of time and I see myself getting a little drunk every night and waking up in the morning to the familiar repulsive self. . . . I wish anyway that the sun would come out. It's true that a man after 30 is dead. In my case death occurred at the age of 38, the day that I said goodbye to E at 32 Grosvenor St. The formality of my actual demise however seems to postpone itself indefinitely – and there are ghostly returns – like that week at Bowen's Court, that morning in the park. The sun has come out. It's too idiotic writing down all this dreary nonsense.

Charles was soon busy both professionally and socially, making friends and acquaintances in the worlds of politics, literature, the arts and high society. He sat next to Greta Garbo at a lunch, and became a confidential friend of Lady Diana Cooper, whose husband Duff Cooper retired that year as British Ambassador in Paris.

During this period, Charles had an affair.

2 April

I don't know yet – I just don't know. Is it another illusion or could it be 'love'? When she said 'I love you', I said 'There is nothing there to love.' But I was shaken. The green arches of the Parc de Chantilly in the April sunshine, the breeze blowing the paper tablecloths . . . the sight of M standing beside the car her plaid rug over her arm. She is like a statue carved in ivory, her beauty severe and classical. It is dangerous this happiness. It is the treacherous sweet poison of this spring.

Oh God what a fool I am – at forty.

1 May

As for M I know that I could stop tomorrow without leaving a trace on either of us. I have nothing to give her except a little pleasure and she is beginning to see that, for she damn it all is extremely intelligent too and <u>too</u> competent. It gives me a little shock of distaste to have a competent woman about. I like women extravagant, late for appointments, wilful, fond of showy clothes and society, vague drifting dreamy, and yet of course all that is v. tiresome. But I don't like competence, intellectual honesty, intelligent sensuality.

4 May

Have just been reading *Romeo and Juliet*. It produces the same effect on me as the love-stories of Turgenev – intoxication and a wild and silly feeling of despair which I have never been able to analyze or describe. It is purely subjective but this essence of youthful passion, romance, disinterestedness is what I have missed and always longed for. Yet in life whenever it has been offered me I have refused it. Even now once more – perhaps for the last time I might have it and as usual I will refuse.

7 June

In the meantime this love-affair has come and gone. . . . It broke with the weather. How much good is it to have been so happy when it has ended so painfully? I am a 'crook', 'torturer of women', 'murderer' – almost, and indeed she has made me feel a monster. Besides there is the distress of the body, the nervous system, every faculty, eyes, touch smell at being separated from her. A deep animal distress much below the mind level or the will.

15 July

An empty day. I keep telling myself that I have it coming to me – this loneliness. . . . It's another 6 weeks since the last entry but I haven't been back to her.

9 September

The trouble is that when I begin to ask myself the question: What woman do I love? I am overcome by a sort of mental dizziness. Put in those terms I can find no answer to the question. I feel capable of loving any woman – up to a point – and in one way or another. I cannot say of my heart (like Cyril Connolly) *les bêtes l'ont mangé*[120] but – more prosaically – I have parcelled it out. And it hurts me to lose the smallest part of it.

20 September

Paris has given me back my pleasure in the texture of life. It has made me feel that I want to go on with life just for its own sake – not to achieve anything remarkable but to enjoy. . . . But I wouldn't have thought that I could feel that shaft of joy that shot through me today as I walked across the Tuileries Gardens with this autumn wind blowing the first falling leaves.

When I left E at the Hotel de Condé today I got caught in the porch of the hotel in a violent downpour, the wind blowing the rain in swirls down the narrow street. . . . I think less about X.[121] I am passing out of her orbit into that of the other woman. I am a v. consolable character.

Bowen's Court, Sunday, 26th October 1947

Darling,

Your letter came yesterday morning and made me very happy. I'm glad you've taken to spending your early mornings in the dining-room – I remember it's always full of sun then, I've seen sun

---

[120] The line '*Ne cherchez plus mon coeur, les bêtes l'ont mangé*' ('Stop trying to find my heart, it has been devoured by animals') is from the poem 'Causerie' in Charles Baudelaire's *Les Fleurs du Mal* (1857).

[121] Unidentified.

in there streaming away, and it seems a pity not to enjoy it. The striped chairs and room in general are pretty, early, too. I remember having breakfast and eating fruit in there one Sunday morning before we set out for a day. I don't think I'll ever love any place, I mean any interior on earth, as much as I've loved 218 Bd St G.[122] If it doesn't sound silly to say so, please give everything my love.

. . . I have been working very hard. Actually, though my brain or imagination are strung up, I don't think my nerves are – not like they were when I was alone here working last spring (as we were saying, that's the same with us both). Also, being in a great rush of work is exhilarating, as you know. (I mean, internal rush, impetus.) Most of all, because of you I am happier than I've ever been in my life.

I've been thinking, why has it been accepted (by Anglo-Saxons at least) that being in love should come so early, almost before one is oneself at all, and then be expected to be put behind and done with?

. . . I'll put the measurements for the ring into the envelope with your fork (which also contains your motto which we wrote out in Paris)[123] and am taking all of them up to Dublin with me next Thursday. . . . There is a place called Weir[124] in Grafton St I've got great confidence in. The only thing that worries me is the unlikelihood of having your fork back to give you by the time you come here – unless I really can persuade them to take the impression from it immediately, as I'll try to do. Failing that, I'll lend you a fork out of my silver-chest, and return yours to you from London via the [diplomatic] bag.

---

[122] Boulevard St. Germain

[123] EB wanted to give CR a ring engraved with his family crest (copied from the fork) and his family motto, 'Virtute Aquiretur Honos': 'Let Honour be Acquired by Virtue' – 'honos' being early classical Latin for 'honour.' The Ritchie family crest is decoratively complex. It is not known whether this ring was ever made.

[124] Weir & Sons, established 1869 and still there.

I do also long to have the ring to put on your finger, not just post. . . .

I do miss you very much, all the time, more than I dare often allow myself to feel. It's 3 weeks today since our Fontainebleau Sunday, I think? I have been thinking about that day all today. Today as to weather and place is so very different, but in its own way it's a sweet kind of a day, too: we should be spending it together.

. . . I can meet you with the car at Shannon any day, or night.

Goodbye for the moment
All my love
Elizabeth

Bowen's Court, Friday, 28th November 1947

My darling – your 'in hospital' telegram was telephoned through this morning while I was dressing. I <u>am</u> glad you've coped with that in this intensive way, boring as it must be being in hospital. All other things I suppose could have been only temporary relief, not cure: and the thing dragging on would have maddened you. I pray this <u>does</u> work: I hope they're not doing anything too disagreeable to you, my patient angel? . . .

Your beloved letter came on Tuesday. How near each other we are. How deeply I love you: this is such a joy, such a joy we share. Charles, you are so dear and so beautiful: I keep seeing you, I can see nothing else. Love isn't really an illusion, it's a reality. As far as I'm concerned, it's you. Something about you dazzles me, and yet most of all I have the feeling of repose and strength. I have lived with you every moment since you left here; I don't feel lonely. Though at the same time it does hurt
[Ends]

Bowen's Court, Saturday, 6th December 1947

My darling – what a nightmarish frustration this French postal strike has been . . . I've been longing for a sight of one of your beloved blue envelopes. Also of course badly wanting to know how you got on in hospital, how long you stayed there, how that worked. I suppose I'd have been in still more of a frenzy if I didn't feel so one with you, so indissolubly wrapped up in you: the feeling of closeness I've had to you here, day and night, since you left has been extraordinary. You do completely colour and fill my life.

Even so, how I miss you: it's inevitable. Love is a life, and a life does cry out to be lived. . . .

Meanwhile, everything here goes on just the same. There are only a few chrysanthemums left in the greenhouse, bronze ones, and the days are getting every day a little shorter. I do love, though, these long pale damp winter evening twilights: something about the whole quality of life here is so tender and soothing. It seems inhuman to be going away to London and shutting up this house. Every time I have to do it I feel as though something died in me – or even as though I became a degree less virtuous. Fortunately whatever it is renews itself when one comes back – but I suppose I have a sort of fear, every time I go away, that I shall die in England and not come back.

I love the evening life of the little towns round here in the winter. All their listlessness or shabbiness disappears when the lights are lit – all those rows of funny little incoherent shops simply blaze – one really does have a 'Here I come to town' feeling, driving into Fermoy or Mitchelstown about 5.30 on a winter evening. The bars packed with drinks and the people packed with smiles. I wish it hadn't been early closing day that evening you and I were in Mitchelstown: we must go in again.

Chiefly of course my life has been lived round the edges of working at the novel. I'm now about half way through the last chapter.[125] I am working at it about 8 hours a day (including the 2 or 3 hours I do after supper in the evenings). Working too late into

[125] Of *The Heat of the Day*

the night doesn't pay, as I then feel tired next morning and so lose ground.

You said you felt a new growth and strength in my writing. If that is so, and I think it is, you know that has come to me from you, don't you? You've given me not only greater comprehension but clearer vision than I had, and made me more fearless. I feel this in my life: it would be strange if it didn't show at least to some extent in my writing. . . .

Of course the one thing I think of is when and how I'll see you. I'd gladly come to Paris for a weekend, as I told you, but that absolutely and completely depends on you. . . . If you say better not, beloved, I'll understand. But somehow, some place in the not too far distant future let me see your beloved face? . . .

Bless you and keep you

Elizabeth.

1948

Charles Stewart Almon Ritchie and Sylvia Catherine Beatrice Smellie were married in Ottawa on 16 January 1948. They returned together to Paris after their honeymoon, and set up house in a small eighteenth-century villa in the leafy suburb of Passy.

Elizabeth Bowen, while clinging to the belief that nothing would change, courageously entered more fully into outside life so as to remain vital to Charles Ritchie and in order to ward off her sadness. As she would write to him: 'The moment one is sad one is ordinary.' She went on a lecture tour for the British Council, to Czechoslovakia and Austria, lecturing on 'The Technique of the Novel,' 'The English Novel in the Twentieth Century' and 'The Short Story.'

Prague, Sunday, 8th February 1948

My darling –

Here I am. You got my telegram? I have spent a sort of ghostly replica of a Paris Sunday morning walking round old streets. Prague couldn't be less like Paris, but the sheer basic resemblances of one continental capital city to another upset me – the long drive in from the airport on Friday afternoon, along cobbled wide streets with blocks of working-class flats was somehow like the drive in from Le Bourget. I thought it would make me feel better – I mean, less lonely for you – coming abroad: actually up to now it has made me feel worse.

It must be true that travel broadens the mind – at any rate this rush of the sensations of Central-Europeanism is most peculiar. This is utterly unlike anywhere I have ever felt or been. For one thing, there's such a funny light: clear and pale and yet somehow dead. The stocky intensity of the people is so odd – excitement without excitability. The noise of the modern part of Prague is terrific: clanging trams, bellowing people – it begins early in the morning, when all the Czechs seem to get up early in order to do the odd spot of carpentry, while their children, to whom they are devoted, wail and scream. My room in this hotel looks out into a courtyard which is comparatively quiet, but it echoes like anything.

Yes, the light is extraordinary: it gives me a feeling of unreality. The buildings are many of them rather extinguished-looking lovely colours – peach, parchment, honey, a pinkish grey. When there's no sun, or under mistiness, the whole city blots out – it looks like a photograph with just a few details, red-brown roofs, occasional lawns of gardens, tinted in. That is, looking down on it, as I did this morning, from the top of the cathedral hill.

I hear letters leaving this country are very much censored. So this is not more than just a description of what I see. Many of the men are not bad-looking, in a thick-set way. They never never, however, seem to take off their overcoats, which are tremendously cardboardy and make the wearers look even thicker than they are. One gets the impression that they make love in them and will probably die in them. The women poor dears look awful: very fat, very dowdy, and they walk in God-forsaken-looking high boots as if they all had corns. The very rich are very dressy but look common. Everything here that is not very old is art nouveau.

By contrast, the old town up the hill is dead silent: it is spectacular but a little frightening. One gets a queer feeling that something unspeakable has happened, one couldn't say how long ago, at every turn[126]. . . .

If I were here with you it would be extraordinary: I keep wondering what sort of life you and I would lead here. Actually I think we would get to love it. It is beautiful; and the strangeness itself would grow on one. But the fact is I'm lonely: I do not feel quite myself, quite in balance, quite in command of anything apart from you.

I am seeing an immense amount of people, whose only fault is that they are too many of them. The Czechs are very touching – they hope so much, one doesn't quite know what for. The British Embassy people, all of whom I met at a party the day I got here, are very sweet: all of them bursting out of their skins owing to the local food. I've never seen so much food, or so much that I so much didn't want to eat. I'm not madly hungry anyway, but it seems so ungrateful. . . . I stay here till Thursday, then go [on] this trip to Olomouc and Brno and Bratislava. I get back to Prague again on the 17th then on the 19th go to Vienna. But I shall be writing again long before that. . . .

I am dying for a letter from you. The idea of having lunch with you in Paris on Friday 27th is what I'm living for. When you write, send me the telephone no of your Embassy. I might have a try at ringing you up from somewhere. And anyhow, I'll ring you up when I get to Paris that Friday morning, to know where and when to meet.

I think so much about you. You are happy, my darling beloved, aren't you? And your new house is nice, and everything goes well? I long for the sight of one of your blue envelopes.

---

[126] EB was prescient. She left Prague just a few days before a Communist coup (see following letter) which was followed by the death of the Foreign Minister, Jan Masaryk, on 10 March. He was found dead beneath the windows of the Foreign Ministry in the old town, assumed either to have committed suicide or to have been murdered by the Communists.

I wish you were not going back again across the Atlantic at the end of this autumn: the idea of your being so far away again torments me.

Goodbye for now, dear love
Elizabeth

Craigforth, Stirling[127] *as from 2 Clarence Terrace, Regent's Park, London NW1. 10th March 1948*

My dear Mrs Ritchie,[128]

I loved getting your letter from Ottawa, and was so touched at your writing to me during what must have been such a busy, crowded week. I have been wanting to write to you for so long – and now, on my return to London after my central European travels, I found my household rejoicing over your perfectly lovely parcel. Really it was good of you! The quite childish – though also practical – pleasure of having such things as you sent can't be described. Also, you can't think how much the kind thought means. One gets so bored, in London, by the monotony of life.

Not that I really ought to complain of monotony – first, my play coming on, then all those travels. Yes, I have been so pleased about the play.[129] I can see, now it's 'on', that it's a mass of technical weaknesses, owing to my inexperience, but I do think the acting's first-rate (most people seem to agree) and the play has at least one merit – good actors' parts. Most of the cast are still young, still with their

[127] EB was staying with her friend Gildie Morden in Scotland.

[128] Lilian Ritchie, née Stewart, CR's mother. She was a woman of charm and character, whom EB had never met. No doubt at CR's suggestion, Mrs Ritchie had sent a parcel of luxuries. In England, three years after the war, there was still food-rationing, and shortages of even everyday commodities.

[129] *Castle Anna*, which EB wrote in collaboration with John Parry, who was managing the Lyric Theatre, Hammersmith, where the play was premiered in late February 1948. It had only a short run, and has not been revived.

names to make, and I must say they have worked, putting all they have into it. The rehearsals, and the working-out of the production, were fascinating. I had never had much to do with actors or theatre-people before; and had been inclined, I'm afraid, to think of them as rather boring show-offs, but my weeks of work with this particular lot have left me with a solid respect for them.

Charles tells me he is hoping he may be able to get over to London and see the play,[130] it will be lovely if he can, as he's been so very interested and sympathetic.

I set off to Czechoslovakia and Austria early in February – one reason why I haven't written before, as I had such an awful rush before starting. I was a fortnight in Czechoslovakia, a week in Austria. I had left Prague for Vienna a few days before the Communist coup. I must say I did think everybody in Prague was in a very peculiar state, but not having been there before I thought this might be normal. . . . And really (though it seems a frivolous thing to say now) if I lived in Prague I could almost imagine becoming a Communist out of sheer boredom with the drabness already produced by Socialism. No romanticness, no gaiety, hardly a handsome person to be seen! I suppose it was coming from the already sufficient drabness of London, under our present regime, that made Prague almost impossible for me to take. . . .

But the place I really did lose my heart to was Vienna – as I imagine everybody always has and always will. Even in its present tragic state it makes one catch one's breath with wonder and sheer pleasure. Do you know it? I expect so. Charles says he's never been there, and I've been urging him to get there sometime, somehow: I know he'd love it. I got the feeling that all the gallantry and the grace that's been gradually fading out of the world since 1914 is still holding out in a last little pocket of resistance, in Vienna. The

---

[130] He did.

particular kind of courage the Austrians, particularly the Viennese, show appeals to me so much – the way they wear their clothes and carry themselves: their air of having life (in spite of nightmarish conditions) under control. And the way they go on being gay on half a glass of wine, by the light of one candle. Really they are a lesson to one!

I'm staying here with a friend for a week, going back to London on Saturday. This is a lovely place, a 17th century house on a wooded hillside. I do hope this long letter won't have bored you. I should love to hear from you again. I had lunch with Charles on my way back across Paris: he was very well except for a cold.

Yours affectionately

Elizabeth Cameron[131]

Bowen's Court, Easter Sunday, 1948

My darling – how are you? I am thinking about you so much, all the time here. How lovely last Sunday, in London with you, was. I am longing for a letter from you – such an unconscious practical joke played itself on me yesterday, when the post came: a letter appeared to be from you and was from Shaya.[132] I should never have thought your and his writing were at all alike, but on this occasion his did look just like yours, and even his envelope was blue. . . .

I feel in such a curious state; not sad, just astray among all these sensations of spring. I think spring brings one's soul to the top and doesn't satisfy it; autumn also draws one's soul up but does satisfy it. I feel disturbed by something at intervals and wonder if it is God. I feel, my darling, that He has marked us both down This curious alternation between joy and dismay, and looking at everything as

---

[131] Except in circumstances connected with her writing, EB always signed herself 'Elizabeth Cameron,' and was always addressed as 'Mrs Cameron' or, on envelopes, 'Mrs Alan Cameron.' To use her maiden, professional name would have seemed to her vulgarly unconventional.

[132] Isaiah Berlin.

though it had a double significance . . . A day or two ago we went over to tea at Annesgrove: walked about the garden there afterwards with Hilda Annesley: there was a magnolia tree in flower – too beautiful in the brilliant spring twilight. She talked about flower-snobbishness, saying her husband Dick is a flower-snob. His must be just a degree more curious than other people's flowers, they must be rare. Rather a fascinating obsession, I think. Certainly they have a bed of the most beautiful pure-ivory daffodils – not a touch of yellow in them at all.

It also made me melancholy-retrospective getting Shaya's letter. He and I used to write these long letters about nothing particular so often – as, indeed, one used to do to so many people. Now I feel he is just trying to renew something, and how right he is. I think the trouble with me and all my friends is that we have all got on in the world rather too well; and though we haven't actually lost innocence, so many of the things we used to enjoy so much together, principally each other, have got crowded out. We all used to be so happy. I think really all that's still there, a frozen asset. But we all need time, peace. Even Oxford – as Shaya says in his letter – has got noisy (psychologically as well as everything else) and high pressure, and full of worldly issues.

If I could live here continuously, and see my friends *here* more, I think everything would be better. I must try and get Shaya to come here again. But he's always so *fussed*, these days, with so many irons in the fire and so much up his sleeve – but then so, I daresay, am I too.

I feel sometimes I have let the whole weight of my life lean too heavily on you. But you see apart from everything else you *are* such a friend. . . .

I feel sometimes – talking as friend to friend – that I may have failed you, or seemed to fail you in understanding. You are extraordinary, I am extraordinary, we have been extraordinary together. I *ought* (I can see how you could feel it) to be able to take one more extraordinary thing (your marriage). The incalculable thing is sadness – how it shoots one down. The moment one is sad one is ordinary. If you notice, nobody in Shakespeare (Shakespeare having no use for ordinary people) is ever just sad. They have moments of interesting melancholy, listening to music and referring to violets, but once there is any question of being just <u>sad</u>, they step right off the edge of that into one or another kind of lunacy.

Sadness seems to take away all one's powers – it's like getting something into one's eye so that one can't see properly, or losing teeth so that one can't bite properly on anything, can't bite on what happens. It not only queers one, it somehow dulls one. I can analyse sadness now that I'm not sad. I would not write about sadness if I were . . .

I've got to go to London for few days in the middle of April. Would you think it entirely hare-brained of me if I flew over to Paris for a day and we had lunch? We might even have an evening drink, too. Then I'd catch a late plane back. It would be heaven for <u>me</u>. Let me know what you'd think. I'd suggest Monday 12th, or Saturday 10th, or Tuesday 13th.
[Ends]

Bowen's Court, Monday, 13th May 1948
My darling. . . . I'm still longing for your next letter and hope one will soon be forwarded from London. Oh <u>how</u> I wish you were here. Wandering round the woods and the garden all yesterday, I imagined you were. <u>What</u> a time of year – birds singing all day long in the light green woods. The garden is full of apple blossom which looks like a dream against the stone walls of the garden with the mountains behind. . . .

Coming up the estuary into Cork in the early morning sunshine (7a.m.) was very poetic. Complete silence – the people were still all asleep in the houses; not a sound from the ship – the engines were cut off; we were moving in on the tide. Only, at each side of the river, the very loud singing of the birds in the trees of the gardens. It was really like the arrival of a shipful of bless'd souls in

Paradise – and such a religious, ecstatic feeling seemed to suffuse the passengers on the top deck that no one spoke, or spoke above a whisper. . . .

There is, for the first time, a slight whisky shortage over here. The Duke of Westminster is said to have sent out, during his months here, and bought up practically all the whisky in these southern counties. If the Windsors, as has been rumoured, are also to join us, I suppose there will not be a drop of anything left. I hope we shall not have too many of these rich refugees from red England – I have always liked, in this country, rambling along in one's own shabby and seedy way; and I should hate the whole place to go Kenya-type smart.[133]

I hope to spend any of my spare time here reading Mauriac.

Darling Charles, I am longing for more news of you, for the sight again of your beloved writing; and still more consumingly so, for the sight again of your beloved face.

All my love

E.

2 Clarence Terrace, Saturday night [Spring 1948]

My darling – this is a funny silent London rainy evening, the end of a day in which I've at any rate heard your voice. The journey back seemed unnatural – why should I deliberately cross the sea in order to put myself in another country from you? Flying, I don't think one feels that so much: there's a sort of dopey unreality about the whole thing. But in a land-and-sea journey, every jolt of the train, every lollop of the ship on the waves seems to drive something

---

[133] With the Labour Party in government, some wealthy and right-wing English people moved to Ireland, fearful of high taxation and the march of democracy, and seeing Ireland as providing fine country houses, plentiful domestic help, and a 'traditional' way of life. This was known as the 'flight from Moscow.' The Duke and Duchess of Windsor did not move to Ireland. Kenya was, notoriously, another playground for the rich English.

into one – the physical sensation of doing something that's against the grain.

But in what really is reality I still feel completely where you are. I see your face against the background of trees, where we were having drinks opposite the end of the Bois lake yesterday. My beloved, we're like creatures pinned together. No, because a pin means pain. At moments love is like a pin through both of us, because it hurts; but what I feel most, and most of the time, is a feeling of having run together and of running on forever together like two rivers which have joined.

Bless you. I am so infinitely glad I went to Paris. . . .

It means a lot to me to have seen your house, the circumstances of your life. It was so inhuman not to be able to imagine and see in my mind's eye the place you came back to in the evenings. And you know I feel a regard for Sylvia, don't you? I think 'regard' is the word: at any rate, I mean something by it.
[Ends]

Bowen's Court, Thursday, 17th June, 1948
My darling – I do miss you most agonisingly here. For one thing, being further distant from you in space; for another, being out of sound of your voice. And this place seems so made for <u>us</u>: I think about you when I walk about out of doors after dinner in the long light June evenings. It was lovely getting your letter the morning of the day I left London. What a heartbreaking disappointment it was your not being able to get over. I <u>told</u> myself, to stabilise myself against disappointment, that your suddenly being in London and our seeing each other <u>was</u> too good to be true; but all that Thursday when I was spending the day in Hampshire with the Jane Austen Society people at the Jane Austen House,[134] I was wondering and

---

[134] At Chawton, near Alton.

wondering what message from you I should find when I got back to Clarence Terrace that evening. . . .

I loved another letter you wrote me, about my novel. How extraordinarily that is your and my book. Short of there having been a child there could be no other thing that was more you and me. It would have been terrible if you hadn't liked it.[135] I miss that book, very much: I'm glad to have finished it, but I miss the continuity of the writing. When I come up here to the Blue Room and sit down at this table (which I associate with the novel) to do other work, I could almost weep.

. . . Oh darling, I wonder if there is any chance of your being over before I go to Paris? July 12th. Seems so horribly far away.

I was over at Annesgrove yesterday. Hilda Annesley who takes a passionate interest in Sylvia (in the rather touching way the older generation do take an interest in each other's nieces) promptly asked me if I had heard anything more of Sylvia. So I was able to say, oh yes; I had actually been in Paris and had met her. I said how much I'd liked meeting her, and gave a full and I hope satisfactory description of the house, what she wore, what she seemed to be doing and everything I gathered that she was doing. Hilda drank it all up and said 'I must now write at once to Beatrice Ritchie: she will be so delighted to hear.' . . . I also thought, what another typical comedy of that generation that was – I imagine Sylvia often writes to Lady MacNaughton;[136] but for some reason they always set more store by second-hand accounts. I have in my time written vivacious

---

[135] *The Heat of the Day* is dedicated 'To Charles Ritchie.' EB had sent him a copy of the typescript. The love affair between her characters Stella and Robert mirrors that between EB and CR. Regent's Park and its rose gardens are among the settings, and the edgy, heightened emotional atmosphere of their wartime London is immortalised.

[136] [*Sic*] for Macnaghten. Beatrice Ritchie, Sylvia's maternal aunt, was Lady Macnaghten. She lived all her married life in Northern Ireland.

pages and pages to my aunts: all the reply I get is 'I was glad to hear from Lady Brown that you are well: she says she saw you the other day in Oxford Street.'

I must stop. Oh my love my love, I wish I could see you, touch you, hear your voice

Your E.

22 June

The expression 'in the hand of God' – high in the hollow of the sky you are in the hollow of his hand. Who could be an airman and not believe in God? . . . I thought in the plane perhaps my death would simplify things. It's an idea I have sometimes since I left E – for isn't that what I did?

10 July

Our house is made for summer. Now it is dank and dark as a potting shed. I can think of nothing to say when I sit down for lunch and dinner in the gloom of the dining-room with rain rattling on the tin and glass of the gallery roof. Sylvia struggles manfully with the conversation or shivers with a pink jersey coat over her dress. We have to go out to warm expensive little restaurants to be able to talk.

17 July

E has come and gone. She said, 'Now it is at once too high and too low for me – too idealistic and yet this waiting at street corners. I have no technique for this.' I said our fear was 'we are clinging to something as middle-aged people do.' She is forty-nine and yet the life we have when we are together is still the thing that keeps us alive. The sun came out for ten minutes when we walked in the Luxembourg [Gardens].

Farringdon, Berks,[137] *Sunday, 1st August 1948*
My darling – It's lovely to think you'll be back within at any rate ear-shot soon – I mean, that I'll be able to hear your voice on the telephone. I hope your travels have been fun, and a rest: I wonder whether the time has gone fast or slowly. I was glad you went to Florence, both because I love it and because I don't love it too much. I wonder how long you had there, and by what routes you went and came.

I'm here for the week-end; it's absolutely lovely, I must say; a sort of general impression of sitting on the terrace tangled with loops of honeysuckle, drinking champagne, with this enormous smoke-blue Berkshire distance reaching away below. It was still the heat-wave when I arrived, but has cooled off now to ordinary English August weather, which is rather a relief. Robert Heber-Percy's[138] exquisite 5-year-old child Victoria is here; all the Betjeman[139] children arrived over, and we spent a very nice demented midgy afternoon boating on the lake.

. . . Oh by the way I've seen Anne Marie [Callimachi]: you'll probably have heard from her as she's now bound for Paris. She said gloomily, 'I suppose it is never possible to see Charles alone now?' So I said oh no, nonsense. She began to thoroughly third-degree me about your life, so I said anything she wanted to know she had far better ask you. And I've been seeing Shaya, who's been in London. . . . I shall now go downstairs and drink some more champagne: I can hear corks popping down on the terrace.

Monday: Clarence Terrace

Also, I went to Johnnie Tweedsmuir's[140] wedding. The bride in spite of being that high-boned Scottish type, was in her own way, I

---

[137] Faringdon [*sic*] in Berkshire was Lord Berners' country house.

[138] Robert Heber-Percy lived much of the time at Faringdon with Lord Berners.

[139] The poet John Betjeman and his family were living nearby at Wantage.

[140] John Buchan's eldest son, by then the 2nd Lord Tweedsmuir. His bride was Priscilla, widow of Sir Arthur Grant Bt. She was an MP, later elevated to the Lords.

thought, quite elegant and very suitable. I hope there is some money in her family – from the magnificence of the wedding I thought there must be. It was really rather a technicolour scene, on one of the hottest of the days – sky blazing in through the stained-glass windows (St. Margaret's, Westminster), vast vases of flowers, gladioli and roses, and a flowerbed of differently coloured though I am sorry to say far from smart hats. The most moving touch were the bride's two little girls, in white muslin dresses and rose-wreathed round straw hats: the doglike and yet cryptic, critical attention with which they watched their mother come up the aisle, as a bride, was fascinating. There is something uncanny about the wedding of a woman whose natural husband (as one can't help feeling) has been killed young, in battle. One feels the queer, sardonic presence of the young dead man....

I must say that this wedding unnerved me for a quite different reason – it was the first that I had sat through since you played your part in the Cathedral at Ottawa.[141] Such a sense of the enormity of that occasion came over me that I literally nearly fainted. In the middle of the Wedding March I turned round and gave Norman,[142] who was seated exactly behind me, the dirtiest look that blighter has probably ever had in his life. I think he must have realized its context subconsciously if not consciously. Afterwards he and I met in the courtyard of the House of Commons, outside the Speaker's House where the reception was to be. We milled around in the heat-wave, exchanging affectionate but slightly under-the-skin remarks. He was alone, Jetty[143] having characteristically twisted her back and gone to the country.

Alan is having a most successful reaction to the diabetes treatment at the London Clinic. He is allowed out by day, comes

---

[141] EB is referring to the wedding of Charles and Sylvia.

[142] Norman Robertson (1904-1968), close friend and senior colleague of CR, was Canadian High Commissioner in London 1946-1949, and again 1952-1957, and Canadian Ambassador in Washington 1957-1958.

[143] Norman Robertson's wife, who was Dutch.

bounding into this house, with bronzed face and shining eyes, looking like a participant in the Olympic Games. I've never seen anything like it. He did get rather a shock, as the specialist told him that if he'd left things any longer he'd have been dead within the next 3 months – he'd have fallen into a coma from which he never recovered. I must say this makes me sound rather negligent; I did keep on asking him to go and have a diabetes test (as they told him at the Eye Hospital last year that he seemed to be diabetic), but he never would, for long complicated reasons. . . .

Darling, now you are back in Paris do stop hacking round and round, automatically, to all those dreary parties. The only reason I have to say they are dreary parties is, their drearifying effect on you. I expect anyway Paris will be quieter in August, but do on any account stop. The glimpse I got of your existence last time I was in Paris was the most awful shock. Sometimes I worry about you the way I've seen you worry about Roley.[144] I believe really I'd rather see you dead at my feet than dead on your feet: If you keep on grinning like a dog and running about the city you'll wake up one morning and find you've lost your looks, your hair, your fascination, your wits, your brain, everything.

However, I hope you have now perhaps come back from your holiday like a giant refreshed.

Well, I long to hear your voice. . . . On Sunday I go to Folkestone to take up my duties as Principal (of that summer college)[145] so I do hope I'll have heard your voice before that.

I do pray you can come to B Court at the end of August. It seems a disproportionately long time – longer than it actually is, really – since I have seen you.

---

144 CR's younger brother.

145 For three years, 1948-1950, EB acted as Principal to the Kent Education Committee's summer school for teachers of English at Folkestone.

I won't write again till I either have a letter from you or hear you're back

Love from Elizabeth

Kent Summer School, Coolinge Lane, Folkestone. Friday, 13th August 1948
My darling. . . .
Oh Charles, I've just got your beloved letter. I feel that awful anguish of loneliness for you, suddenly, like a whiplash. It's the most extraordinary feeling, terrible, sometimes at moments – as though one's whole spirit tottered.

Darling, what you say about the empty hotel at Bellagio[146] is so extraordinary. It feels like my experience, so much so that I can't believe I wasn't there. I could write a story about it – in fact, shall I? Your experience sometimes – and this is a case – seems realer to me than mine. Perhaps I was there – all that fortnight while you were away, I had a curious light-headed, not-quite-all-there feeling – perhaps that was why I was in the superficial sense happy, or at any rate enjoying myself – nothing (I mean nothing immediately round me) mattered.

It was a question (that fortnight) of holding feeling at arm's length; because if I ever had let myself feel I should have felt desperate, as you knew so well that it was not a thing to be said, I couldn't bear your going to Italy, which I've always felt is your and my country, without me. But obviously you had to go, I'm glad now you've been, because to have been in the same places, even though separately, is a bond between us. And it was too big a matter to feel bloody-minded about – one can only let oneself feel bloody-minded about smaller things – ideally one shouldn't feel bloody-minded at all, but that's impossible.

---

[146] On Lake Como in Italy.

I dare not, even now, set too much store on your coming to B Court at the end of this month. It would be unfair to say 'It will kill me, I think I shall die, if you don't come', because I do know you will come if you humanly can. It would mean all the world. . . .

I'm so haunted – happily – by your picture of Bellagio.

I was (as I said on the telephone) at Mennaggio for a month, with [Aunt] Edie Colley and the (as they then were) children, just after I grew up. It was May. And, the year after, Joan (Reed now) and I stayed at Cadinabbia[147] for a day or two on our way back from Florence. Both times, I was thinking 'How lovely to be here with someone one was in love with.'

This is an extraordinary life! So utterly unlike mine that I'm enjoying it. The 'Summer School' is in a group of large ex-private schools (luxury type) scattered about a plateau to the west of Folkestone. The participants – 230 students, 50 staff – spend much time galloping from one scene of activity to another. The idea is, a refresher course for teachers – and I must say it does seem to be a good idea . . .

My role, at the outset, completely baffled me – it was hard to see what I'd been hired (at a very generous salary) to do. I hope my personality is enough, because as far as I can see that is all they are getting – though I must say even that keeps me on the run from early morning till late at night. They certainly all are an awfully nice lot of people and I like being with them. As I think I've told you, I really do like (for limited periods) community life – being among a humming hive of people.

Really such duties as I have evolved for myself are those of an air-hostess on a rather larger scale. I also keep people's amour propre smoothed down, which is quite an operation in itself.

---

147 Mennaggio and Cadinabbia are also on Lake Como.

In the evenings it is rather like a liner – movies and dancing. Also from time to time some of us pile into a hired bus and go on the most fascinating expeditions. . . .

Bless you, my dear darling – bless your beloved heart. Your E.
p.s. Had no time to read this through, so if anything doesn't make sense you must guess.

Bowen's Court, Saturday afternoon, 4th September 1948
Beloved – Your telegram has just been telephoned through. It's just past half-past four, just getting dusky outside, and I'd turned on the writing-table lamp. You've never been out of my thoughts – I was thinking of you arriving back,[148] yesterday evening, wondering what you were arriving back to. . . . It makes me sad that I can save you so few of the worries of life. Such a feeling of tenderness for you goes through me that it nearly bursts my heart. It's a tenderness that deepens every one of these times that we are together. I wonder whether any other being can ever have been so sweet to love, so creating all the time of more and more love, as you are.

You even seemed to be with me yesterday afternoon in the coming back alone here I'd been dreading so much. It was about 5 when I got back, a very clear glassy sky with a half moon over the trees already and the rooks beginning to rustle across it. Getting out of the car and coming up the steps I did shudder at the idea of walking into the house you weren't in, but the moment I was in everything was so sweet and kind, the fire burning brightly, the last reflections from outdoors coming into the room, and I felt happy – really as though you had left part of yourself behind and were in some way waiting here to greet me. The fact is that happiness and tenderness and love don't evaporate from the place where they've

---

[148] Back in Paris after a visit to EB at Bowen's Court.

been strongly; one's left with something better than memory, a feeling of something still going on – don't you think?

All the same, all today I've worked very hard, hardly letting myself look round or think. Because occasionally the agonising full force of missing you can't fail to come over me.

I wish I were an Impressionist painter and could paint pictures of you as you were here – halfway up or down on the stairs, coming in through doors, standing leaning against the mantelpiece. The things I think of you and the ways I see you would sound foolish said or written even to you. I wish I could show you the pictures I would paint.

. . . I wonder what your Shannon-Paris flight was like – good visibility; did you see that half-moon; was the picture a nuisance? Most of all and as soon as you can I do want to know about your Job affliction – what that doctor prescribes now, whether you're going into hospital. Unless that doctor does seem really able to get a grip of the thing do, and as soon as possible, also see someone else. I wonder if Dr Bourke's ointment has gone on doing any good? I'll get the prescription on Monday and send it to you. How very very good you were, you know. A thing like that must have made you feel so frantically tormented and restless the whole time, and you've no idea how little you showed it. The most slight physical irritation at once makes me so irritable in the other sense.

It's now 5.15 – quite dark outside (I haven't yet drawn the curtains) and the rooks now right over the house. It's been the most lovely, beautifully-coloured day – rather like it was yesterday morning when we were driving into Limerick. Only, this afternoon, still more theatrical – vivid smouldering sapphire-blue distances, strange gashes of light across the mountains, the yellow of the trees looking at once burning and diaphanous. I did wish we could have had this day while you were here. . . .

Poor Jim, back again without [his family] from Shannon, on the telephone sounded very low. I am taking him up on his kind offer to go up to his place and have a bath,[149] though as a matter of fact I should just as soon stay here. Tomorrow (Sunday) I'm going to lunch at Annesgrove; I shall spend the rest of the day catching up with letters; and then on Monday I shall go back again to the novel. I can't tell you what it has been for me, your reading it. It's cleared my mind, given me still more confidence and a sort of burst of inspiration for the last lap.[150]

I must stop now. Bless you and keep you, my darling love. If I could know you to be as happy as you make me, I should be satisfied – even I couldn't wish you more than that.

Your E.

5 September [Paris]

What a skeleton in the cupboard Mary is.[151] I feel as if I had put away a wife or two to make my present marriage which puts a strain on the marriage.

The rooks' feathers on the walk at B Court. In E I have for the first time in my life come to a full stop. I can go no further. She bounds my horizon. In every relationship I have thought beyond the person and the present, back into the past or forward into the future towards another care known or still unknown, towards a different experience. She is the goal towards which part of my nature, the deepest laid and most personal part, has always been drawn. She is the meaning of my life.

Always the same, for all my preoccupation with politics, my love affair with God, it is always the personal relationship which obsesses me. The dream and the realization of the dream. The Irish say,

---

[149] The Gates's bungalow had a modern bathroom with running water. At Bowen's Court, water was carried up by the maids to the bedrooms in cans to fill tubs placed in front of the fire.

[150] EB was working on *A World of Love.*

[151] Mary Adlington, a cousin and former love of CR.

'This breaks my dream.' Bowen's Court has that effect. It cannot last, but it can be returned to. A 'revenant' – what is so horrifying about that?

Bowen's Court, Tuesday, 7th September 1948

My darling – I got your beloved letter yesterday morning: I hope you'll have by now got mine. Oh, I am missing you. But like you I am happy, too: I feel so built in to our love and so much, also, I'm living in the perfect happiness of our days here. I see you in every room, at every turn of a path out of doors, and in the fields and places where we walked. It is in the happiest sense a haunting. How sad it would have been if we had never had these two places in their different ways so completely our own – this house, and your Bd. St. Germain flat (I shall always believe you and I'll haunt that, too: I hope whoever lives there now likes us).

... Thank you very much, darling, for ... the cigarettes (which I'm still smoking, as I meanly never offer one to a human soul), and the ENORMOUS supply of soap, which couldn't be more appreciated, as so many people are coming and going.

The house party goes on well: everybody seems very happy and harmonious. Loren[152] is sweet, and I think enjoying himself in his own queer little impersonal way. He sleeps like a dormouse till lunchtime every day. He and Eddy[153] have taken a great shine to each other, which is nice. Eddy is I must say an angel on occasions like this – so house-trained and considerate and amenable and chatty. More and more do I think fully-developed social instinct is

---

[152] A young man from the Canadian Embassy in Paris.

[153] Edward (Eddy) Sackville-West (1901-1965), later 5th Baron Sackville, first cousin of Vita Sackville-West and heir to Knole, her ancestral home in Kent. (Being a woman, Vita could not inherit.) Clever, physically fragile and sociable, Eddy was the author of five novels and a biography of Thomas de Quincey, all published by 1936. A dilettante of all the arts, he was on the staff of the BBC, and wrote art, music and literary criticism.

one of the most attractive and even virtuous things in life; it almost seems to me like the modern version of Christianity. I can say this to you as you so much have it. . . .

Eddy has got a passion for driving the car, which is a good thing, as I feel so bemused with all these people that I think if I drove I should go head on into a wall. We career about the country going to lunch, tea or drinks with the neighbours: I am so slack about being sociable when I am by myself, so this seems quite a good time to explore a lot of houses I hadn't been to before. My heavens, how rich some of these newcomers to Co Cork are, and what they have done with their houses! Some of the houses, I must say, are marvellous.

This evening Loren leaves, tomorrow Alan and an American girl called May Sarton[154] arrive . . . on Saturday we drive May Sarton to Cobh harbour and place her on a liner to return to America. So after Saturday the party

[Ends]

There are no more surviving letters from Elizabeth for almost seven months.

---

[154] May Sarton (1912-1955), from a Belgian family who settled in the US, a lesbian poet and novelist who spent much time in Europe. Sarton fell in love with EB in the 1930s, there was a brief romantic episode, and they remained friends. The impersonal manner of EB's identification of her to CR confirms that she did not always tell him everything.

1949

Bowen's Court, Thursday, 14th April 1949

My darling,

. . . Keep me in your mind – that's where I feel my only real existence is.

I forgot to ask what you'd be doing at Easter: I wish I had, as I'd like to know now, and wonder. Are you, I wonder, going out of Paris? I have this envy of Sylvia all the time – nothing to do with anything <u>against</u> her, which I haven't. But how lovely to be living in the same house, getting into the same car, driving to the same places.

No news, really, here everything very agreeable. Two days ago I spent an exhausting afternoon in Cork shopping. But really it's worth going into a town for the pleasure of getting back here again. This afternoon I'm driving into Fermoy to get my hair washed and bring back some patterns of tweed for an overcoat Alan's decided to have. On Saturday morning I shall decorate the church for Easter. Such heavenly dullness: it drips like eggnog over one's nerves. After Easter I must start working again.

Write again soon, if you can, beautiful and beloved. The joy of one of your blue envelopes . . . I shall write often, just in scraps like this.

Your E.

Large batch of American press-clippings came in today. H of the D[155] still well in the best seller lists, I am glad to see.

Bowen's Court, Thursday, 26th May 1949
My darling – how are you? . . . I wouldn't have imagined ten years ago that it was possible to be so lonely for anyone. The fact is that apart from everything else you are my dearest friend, so much my dearest that you've become my only friend: every day without you, however happy in itself, seems meaningless and imperfect. I realize that in love one really hands one's sense of identity over to another person. Only, you don't seem like another person: you seem more real than me.

Have you ever lived in the country for months on end? I hadn't, till now, for so long. It does something to one: I suppose, though it sounds absurd to say so, it enlarges one's soul. I know one needs Nature – the changes of the season, the rhythm of things re-happening, and the knowledge that they will go on happening. All one's thoughts become larger, slower and milder. But alas, in this state one also cries out more for the completion of Nature and all the beauty, which is, to be with the beloved.

When I drove with Eddy [Sackville-West] to Shannon on Monday, to see him off, I longed to hang about Shannon till a TWA[156] or something came in, and then board it as casually as one would a country bus and get back to where you are. I drove away from Shannon (having put Eddy in his plane) very fast, miserably, very badly, as though all the devils in hell were after me. I couldn't bear putting even 58 miles more of distance between me and you. Turning my back on the airport seemed to be turning my back on the possibility of seeing you. I arrived home quite dizzy from having driven so fast, and with a ghastly stomach-ache . . .

---

155 *The Heat of the Day* had recently been published both in the UK and the US.
156 Trans World Airlines, major US-based airline from 1930 until its acquisition by American Airlines in 2001.

Alan has come back from London rather ill again: more of that wretched heart-trouble. He's in a very sweet and touching, uncontentious mood; wanders about the place in a sort of dream. Deprived of his cat, he is now falling in love with trees, the trees here. A most curious development. He's got particular ones he's got an obsession about; he not only walks to where they are to gaze at them but talks and talks about them. Then, he wrung my heart by saying suddenly, 'Do you realize these are being the happiest months of my life?'

I've just finished writing for the New York Times a review of a book about Virginia Woolf. How difficult she is to write about, and how the attempt stirs up all sorts of impressions of her. I can't believe she's dead; she was so fascinating and lovely. I think I must have had something akin to an in-love feeling for her. Oh, supposing the horror if you were dead and somebody wrote a book about you and I was asked to review it!

This is a rambling sort of a letter – but it is to me as if I were talking to you before lunch. Oh if I were! I got so fond of that place with coloured umbrellas outside it, down at the end of Avenue Foch, near the Bois.[157] I hope next time the weather will be good enough for us to sit again in our Bois place near the lake.

Write if you can soon.

All my love. Your E.

Royal Kent Hotel, Friday, 2nd September 1949
My darling – I got your letter, written just before leaving for Strasbourg. I do wish we could have met in Calais, but thought it rather a flying hope and do understand about the Ambassador. I love and love you, and long to hear your voice and set eyes on your beloved face. I've moved down for 48 hours rest-cure to this nice

---

157 Bois de Boulogne, Paris.

and funny hotel in Sandgate – it has a garden-terrace running down to the sea. I felt like a squeezed sponge when the Summer School was over (it finished yesterday morning) and quite incapable of speaking another word to anybody (other than, if it could have been so, you). In fact, I came here rather than to the usual White Hart, Hythe, which is only one and a half miles down the coast, because I know the people at the White Hart so well that staying there would have been in the nature of a social visit, involving talk.

I go back to Clarence Terrace tomorrow morning, Saturday; feeling I hope by then more human after this nice time of looking at the sea and sitting in the sun on the terrace doing absolutely nothing whatever. There's also a very nice little bar here. This is so much at the edge of England that it feels somehow like being in France – I can just see the French coast from this writing table, which is in a ramshackle gay slightly louche glass lounge, full of broken-springed sofas, with urns of coral-pink geraniums full of sunshine and quivering in the sea breeze outside. It's a queer de-personalised sensation simply putting in a meaningless but happy day here with no reason except recovering from fatigue.

It's been really quite an experience, the last fortnight – very much more so than last year. It struck me that all my colleagues and the students were in a slightly peculiar psychic state: it may simply have been the prolonged and almost relentless fine weather, which floated everything in an atmosphere of illusion. I observed people falling in love with one another left and right. In a way I knew it was rather a projection of my own: 260 people of both sexes were living, consciously or unconsciously, inside an Elizabeth Bowen novel. I could say this only to you, and I would not say it even to you if I had found the situation unhealthily gratifying. But the fact is that I would rather write a novel than project one.

I didn't realise you'd never read *The Hotel*, and I'm glad you like it – for what it is. You know it was my first (I mean, novel as apart from collections of short stories) and I wrote it when I was 25. I know the idea of a hotel scene came from Proust – I was reading the Balbec hotel part in *A l'Ombre de Jeunes Filles en Fleur* when I suddenly remembered the (at the time) appalling hotel at Bordighera[158] where I had spent a winter, 3 years before, with the Colleys. Never was I more bored and depressed – never have I been since – than during that Bordighera winter. But I afterwards saw this was a case of what Proust says about boredom being (subsequently) fruitful.

I expect I was in ways rather like Sydney[159] – only outwardly less clear-cut and intense. And a complete difference as to physical personality: and physically, personality goes deep.

Knowing you and loving you has so much changed me that I can't remember what I was like before. I think that until I fell in love with you I had gone on inside being 25. I really did rather live in a world of dreams and theories. And I realise I always really was rather cautious and cagey, always holding something back without knowing what. Any of the successive people I thought I loved were always turning on me, disconcertingly and saying 'You don't love me

[Ends]

16 October [Hotel de la Paix, Geneva]

To understand one's own destiny, to have some framework in which to see this floating shifting mass of experience, to chart these currents, these shocks and depths and dangerous rocks, not to die without knowledge. Oh E, how can I live separated from you? What have I done to us? If I stopped caring, I should never care for anything. If I stopped fearing this, I should fear nothing again. . . .

In a dim way I like this feeling of being alone and taking up this monologue. I miss my wife. I want her. I am waiting for her. Yet this time of recuperation is quietly, sadly pleasant.

---

158 On the Italian Riviera, near the border with France.

159 The young heroine of *The Hotel*, published in 1927.

Bowen's Court, Monday, 24th October 1949

Dear love. . . . I was sorry to think of you leaving Geneva, because I felt you'd been happy there – relaxed, apart from the work, and very much yourself, walking beside the lake. Though I don't, as you know, know Geneva, I feel sort of lonely for it now you've left it. . . .

No, beloved, don't be frightened by the Constant[160] story, or any other about the decline of love. I think with us what we must recognize is that our love is growing more formidable as it grows stronger and deeper, and more deeply rooted in every fibre of ourselves. But with all its formidability, its whole essence is gentleness and tenderness and unshakeable belief in each other. I do know there is a fault in me, and I bless you for your forgivingness and understanding. I depend on you more than perhaps even you know – or indeed perhaps more than even I know. The way grace (I mean in the almost divine sense) renews and renews itself, in us and for us, <u>is</u> extraordinary.

My inability – though this only breaks out from time to time – to 'take' the fact of your being married to someone else is a sort of deformity in me, like my stammer. Help me with it. The thing – the un-resignation – takes such complex forms: I never know at what moment it isn't going to leap on me like a tiger. But the root of it is so simple: I should have so loved to have been married to you myself. Keep that in mind when I seem at my most horrible. I know you really do. The light of you, and of our love, is the only light for me. I do so love you, my darling. . . .

Of course, the paradox of this dear nice house is that I would feel rather mean in occupying it alone: and yet how much I do like being alone in it! In a priggish way I feel that in these days people are owed any pleasure or rest, even in the dimmest sense, they can have, and that if they enjoy coming here they ought to be able to.

---

[160] Benjamin Constant (1767-1830), Swiss political writer and novelist, lover of Mme de Stael. CB was reading the new biography of him by Harold Nicolson, published 1949.

Don't you agree? I've backed down on an awful lot of people I ought to have had to stay this autumn, all the same.

I must stop this particular letter, as there's early lunch as I am taking Elizabeth[161] into Cork: we both need to do shopping. We must go into Cork next time you're here: it really is an amusing peculiar place.

All my love, beloved

E.

When I say 'this particular letter' I mean – think of it as a page or two of what's really a continuous one.

Bowen's Court, Friday, 28th October 1949

Darling, this is just a continuation of my last letter. . . .

I wonder what you made of the Hundred Days part of *Benjamin Constant.*[162] Do you see why I think it would be a subject for you, as well as being a subject for now? ('Now' being the next 5 years or so.) I suppose the value of a historical study is its relation to the time it is written. . . .

Elizabeth Jenkins left yesterday. My cousin Charles Bowen is staying here for 2 nights. (He's come over from Kilkenny, where he's with the Butlers, beginning to learn to farm.) He is a nice young creature, quite good-looking in a tall, fair way. 6 foot 2. Curiously jerky and nervous in his manner. I'm driving him back to the Butlers' tomorrow, and spending the day there, in order to have a conversation with Gilbert and Noreen about his future. I've a feeling they don't quite know what to make of him; and I'm not sure that I do, quite. But there's something rather touching about him. Oh how I wish I could send him to you, for a year. You could

---

161 The author Elizabeth Jenkins, who was staying with EB at Bowen's Court.

162 The Hundred Days (actually 111 days) in 1815 were between Napoleon's return to Paris from exile and the restoration of the Bourbon monarchy. During this time Benjamin Constant worked out, with Napoleon, a new constitution for France.

teach him – by example rather than precept – so much. He might bore you, but I think you'd make allowances for a lot.

I've emerged from my torpor and am giving an enormous lunch-party today. Half the countryside, I seem to have asked. Unusually, for Co Cork, I've got more men than women: one family have a nice Army son home on leave. 2 beautiful bachelors therefore (one being Charles) and no girl for them. Too irritating, when I think of all the girls I've had languishing here at one time or another. Anyway, Charles will have to act host. He's had so little social life, even of this mild kind.

Next Wednesday, November 2nd, I go back to London. Except for the possibility of seeing you there I do dread it. Really one of the things that makes me tend to feel a bit unbalanced is this perpetual shuttling to and fro. Yesterday morning when I was in the middle of dressing I suddenly stood still in the middle of my room and said 'Oh God, oh God, oh God!' Do you, ever?

I live for your next letter. One thing about London, I shall be able to hear your voice on the telephone. On Thursday and Friday, Nov. 3rd and 4th, I shall be out all day at the Royal Commission,[163] which will by then have rolled round again. . . .

Two days ago there was a most exquisite crystal day here, with a turquoise blue sky. Elizabeth and I drove off in the early evening to look for an exquisite Nash castle I remembered, not far from here (somewhere under the other mountains, on a bye-road off the Mitchelstown–Cahir road). It was so difficult to find that it

---

[163] In 1949 EB (under her married name Elizabeth Cameron) was appointed a member of the Royal Commission on Capital Punishment, which met regularly and frequently to determine 'whether the liability to suffer capital punishment should be limited or modified,' before reporting in 1953. Their report favoured abolition from an ethical standpoint, but in view of their remit and of public opinion, largely in favour of the death penalty, recommended certain modifications. The work of the commission included visiting prisons in the UK and the USA. EB did not actually witness a hanging.

reminded me of the chateau in *Le Grand Meaulnes*, which the boy was haunted by but could never find again. When we got there it was too extraordinary – a pale-stone building in the brilliant sunset light, empty, shuttered, dead-silent, with grass growing on the terraces. From the terraces, a fairy-tale view of blue velvet mountains, with knolls of trees, all bloomed over on their tips by the sunset, in the foreground. It's very modern-ness (1820, I imagine) made it more uncanny. The gardens were laid out in a rather French way, with perspectives of slender trees, and little court-like sub-gardens enclosed in hedges of box. It was more ghostly than I can say. I always think sunset is a hallucinated hour. The upstairs windows were not shuttered, and one could see blades of yellow light striking through the rooms. It was as precise as a building – though utterly different in style – as Bagatelle.[164] I thought of you so much, and longed to be sharing my curious shivers with you. It would be the perfect dwelling for two people who, in love, had deliberately decided to enter forever the world of hallucination, even at the risk of madness. The name of the castle is Shanbally: inappropriate, there's nothing particularly Irish about it.[165]

I must stop now, my love

Your E.

Charles Ritchie was recalled from Paris to Ottawa and promoted to Assistant Under-Secretary of State for External Affairs, to take effect January 1950.

17 December [*shortly before he and Sylvia left Paris*]

Indeed the great revolution in my life is my altered attitude, particularly since my marriage, but I was ripe for it even before then,

---

164 Château de Bagatelle, the eighteenth-century folly in the Bois de Boulogne, Paris.

165 Shanbally Castle, Clogheen, Co Tipperary: designed by John Nash with improvements by John Repton, was built around 1812. In spite of a campaign for its preservation by Edward Sackville-West, who tried to buy it, Shanbally was demolished in 1957.

in my attitude to people, my growing incapacity to take pleasure or interest in them and as a result the lessening interest and pleasure which they take in me!

This is one reason why E is so necessary to me. Without being 'social' she makes me believe in people's feelings and she re-awakens my sympathies and my curiosity and humanizes me. I fear the gradual drying-up of these feelings, a thing which marriage produces and which I see happening to many others.

Bowen's Court, Monday, 26th December 1949

My darling – I was thinking of you all Christmas morning I felt very near – did you? I wondered what it was like (weather, I mean) at Chantilly.[166] Here it was rather beautiful – pale beaming winter sunshine on what have become fawn-coloured fields. The grove of trees in the lawn in front of the house is now in its winter shape – more symmetrical than it looks in summer. A sort of winter drowsiness has settled down on the sheep and cattle. The holly this year is covered with an enormous number of very red berries, like Christmas-card holly. Christmas service in the church was as usual rather too short (an unusual fault) as Canon Osborne had to tear on and take another service. I so much miss carols and hymns that I turned on the wireless. I also turned it on in the afternoon and heard the round-the-Empire Christmas broadcast. I was in such a state that the sound of Australians celebrating their simple, homely Christmas reduced me to tears.

People came in to drinks before lunch, and again in the evening. In the afternoon, when I had switched off the Australians and blown my nose, Alan and I went for the usual Christmas afternoon walk round the fields. In the afternoon it clouded over a little, and the landscape and mountains looked quite colourless,

---

[166] The Ritchies were with Lady Diana and Duff Cooper at Chantilly, north of Paris near Senlis, where the Coopers remained living after his retirement.

like a photograph. In the evening I read a book about Rilke – Nora Wydenbruck's.[167]

Already I have to struggle against the wound of not knowing what you do at every moment. Everything you do and say and hear, and the people you see are more important to me than anything in my own life. Will you, when you get settled into Ottawa, try and keep a sort of diary-letter for me? Really, from what you've told me about things and people there, the scene there has become so real to me that if I have the shortest notes or outline of daily things, my own imagination can fill the rest in. I wish there were cafés in Ottawa: I know there aren't, but I mean I wish there was some place where you could sit between leaving the Department and arriving home, and write to me? The writing-room of a little hotel, or something. That place would then become in a way yours and mine, like all the places in London and Paris where we have met and sat down and had a drink and talked. Does this sound very fantastic? But somehow (or so I always find) the place where one writes a letter becomes so much connected with the person (if it is the beloved) one is writing to. So much so that that funny glass-fronted lounge of the Royal Kent, Sandgate, had been, for me, you and me before you and I actually arrived there, because of the long sunny morning last September after the Summer School broke up, when I sat there looking through the glass at the sea and the coast of France, thinking about you and writing to you.

But I realise one difficulty about Ottawa is – isn't it – that owing to some law one can't just drop in any place at random and order a drink and – as one does do with a drink – settle down?

The idea of your leaving Paris is torture to me. It seems like a queer sort of injury to Paris. Do you see what I mean? I can't bear to think of that city empty of you – deprived, made poorer by the

[167] *Rilke, Man and Poet* (1949).

susceptibilities you have taken away from it with your physical presence. Paris, as you've said, is so like a person, so like an object of love. It seems to draw its existence from the illusion it sets up. . . .

I do long to know, though, retrospectively, about several things (will you, if you can, write me a longish narrative letter from the Queen Mary?) Did you and the others give Diana [Cooper] that cage of birds? What did Nancy M say about *Love in a Cold Climate*?[168] What was the old girl like, with you, altogether?

I want to talk to you about the Rilke book – or rather, about Rilke, and all sorts of things arising out of his view. But I think I'll keep that for another letter. It is a scourge not being able to read German. It's extraordinary that such a hideous language should be so perfect for poetry. I feel certain he would be your and my poet. Shall we both try and learn enough German to read him? (I do hate and mistrust translated poetry.) I know just enough German to see how utterly 'off' and false the rhymed English translations given, in this book, to the originals (quoted) are.

I feel that in this time to come Rilke could be a great strength and stay to both of us.[169]

I'll stop now.

Sweet Charles, the whole of me is with you. Don't be sad.

Your E.

---

[168] Nancy Mitford (1904-1973), who lived in Paris, was the eldest of the six Mitford sisters and a good friend of CR. Her successful novel *Love in a Cold Climate* had just been published.

[169] The main preoccupations of Rainer Maria Rilke (1875-1926), a lyric poet with a distinctive voice, are death, love, solitude, and his impassioned quest for spiritual transcendence in an unsatisfactory world. He was much translated; Eddy Sackville West, with Vita Sackville-West, had published a translation of his *Duino Elegies* (1931).

1950

2 Clarence Terrace, Thursday, 5th January 1950

My darling – I see you and feel you so distinctly that I can't realize you are on the Atlantic now. Partly you are in this room – the downstairs front room at Clarence Terrace, sitting on the other end from me of the red sofa, leaning your beautiful head back against the back. Partly we're walking up the Avenue Foch, just having left that railway-station café at the edge of the Bois, having had a before-lunch drink, walking towards the corner where I turned off to Rue Spontini and the Carrolls', past an iron railing with ivy hanging out through it. Your beloved hand is against mine and it's very cold – your hand.

I'm sorry I was so wet and low yesterday morning when we talked on the telephone. I had woken up that morning, the day you were sailing, feeling as though my insides were being torn out by pincers. I hadn't expected you to come through so early, so to hear your voice was both a joy and an agony.

Yesterday evening I kept imagining the Queen Mary pulling out from Cherbourg. I imagined you went below and had a drink so as not to see the last lights of France. Ever since then I've heard the soughing noise of the sea, like an hallucination.

This sort of double goodbye has been so awful. A sort of two bites of the cherry of pain. First the goodbye to you in Paris; but at the same time all these last 3 weeks I've thought, you are still <u>there</u>. Then yesterday, knowing that you were actually physically leaving that beloved place where we've been together. But I'm not so down really; I'm not truly, darling Charles. This is only one more thing to be endured and got through, and we've endured and got through so many things. Though it hurts more, it <u>matters</u> less, to be parting now than it has at any other time. The parting is only geographical (though all the same I hate geography, oceans, space). Your dearness, and our absolute, unassailable happiness fills me, like a strength. You feel that strength too. Our love is like something that we have given birth to: it has an independent existence of its own, outside temporary anguish and loneliness. It is like an angel (only could you and I have given birth to an angel?) able to comfort us and bless us.

It's a good thing you and I both work hard and are always in a hurry and at high pressure. That's a great anaesthetic. You will be reading this, I suppose, in your room at the Department. I wonder whether it's a new room or one you had before?

Only, we mustn't over-anaesthetise ourselves. Don't let us let anything, while we are apart, blunt our imagination and tenderness, even if those are sometimes a cause of pain. See me – I wish I were more beautiful – and feel me, even if it hurts. Really one comes through the momentary pain of envisaging the one who isn't there (actually, physically) into happiness. . . .

You beautiful and precious creature, take care of yourself. You are the whole meaning of life. Don't let your hands get cold, and most of all don't get a cold in your soul. All my love – Elizabeth

2 Clarence Terrace, Saturday, 7th January 1950

My darling – I'm going to type part of this, if that (my typing) won't drive you mad; because typing takes up less room.

Two days ago, Thursday evening, I heard your voice from the ship.[170] That has made all the difference in life to me – all the difference of life. I keep imagining you at every moment in that great pitching rattling QM, in the middle of storm.

. . . The last 2 days, Thursday, Friday – have been extremely legal and fascinating. They've been the sessions of the R[oyal] Commission on Capital Punishment. On Thursday morning, the Lord Chief Justice, Goddard,[171] gave evidence. He is the most entrancing, witty tough – slightly Bowra-type.[172] In a separate envelope I'll send you a press cutting gist of what he said. He then came back to lunch with us (the Commission) and I was lucky enough to be put to sit beside him. Conversationally he was a great pleasure. Like all people high up in what they do he gave the impression of being indiscreet, though no doubt he was not really. He also came out with one of the least boring stories about a cow I have ever heard: you know what a flood of stories about cows artificial insemination has given rise to.

Mr. Justice Humphries,[173] who gave evidence on Thursday afternoon, also lunched with us. As you would know, he is 82, with – he says, and they all say – 60 years practice at the Bar behind him. How anyone could be a practicing barrister at 20 beats me – is it really possible? He is a gay nervous flexible old Welshman, looking very much younger than he is, with light, and light-looking, blue eyes. As cute as a pet fox. I must say both he and Goddard struck me as absolutely cynical . . . It was a most exhilarating but exhausting

[170] By radio telephone, not in her head.
[171] Rayner Goddard (Baron Goddard), Lord Chief Justice for England and Wales 1946-1948, had a reputation for heavy sentencing and reactionary views.
[172] Maurice Bowra (1898-1971), the witty, bisexual classical scholar, Warden of Wadham College, Oxford, from 1938 and one of EB's group of close friends from the time when she and Alan lived in Old Headington, Oxford.
[173] [*Sic*] for Humphreys, a former Lord Chief Justice best known for presiding over the post-war Treason Trials in the UK.

day. I came home completely exhausted and had a bath and 2 very large drinks and had supper in my pyjamas and went to bed.

On Friday we had Mr. Justice Byrne, who is more serious and younger. I should think, a Wykehamist. But very nice.[174] Being more of a contemporary and less of a star he was more possible to ask about various legal points which have always baffled me. He says, for instance, that the Law has no interest in motive: it is enough for the prosecution to establish intention. (He also came back with the Commission for lunch, at which the conversation in which I elicited this took place.) Of course, the trouble is that the public, following any trial, thinks entirely in terms of motive. Unless motive's shown, they find it hard to accept that there was intention. Byrne said what really worried him was the appalling conditions in prisons. Overcrowding – the prisoners fungus-like from airlessness, lack of exercise, constipation, absolute mental blank. I must say even the unformulated idea of all that had always worried me, though I had never really visualised the revolting, deadening details until he told me. I have an awful feeling I shall end up by burning myself out being a prison reformer.

No, I'm mad – it was on Friday you rang up. Because I know when we talked I was dressing to go to a party, and that was on Friday. I had been feeling low and unlike a party, but then after we'd talked I felt different and put on one of a pair of lovely sheer nylons the Knopfs[175] had sent me from New York, and felt in quite good form, and when I got there enjoyed myself very much. The

---

[174] Sir Laurence Byrne (1896-1965), judge of the High Court 1947-1960, chiefly remembered for having presided over the prosecution of D.H. Lawrence's *Lady Chatterley's Lover* in 1960. Wykehamists – former pupils of Winchester College, a leading public (i.e. private) school – were sometimes stereotyped as brilliant, cerebral men lacking in emotional intelligence: hence EB's 'But . . .'. Sir Laurence was not a Wykehamist.

[175] EB was published in USA by A.A. Knopf. Alfred and Blanche Knopf became her good friends.

drink was all champagne (I mean literally, not only I felt it was).

The party was my new girl friend Nancy Spain's.[176] I can't think how she does it – the champagne, I mean. She writes very enjoyable crazy detective stories. Someone called her the Firbank[177] of the detective story world. I think I will send you one or two of them: I know you don't care for that genre as a rule, but there really is something very attractive about hers. I had a vacancy for a girl friend, and she just fills it; tho' she's a great deal younger than me. She's nice and gay and rattling. . . .

Leslie Hartley's new novel *The Boat*[178] has also just reached me. I'll send you a copy of that too. I haven't had time to read it yet, but it looks enjoyable. A great deal, of it, I believe, is about servants. I wonder if that mad housemaid incident you and I got mixed up with when we were staying with him comes into it. I think too I'll send that Rilke book I was reading in Ireland: it seems funny to get wrapped up in a book about a poet one doesn't (or at any rate I don't) know direct; but the whole story, and the outlook in it, fascinates me. In a queer way something about the man and the story seems like a by-product of your and my experience.

I realise – à propos of my being amused and made happy by Nancy Spain – that one of the reasons I long to live in Ireland is because I feel so much happier with Anglo-Irishwomen than with Englishwomen.[179] The latter always seem, in London at any rate, to divide themselves into the slightly intellectual, who always come to seem to me either <u>bourgeoises</u> or backgroundless, or else into

---

[176] Nancy Spain (1917-1964), broadcaster, journalist and novelist, became a media celebrity and something of a lesbian icon. EB's friendship with her came to an abrupt end.

[177] Ronald Firbank (1886-1926), a camp novelist and great stylist.

[178] L.P. Hartley's *The Boat* was published later in 1949.

[179] Nancy Spain was not Anglo-Irish, though she spent much time in Ireland. She was English, from Newcastle upon Tyne.

tremendously streamlined and rich-thinking types (under the L Westminster[180] heading) who though I admire them and am all for them and for anything they can get out of life, I am neither smart enough nor organised enough to be able to cope with, or to be with without a feeling of restlessness for long. Analytically, I can see I'm that awful paradox, a dowdy snob. I had a particularly cosy ten days in Ireland this last time, Christmas, seeing quite a lot of several of my contemporaries – all rather like me, with make-up put on one-sidedly and generally a button off here or there, or having forgotten to put on one earring. Heaven knows I don't admire this, but it does make me feel I've come home again when I meet it. . . .

Thursday Jan. 12th

The week-end and the early part of this week was made awful by my having accepted an offer to write a short story for the price of one hundred pounds; unfortunately it had to be written against time. I was too mercenary to turn the offer down, and was stupefied by an English magazine offering so much money. I'm not yet actually in a financial crisis, but I can see one ahead if I don't do something – I can't go on living indefinitely on *The Heat of the Day*, and I shall need money for America. Since I sent the story in, my agents told me that they could place quite a lot of others for the same money. So I suppose I had better do some more. But the fact is that writing so-called 'light' stories is as much as a sweat to me as writing any others, and less pleasure. And less long-term value, because though not ashamed of the light-type ones I wouldn't want to reprint any of them in a book.

. . . Angelic Nancy[181] comes round almost every day from her new flat, with her baby Marian under her arm, and tidies up and

---

[180] Loelia, Duchess of Westminster.

[181] The Camerons' long-time maid at Clarence Terrace. Before she married, she 'lived in.'

organises. I must say, I've never seen anyone manage a baby better than Nancy. On arrival here, she simply opens one of the kitchen drawers, puts the baby into it as though it were a pair of gloves, and that is that for all the rest of the morning – she leaves the drawer open, of course.

Also a very nice avuncular male char called Mr. Waddling comes in to clean. But all the same there is a hideous amount of rushing up and down stairs to do, in the evenings and early mornings. It would probably be simpler to let things slide, but I do loathe, don't you, living in squalour [*sic*]. My idea of squalour is un-emptied ash-trays and glasses with dregs of drink in them all over the place, or discovering there is dust on a table when one turns a lamp on. In order to avert this kind of squalour, which gets on my nerves and makes it impossible to relax, I find I'm perpetually in the vaultlike kitchen cantering round and round. In the mornings I make the family coffee down in the vaultlike kitchen, then solemnly bring myself up my own breakfast tray and go back to bed. I think having breakfast out of bed is the last horror. I now see why housewives get so aggrieved and bleak and are always having to be ginned up by the BBC or flattered by politicians. . . .

Friday 13th.

. . . The other day I walked in, and all round, Regents Park. I hadn't for ages. Already small green buds are coming out on some of the bushes. I wish you and I'd made time to walk in this park when you were last in London. A particular gentle tract of our happiness belongs to it – walks after lunch, walks when we were coming back here to this house for tea. So much so that the park has become you for me. A sort of absolutely opposite parallel to the beloved Luxembourg. Do you remember how often, at all times of year, we walked down that long straight avenue of chestnuts – here, in this park, I mean?

I long to hear about your place you will be living in in Ottawa, and your day – your days. Oh my love. E.

Bowen's Court, Tuesday, 17th January 1950

Beautiful one – thank heavens your letter of Jan. 12th has just come, and made me again happy. I don't know why I was getting into such a state (see the rest of this letter, written last night.[182]) I suppose I've been feeling in psychic waves or something, that you are not happy, that you've been, as your letter says, in an uncertain mood, or a 'state' of some sort. So have I been. Eddy and his house-shopping[183] proved actually a welcome distraction.

I wish we could help each other more with our lives. We do help each other by the very fact of existing – in fact except for God I have no help but you. Oh my love, though, something not only so sad but so frantic comes out from between the lines of your letter. I wish I were there. . . .

All my love – Your E.

Sunday evening, 22nd January 1950 [2 Clarence Terrace]

Dearest – how are you getting on? This January's getting into my very bones: I'll be glad when it's over. Tonight I went to bed early, but then couldn't sleep: I got up and leaned out of my window and looked into the misty Park darkness, the lamps with hazes round them, and suddenly such a miasmic feeling of loneliness, and terror – absolute terror – of not seeing you again, came up to me out of the night air that I came out of that room into this (the upstairs front room where I work, the former drawing-room) and turned the lights on, and am writing this. . . .

I certainly have had a most peculiar week. I wrote last, last Tuesday. The following afternoon I spent a long time visiting Maidstone jail. This was the first prison I'd ever been in. Except for

[182] Not in the collection. CR presumably chose not to preserve it.

[183] Eddy Sackville-West, who converted to Roman Catholicism in 1949, was looking for a house in Ireland.

the noisy symbolic clatter of heavy keys as we were admitted . . . none of the sensations were quite what I had expected – tho' I don't exactly know what I had expected. This is not a typical prison, as it's an experimentary one run on advanced lines. The Governor is a terrific talker with a cavernous lantern-jawed face and a shock of hair. He wore a baggy tweed jacket and choker scarf – the latter made him look rather like an apache. After tea in front of a roaring coal fire in his room (I have never met any where else, in England, so superheated as are scenes of guilt and misery: the Old Bailey is the same) he took me for a tremendous sprint round the prison. It seemed enormous: the Governor and I proceeded at a double across dimly-lit quads. We went into workshops, class-rooms, recreation-rooms, an immensely theatrical-looking chapel, a concert-hall, then dashed inside and up the spiral stairs of an enormous nubbly-looking building like an outsize Martello tower. In the rooms of this, which were shaped like slices of cake, groups of prisoners were spending the evening by engaging themselves in culture and hobbies. There were, once again, roaring coal fires.

After the darkness of the succession of quads, or campuses, outside (and these, moreover, cut across by an icy wind) the inside parts of the prison lit by row upon row of powerful hanging bulbs, seemed almost hysterically bright. I felt I was right in the middle of a Kafka nightmare. The prisoners, who were very chatty and obviously pleased (I thought) to have somebody coming around looking at them, looked rather like troglodyte undergraduates, until, at the second glance, one realized that each and all of them, in some indefinable way, was a bit off. They were dressed in grey flannel suits, shirts with soft collars, flopping ties – the only queer thing was that the shoulders of their coats were unpadded, so that they flopped down and made each man look as though he had been deboned. And, though they acted so frank and kept staring one merrily in the eye, there was a stench of squalour and slyness about them all.

The whole place got me under the skin, with an unspeakable feeling of enormity.

This, however, was nothing to the way I spent the 2 following days – Thursday, Friday. I have been – in fact still am, for there will be 2 more days of this week before it finishes – sitting through a murder trial at the Old Bailey. I am there representing the R Commission on CP.[184] This is not a thing anybody would do for pleasure, one would have thought, though as a matter of fact any spare accommodation in the Court is packed with what journalists call well-dressed women. The thing I can't get used to is that the whole inside of the Court we're in is like the inside of Harrods – light oak panelling, Edwardian baroque plaster ceilings (extremely clean) and tasteful lighting. It's small, and doesn't hold many people. The acoustics are bad.

The man on trial is [Donald] Hume, 29-year-old, charged with the murder of [Stanley] Setty, a Jewish dealer in second-hand cars. I'm relieved to find that one is far less conscious of the prisoner, and that he – or at any rate this particular young man – is so riveted by the to-and-fro of the trial that he seems unconscious of himself. His head turns to and fro, as though he were watching tennis.

I don't know whether you read the Hume-Setty case? Everything happened early last October. Setty disappeared, and dismembered portions of him were found in the Essex marshes, having been parceled up and dropped from a plane. Hume – who had been making a living by air-smuggling – admits to having dropped the parcels (to oblige friends, who gave him cash down for the job) but swears he had no idea what was in the parcels. The police claim Hume stabbed Setty to death in his (Hume's) Finchley Rd flat, in order to rob him.

. . . Hume moves me and haunts me: he's a sort of an international age-group type; could easily be Canadian, French, or indeed Irish. Tall, well-made, a little soft in the face and body, a nubbly teddy-bear profile, a shock of hair. Was in the RAF. Has a very pretty young

---

[184] Royal Commission on Capital Punishment

wife, whom he's much in love with, and a baby daughter. If he did do it, I imagine it was because he was not only exasperated but chagrined by lack of cash. He's what in Ireland's called a boy-o – a beau garçon, though of a bumble-puppyish, lumpy kind. And obviously a show-off – mad for good times and luxurious, pleasing things.

I pray for him – both when I'm sitting in the Court looking at him and every night. Oh God I don't want him to hang.[185]

Well, there are 2 days more of this. I don't think the whole thing suits me: I feel strung-up, upset. Pray for me, darling. Darling lovely Charles Your E.

Berne, Thursday, 23rd February 1950

My darling – I got your beloved telegram yesterday morning at Geneva. Oh I was thinking of you so much there. I had a lovely front room (no 48) at the Hotel de la Paix, looking on to the lake. When I woke up there, yesterday morning, just before dawn, I went and looked out of the window and it was too lovely – the whole sky glassy and lemon-yellow lights of the town and along the quais still all blazing away, reflected in the water; the outlines of the mountains like black glass, mysterious, and steamers anchored along the quai opposite the hotel could just be seen in the half-light, and looked ghostly; and a wonderful cold sharp breath came up from the water. Did you ever happen, when you were there, to wake up and stand at your window at that particular pre-dawn moment of a very fine day?

The only snag – did you find? – about the darling Paix is that there seem to be almost no bathrooms. My otherwise perfect room

---

[185] Hume, who was guilty, was sentenced to 12 years in prison as an accessory after the fact, after the first jury failed to agree. Released in 1958, he led a life of fraud, subterfuge and violence before being arrested and tried for a second murder, in Switzerland. He ended up in Broadmoor (maximum security psychiatric hospital). Rebecca West followed the 1950 trial and researched the background for her vivid account 'Mr Setty and Mr Hume,' published in *A Train of Powder* (1955).

had not got one of its own, and I could discover only one on the whole floor. In order to enter that it was necessary to ring down to the hall porter and get him to contact the chamber maid, who would then 'preparer' it. All this was explained at length. I so much hate a hoo-ha about a bath (instead of being able to drift into one whenever one feels inclined) that I didn't have one at all. I was there I must say less than 24 hours, and had been boiling myself in baths in my previous Lausanne Hotel 2 or 3 times a day.

. . . Darling Stephen T[186] was at Lausanne, at the Beau Rivage. It was sweet having him, and a great antidote to professorial society. He came everywhere with me, and was a succès fou with otherwise speechless professors' wives. On Tuesday morning he drove me in to Geneva in that enormous car he always acquires.

On Tuesday I went to lunch with the British Consul and his wife, who have a very nice villa uphill some way out, formerly occupied by Beckford.[187] Still better, the Byron Diodati[188] is only four minutes walk away along the road. I remembered so well your telling me about it and how you'd seen it. So both for your sake and B's I was longing to. The Lamberts (my hosts) very kindly got the key and we not only walked all round Diodati but went inside it. Oh how lovely it is. Don't you think it would be very nice if you and I lived there – perhaps not for always but for some time? It is a place which gives one the feeling that it ought to be a chapter of one's own life, and life to me is our life.

I loved that long narrow salon stretching across the width of the house with windows overlooking the lake; and the iron balcony outside those windows, which seems to overhang the view of the whole world. And the little study, with the bed-alcove, at the side;

---

[186] Tennant

[187] William Beckford (1759-1844), writer, collector and designer, spent more than a year in Geneva, with a tutor, in his late teens.

[188] Byron was at the Villa Diodati, on Lake Geneva, in 1816. It was at Diodati that Claire Claremont conceived his daughter Allegra.

and the great dank dining-room. All through inside, it had of course the ghostly chill of a house shut up for a long time, darkened by the shutters. I kept imagining Byron on those rather clumsy, conventional stone stairs. Do you find that when you imagine anyone living in a house you always visualize them on the staircase, going up or down?

I enjoyed even the academic part of my Geneva time. . . . In the afternoon I lectured in the University, and in the evening to a society. A young Englishman called Anthony Rhodes, who during the war wrote a very funny book called *Sword of Bone*[189] (I think you liked it) was there too. And a little American called Johnnie Widdicombe whom I first met in NY and have known off and on since was there too, working in ILO.[190] He had just come from Poland where he'd been for the last 3 years: he had loved it.

The awful thing for poor Johnnie (who's a queer) was that he'd been having a tremendous love affair with a young Pole, and was snatched away in the middle of it. And worse, he fears that his young man, having been compromised by relations with the West, may now be in the hands of the police. Oh, may the Iron Curtain never divide us, darling!! What appalling things can happen to people in love, these days.

I was cross at having to leave Geneva, but actually Berne is rather fascinating too. I cannot remember if you've ever been here? I like its arcades and provinciality, and cobbled streets (in the old part) and all the 17th and 18th century houses – especially the ones backing on the ramparts, with hanging gardens. All the non-Swiss who live here seem almost dotty with boredom and say it is hell for long. Apparently compared to the rest of Switzerland Geneva is Babylon – your friend there was right. But all the same

---

189 Published 1943.

190 International Labour Organization, an agency of the United Nations.

like all dull peoples the Swiss do cast up a few rather fascinating neurotic types . . .

I hope in London, to find that my affairs with the British Treasury are clear,[191] and that I may take up my air passage to NY on March 8th.

In that case, oh my beloved, I shall be seeing you sometime within the next 3 or 4 weeks?? . . .

This is the day on which the great British nation decides its fate. I must say I do wonder what happens. The Swiss seem in a greater state of excitement (so far as they are capable of excitement) about the British elections than the British themselves even when I came away. I do get a feeling that the British being socialists has bored everybody. They don't feel it's quite the thing; and I must say I do agree.[192]

Oh I feel so much about the possibility – the certainty I hope it may soon be – of seeing you that I can hardly speak of it; I dare hardly think of it. Charles, Charles, Charles

All my love, my love Elizabeth

139 Oxford St, Cambridge, Mass. Tuesday, 21st March 1950

My darling – except that I remember every moment of those 3 days,[193] I could hardly believe they were true, they were so perfect. A continuation of chains of other perfect days, in so many places, but always encircled in our own curious world, which has been our history. I don't know why our happiness together should surprise me, each time it recurs: it doesn't, really surprise me, because it is what I remember and live on and live in while we're apart. When

[191] In the post-war years there were restrictions on taking currency out of the UK.

[192] In the general election of 23 Feb 1950, the Labour Government retained a majority of just five seats, and called another general election the following year.

[193] They had three days together in Montreal after EB arrived in New York.

I say 'surprise' I mean there's each time we meet, a sort of shock of sheer happiness, of utter reassurance, of returning fullness of life. And the only equivalent of that shock is a sort of surprise: What is lovely is that always about our meetings there is something still more than one expected. A fresh revelation – of happiness, of love, of each other? – every time.

I suppose it is the full tide of happiness that makes the partings bearable – I mean bearable at all: I must say they are barely so. I went into a sort of abeyance, a stupour [*sic*], for a short time after we said goodbye outside the station, then thawed awake again into happy thoughts.

You're right, to have met on this side of the water has been a tremendous thing. It could not have been better. A sort of rational build up to all the belief we both already so strongly had in our continuity. Dear beloved. Montreal – we could not have been in a happier or more friendly-to-us place, could we? It seemed to be opening itself to us, and be giving us something, like Paris did, only so very much in its own way. I shall never hear its name spoken without love; I imagine, my heart will turn slightly over whenever I read the word 'Montreal' in a newspaper. The coloured houses in the snow and the icicles and the coloured awnings and the puffs of snow blowing down the streets, and that wonderful 6.30 p.m. glass-clear evening sky we used to see from your window while we were having drinks.

My journey to Boston was comfortable and uneventful. This (Boston, Cambridge)
[Ends]

24 W 55th St, NY. Sunday, 26th March, 1950
Beloved,

... So here I am, writing to you on a Sunday night, midnight, in Blanche Knopf's apartment; which, being herself out of NY for some time, she has loaned to me for the weekend. It is very nice, the apartment; curiously harmonious and restful and quiet. I am sleeping in a little study – one wall coral, the others grey. A lot of lamps, and one extremely intellectual picture of a pink cow hanging over my bed.

I was homesick leaving the Wrongs and Washington.[194] Did not at first feel at all in the mood for the NY racket when I got back here.

I have kept thinking of, and in fact living in, every moment of last weekend. All this weekend I keep thinking 'this time last week, in Montreal . . .' . . .

Well, I want to tell you all about the time with the Wrongs. . . .

That evening the Wrongs had a dinner party – the Franks, and my friends the Frankfurters, and 2 other very nice couples, and one clever little odd man. I liked Sir O Franks, whom I sat beside very much: he would not have been my idea of a British Ambassador to Washington; but times, as we know, change; and I understand he's a great success.[195] The food was divine and the dinner party extremely enjoyable. I wore that smoke-grey chiffon dress I bought here in NY and had meant to show you.

Hume [Wrong] was saying – when we were en famille the night before – how much he had wanted to have you there with him, and how frustrated he had felt about the whole thing. – I suppose you should really, ideally, go there as Minister, shouldn't you? It would make me happy to think of you there, among those people who love you so much. Although inevitably I cannot but want you back in Europe. . . .

The following (I mean, the last) morning, Friday, Joyce [Wrong] and I spent a fascinating and fruitful morning in a lunatic asylum

---

[194] Hume Wrong (1894-1954), Canadian Ambassador in Washington 1946-1953, associated with Norman Robertson and Lester Pearson as one of a particularly gifted group in the Department of External Affairs, and an early mentor of CR in the Canadian diplomatic service.

[195] Sir Oliver Franks (1905-1992), academic philosopher and public servant, British Ambassador in Washington 1948-1952. He became Provost of Worcester College, Oxford, and a life peer.

– St Elizabeth's. This arose because Felix Frankfurter,[196] who's been following the proceedings of our Royal Commission on C P with close and fascinated though enraged interest, fixed up for me to go and talk to his friend Dr. [J.] Overhauser, who's the head of St. Elizabeth's, about the insanity element in crime. Dr. Overhauser was most interesting and helpful – a striking and noble man. St Elizabeth's is a vast place, a colony in itself, occupying a sort of park. It was a beautiful gay sunny springlike morning. . . .

The lots more things I have to tell you about NY I'll write from London. Will you write to me as soon as you can to Clarence Terrace? . . . Good night, dearest heart, for now.

Your E.

North British Hotel, Edinburgh. Tuesday, 4th April 1950

Beloved,

This is only an interim letter of love in exhaustion. Exhaustion due to listening to these frightful Scots. I have been miserable since I got back, and particularly miserable here. By miserable, I mean homesick for the N American continent – for being even in the same piece of land as you; able to hear your beloved voice on the telephone. . . .

I couldn't write from London, because the same afternoon as I arrived off the plane I had to go down to Kent. I felt almost mad with flying-tiredness and unfocussed nerves. On Saturday afternoon when I got back again to London I went to bed and slept for 18 hours and felt slightly better; but then had to heave myself up and pack and come up here to Edinburgh with the Royal Commission . . .

---

196 Felix Frankfurter (1882-1965) born in Vienna, prominent authority on US Labor Law, professor at Harvard Law School before becoming Associate Justice of the Supreme Court (1939). A Zionist, he was also a strong advocate of civil liberties and of the desegregation of public schools in the US.

This hotel is slightly like our Windsor Hotel, Montreal, which at once makes me happy and disturbs me. About the same period – with those long darkish wide thickly-carpeted corridors. Without you here I feel ghastly. I do think Edinburgh the absolute end. Its dreary romantic skyline and Albert-memorial architecture and pallid low-pressure and dowdy shops and people. All the dreary healthy lassies trooping about. And the smugness . . . At least 2 of my chers collègues on the Royal Commission hate Edinburgh as much as I do, I've discovered; but it is impossible for us to relieve our feelings to one another as we are perpetually surrounded by beaming Scottish spies, popping up beaming at our elbows and pointing out how lucky we are to be here and how beautiful it all is.

Of course I expect I am slightly biased: this is the very worst city to land up in straight from NY. The drop from very high pressure to very low pressure makes me feel slightly mad – as may appear from this letter. I lie awake brooding over the fate of Mary Queen of Scots; a character I never thought of before. But fancy being snatched out of France to govern this dump!

I remember liking Scotland and the Scots when I was staying with Gildie Morden in that nice big house in the country outside Stirling. It is these middle-class Edinburgh ones who are so appalling. Compared to them the Swiss are glamorous and the Czechs a riot. . . .

I'm now going out to dinner with one of my RC[197] colleagues to spend a cosy evening discussing diseases of the brain.

You'll write next to Bowen's Court, won't you. I shall be there till the end of April. . . .

Dear beautiful gentle one, I love you and miss you so. E.

---

[197] Royal Commission

Bowen's Court, Tuesday, 11th April 1950

My darling – Your letter of April 4th came this morning: I came downstairs and, with such joy, found it there in a patch of sun on the hall table . . .

All this Easter here has been an uncanny mixture of brilliant sunshine, interspersed with scuds of rain, and this roaring, knife-like, 80-mile-an-hour (they say) gale. In a way it makes one rather restless, as the sunshine makes one want to be out of doors the whole time, but the gale, as soon as one goes out, stifles one and knocks one silly. The country is looking most beautiful – a mist of green over hedges and smaller trees; the larger, great trees with that pinkish look which means sap rising, readiness to bud. It's also lovely to come back to the singing of birds again – a curious depth of singing and chittering and bird-movement right back through the woods.

All this is, in a way, unbearable; because it all – even the soughing gale – plucks upon every nerve of love. I am torn and demented by longing for you. For our being together. I feel as though my mind and my soul and all parts of me were sealed up while we are apart. I miss the naturalness, my darling, of all we have; all that mixture of aliveness and joy and calm. I think you are my soul. I do so love you, adore you, miss you so much – need you. . . .

Yes, I suppose it is best to have one's children when one is young oneself. And yet in your case I can see that – as you yourself felt at the time – yours would not have been the temperament for a young marriage. My beloved, in so many ways you are so young still. I think you would have a very natural, equalitarian (inwardly) relationship with a child, a son, if you had one now. Somehow I feel convinced that you will – soon, or in the not too far distant future. I don't say this merely comfortingly: I feel it. And you know how I wish it. Dear one, there is a genius in your nature that I feel is, somehow, bound to go on. . . .

It was such a joy getting that other letter of yours in Edinburgh – I can't tell you. It was handed to me just when I was tearing out of the hotel to the morning session of the Commission; and, owing to the matey communal lunch, I was unable to read it until the afternoon session had broken up, which was torment. When the session *had* broken up, I then dashed round the corner into a Prince's Street teashop – a gloomy place in itself, but how happy I was there, reading and re-reading your letter. That teashop's the only spot in Edinburgh I remember with tenderness.

Oh dear, and how horrid I was – in the letter I wrote to you from there – about poor Edinburgh and its inhabitants. I really can't see – in perspective – *why* it got me down so completely. Everybody was very nice to me personally, so I was not suffering from pique. But I think it was the deadness. In *all* the places and cities I've rambled round in these last, post-war years, I don't think I've struck anywhere that didn't generate *some* kind of life.

The real trouble I think is that those Scots really do *need* Home Rule, self-government. And *do* they want it! I think the situation's growing quite serious: mounting up with a really bitter resentment of England. I was let in on this because of being Irish – 'the sort of bloke who would sympathise'. The people who talked to me about it were of the most serious – Lord Cooper,[198] their Justice General (equivalent of the English Chief Justice) for instance. Do you – I mean, in the Department – have any situation reports on this? I don't think the situation's negligible *at all*. Lord Cooper said to me: 'It seems impossible for us to make the English realize how serious the situation *is*, and how soon it will have to be faced and dealt with.' Of course the whole basis and backing of the thing, with the Scots, is economic grievance; plus resentment against the 'centralization' in London.

---

[198] Thomas Cooper (1892-1955), from 1947 Lord Justice General for Scotland and Lord President of the Court of Session. 'Lord Cooper' was a judicial title. He was given a life peerage in 1954.

In an atomic age, this whole matter might seem derisory. But I don't think the moral effect (on the rest of the world) of an outbreak of Scottish-English bad blood would be derisory – do you? It would split – at a moment when any concept is so important – the whole 'British' concept. Oh dear, if only I had more time I would drift around Scotland for 3 weeks or so, and then send you in a quite imposing (<u>and</u> dependable, because I am quite good at that sort of thing) situation report.

... Meanwhile, all my love, dear beloved, my dear soul. E.

11 April [Ottawa]

It may be that this return of mine to Canada has had an effect which up to this moment I had not recognized. It has restored my effectiveness. Perhaps I am more Canadian than I had thought.

2 Clarence Terrace, Saturday, 6th May 1950

My darling – it was so lovely and warming getting your letter yesterday morning. Every time I move it brings on a renewed stab of longing for you – every time I move from place to place, I mean. My lack of you is like a lurking latent physical pain – which anything happening to the nerves or sense, such as a journey, brings on with violence.

Well, here I am. Darling Yves[199] is to arrive on May 15th. I am tensely excited – absurdly so! It will be too awful if, having arrived, he shows signs of wishing he'd never come. I am preparing things so as to be as agreeable as possible for him, within limits. I mean I think he would take a low view of <u>fussy</u> preparations – good servants always do, I notice.

I am going to stay on long enough to induct him; then I shall go back to Ireland probably about the 19th leaving him and Alan

---

199 Yves had worked as a domestic servant for CR in Paris in 1947 and was coming to London to work for the Camerons.

to shake down. He's bringing his bicycle, at his own suggestion, which I think is a good plan, as it will both get him out of the language-difficulties involved in public transport, and make it possible for him (if he wishes to) to cruise round and explore. I am laying in, for him, a map of London, a guide in French to London (if to be found) and a French-English phrase-book. I know – and respect the fact – that he hasn't either the slightest wish to or intention of learning any English, but he might be glad to be able to use a word or two just in a crisis. . . .

I forgot to tell you, because I hadn't realized myself that I've once again become a mother – I mean, got another book out. It's called *Collected Impressions*, and is that collection, of which I think I vaguely talked to you, of reviews, prefaces, broadcasts, occasional pieces, etc. Its interest is mainly historic, I consider. I suppose it's for that reason that it's coming out doesn't excite me more. Still, I can't feel indifferent to it – any style it has, I think, is in the arrangement: it was interesting arranging the stuff, like making a sort of scrap screen out of my own work. I've posted you off a copy from Cardiff: it was my first opportunity to buy a copy. . . .

Oh I adored Cardiff. Darling it is the most fascinating place: I was trying to remember if you'd told me you'd ever been there? . . .

Cardiff has got a completely Continental feeling. The vitality nearly knocks one down. It was a vivid May day, I must say, of the kind which dramatizes anywhere, but even so. Architecturally, it's a sort of Osbert Lancaster nightmare; prevailing style Turkish-bath-type.[200] At the end of fantasmagoric streets (always a little out of the straight) chestnut trees in flower tossing in the wind and sun. And I was so fascinated by the Welsh en masse themselves. I've got a lot more to say about this, but will go on in another letter as I must in a minute catch an underground train out to New Barnet,

---

[200] Cartoonist and designer Osbert Lancaster (1908-1986) caricatured styles and trends in architecture in illustrated books such as *Homes Sweet Homes* (1939).

Herts, to see my old Uncle Mervyn Bowen, who is dying. What a thing to do on a wet gloomy London May afternoon. However it's worse for him (dying, I mean), poor old boy.

Oh I loved hearing about the weekend at the Masseys, and about their house and the general lay-out. Beautiful, don't kill yourself on the Atlantic Pact.[201] You know really I am rather afraid of your over-working past the point that you should – partly due to interest and absorption in the work itself (which I can well see) partly out of general frenzy. Yes, isn't it a queer feeling when one has been absolutely concentrated on a thing to the exclusion of all else, and then has to snap off and go to a party, where one's supposed to talk. It always makes me feel like an owl in daylight. . . .

Write as soon again as you can, dearest. Do you really love me as much as I love you? Yes, I think you do, but why should you? I love you so. E.

Please ask Norman [Robertson] to come and see me, if he can possibly spare a moment.

Sunday, 14th May 1950 [2 Clarence Terrace]
My darling,

. . . Paris arrives here tomorrow evening in the person of Yves. Queer, he's the 'carrier' of that one year, that only year, I ever loved Paris. Oh my darling, what a year for us to have had!

We are always near each other, close to each other, all the week round, every week, but naturally this sense of each other floods in most at weekends, doesn't it, because of the sheer fact of the stopping-off of the use of our brains and faculties in sheer work. I never know whether work is an artificial tension or a natural one – which do you think? It's natural to both you and me to have some sort of tension: if it didn't create itself by work I suppose it might create

---

[201] Canadian diplomacy was central in the formation of the North Atlantic Treaty Organisation (NATO).

itself in some more crazy, even slightly pathological, way. I never can, even so (I mean if we weren't working) imagine tension between you and me. But I imagine that if we were together and not working we'd embark on some series of wild hunts. Which might be enjoyable.

... My darling – I've so often thought what you put into words in your last letter: how do people who do not love, exist? At least, they may exist but they do not live, surely?

... Cumulating, all milling about their own city, what a fascinating, electrical, dubious race they [the Welsh] are. Cardiff had such voltage that even New York, in retrospect, seemed pudding-y by contrast. Almost everybody who passed me in the streets gave me a queer sensation of mixed méfiance and attraction. I began to think I could trace in my own writing a sort of Welsh hereditary streak. Surely quite a lot of the men, particularly, in my books are slightly Welsh, though I don't call them so – and never recognized them as such?[202]

You gave me such a picture, so much the feeling of that house where you were last weekend. It did all sound very fascinating; especially those islands with 'Charles Adams [*sic*] houses' on them.[203] Oh, I'd love to see it all; oh, I never can see enough places: all these scenes of your life, at this time, how I long to share them with you!

This letter would have been written yesterday (Saturday, after tea) if it had not been for and just as I got up from the divan (in the room upstairs which used to be the drawing-room, now my work-room) and went across to the drawer to get some of this blue

---

[202] The founder of EB's family in Ireland, Colonel Henry Bowen, who arrived in the seventeenth century with Cromwell's army and acquired the lands in Co Cork where Bowen's Court was later built, was a Welshman from the Gower Peninsula in Glamorganshire.

[203] Charles Addams was the *New Yorker* cartoonist specializing in black humour and macabre settings and characters. CR had been with Sylvia's brother Peter Smellie and his wife Fran at their country place on the St Lawrence River near Brockville, Ontario.

paper, the telephone rang. And I thought, 'Why, how, now, if that's Norman?', and it was Norman. He came round about 20 minutes after that. It was heaven for me seeing him, for all the reasons you know – apart from the fact that he's such a darling himself.[204] We had (or at least I had) a heavenly time talking. I felt what fun it would have been to have finished by going out to dinner together, but he had to go back and join up with the boys again; and Alan, it being Saturday, was all over the place. So the question of dinner never even came up, but I just felt it was, wistfully, at the back of both our minds. Not in the romantic or sentimental sense; just that he and I were both in the mood (it being such a heavenly bright gay May evening) to have done something that might have been amusing. I felt quite melancholy after he'd gone; and by the way he glanced round at the sunset and all the people good-timing out in the Park, and the chestnuts and tulips in flower, I could see that he temporarily was not in the mood to resume what would end in an all-night session with the boys. . . .

I'll read *Jalna.* Don't send it to me, darling; because I can get it here; it's such a classic that it's all over the place. Like you, I'd always heard of Mazo de la Roche books – heard of them almost to saturation point – but had, equally, taken it for granted they wouldn't amuse me. I'll now go straight for *Jalna*; and probably afterwards read the rest: there's a whole series of them, isn't there?[205]

I'm sending off to you, from Bumpus,[206] the new Henry Green, *Nothing*,[207] which I did think, in its best parts, quite brilliantly funny and to-the-point: it lags, perhaps, just a little towards the end. What

---

204 Norman Robertson, CR's colleague and friend, on a visit to London, was then Clerk of Canada's Privy Council.

205 Mazo de la Roche (1879-1961) was a phenomenally popular Canadian writer. Her series of 'Jalna' novels – there were to be sixteen in all – chronicled a family's history over a hundred years.

206 Bookshop in Oxford Street.

207 *Nothing* was the eighth novel of the idiosyncratic Henry Green (1905-1973), born Henry Yorke, a writer particularly admired by fellow-writers.

I do wish I'd had the gumption to send you from NY (because it's published there but not yet here) is Eudora Welty's[208] latest, *The Golden Apples.* Do get hold of it if you can.

It was such a pleasure to me, as I told you, when she came to B Court, to find her as much heaven as a person (in a quiet way) as she is as a writer. I think that the queerness, or inspiration, of her vision comes out in the photographs she takes: here's one she's just sent me (which do keep) of Bowen's Court. Odd; I've never seen, visualized or remembered the house from that particular angle. So it looks more like a house in a dream or in a story, to me – the house in the photograph, I mean. The windows are the side windows of the library.

I'm just reading Eddington's *The Nature of the Physical World.* In an extraordinary way, it illuminates what is the matter of my novel.[209] I now can't read anything that isn't in some way relevant to that novel. I keep dashing to the Bible, for instance. At other all-out moments, I read, as ever, detective stories. They are a sort of lazy substitute for movie-going, I suppose. All action and images, no bother with words.

I'll write you every word of the epic of darling Yves' arrival. Oh I do hope he'll like it here. I've been so touched by his determination to come, and by the way he's accommodated himself to endless delays. Certainly he's arriving at a pleasant time of year. I'm going to Victoria station to meet him. How we shall get his bicycle in to a taxi, God knows.

. . . Dear beautiful, I live from one to another of your letters. I rather listlessly went out and bought summer clothes yesterday. It's depressing how little interest attaches to clothes you won't see. Bless you and keep you! Elizabeth

---

[208] Eudora Welty (1909-2001), fiction-writer and photographer based in Jackson, Mississippi, and a friend of EB.

[209] Arthur Eddington's book was published 1929. EB was working on *A World of Love.*

2 Clarence Terrace, 18th May 1950

Darling – This begins to be a happy time of the week when there may by any post be a letter from you. So, this is an interim one from me, just to tell you about the arrival of darling Yves. . . . He's sweet. Seldom have I been gladder to have anybody in the house. He seems happy so far. He liked his room, I'm very glad to say: I mean, I'd been rushing about trying to make it as much what he'd like as possible, and he greeted it, on arrival, with an unforced grunt of approval. I think he appreciates having a gas fire: he retires in there in the evenings and writes innumerable letters. I long to know whom to, and what about.

His work in the house is heaven: done with all-out passion and concentration. He's made the floors of these rooms shine so much that I almost feel like taking off my shoes like an Oriental entering a mosque each time I come in from out of doors. His cooking also seems to be in good form. He required, in order truly to express himself, saucepans, vegetable-grinders, ladles, etc other than we have. In fact what used to be called 'the kitchen battery' in this house had run extremely low, and I had been hanging on before buying anything to know what Yves would want when he arrived. So he and I spent the morning riotously (and hellishly expensively) shopping in Selfridges kitchen-outfitting department. 2 or 3 minor objects he'd wanted were not to be had: I don't believe they exist in England at all. To this I could only make what has become my stock comment, 'qu'en Angleterre, évidamment, on me sait pas vivre'.[210] However, he's most indulgent and benevolent. We collected round us, in the course of our shopping, almost the entire staff of Selfridges, who were I think convinced that a master chef of international reputation had arrived in London. Certainly Selfridges went all out – 'We must do our best to satisfy him', the assistants kept murmuring into my ear, while Yves examined object

---

[210] [*Sic*] for évidemment, French: 'In England, of course, we don't know how to live.'

after object, tapped it, blew through it and put it down again, with a courteous indulgent but slightly pessimistic air. Finally I think I got at least the equivalents of what he'd wanted: he seemed very gay about it all. We emerged from Selfridges clattering all over with aluminium objects, like the White Knight. Then we raced home and unpacked them all on the kitchen table, to the amusement of Nancy.

Nancy is to go on coming in for a few hours every day, to look after my clothes and do small things about the house . . .

This oh my darling isn't as you can see a letter, simply a report. But Yves means so much to us both. I'll write a letter in a day or two. Your E.

No letters from the next two and a half months have survived.

Eversley, Coolinge Lane, Folkestone. Tuesday, 1st August 1950
Oh my love. . . .

It gives me a pang of loneliness looking at the sea and thinking you're not on the other side of that sea, as I've been able to do in other Summer School years when you were in France. . . .

I feel, as you do, my darling, a terrifying feeling of fatigue and inanition and a sort of lost-news amounting to dementia when we haven't been together for a long time. Yes, I too can live, for some weeks or even months after we've met, on the store of joy and freshness and energy and vision (even) that your presence sets up. After that, I begin to feel almost ill with longing for you, and life becomes an almost unbearable strain.

Yet, through all these long absences you never seem less close, or dear, or clear to me. You never 'fade' – that would be the one unbearable agony – the agony of wondering whether you really existed at all. On the contrary, the very fact of my longing for you gives me an almost hallucinated, sharpened sense of you. I see every expression of your face and hear every tone of your voice. I feel that these absences from each other are a bitter injury to us, but somehow they cannot injure our love – it has too much depth and strength.

But oh, I not only miss you so terribly but need you so terribly.

There are some very fine women on the Summer School staff – Durham University professors of education. They are obviously completely 'sublimated' – keen on their subject and at the same time very well-balanced. I mean they are not at all repressed or spinsterish or coy. Obviously love plays now – if it ever did – no part in their lives at all. Their complete self-confidence and cheerful satisfaction with themselves and the world makes them in their own ways quite attractive – they are friends to people but at the same time quite impervious to them. I marvel at them with anything but scornful wonder: how can people arrive at that – especially women? I could never get sublimated like that – though after all I am quite an enthusiastic writer. But I could never (I don't think) live for my work. I suppose if you died I should try to, as a means of trying to preserve my sanity.

But I don't think I should succeed. I might 'live for others', but I could never live for my work.

Perhaps women (other than me) do 'sublimate' more completely than men. I've seldom met a man (or much more seldom met a man) whom I felt somebody couldn't upset if they really tried to.

If there are men who are utterly un-upsettable and impervious, they're generally of the slightly repulsive smug civil servant type, whom nobody would ever want to upset anyhow.

I was quite glad to get into this bracing (in the climatic and all other senses) atmosphere, out of the emotional steam-heating set up at B Court by my recent house-party – Rosamond [Lehmann] and the McCullerses (Reeves and Carson.[211]) All three lived and

[211] Carson McCullers (1917-1967), American novelist and short-story writer. Her most recent book was *The Member of the Wedding* (1946), which she dramatized in the year she visited Bowen's Court.

moved in a haze of intensive subjective emotion – plus, in the case of the 2 McCullers, a haze of alcohol. They were all dears, but I got emotionally bored by them. They produced an atmosphere compounded of mixed Dostoieffski and Michael Arlen.[212] At intervals, putting down their glasses and mopping the tears of agonized introspection from their eyes, they would remark that Bowen's Court had such a happy, happy atmosphere, hadn't it, and that that
[Ends]

[212] Michael Arlen (1895-1956), Armenian in origin, was a satirical novelist of London society life, best known for *The Green Hat* (1924).

1951[1]

Between Elizabeth's last letter of 1 August 1950, and Charles's diary of 10 October 1951, there is a gap in both letters and diaries. They were either lost or destroyed.

10 October [Ottawa]

It is these evenings at home that I find hard to deal with. Not lonely – no. Oh don't tell me I am going to be miserable again, but tonight is too much like last night. Think of a winter of such evenings. Yet I feel guilty when I write this, as if it was Sylvia's fault. It is no more hers than mine. Nobody could be 'better company' than she is. It's just that I haven't the habit of home life. I suppose I could go through old letters, clean my shoes, read the Economist, do my accounts. What do long-settled married men do in the evenings at home? Search me.

11 November

Coming round the corner by the Chateau Laurier[213] to go up to my office, I thought that what I would like would be to find myself

---

[213] The Château Laurier hotel at 1 Rideau Street, Ottawa, close to the Parliament Buildings.

in a big double bed with a woman, with the curtains drawn and pink-shaded lights, and to fuck and smoke a cigarette and talk a little and stretch out my arm for a bottle of champagne on the floor beside us and drink a little and fuck a little and have a hot bath afterwards in a luxurious hotel bathroom, like the one at the Dorchester [in London] where there were lots of large size bath towels.

I should like to write to Sylvia and tell her how much I wanted to be in bed with her, if we were on those terms, but I can never talk to her about my desire for her.

Hotel Finlen, Butte, Montana. Wednesday, 21st November 1951[214]
Darling – I have not yet (that is, at time of writing) got to Jackson, Miss., to find your letter for which I so much long. I am hung up, snowed up, by these ungodly North-Western snowstorms. I am in a frenzy, you can imagine. By this time today I should have been within a few hours of arriving at Jackson in the nice sunny South, and here I am in the most terrifying fantastic scabrous hill town, Butte. Apparently it was lunacy of those New York people who have been planning my journeys to attempt to send anybody by air in this region at this time of year. . . .

Oh I wish you were here – not that it is a spot designed for pleasure, but it is so curious! Louche. A half-rotting, half-flashy mining town (copper mining, I think) scrambling up and up the sides of a steep hill surrounded by vast appalling mountains. The most modern buildings are circa 1920, and many are cracked and sagging and falling down. The pavements are cracked and fall here and there into deep declivities, as though the whole place had suffered an earthquake shock. And the uncanny thing is that the whole place, which is obviously a tremendous pleasure centre, with street after street of bars and saloons, blazes with lighting all night:

---

[214] EB was on a lecture tour of American universities, ending up with a few days with CR in Montreal.

there was a viscous glare all over it, bright as day light – fluoures-cent [*sic*] lighting and whirling neon signs – when I arrived at this hotel at 3am last night. It is in Butte that the original strip-tease act is said to have originated. And my room in this hotel was so peculiar. I say 'was' because I have just checked out of it, <u>trusting</u> not to be here another night. The room was quite unlike those ultra-respectable, hyper-hygenic hotel bedrooms in which I've now spent so many blameless nights. I got the feeling that someone had lately cut somebody else's throat there after a drinking-and-sex orgy, and that the blood had only just been scrubbed off the walls.

However, all this makes a nice change.

As I say, anything seemed better than getting permanently stuck in Missoula,[215] eating Thanksgiving turkey with the University faculty, nice as they all were.

Before Missoula, I was in Portland, Oregon, which was enjoyable; and before that in Seattle – along with General MacArthur. Seattle was enjoyable too. The North-Western people are handsome – the women Junoesque, Edwardian-looking, with temperamental faces and magnificent eyes. But I found the English-type climate of Oregon and Washington unexhilarating. And as I think I complained in an earlier letter, there was too much scenery – coniferous forests, rushing torrents, etc . . .

Goodbye for now, my darling love – E.

2 December

The most extraordinary phenomenon seems to be taking place in me. I seem to be falling in love with my own wife. It's not the first time this has happened, but never before, I think, with the force of this time. I find her beautiful. I want to go to bed with her all the time, and I don't grudge her this hold over me.

---

[215] The University of Montana, Missoula.

1952

9 February

I think that part of my reaction of boredom and distaste for Spender's book[216] comes from being reminded by it of countless pages of similar self-absorption in my own diaries. When I first knew E, I was surprised and rather disconcerted by her lack of concern with her own 'interesting personality'. I found it difficult to accept when she, the leading psychological novelist of the day, told me that she was not interested in people and their motives and characters. I now understand what she meant. The exercise no longer amuses me. In fact it is only from obstinacy that I write this private diary at all.

19 March

I come back to this diary because of the need to attach myself to this daily life in Ottawa from which every fibre revolts. One must regard one's life enough to want to record it, even with resentment. The worst would be to admit that it is just a question of 'getting through the day'. . . . Of my visit to Europe I write nothing; it was

[216] Stephen Spender's autobiography *World Within World* had just been published.

too interesting to leave me time to write. When I am living, I have no time for a diary.

26 May

One comes to disbelieve in the possibility of happiness, to make a stoical virtue out of continuing to endure what one has not the courage and imagination to change. But the deterioration in one is visible to others and gives the lie to the notion that this kind of passivity is a virtue.

Charles deliberately left one of Elizabeth's letters where Sylvia would see it:

7 June

And this decision seemed to me a very important one. What was my motive in first wanting her to see the letter? To move her? To make her cry? To shatter the shell?

18 August

With me love for a woman is always linked with a need to betray that love; a compulsion which I dread and desire.

But there are times when that interminable dialogue of marriage seems interminable. It gives one a feeling of pure pain to think that it must go on and on and on. I am pretty sure that I should feel that whoever I had married.

Alan Cameron had been unwell since a heart attack in spring 1951. In early 1952 he and Elizabeth gave up Clarence Terrace and made Bowen's Court their only home.

During the night of August 26 1952, Alan died in his sleep, in bed beside Elizabeth, at Bowen's Court.

He was buried in Farahy churchyard, beside the gates of the avenue leading to the house, close to the grave of Robert Bowen, Elizabeth's father.

part two

1953-1958

1953

Charles Ritchie did not keep any of Elizabeth Bowen's letters about Alan Cameron's death. Nothing more from Elizabeth to Charles has been preserved until March 1953, when she was with friends in Italy, and the surviving correspondence remains sparse until mid-1954.

Perugia, Friday, 27th March 1953

My darling – that little house up in Settignano was made lovely by a letter of yours arriving the day before I left. . . . The weather was of the sort of glory one associates with May, and the beauty of those hills all round, either tumbling or terraced down to the Florence plain – cypresses, olives and flowering fruit trees – was indescribable. The villas, farms and churches, are beautifully nitched – all stucco, and in the sunshine they gleamed golden. Also that burning pale-emerald of the young wheat planted at the foot of the olives is so lovely.

I was glad to get to Settignano, and thankful not to be down in Florence, which, except in the cool of the early mornings, seemed noisy, dusty, tourist-y and hot. Actually I suppose I was in Florence rather too little – I succeeded in seeing nothing but the Uffizzi: though that in itself's enough. But I should have revisited all the things that gave me such an intense joy when I was young, and first went there as an eager tourist with Joan [Reed]. We did go to San Miniato, up on the hill; and how lovely that is – surrounded by light and silence (all but the singing birds) and cypresses. Of course part of the joy of existence there is nothing – at least in fine weather – seems in the drab sense quite real: one seems to be living in that world which is the background of an Italian picture.

I had been glad to get out of Venice; I've never really liked it, and this time got the creeps there – partly, I expect, because of being alone. I only had 2 nights and a day there, but that was enough. My hotel room looked out on to a spectacular part of the Grand Canal and ought to have been marvellous. But for some reason Venice gives me the feeling of being exhausted – too many sensations have been wrung out of it by too many people, or something. I can't look at anything with a fresh sensation, a sensation of my own; I'm already thinking of Guardi or Henry James or Canaletto or Proust. The uneven pavement of San Marco – Proust, for instance.[1] Of course as I realized the day I left and took a gondola to the station, the place should be seen from the water – the quivering upcast reflections of light are like nothing else. But on foot it's hobble, hobble, hobble along those bloody calle,[2] all much the same; and one can seldom find anything one is looking for . . . the most pleasing thing I remember about Venice is sitting in the Piazza S. Marco – where I spent much time; it really is, as someone said, like an enormous drawing-room – watching a pair

---

[1] Guardi and Canaletto were popular and prolific 18th-century painters of views of Venice. Henry James (1843-1916) finished his novel *Portrait of a Lady* in Venice; his *The Aspern Papers* and *The Wings of the Dove* are set in Venice, and he wrote an essay on the city in *Italian Hours*. *A la recherche du temps perdu* by Marcel Proust (1871-1922) is shot through with perceptions of Venice, most notably in the volume *Albertine disparue*. Proust's narrator tripping on the paving-slab in the Piazza evokes, like the famous madeleine, a flood of memory.

[2] Narrow streets bordering the canals.

of pigeons trying to make love on a succession of the two-narrow ledges provided by the capital of a long row of columns. Each time anything began to be at all pleasurable, they fell off, and went hurtling and bumbling through the air on to the next ledge, where they tried again; and so on till they vanished out of view down the immense perspective of the piazza. I doubt if they ever made it; their stupidity and their persistent desire fascinated me.

Another pleasure of Venice was a fascinating conversation over dinner one night as to whether one thinks in words or not. I said, certainly not; one thinks in images and the language found for them is nothing more than a translation. I was hotly supported by a professor who is a Croce-ite. Apparently this is a topic which splits intellectual Italy to the core: and it's a question I can't leave alone – wherever I've been since, it's started again, and there has been a dog-fight. Do you think in words?[3] . . .

Oh I have so much to tell you, so much to talk about –. It seems to me sometimes almost a horror, a sort of outrage, that we should not be here together. This country gives one a feeling of life for life's sake. But even out of Italy I feel our apartness all the time. And sadness often takes with me, as it does with you, the form of a sort of deathly boredom. I am glad you're going to the Wrongs for Easter. Sylvia too, I suppose: 'not that I mind', as Eddy would say, only I love to think of you alone in that house in that queer state of gossipy companionship with the Wrongs, as I am so often
[*a page missing*]
I go on to Rome this afternoon; Naples tomorrow. I hope I shall have peace to write from Naples. It's all these people; and I am so tired at night. Goodbye for today, my dear love. E.

---

[3] Benedetto Croce (1866-1952), Italian idealist philosopher and politician. The area of Croce's theory which exercised EB was probably the idea that art is rooted in imagination and intuition, preceding thought, which is 'realized' in writing.

Bowen's Court, Thursday, 18th June 1953

Dearest – a week ago was the day you came back here. The bouquet I came back clutching from the Kinsale bazaar is still alive. Oh my love, I did feel ill after you left, slightly – as though your going away (though only temporarily) had done something to my stomach. Such an extraordinary thing, each time – a world of timeless and complete happiness, with suddenly a blade of anguish coming down like a guillotine – you going. But the great thing is that it is so sudden, no other of the days are overshadowed – from the moment you come back into this house the feeling of perpetuity begins again. And in fact what we have is perpetuity, and the breaks in it are shadows – no more are they, really? If only they were not there.

This time had such a complete rounded happiness about it – like the sheen of light in the July trees as we drove down into the plain from the side of the mountain, that afternoon. I love you so much; I love you so much.

I was at Kinsale – as I told you, I would be – at Urssie's house, the night after you left.

. . . As we drove back along the edge of the Kinsale harbour water after dinner at Acton's [Hotel], on our way uphill to Fairyfield,[4] she looked back at the town with its few reflected lights and said, 'Such a beautiful ghost town, to die in, and what more does one want?' I said, 'Oh nonsense, Urssie!' She said, 'Yes, Elizabeth, but you have someone you love.'

Which is true. While you live and are near me in any sense, I'm not really frightened of anything. You are my eternity.

---

4 Urssie was Lady Ursula Vernon, who had been a famous beauty, daughter of the 2nd Duke of Westminster, married to Major Stephen Vernon who had had polio and was in a wheelchair. The Vernons' holiday house was Fairyfield in Kinsale, Co Cork. Like Lady Ursula's father, they were racing people. Their main home, where they had racing stables, was Bruree House in Co Limerick. EB met them through her old friend Jim Egan, who was their land agent, and Urssie became one of her closest friends.

Audrey's here and is very nice, very well.[5] No time for more now – Elizabeth Taylor, my beautiful novelist chum,[6] and her husband (they're touring in Ireland) have been here for drinks and tea, and have damn nearly made me miss the post. . . . Goodnight.

Your E.

---

[5] Audrey Fiennes, EB's first cousin and close friend.

[6] Elizabeth Taylor (1912-1975). Among the best-known of her 12 novels are *A Wreath of Roses* (1949), *A Game of Hide and Seek* (1951) and *Mrs Palfrey at the Claremont* (1972).

1954

In May 1954 Charles returned to Europe as Ambassador to the Federal Republic of Germany and Head of the Canadian Military Mission in Bonn. He and Sylvia lived in Cologne, at 70 Lindenallee.

[Nd] May

Happiness and boredom blended in the motion of the ship,[7] the creaking of the cabin. . . . The growing realization that having married for companionship I am now passionately physically in love. And the companionship? Never mind, I have been happy.

Bowen's Court, Wednesday, 6th July 1954

Dearest love. . . . Oh love you wring my heart when you spoke of walking in that little park near your house. I mean, there I should have been, too, walking in the early morning, when in German fine weather that bloom lies over everything. . . .

Do you know, it sometimes tears at me like one of those iron hooks used (I believe) by mediaeval torturers, our going on being apart like this, week after week, summer after summer. Apart from

---

7 CR was on board the *Queen Mary* between Cherbourg and Southampton.

anything else, there's such a loss in pleasure (even of the most minor kind). I feel so gay when I'm with you – do you with me? Every detail of existence, not only one's own but every one else's, has a sort of enchantment – when we're together. . . .

Well, I had a very enjoyable weekend in Oxford – change of air did me good, and I did adore it. Stayed with Maurice Bowra. . . . And who DO you think is going to be married? Shaya! It could not be more of a drama, and I've been hearing about it all (as you can imagine). He, unfortunately, was away and examining somewhere that weekend. However his and my friends probably know as much or more about it (I got the feeling) as he does.

She's a White-Russian-French-Jewish woman, Paris Haute Juiverie extraction, married, but going to get a Paris divorce. I cannot be clear as to her present name, something like 'Heilbraun'. She's at present married to an Austrian-Jewish atomic physicist, whom she met in Canada. (Not a spy apparently, but a cad.) They live in Headington, in one of the manor houses. She is very rich. The atomic husband is allowing himself to be bought out, at an astronomic price, Maurice says. Before the agreement was come to, he (the husband) was turning ugly – putting detectives on etc. There is to be a Paris divorce, which apparently won't compromise Shaya's position in Oxford. She's about 41. Handsome, attractive, not particularly romantic. Adores Isaiah. He is reputed, too, to be very happy. The marriage is considered (a) very suitable (b) rather surprising – Stuart Hampshire said he'd always thought that if Isaiah married at all he'd make a romantic marriage. The suitability is obvious and they are apparently very good together (socially).[8] The person said to be taking it least well is Miriam [Rothschild].

---

[8] Isaiah Berlin married Aline Halban, née de Gunzbourg, but not until February 1956. They lived at Headington House, her previous marital home. When EB received an Hon. D.Litt from Oxford University later in that year, Berlin gave a great party to celebrate both that event and his recent marriage in the Codrington Library at All Souls.

I said, I thought she liked John Foster,[9] but he [Stuart] said no, her principal interest lately had been Shaya. Apparently her marriage (to Lane) is breaking up,[10] and also her best girl friend has died. So it had been generally thought (and by some, feared)
[Ends]

18 July [Cologne]

After the feverish high-pressure of E's visit and the house party, I am back again in the vacuum. This time the sense of emotional emptiness is heightened by the non-human life we are leading.

29 July

A life to let – this attractive property, old-fashioned, rather rickety dwelling, park encumbered by squatters' rights, lovely views. Owner willing to rent at sacrifice price, would consider sale. Sentimental associations and gravel soil.

14 August

Yes, it is not easy managing this slice of one's life; keeping a lid on the vacuum. Well, E comes to stay next week. She certainly lifted the lid last time, but what is the use? I know quite well already what is under there – nothing, nothing, nothing. Never mind, it's no worse they say than the story of any other middle-aged man.

Epitaph: Married his cousin, went queer in the head from drinking and thinking about himself, no children – anyway no legits.

---

9 Academic, barrister and Conservative politician.

10 Miriam Rothschild's marriage to George Lane, originally Lanyi, a Hungarian, was dissolved in 1957.

Ritz, Madrid.[11] *Wednesday, 6th October 1954*

My darling. . . . Well really this is a most extraordinary country, at once fascinating and repellent. In a way very much like I imagined it would be, only more so, and with that unforeseeable x quality (that there always is) added. The actual glaring staring stripped-down beauty of the landscape, in this searching hard uncanny light, is immense. Quite right to say Spain assaults the senses. I've never heard so much noise – that is, when there's any noise at all to be heard. Even the birds scream. And church bells don't merely break the silence (if there has been silence); they smash it to smithereens.

Since we've crossed the frontier we've stayed at San Sebastian (which is rather like a crazed edition of Folkestone, built round a shell-shaped bay), Burgos, and now Madrid, from which we've been driving out and seeing places such as the Escorial.

Thank God you didn't come to Madrid: to work, I mean. For one thing, all the people look most fearfully common: I suppose it must be the Franco-Fascist atmosphere. It's a much more flary-glary city than I'd imagined, greater part of it modern and rather South-American looking. Great parts of it feel rather like the Tottenham Court Road. It's noisier than Paris, Rome and New York all rolled into one (fortunately the Ritz is restful and quiet). It's also next door to the Prado, and anything anything is worth it for the sake of these pictures – it's nice being able to wander into the gallery for odd half hours at a time.

I feel one would deteriorate like anything if one lived and worked in Madrid. Some of the people I've met here (the Blacks have friends here) have something indefinably moth-eaten about them. Ungrateful to say so, as they've been extremely kind, matey

---

[11] EB was on holiday in Spain with Jean and Barry Black, who had bought Creagh Castle near Doneraile in Co Cork, where EB's friend Dorothy Bucknal had lived, and which was the model for Mount Morris in *The Heat of the Day*. Jean Black was, like Ursula Vernon, one of EB's closest later friends.

and hospitable. I think this would have been no city for you and me. No place for strolling about the streets. And I have a feeling that in this atmosphere all feeling would either wilt or harshen. Not yours and mine – but in general this is a bad place for feeling, an unhealthy place for it, I feel certain. Also the city has no environs – here it stands blazing and baking away in the middle of this bald void plain.

Though you might not think so, I am enjoying myself very much. At once very glad I came, and pretty certain I'll never come here again. There's a sort of crazy element in the enjoyment, and the Blacks are heaven. I mean it's rather like going round Spain with the Marx Bros. Jean is always crawling around the inside of the car swatting at flies with a map, and hitting Barry on the head with the map while he is driving. We are eating and drinking far far too much, and sleeping far too little. I don't think much more of this would be GOOD FOR ME – I mean, it really is exhausting, though also in a way stimulating. And I feel relaxed in one way because of an odd, lulling indifference to my surroundings, including (though I have a warm and ever-increasing affection for them) the Blacks. I think if one were in a state of tension, particularly emotional tension, in this country, one really would crack and go off one's head.

But oh I miss you, I miss you, I miss you – till I can hardly bear it. Write to me soon – I can't bear there being any gaps, however unavoidably, in our letters . . .

Oh my darling, my darling. Think of me, think of me. I think and think of you. Thoughts of you going running through my mind, all mixed up with this Spanish landscape, as we drive.

I stand about in the roomful of El Grecos here. You are as I've always said very like something in an El Greco. The more El Grecos I see, the more I see that. Tomorrow we're leaving Madrid and going on to Toledo, so I shall be seeing a whole lot more.[12]

---

[12] El Greco (1541-1614) painted figures with long slender bodies and elongated faces, which is why they reminded EB of CR. Many of El Greco's mature works are in Toledo.

Goodbye for now, my beloved love –
Elizabeth

151 Old Church St, SW3,[13] *[?] November, 1954*

My dearest – what it meant, hearing your voice again this morning. I've a feeling I went on talking rather too long; and that somebody, towards the end, was trying to come into your room. If so, forgive me: but I wanted to go on talking for hours. I could wish sometimes your Embassy wasn't such a cosy little family party. . . .

Oh if only you were in London today. It is one of OUR days – the look of everything, the sun shining moistly on everything, the leaves drifting in the parks and gardens and gummed to the pavements. When I'd hung up the telephone, I was left so restless and with such an ache for you, and with a what's-the-point-of-being alive-when-we're-not-together feeling. It's funny writing to you in this little tent-shaped room, with the window at floor-level and the outlook on to this Chelsea garden, where we sat and talked those afternoons last May. In a way it seems such a short time ago – I shall never forget the joy of feeling, knowing that you were back 'this side' – back in Europe. I expect in a way that your being in Europe makes me more restless. If I could see you about once every 4 weeks like when you were in Paris, it would be easier. But I quite see that and Bonn being as it is (that is, so much of a village) that is absolutely imposs.

And oh darling, we have the uninterrupted reality of OUR life – the only life that is a reality to me and, you say, to you. Your letter about that dangerous time in the plane did really terrify me – one can feel a sort of retrospective terror. If only I'd known you were in the air – I always have you in mind, I'm always what the Irish call 'burning a candle for you' when I know you are. . . .

---

[13] The house of EB's friend Helen Arbuthnot, where she often stayed when in London.

So now I'm living for the first week in December. I know you will make it both as soon as you can and as long as you can, so I'm leaving it to you. I think the best (that is, least expensive of time) way for you to travel would be, overnight by the Hook of Holland (if you could bear it) then fly by a midday plane London-Dublin, then, having got to Dublin take the 6.30 train from Kingsbridge station that gets you to Mallow – where I'd meet you – about 10pm. But even so it's 24 hours. Your office might be able to track a plane that would get you to Shannon within the day.

Oh Charles I can hardly bear to think of the happiness of seeing you. Please God, nothing stops this!

The Princess Margaret project is off – and, I can now confess to you, to my relief. It's for this reason: she is now not giving any interviews whatever. I saw the Family press officer, Commander Colville, this morning, and he told me. As he says, there's nothing to stop me writing the thing without an interview; but I gathered (during a man-to-man talk in his office) that 'they' would infinitely rather not have anything about her, right now in either the British or the American press – however high-class the article or its author.

In fact, her romance and her feeling about it apparently is intensifying; the whole situation is on hot bricks. He said 'I tell you this only between these four walls', and asked me not to repeat it. But you, my dear dear Ambassador, are accustomed to keeping secrets.[14]

I'm relieved, because I never did, I realize, much want to do the thing. I'd a feeling that it was slightly 'beneath' me. Socially, it would be quite unpardonable of me to do it – however discreet the article was – against the background of what he told me. So altogether this gives me a let-out where the American magazine in question (Holiday) is concerned. I can well use the time, as I'm

---

14 Princess Margaret, the Queen's sister, then aged 24, was in love with Group Captain Peter Townsend, a commoner separated from his wife, with two children. Church and Parliament were against the match. (On 31 October 1955 the Princess announced that she had renounced her plans to marry him.)

haunted by some short stories I want to write; and the short stories should in the long run bring me in as much money (or almost) as I should have got from Holiday. . . .

[Ends]

[*postscript on first page*]:

This is, again, written on the writing-block I bought in Bonn. I used to write scraps of the novel on it while I was waiting for you on the porch of the Königshof [hotel], overlooking that garden.

8 December [Bowen's Court]

Impossible to say what or how I feel about being back here – slightly queasy, can't focus my thoughts, seem to be looking at life through bi-focals. Then this shifting cloudy Irish sky outside these big windows seems reflected in my mind, where impressions shift and blur. . . . I am wary now with E. She says that if my present life continues (she is thinking of course of one side of it) I shall go mad or die. I wonder if I won't simply get dried up emotionally, cease to care or even notice that this is happening to me. I'll get older, harder (towards others, soft always to myself). Anyway I have back a precarious balance and I don't want it undermined by her profound unhappiness, which she only shows to me. Wouldn't it be better if we – oh I don't know . . . I don't want to have any more involved, shaming conversations over the Irish whiskey about my feelings. I am not an adolescent any more, or if I am it's indecent and should not be mentioned. Let's talk about something more interesting. After all I am spending five days with one of the minds of the generation. Can we help each other? It sounds like an Oxford Group[15] meeting. Can we anyway not harm each other? Let's cut our losses and get some fun out of life.

---

[15] The Oxford Group, also known as Buchmanism (after its founder) and as Moral Rearmament, was a Christian organization promoting surrender to divine guidance in public and private life.

9 December

Damn cold in the house. And we come back and back to the same subject [*crossed out, but looks like* 'my marriage'], 'to have nothing to look forward to' and that 'my feelings are getting number' etc. It's quite a sterile subject as well as painful. Yet I am not unhappy here. No, I feel this morning a sort of exhilaration. Being with her does still in a way work – work on me. We sit before the fire in the library, the Scotch whisky runs out, then the rye, we talk on. I feel that gash in our love caused by her in Bonn closing up, but I can't forget that it is there. She says I am older than she is, more resigned, but it's the worldly side that she forgets. I must steer my course. She wouldn't mind a spectacular shipwreck, if she could rescue me, the survivor – but what good would I be to her?[16]

10 December

Yesterday we went into Cork. Also I read her new book, 'The World of Love',[17] which I had only seen in manuscript and which arrived, the American edition, from New York. It is a triumph for her. The blurb says 'written at the height of her powers', and so it is. In spite of loneliness, sorrow, despair, she has written this masterpiece of her art. *The Heat of the Day* was a transitional book. Here is certainty, and to think that she wrote those final chapters in the nightmare agitation of that visit to Bonn, in my sitting-room in Cologne; on the table of the verandah at that small German hotel. If she was as distractedly unhappy over us as she seemed, how could she find the concentration to write this unique book in which her own

---

[16] What exactly happened in Bonn is never described. The inference, from CR's several diary entries, is that EB lost her control, expressing to CR in devastating outbursts, not only privately but in the Ritchies' house, the depth of her misery and resentment about his marriage. The resulting tensions incurred Sylvia's distress and displeasure.

[17] Correctly, *A World of Love*, published in the UK and USA in early 1955.

genius and vision will be found?[18] On the landing outside my door the maids are prowling, they want, poor creatures, to do this bedroom . . . The exhilaration of this book racing through me, the happiness of this morning, it's been bought at a price paid by her, perhaps even more by me. It is our book as it contains our shared illusion of life and could not, as they say in prefaces, have been written without me!

11 December

A snow-carrying wind is creaking and whistling through the house. If the gales begin again all our plans for leaving will have to be altered. Planes grounded. Roads impassable. That would suit me. I am perfectly happy. . . . Yesterday we drove over to Cahir. E bought me two gilt gothick mirrors. We drank in the Cahir Inn; she cherry brandy, I Irish whiskey. . . . We sat before the fire together in the evening saying mainly things we have said before. All the time the fabric of our love is strengthening again. I am coming back into her 'World of Love', only I am aware over my shoulder of that other, and of the world we share – or do we?

12 December

When was all this talk of happiness? Only yesterday – rats. Today, my last day, the sun shines on me as I write, but I feel back where I was. 'An unreal happiness', didn't E say something like that? Well it's the best we can have, either of us. So don't let's be ungrateful. There she's coming back from church, I hear the car in the avenue. I half wish this life could go on and on. Never to say that it was for always, but to drift into it.

---

[18] After a similar painful confrontation with a former married lover, Humphry House, EB wrote to him: 'I am a writer before I am a woman.' Emotional experience, however devastating, fuelled her writing.

13 December

I go today. . . . The rooks round the house seem demented judging from the row they are making, an ill-omened day. E and I go now our separate ways till the next time; now the pattern seems set, to be smashed only by the death of one or the other (or could treachery break it?). Last night we ate a jar of caviar in front of the fire and went to bed early. I felt sleepy, as if we had said what we had to say to each other – different from being bored – but understanding couldn't go further. All we have to do now is to live our lives without too great discredit.

14-15 December [Cologne]

The main thing is constipation of a peculiarly uncomfortable sort. I feel 'egg-bound'. Also the come-down is bad this time. The house is stifling with central heating after the cold of B Court.

20 December [Paris]

Well here I am, on the move again . . . It is a week today since I left B Court. The life there seems a remote happiness, yet one to which I cling. Where is the exaltation, the feeling of rest and health and quiet happiness? A middle-aged paradise; perhaps the only paradise which is now not a false one.

1955

1 January [Cologne]

Oh these Rhine landscapes. 'Ruhig fliesst der Rhein'.[19] E said she would write a story called that. At the height of last summer's climax, she said it. The night we were dancing together at the Berards. She said our life – our dancing life – was over, and there was nothing left for her but to go into a convent.

Bowen's Court, 4th January 1955

Beloved, I so loved getting that post-Christmas letter of yours. . . .

I am glad you've got that dachshund puppy. I really think dachshunds are darling little dogs; I love the way they tuck their long noses into the crook of one's arm.

I think I wrote to you on the eve of our Hunt Ball. It really was great fun. Noreen Butler (I wish you had met her) looked really dazzlingly lovely: I was so proud of her. It was such fun here, starting off for the party – fires and flowers in every room, and a sort of hum of excitement as we all got dressed. We then dined with the Blacks: a party of 10 in all, all very in the mood and gay. The ball

---

[19] From the old German song 'Die Lorelei.'

itself was in Mallow – rather like those old 'Assembly Balls' must have been. I looked handsome (I was told) and certainly enjoyed myself very much.

Oh, how I love pleasure!

I think Ireland's rather a place for pleasure. I mean, the real kind – slightly dashing, more than a bit ramshackle, but totally without calcul and unsnobbish.

New Year, with the Vernons of Bruree, was fun, too. The inevitable champagne, very glamourous [*sic*] crackers, enjoyable sentimental tears and kisses.

But you see, WHY are you not here, oh my dear love. What are we doing, spending these months of our lives apart? Well, it can't be helped, I know.

I am still living in the happiness of that perfect week. Your sweetness, and our hours, and your dear presence. 'Benign' seems such a funny word to apply to you, but there's no other (that I know of) for some particular quality that you have. You shed light round you (does that sound ridiculous?).

I'm so glad we went to all those places together – Cahir, Cork and that bar. They are now all part of us, part of our experience, and I love them. I shall be going into Cork again in a few days, and I'll sit and have a drink at that bar.

Next letter, I must tell you about my PLANS. I shall be here till the 17th, anyway. I haven't yet started organizing myself in any way about getting to Rome; I don't think I've really realized I am going.

There's a whistling blizzard. I'm writing by the library fire, in the chair you sat in. After tea, I'm driving to Bruree, to stay 2 nights and help Urssie with a parish social.

Darling old [Jim] Egan loved your letter. Oh my darling, write to me soon again, will you? Your E.

18 January

I am beginning to wonder if I have finally settled into a kind of semi-senile quiescence, and I am getting faintly worried about my entire lack of interest in sex. Is it the climate? Or have I had a change of life? Quite a contrast to last autumn. Not only have I no emotional interests, but I feel that I shall never have any again. . . . That is a thought that drives me to panic. Is it my marriage that is doing this? I don't know. I can't think about my marriage any more. Yet I am not unhappy . . . The only thing that has a little penetrated this apathy has been reading an unfavourable review of E's new book in Time. It hurt me and saddened me. I do want this book to be a success in the most obvious vulgar way, to bring in money, publicity, to make her feel on top of the world.

25 January

Rang up E today. It was like talking to someone on another planet or trying to communicate with the spirit world. I feel as if I was in limbo in this place and will never escape from it again.

Albergo d'Inghilterra, Bocca di Leone 14, Rome.[20] *Wednesday, 16th February 1955*

Your beautiful postcard with the sledge in the snow arrived this morning. And I sent a telegram to you, to 70 Lindenallee,[21] with my, this, telephone number . . .

I feel I wrote you a rather 'low' letter yesterday evening: it was a mixture of post-journey anti-climax, stage fright about arriving in Rome – such a terrific thing to be doing, really – and not liking my room in this hotel. I liked the hotel at sight, but not the room. So that fussed an old atmosphere-queen like me. The solution was of course perfectly simple. I went downstairs and asked the charming management if I could have another. They said, yes certainly,

---

[20] This was the first of several visits to Rome in connection with her book *A Time in Rome*, which she wrote as if it were an account of a single sojourn. It was not published until 1960.

[21] CR's home address.

another would be empty tomorrow (today, that is) and I could have a look at it and have it if I preferred. So this morning I did, and it's heaven: all I could want. A quite big, rather gay, light corner room – with two windows therefore, each in a different wall. Sunshine, made more yellow by being reflected off the ochre buildings across the narrow streets. And over the windows, voluminous cream-coloured starched lace curtains. A honeymoon suite, really, with twin beds covered in rosy cretonne, and armchairs covered to match. And a nice big bathroom off it. Plenty of lamps – though the bulbs are rather dim; I think I must do something about that . . .

The reason I hated my first room, I can now tell you, was that it was claustrophobic. One small high-up window, looking across at a practically blank wall. And below it, to look out at, nothing but a small yard with ash-cans. It was quite luxuriously furnished, but too small – almost entirely filled by a vast (I must say, it proved, very comfortable) letto matrimonio, which had the effect of making me feel lonely – and the rest of the room was just a path round the bed. And the furniture consisted too much of cupboards: every time I opened one of them I banged myself. And the plug in the bathroom quite often wouldn't pull . . . So all that got me into rather a state.

I think the hotel think the better, rather than the worse, of me for having wished to better myself. I explained that I am a scrittore and must have pleasing working surroundings (which is true). And a lot of mail, and flowers, which hotels always think well of, have arrived for me . . .

This morning, after I had settled myself into my new big room, this one, I went out and bought maps, a dictionary and an extra guide-book. I had brought with me Augustus Hare – very rare now, as he's out of print[22] – lent me by a woman in London. The

---

[22] Augustus Hare, *Walks in Rome*, 2 vols, first published 1874.

sun shone and everything was lovely. When I'd done shopping I climbed up the Spanish Steps and looked at the view, walking along past the Trinita, under the balustrade of the Pincio gardens. I found a delicious little nitched terrace café, with one or two flowering oleanders, where I sat outdoors at a table in the sun – it was almost empty; no Roman would be such a fool, at this time of year – and looked at my maps. At the moment I don't in the least mind looking and behaving like a tripper: I expect later I shall develop a residential snobbishness . . .

Write when you can, oh write when you can. And sometimes ring up?

Oh Charles, Charles, Charles . . .

Your E.

Albergo d'Inghilterra, Rome. Friday, 25th February 1955

My love – it was agonizing when your call from Cologne began to come through this morning, then got held up. Will you try again tomorrow, I wonder. I'm dying to hear your voice again – so far, the lines have been so awfully good. . . .

I am walking around Rome like a maniac, in a daze of excitement. I don't know how many miles a day. Not at random: I work myself out a route everyday. It's a most thrilling feeling, opening up a city. Totally different from any other time I've been here before. Also I'm being very social – though in the evenings only, if I can possibly manage it. Everybody's being very kind and hospitable to me – which considering how many visiting firemen there are, and what nightmares their arrivals are to the residents, is very nice of everybody. . . .

The only thing that is making me sad, and very sad, is that I suddenly saw in the Times that Humphry House, that friend and long-ago former love of mine, is dead. At 46. The announcement just said 'suddenly'. I've written to Maurice Bowra to ask the details. How people come alive, almost unbearably, when they're suddenly dead. And he was a darling, and a great, though an odd, character.

Oh, don't die. Don't die. I can measure by what I even feel about Humphry, how much greater, how absolute and utter, a desolation could be.[23]

Goodbye for now, for a day or two only.

All my love, Elizabeth

27 February

Obstinately the adolescent remains alive in me. Still I dream of one more fling. Still I am unreconciled to being an Ambassador, to going out for Sunday walks with the pet dachshund, to my own incapacity to write a book, to the middle-aged hairs growing out of my nose . . . If anything could get me down, it would be marriage. Not Sylvia, but marriage. Sometimes I have a panic fear that it will, it and diplomacy between them – the inner and the outer conformity.

13 March

[*Sylvia is away*] Of course the truth is that I am enjoying this bachelor status. Yes, enjoying it. I feel my faculties coming alive again. It is not that Sylvia bores me, but that she makes me feel like a bore; and that is hard to forgive. . . . The almost disquieting part, only it doesn't disquiet me, is that I have no impulse to have a love-affair, am so indifferent to letters from my loves (E of course apart, but that is always apart) that I can hardly read them.

---

[23] EB and Humphry House, a fellow of Wadham College, Oxford, were lovers for three years from 1933, when EB and her husband Alan Cameron were living in Old Headington. The Camerons' marriage was not fully consummated. Humphry House was her first real lover. He married soon after their affair began, and EB's high ambitions for their relationship, and her attitude to his marriage as unfulfilling of his true nature and potential, was not unlike the situation with CR. The affair ended when House took a post abroad.

Antico Caffe Greco, Rome. Wednesday, 16th March 1955
My darling. . . . Do you realize that going about by yourself you're a different man? And your voice from in bed in the Hamburg hotel the other night sounded so warm and gay and happy. The voice of someone 20 years younger. You beloved love.

. . . Yes, *A World of Love* is having a tremendous impact, isn't it. I can hardly believe it – oh yes I can though. I meant to send you Leslie Hartley's review of it in The Spectator – a paper I don't believe you see – but the review's back in the hotel: I'll send it in my next letter.

Yes, I agree: that struck me – the book does frighten people!

I feel so close to you; so in touch with you. The telephoning, and letters. (I loved the Hamburg postcard.) Oh my love I so love it when you are happy, even when you're happy without me. That is your natural element – gaiety, élan, amusement.

Yes, and I am simply adoring Rome. Each day seems too good to be true. Doing the most extraordinary things – today, having come back from a lunch-party and changed my clothes – into the kind comfortable for walking-about, I mean – I spent the afternoon and evening into and part of the sunset walking about the enormous Rome cemetery, Campo Verano. It was begun in the 18th cent. And is used now – the place streamed with pompes funèbres while I was there. I cannot tell you how cosy, in a thoroughly morbid way, the place is. A marble epitome of family life. Everything tells a story. The setting sun streamed through the crimson glass globes of lamps on the graves. And often, in the marble hands of the statues – young brides reclining, little boys in sailor suits – little touching bunches of flowers, beginning to wilt at the end of the day's sunshine, have been laid. An immense piety, to the groups of the dead . . .

Well, so when you get this Sylvia and the aunts will be there. Here in Rome where all families of all classes seem to live in hordes on top of each other, it doesn't seem so odd. But of course the key of the Italian family system is that the man of the house is a free agent. A respected prowler. He looks benevolently round at the assembled faces of his womenfolk, then civilly rises, bows and goes away – off with his mistress, out with his boyfriends. And how indeed could he endure life if he did not.

In this country women though decorative seem to be less of a nuisance, less of a bind, less bossy than they are in countries where they are less decorative. . . .

<u>Every</u> day, at all times and so many places I think of you. I love you, I love you. Telephone soon – just to talk. <u>Elizabeth</u>

Rome, Tuesday, 12th April 1955

My darling. . . .

I hope you liked Vienna; I did love it – though I saw it in snowy winter, and so soon after the war. Feb 1948. Do you remember I told you, I ran into Graham Greene there when he was just beginning to make the *Third Man* film.[24] And the film was so like Vienna as we saw it at night. But also I have a wonderful daylight impression of it, those great plunging statues and fountains, and stupendous perspectives. It's really a more spectacular city than Rome. And the country round so lovely. I hope it was warm enough to sit out of doors and drink wine. Lilacs out. <u>Oh</u> such a gay place, even after all this ruin and misery. Unquenchable gay, I thought.

And how funny your staying at Sachers.[25] I was there do you remember when temporarily it was a British Military Transit hotel, full of specially imported black leather armchairs and, as Graham said, decaying marriages (the Occupation people and their wives).

---

[24] *The Third Man* (1949) directed by Carol Reed, screenplay by Graham Greene, with Orson Welles, Joseph Cotten, Trevor Howard, Alida Valli.

[25] The monumental 19th-century Hotel Sacher, in central Vienna.

It was true that one heard fractious murmuring grumbles behind each door as one walked down the corridors. And they, the Military, wouldn't let one have breakfast in one's room; one jolly well had to come downstairs fully dressed and drink stewed black tea and eat baked beans. At least I didn't eat baked beans, but one was supposed to. And all that among that elegant glory – the whole of Sachers had such a marvellous atmosphere of former grand dukes and parma violets. I hope all that's been restored now. I remember I didn't write to you from there because I was on my way home through Paris, where we then met and spent a day.

... Easter morning was pure and dazzling. I longed to kiss you on the forehead and say, 'Christ is risen.' They have banked the Spanish Steps with azaleas, mostly white, which gives them the effect of being flowed down by a white lace veil. Lovers get in and sit among the azaleas, blinking in the sun. Coming out of 8 o'clock church I for a moment had an attack of loneliness, then somebody said softly in my ear, 'Happy Easter, dear dear Elizabeth.' It was old pussy-face Roger Hinks,[26] but very sweet of him. Then outside the church I was gathered up by a New York family, the Taylors, I'm very fond of – father (he used to be Director of the Metropolitan Museum, but has just retired and taken on a smaller one[27]), mother, a very pretty woman, and two very charming serious teenage daughters. So we all went along to Babbington's English Tea-rooms and had an enormous and rather gay breakfast, inside a window open on to the sunshine – American coffee and Scottish scones

---

[26] Art historian, whose post as Assistant Keeper in the department of Greek and Roman Antiquities at the British Museum was terminated over a public scandal about the cleaning of the Elgin Marbles. In 1955 he was the British Council representative in Greece.

[27] F.H. Taylor was director of the Metropolitan Museum of Art in NY from 1940. In 1954 he returned to his former post as director of the Worcester Museum of Art in Massachusetts.

and marmalade. A very cosy and happy thing to do – just exactly what I had been longing to do when I came out of church.

Then I drove out with some people to lunch at Ninfa with the Sermonettas,[28] who have turned the whole of that dire mad little 13th century ruined town at the edge of the Pontine marshes and under the steep mad mountains into a garden, and live at the edge of it at the edge of a brook. We had lunch out of doors by the brook, under a vine . . .

Oh by the way a book you must read, I implore you, is *Bavarian Fantasy: the Life of Ludwig II.*[29] All the material for it came out of the secret archives of the house of Wittelsbach. Diary, his, and love letters. As you know, he was a queer, and went mad eventually, so it's quite a depressing book. Full of the most ghastly Bavarian castles. It's not at all well written, indeed more than trite. But in a way that rather heightens the effect. Author, Desmond Chapman-Huston. He's dead now poor chap, too. A friend finished editing the book for him; it's just newly out.

At midday today, for the first time since I've been in Rome, a really full blast sirocco struck Rome. Have you ever been in one? I can't tell you how awful it is – a hot wind like an unceasing blast from a grey furnace, with all the filth and debris in the world flying through the air and into one's mouth. Everything seems to go colourless and evil: it's like seeing someone one loves in a bad mood. The awning of the outdoor place where I was having lunch yanked, heaved, flopped like a big mad bird, almost split across. I decided it would be hopeless to go on with the day; even the idea of moving from place to place filled one with dread. So I took a very expensive taxi and came home, and have been lying on my bed reading Roman history. I also went to sleep. It's quite a thing

---

[28] The famous gardens of Ninfa, now open to the public, belonging to the Sermoneta [*sic*] family, about 70 km south of Rome.

[29] Republished as Ludwig II: The Mad King of Bavaria, by the Dorset Press in 1990.

to have lived through a sirocco, but I hope it won't happen again. They say it always causes a crime wave, and I don't wonder . . .

Very much love

Elizabeth

Oh by the way, where am I to send telegrams to now? Let me know. Now you say you've stopped Erik[30] opening them and laying them out on the hall table, hadn't I better send them to 70 Lindenallee again? Rather that, surely, than having them thumbed over in the embassy in case they happen to arrive when you're not in . . .

15 April [Venice]

Dearest E, this is the letter I would write to you if I still dared to tell you everything – if your hatred for S did not frighten me (that hatred is eating into you, you said it was like a cancer). I am in this situation – indeed in the midst of it – between the two of you. Today when I came out of the Church of the [?] into the sunlight, leaving S to look a little longer at the monuments, I felt possessed by you. I mean possessed as people are by God or the Devil. I saw that our love has twined roots of good and evil, that it lives in the darkest places of my nature and of yours, as well as on the pleasant surface. Shall we end by destroying each other? But you are the stronger. You have the deadly weapon of the artist . . .

16 April

It is 9.20 in the morning and I am waiting in the hotel lounge for a telephone call to E in Rome. I talked to her yesterday morning. . . . The pain in her voice – the awaited reproach which yet is not a reproach but the response of her nature in love – 'Oh you are NOT in Italy' – what am I to say[31]? . . . I cannot breathe for long the air

---

[30] The Ritchies' butler at 70 Lindenallee.

[31] EB was stricken to discover that he was in the same country as she, with no plans to meet her. He was with Sylvia.

of guilt, conspiracy, love – and yet I cannot breathe without it. E and S are getting too old, falls and bruises which used to heal in a day go on giving pain and earlier wounds reopen at a touch . . .

Now this morning she had time to collect herself – it was like talk between two married people of plans and dates and friendly loving messages.

Bruree House, Monday, 21st May 1955
My darling. . . .

I'm writing with the gold pen that you bought in Cork, that afternoon we were there. In fact, it was a Monday afternoon, exactly a fortnight ago. Oh I cannot get over this missing of you, it eats me. In a way I wish I were at Bowen's Court today, where I should be at least among our surroundings. . . .

I have just finished my Tatler review: tomorrow when I get home, I shall I hope go back to writing the Rome book. The only thing for me now, for these next weeks, is to work very very very HARD.

It's now 4 in the afternoon; the house is full of lovely ticking clocks and dozing people . . . Urssie is padding in and out of the garden (in spite of the rain) in slacks and a beautiful tarty-looking ex-evening black beaded jumper.

Do not, DO not let it be too long Charles, before I see you again. Having to face the idea of not seeing you again for a long time would almost kill me. I live now in the memory of our every moment. Oh my darling, I do love you so much. Elizabeth

18-20 August [Bowen's Court]
This diary is a clinical document; the story of a struggle with an obsessive cycle of boredom, dissipation, remorse, apprehension, boredom again . . . but the attempt to escape from this cycle and with God's help from my own self-obsession is the real object of the exercise of which this is the record.

E is in her room writing her Tatler review. Oh now that these days with her have begun to run through our fingers, I know they will go so quickly and begin to dread that last morning – the packed bags and the drive to the station – as if it was today. Patches and tatters of complete life together.

28 August [Montreal]

. . . I took a walk up the Montreal mountain where last night I sat on a bench smoking a cigarette and resolving to have another go at It. Under the controlled surface of my mind were thoughts of E, of the sad, disturbing, fearful love which I half hate and without which I am not alive. The perpetual dialogue between us, which it seems must continue into eternity. How often have she and I walked up these steep streets to the mountain talking together, her hand on my withdrawing arm and down again to iced martinis at Restaurant Carol on a snowy day? How unbearable Montreal would be if she was dead, and how could I bear her saying that she wouldn't give a damn if she was told that she would be dead in a month's time? But I only said that it was true for me too. But was it true for either of us?

Bowen's Court, Thursday, 1 September 1955

Beloved. . . . I so clearly saw you, my beautiful one, in Montreal, walking up what I can't help thinking of as our mountain, up those dear steep streets, and eating at the Eiffel Tower, and going, when you'd finished the letter, to drink coffee and orange juice in our glassed-in downstairs place. Oh how happy we have been in Montreal – for me, I suppose, it's the one city in the world which has nothing but those associations: our life, you, our happiness, those lovely hours and days that though so few (few at a time) were also so full, all those moments and things we did, the same things, each time with even more joy, like the morning martinis and the afternoon movie (I don't think we ever didn't go to a movie when we were there, did we) and then back to drinking and talking before dinner in a Windsor [Hotel] room. Bless beloved Montreal.

When you said (in your letter) that you felt so much more than half at B Court, still, it was exactly what I felt. . . . I really could almost see you, in fact did see you, sitting in that drawing-room chair, the yellow armchair. . . . Charles, everything lives so when you are here. You know that line about 'the city now doth like a garment wear the beauty of the morning'[32] – well, this house and everything around puts on some sort of extreme garment of beauty when you are here. Summer, autumn, winter – I always feel that when you are here. The only season you haven't been here is spring, I think.

A week today since we raced to that Dublin airport. . . .

The church so triste[33] and bare, ugly, no candles or flowers (other than on the coffin) and the whole place filled with stark cheerless light. I prefer dark churches. Oh really the Church of Ireland is too depressing: RC funerals are much gayer. All those present at the funeral were old – do you know, except for one or two people I think I was the youngest there. And most of them, instead of wearing black, which I suppose they didn't possess, had compromised by a sort of ghastly drabness. We followed the coffin to the grave along a narrow path out through forests of weeds.

I said to [Aunt] Edie, as we drove back to Corkagh, that if I ever had a funeral I should like it to be a very pretty one. More like a wedding. I'd like to be followed to my grave by a string of beautiful girls carrying roses, each attended by a charming and ardent lover. I should hate to be seen off by people who looked like hell and depressed each other . . .

Well, after the funeral I . . . got to the Vernons' about 6.30. That evening the house there was full of bats. Faulkner (that valet) came in after dinner, coughed, and said, 'The light on the upper landing

---

[32] William Wordsworth (1770-1850): 'This city now doth, like a garment, wear/The beauty of the morning. . . .' from 'Composed upon Westminster Bridge, Sept 3. 1802.'
[33] EB had been to a family funeral.

has failed, and there are six bats in her ladyship's room.' Stephen said, 'Fortunately her ladyship likes bats.' And indeed she does. When we all went to bed, through her open door I saw her gazing up at them ecstatically, looking more Charles Addams than ever. In fact there were only three bats, but their (to me) horrible shadows on the ceiling multiplied them. Fortunately there were none in my room – the same room as I'd had before, which I was glad of. Next morning when I went in to say goodbye to Urssie before making an early start back here, I asked 'Well, how did you and the bats get on all night?' and she said, 'Oh, they were heaven' . . .

Dear beloved joy of my life, now I must stop. Elizabeth

Bowen's Court, Tuesday, 19th December 1955

Yesterday morning I had your letter from Paris, the one written in the early morning, my love. You said it was short, but so much came out of so few words. I stood by the library fire reading it, and such love for you and such a great wave of gratitude for our happiness rose up in me, almost choking me. I re-live the minutes and hours of those blessed days in London, and the things we did. This time last week, Tuesday evening, we were still together, having dinner at that dear glowing Ecu de France[34] . . . And all Sunday, this last Sunday, here, I was thinking about our Sunday in London. A pouring-wet black-dark Sunday in a totally empty London in mid-winter: could anything in principal sound drearier? And I think it was somehow the happiest and most perfect of the happy and perfect days we have lived.

I wanted to write to you on Sunday, but what do you think, I had to do the Tatler review. You, and all the things I was saying to you in my mind, kept becoming between me and my typing. I got on (with the review) very slowly, and all the time cursed and swore.

---

[34] Restaurant in Jermyn Street.

I was in the drawing-room, which was filled with sweet-melancholy winter light, the sun coming in from the west through the bare woods. That has become so much your and my room. I'm sorry to say it has also become, while I've been away, extremely damp – in spite of the blazing fire and several stoves, a chill humidity haunts those yellow satin armchairs. I removed the (loose) cushion from the small of my back when I'd been sitting some time reading one of the books I had to review, and held the cushion to the fire, and clouds of steam came out. So at the end of the day I took all the cushions out of the drawing-room upstairs and stuffed them into the hot press – I'm leaving them there to bake for the next day or two, till I use the room again. Yes, this is a darling but DAMP country. . . .

Soon I'll write again – Elizabeth

170 Ebury St. SW1,[35] *31st December 1955*
Last day of the Old Year. May we both have a very happy 1956 – and by happiness I mean seeing each other, being together, as much as possible. Oh I do pray, literally pray, that may be so . . .

London feels very ghostly without you. I realize that it has come to be, for me, simply a place I come to see you. It's a brilliantly fine pale-sunny day – or rather has been; it's about 5 p.m. now. I am writing this in bed, in the course of an afternoon rest, in my funny little tiny dollshouse room at 170 Ebury Street. It has a paper striped in two shades of dark green, and a bed with a very ducal crimson-brocaded head. The electric fire is full on, the window looks out (at the back) over dusky gardens, and I can hear electric trains rumbling in the distance. For the afternoon, I have this tiny house to myself; Urssie is out hunting (in Surrey), Stephen has gone to a funeral (an old horsey friend's) in Cambridge – no, actually it's a cremation. Tonight we are going to make a NIGHT of it

---

35 The Vernons' London house

– going to the opening of the ballet at Covent Garden, then on to Quaglino's when I imagine that Urssie's objective will be meeting up with Douglas Byng[36]. . . .

Charles, my tortoiseshell powder compact is an active joy each time I use it. I love feeling it on the palm of my hand; I love stroking it with my thumb.

I know what you mean by dropping toads. I mean, I find myself doing that myself – it quite scares me. I am afraid of saying something quite evil, which might stick, or be repeated. It's the result of this agonizing impatience with life, this restlessness, this sense of things running to waste I so often feel, and I know why, it's being apart from you. Sometimes my missing you is almost like an illness.

And I fly into tantrums over quite small things.

And, back again on Friday next to Bowen's Court, like a homing pigeon, who do you think is coming speeding? Eddy. Chiefly he says in order to order carpets for his new house.[37] And the awful thing is, I feel the most raging claustrophobia at the idea of his coming. I don't want to sit over the fire with him evening after evening. Oh how beastly I sound. But do you know it sometimes drives me nearly off my head seeing him sitting there smugly in your chair. He says it is for only 'about a week' this time, and I do hope so. Oh I know it's selfish of me, but if I can't be with you I'd so much rather be alone. . . .

Your E.

---

[36] Comic singer and entertainer, famous for his drag acts.

[37] Eddy Sackville-West had bought a house, Cooleville, at Clogheen in Co Tipperary, about 18 miles from Bowen's Court. EB's presence nearby was a factor in his decision. He was to spend about five months in every year there.

1956

Bowen's Court, Friday, 6th January 1956

My darling . . .

How you could ever think you could disappoint me . . . Well you don't think that now, so we needn't go into it. You must really realize that loving you is like being absorbed in something that though it never changes always moves forward; you are always a new marvel to me, the things you think and do and say, and your beloved alight alive face. Although I more and more love you I've also never fallen out of love with you, indeed fall more and more in love with you. I say 'although' because one hears in some relationships how the first wild flame gives place to something steadier, etc. But for me there is always the flame. I do feel the steadiness of trusting you and believing that you love me, but that goes on being a miracle, too. Dearest, do you not know you are very fascinating (that has become such a cheap word, but I can think of no other and I do mean it, in its pure original and unspoilt sense). Your moods, and the darling activity of your mind. Being with you sometimes is like leaning over a bridge looking down into deep sometimes bright sometimes dark moving water. You never will be old. Oh my heavens what terrifies me is that you'll die before you even are old in years. You have promised me that you won't – you've promised, promised. It would be very hard for me not to feel that that was my death . . .

Oh my love, all my love E.

Bowen's Court, Monday evening, 16th January 1956

Oh my love. . . .

Poor Eddy, how beastly I was about him before he came: he was so harmless and happy and nice when he arrived that I now feel rather a cad. It was the idea of anybody coming here which irritated me. The week he was here he dashed to and fro to Cooleville, Clogheen, his newly-acquired house, and was no trouble. Twice, once for a whole day, once for an afternoon, I suspended my fierce writing and he and I went into Cork to do his house-furnishing shopping. Almost everything, from the drawing-room carpet – of a colour and pattern he was jolly lucky to find in Cork; it's the same as Cecil Beaton[38] has for his front stairs – to servants' bath mats have now been acquired . . .

Oh, Charles, it's so Cold here! It's cold in a way that gets me under the skin: at intervals goose flesh tears up and down me and I imagine I am going to die. My great big bed gets so icy in the small hours of the morning, like a tomb. What's it like in Germany? Having begun the winter in heated houses, I do now feel like going to pieces in this raw air – oh dear, what would my doughty Bowen ancestors have thought of me? Really, somebody with not only an Irish but a Welsh ancestry ought to be able to stand up to dankness better than I do. Perhaps it's age? It isn't really as dreary as it sounds: I keep up roaring fires and stuff the corners of any room I am in with portable stoves.

---

[38] Cecil Beaton (1904-1980), fashion and society portrait photographer, stage and costume designer, diarist.

The fact is, I am so lonely for you that I'm nearly off my head: it undermines my physical morale. Oh my love, I do want you and miss you so.

Bowen's Court, Wednesday evening, 29th February 1956

My darling. . . .

It rather made me miserable, leaving the flat 16c West Halkin St, on Monday morning. At all moments and up to the last moment, the place remained so full of you. Because of that, it was such a wrench turning my back on it and leaving it that I banged the door behind me and pitched down stairs with tears in my eyes. As a matter of fact I think and hope that my relationship with that flat is by no means over. The nice maid Mary, saying good bye to me, repeated 'You will come back, Madam, you will come back, won't you?' and I said that at any time when it should suit Mr Knollys[39] to let me have the flat again, I certainly hoped I should. It was lovely, wasn't it? It was so very very much our home. We can be happy in London at other times and in other ways, but I do like to think we shall be back again in that flat some day . . .

I am finding it rather difficult to adjust back again to life here. The fact is Charles that saying goodbye to you this last time has made me feel as though my inside had been torn out. Sometimes I feel as though I didn't know where to turn. I walk about rooms by myself saying 'Charles, Charles, Charles.'

I spent today in what was rather a good brisk extraverted way – taking part in a jumble sale held at Doneraile [Co Cork] in aid of the rates to be paid on Canon Osborne's Protestant rectory. The morning was spent in a basement room of Doneraile Court,[40] marking the prices on for things to be sold, then I went back to

---

39 Art dealer Eardley Knollys, whose flat in West Halkin Street EB borrowed.

40 A major country house, until 1975 the home of Viscount Doneraile. EB was a friend of Lady Doneraile (Mary).

lunch with the Blacks, then we dashed back and sold the things (very successfully raising sixty pounds) to the RC population of Doneraile. Jean Black had put all her trousseau clothes into the jumble sale: it was rather touching – the really very beautiful, brilliantly-coloured and expensive clothes of 15 years ago.

A few days before I left London I went to lunch with Raymond Mortimer and his chum Paul,[41] in their wonderful and exotic Georgian house in Canonbury – uphill above Islington. The surrounding ground was covered with snow. You were right in thinking Raymond was burning to have a chat about Eddy's affairs. He was not hostile (to me) but he was extremely fussed and deeply agitated. After some humming and hawing, he said: 'What we fear is, that when Eddy goes to live in Ireland he may Take to the Bottle.' 'Good heavens, Raymond,' I said, 'why?' 'Because, Elizabeth, everybody in Ireland drinks so much.' 'Really, Raymond, do you mean that I am a drunk?' 'Good God, no . . . but the fact is that in the last two years, since Eddy has started being so much in Ireland, he has started Drinking Far More Heavily.'

Yes, he said, they (the Long Crichel[42] boys) had observed that the whisky at Long Crichel was steadily going down. At first they had thought it was Deverell (the butler) but finally it had become plain to them that it must be Eddy.

The idea of those dear old sissies at Long Crichel all rushing to measure the decanter with their thumbnails, each time poor Eddy has one then goes out of the room, really did seem funny. But also grim. It really is time poor Eddy did have a house of his own! And really they need not be so fussy; this is not the first bolt he has

---

[41] Paul Hyslop, architect, who lived with Raymond Mortimer at 5 Canonbury Place.

[42] In 1945 three gay men – Eddy Sackville-West, Eardley Knollys, and the music critic Desmond Shawe-Taylor – bought a weekend home, Long Crichel House, at Long Crichel near Wimborne in Dorset. Knollys was then the National Trust representative for South-West England. Raymond Mortimer had recently joined the trio. They kept a hospitable house where EB often used to visit.

made – did he not [pop] off and quietly join the Church of Rome?

I laughed inwardly during the conversation and out loud when I was alone afterwards, at finding myself cast in the role of an elderly Irish rake. I think this must be the result of poor Eddy's artless unwitting prattle. I said somewhat briskly that I thought Eddy was well able to take care of himself. 'Yes, in a way he has a will of iron,' said Raymond, 'but he is also rather easily influenced.' I said: 'Of course, Raymond, you are the great influence in his life.' Which at once mollified the old boy and spiked his guns.

It is late at night; I must go to bed. A log fire is burning in my room. Goodnight, my love. E.

Bowen's Court, Thursday, 8th March 1956

Dearest,

Yesterday I got your lovely letter, about wearing your new suit (I would very much like to see you in it, my angel, I am glad it is such a perfect success, I love dark grey flannel, and I know the sublimated look you will have in it: I know you love a new suit) – and Frank Ziegler[43] having appeared again, and your having read the K. Mansfield preface.[44]

It made me very happy, what you felt and said about the KM piece. Very happy – all day I was in a glow. I did have a curious feeling about writing it – a more personal feeling than I've had for a long time (about writing anything, I mean). At the outset, it seemed just a chore and a sweat having to write the preface at all, specially when I wanted to be getting on with my Rome book. Then a curious sort of undertone from the subject, and I suppose also the personality of the woman, caught me. I became so deeply involved that the thing became more and more difficult to write – I could

---

43 An old Oxford friend of CR.

44 *Stories by Katherine Mansfield* selected and with an introduction by Elizabeth Bowen, NY 1956, UK 1957.

not have got into more of a fever if I had been G Flaubert:[45] literally at one point I sat up the whole of one night. So I am VERY glad that you, objectively, find it good.

I really am delighted about Frank Z. having turned up again! It does sound tremendous fun. What I've been so longing for you to have (there where you are) is a BOON COMPANION. And he sounds like one. Plus the interest of the past. I hope you'll keep going with him just in an easy-come, easy-go sort of way: neither of you becoming involved, I mean, in each other's home lives. I often think the French and other Latins are right in seldom bringing or asking their friends to their homes. It always annoys Anglo-Saxons so much. But really in homes, with wives having to be talked to, everything tends to bog down. (I don't mean your home, my home, any home particularly, just homes in general.) I notice Irishmen – Irish-Irish, I mean – tend to be like the French in that way. They are in tearing form when around the town, but rather subdued, cross-ish, and on the defensive (or facetious) when among their dear ones.

Oh, how I like having boon companions. Really at present they're all I need – I mean, in my everyday existence. As I've often told you, I don't seem any longer able to cope with friendships: I always feel I disappoint people who expect much of me. Eddy has got quite a streak of the boon companion (it's probably the development of this racy, noisy, high-spirited streak in him, lately, which has upset Raymond).

Eddy arrived yesterday evening, and is here for a week, till the 14th, tearing about doing his Cooleville house furnishing. . . . I am keeping as static as possible, as I simply MUST get on with my Rome book. So I confine myself to hearing about everything in the

---

[45] The French novelist Gustave Flaubert (1821-1880) was a perfectionist, struggling obsessionally to find the right word, the right phrase, sometimes taking a week over a single page.

evenings. However, I'm going over to Cooleville with them this afternoon: it is fascinating watching a place grow, and I hear there are great pools of purple and white crocuses under the trees, which will be lovely to see.

This house, having been totally flowerless, inside, for 2 months, now looks like Fortnum and Mason's – all my hyacinths in bowls have come out, and Jean Black has given me some pots of flowering petunias, very voluptuous, and Jim[46] brought over some pots of primulas, pink-mauve, from the Cooleville greenhouse, where they were wasting their sweetness, doing no good.

Oh if only you and I were sitting in the yellow chairs in the drawing room, in front of the fire, among all these flowers . . . The heat of the fire draws out the smell of the hyacinths. These early spring evenings seem meant by Nature for you and me. Every time a bird sings, I feel a pang – and now birds are singing most of the time . . .

Already, I'm beginning to live for May. Please GOD, there is now only one whole month left (I mean, April) in which I do not see you. Charles, I do love you so very much. Elizabeth

Bowen's Court, Thursday afternoon, 13th March 1956

What I did love, my darling, was getting two letters from you. . . .

I am writing this in Jim Egan's van drawn up on the gravel in front of Cooleville. The house is in the course of being painted salmon-pink – that sort of Italian colour. The front door is open and the house is humming with workmen, and with Eddy and Jim shouting from room to room. The sun is shining, which keeps me warm in the van; rooks are whirling about the sky, at one edge of which some sinister storm clouds are piling up. There are large pools of purple and white crocuses, and there are wide shaven

---

[46] Jim Egan, EB's friend and the Vernons' land agent, was also acting as agent for Eddy S-W.

lawns. A vast ruined mill overlooks this part of the garden, and it is full of wood-pigeons, cooing loudly. The van is turned with its back to the mountains, which when I turn round look enormous (which indeed they are) and are misty hyacinth blue. It really is a very nice place indeed; I do think Eddy has every prospect of being very happy here.

The only thing is, I'm afraid Raymond *has* got something in this thing about Eddy and the bottle. I don't mean he really drinks such a lot – I mean, by what I regard as normal standards – but it does *affect* him tremendously: the last two or three evenings he's been what I suppose anyone would call tight: not stupid but madly exhilarated. I think the explanation is that he's already punch-drunk with excitement over this house. Last night we were over at Creagh Castle, and when we were going away the poor lamb lost his sense of direction and all but drove crash down that steep place overhanging the river opposite the Blacks' front door. When it seemed to me that our front wheels were well over the brink, Eddy said, 'Let's see, which way *are* we going?' – and Barry who was standing pensively in the middle of the gravel, seeing us off, said with his usual mild detachment, 'If I were you, I think perhaps I'd back up just an inch or two.' This seemed to me an understatement. It's the first time I've ever been alarmed by Eddy's driving; the rest of the way home he was not at all all over the road, but it seemed to me we were going like a bat out of hell. However, *don't* be alarmed, he is going away tomorrow and by the time he's next here I expect he will have calmed down.

If he really is 'drinking', I've no idea how to stop him. I refuse to nag anyone in my house – in fact I refuse to nag anyone. I suppose the fact is, he always has had someone in a nurse-or-governess relationship to him, in one form or another, and is now fairly far on in life, starting off for the first time being a free agent. Really he's no fool, and one would be a fool to treat him as one – he'll find his own equilibrium, don't you think? Only in a sense one cannot not feel responsible, partly because he is so young for his age,[47] partly because he's in his own way so fond of me and does, I know, react to what I do or say. . . .

I've been told once or twice in my life that I 'have a bad effect on people' – it always made me furious at the time (because I do think it's really neither just nor true) but troubles me afterwards . . .

All my love: think of me. You are in my mind and my being, you know, all the time.

Your E.

The Normandie, Knightsbridge, Friday, 23rd March 1956

My darling. . . .

My date last night was being guest of honour at a large literary dinner called the Society of Bookmen. I was rather scared, as I had to speak for 20 minutes, and I always think after-dinner speeches are so difficult – and particularly inappropriate for women. However I got by all right: one old boy Geoffrey Faber,[48] who is a Fellow of All Souls so ought to know, said it was the best speech on any literary subject he had ever heard.

I have spent the morning shopping in Harvey Nichols, which practically adjoins this hotel so is convenient – minor spring clothes. I bought a rather nice banana-coloured heavy-ribbed knitted jacket, and a tangerine Italian cotton shirt, nice and voluminous: I shall look like a plate of dessert. I also bought a toast-coloured woollen suit: I do hope this is a colour you like, as you'll see it often.

I am now to catch a late afternoon train to Salisbury, for Long Crichel. I do hope Eddy's keepers won't start picking me over again. If they do, I shall snap down and change the subject. But I think old Raymond would never do the same thing twice.

Goodbye for now, oh my dearest love. Your E.

---

[47] Eddy S-W was 55, two years younger than EB.

[48] Sir Geoffrey Faber (1889-1961), academic and author, founding editor of the publishing house Faber & Gwyer, afterwards Faber & Faber.

Bruree House, 6th April 1956 [incomplete]

. . . I am enjoying this weekend, so far, considerably more than I enjoyed my last at Long Crichel. There was a considerably poltergeisty atmosphere there . . .

Raymond's having imported poor Hester [Chapman] really put the thing wrong. Deeply and truly as I feel for her in her lonely despairing sorrow at Ronnie [Griffin]'s death, I continue to find her most unpalatable. And the effects of her grief make her more so – she is being 'wonderful' about it, which means that she never stops talking: up hill, down dale, day and night, that voice of hers. And as there is nothing to do at Crichel but sit about and talk, opportunities to be frenzied are endless.

However, it wouldn't have mattered if Raymond, with Hester as audience, hadn't continued his endless needling of me on the subject of Eddy's move to Ireland. I thought it so fearfully indiscreet of him. I mean, she has such a long tongue; she lives for 'situations' and for broadcasting them, inflating them, distorting them, endlessly discussing them with all her circle, such as Rosamond Lehmann. Much as she was enjoying herself at Crichel, I also felt she could hardly wait to whip back to London and start talking. What a fool Raymond is, giving himself away like that.

However, I got on very well with Desmond [Shawe-Taylor]. I forget if you ever met him? He's an Anglo-Irishman: very conventional outwardly, looks like somebody in the Kildare Street Club, Dublin. I remembered being told what indeed became very clear during the weekend, that Desmond can't stand Raymond, resents his having moved into Long Crichel. So I adopted the Russian policy of driving a wedge between the democracies. Desmond and I sat in satirical Celtic silence while Raymond, increasingly resentful and uneasy, was left to conduct a conversational pas-de-deux with Hester. Well did he know I thought he was being second-rate: in that sort of way he is no fool.

I am now clear that Eddy's fundamental reason for wanting a life in Ireland – so fundamental that he either hasn't realized it or doesn't want to – is to get away from Raymond and all that whip-cracking organization. No, I don't think Eddy is in love with me, in any usual sense. He has told me that he does love me very much, but I think it is that happiest kind of love which contents itself with the happiness they have with a person. I think it would be accurate to say that he's in love with my company, my companionship. Being in love, he has told me various times, has always made him frenzied and miserable.

I think the fact that he knows I am not disponible settles his mind. And indeed I think it's that very fact that makes me at the moment the ideal person for him – always happy to see him come, sorry to see him go, pleased when he turns up again, but not wanting anything of him. With me he's outside the area, which can be such a nightmare of exactions, followed by reproaches.

Oh my love, it's you who suffer and have to cope with, so often, the tiresome side of me. But there's no doubt that loving anybody the way I love you does drag up one's whole nature. When it's a case, simply, of great affection, one can be endlessly easy-going, good-humoured, serene. Only you know my wickedness. And yet it's a fact that the very fullness of a love like ours, it's all-inclusiveness, roots us together. And does more, makes of our happiness an entire strong world, a real world, which through all is ultimately a fearless one – don't you think so?

I draw strength from you. If I have any virtue, the source of it is in you . . .

3 May [Bowen's Court]

But here we were at Dublin airport and there was E on the balcony of the airport building in a white sweater, brushing back her flying hair with her hand. I pretended not to see her from the plane window; as usual I wasn't quite ready when life came along, my plans not completely laid. We drove to Bowen's Court after lunch in what the headwaiter commended as a 'cool corner' of the airport dining-room. The country was a confusion of green under a cloudy sky. I have never seen Ireland in May before. At beloved Cahir, we stopped for a drink. We got to Bowen's Court for dinner. 'Welcome home,' said E.

6 May

Today is very different, a dark ugly sky, wind, a malaise outwardly and inwardly. . . . Yet E is happier today. She says that the accretions of interests, of things happening to us in our separation, is disappearing. She says that she felt 'inexpressive'. She hates to be called a 'sensitive' novelist and says that the critics who write solemn estimates of her work miss something coarse, in a way vulgar, in her writing. Last night as, in the evening light still lulled or sated with the green enchantment of the countryside, we drove up to this door, I said to her how frightening this house must have been, looming up over the delinquent behind in his rent or guilty of poaching, summoned up from the village before her bearded Victorian grandfather. It is a house which has a frightening aspect.

There has been much talk of Eddy since I was here. In fact the conversation has come back and back to him, till now E begins to fear that I resent this and was at pains to prove that he was 'only a friend'. We went yesterday afternoon to his new house at Cooleville where he is settling in ten miles from here. Jim Egan and Jo Gibson were moving in the books and furniture. The neighbourhood is agog with his coming, with his man-sized roses on the wallpaper,[49] and his rose carpet too.

As I write, E is working upstairs. I sit before the fire, read, yawn, and look at photograph albums. It might be a Sunday at Lindenallee, except that here she separates herself off to work and I rail as Sylvia does at home. This morning is at home. We went to buy the Sunday papers, not at the NAAFI[50] in Bonn, but in Mallow where the

[49] This wallpaper was maroon flock, with huge white roses on it.

[50] NAAFI runs pubs, clubs and shops for British military personnel overseas.

people were streaming out of mass. Perhaps married life would be much the same anywhere with anyone. It's no use, I can't put a heart back in the hollow where mine used to be.

7 May

E has been working since dawn, while I lay in an Oblomov-like stupor in bed. Motored over last night to the Vernons for dinner. . . . Urssie surprised and even embarrassed me by an outburst after dinner to E and me, but before the company. 'Don't get yourselves cluttered up with engagements, darlings. Be alone together as much as you can, be happy. Do be happy.'

8 May

E and I came home here for dinner and it was coming home. We sat drinking whisky and talking. She said that as she got older she got more recalcitrant. That for years she had accommodated herself to people like a 'sort of Jew', but that now she was getting more like her father. She adjured me to be 'honest'. It's late for me to begin.

9 May

We were to set out right after an early lunch for Killarney, but E had an accident in Kildorrery village where she had gone alone to get petrol for the car – ran into an old woman who rushed out across the street to greet an old friend under the wheels of the car. However it was far from fatal though the only report I could get from the village was that the old lady was not as bad as she might be nor yet as good. So we started off . . .

And all the way as we went along there was the fascinating flow of E's talk, the pictures of places, people, the continual surprise and pleasure of her choice of a word, the funniness, poetry and brutality of her view of people and events.

10 May

Much as I enjoyed it all,[51] I began to feel that this experience of beauty, interest and leisure, the exposedness to impressions, was beginning, faintly, to curdle in me.

How to convey the delight of E's company, the youthful zest of her conversation? She showed me some of the Bowen topography yesterday, the hotel at Parknasilla where one of her short stories takes place, the castle at Ardagh where another one does.

11 May

We came back[52] and sat talking over the library fire. E was perhaps trying indirectly to warn me that if she doesn't see me more often, Eddy may more and more come to occupy her life because of what she calls his adhesive, his impermeable quality, which she says is like Sylvia. She says that she could bear to think of me as in love with someone else, but not unhappy as I am. I say that I am not usually unhappy, but just not happy. She says that our separate lives are not natural.

12 May

When we came upstairs I said, 'All the same it must be dreadfully lonely sleeping by yourself in this big empty house', and she said, 'Yes, but how else to arrange it.' All day running under my pleasure was resistance. I itched with this beastly itch, and popped anti-histamine tablets secretively, felt that I had said everything I could ever have to say in this world, that I was barren, that I could absorb no more impressions, that I was glutted with them, with beauty of scene and joy of communication, that I could take no more but was spoiled for anything else. Yet I dread the end of this like waking

---

[51] The Killarney excursion

[52] From dining with the Blacks at Creagh Castle.

from a strange dream. But E says it is reality, and so it is. Her youthfulness, her childishness, her tearing energy, with what can a middle-aged hypochondriac respond? But she will not let me be that, and that is not what I wanted me to be. While I write the weather outside these big windows in this bedroom has turned again from a hard light to cloud. There is a heartbreak in this place, in this person.

13 May

Last morning at Bowen's Court. I feel a ghost of myself, also rather sickish. The corruption of the heart, the worm in the bud, but the corruption is in me not her? . . .

E talked yesterday of Virginia Woolf. She says her unpublished diaries show that she had no fondness for her friends including E; 'or perhaps', she added, 'her affection was intermittent' (as mine is for so many people).

I have been reading in *Bowen's Court*[53] the terrible account of old Henry Cole Bowen, E's grandfather, an improving landlord and a Victorian ogre who eventually went mad as did E's father. This undercurrent is always here in this place and yet Molly[54] says, 'It is a happy house.' It is both, so is E.

Bowen's Court, Tuesday, 15th May 1956

My darling. . . .

I got home from Dublin about 9.30 last night, Monday. Monday was still a day on which I had seen you (looking for a minute round my door at the Shelbourne) so it had still a character. The evening, all the course of the drive home from Corkagh[55] to here, was what could have been unbearably beautiful, everything liquid gold and the mountains, where there were mountains, looking like coloured

---

[53] EB's book about her home.

[54] Molly O'Brien, EB's cook

[55] Her Aunt Edie Colley's house at Clondalkin, Co Dublin

glass. So I pulled down a sort of iron curtain over myself, and drove along very fast, singing loudly. The bad moment came when I actually got back here, and the library was still full of late day light and our fire was burning. I drank a very large whisky, ate a plate of stewed rhubarb (a strange delicacy, but I didn't feel like anything else) and went to bed and read an American thriller.

A typed message left on the library chimney-piece by Paddy[56] to say that Mrs Finn of Kildorrery[57] was decidedly worse didn't cheer me up. However this morning a Kildorrery friend rang me up to say that Mrs Finn was considerably better, having passed a comfortable night. What ever happens – and really I think it's likely she may die – I will remember your advice, your injunction – it was not my fault; I have not de quoi me reprocher.[58] I did as much to save her from her poor darling senile action as any being possibly could. Thousands of people, through no fault of their own, have been the indirect cause of somebody else's death; and if that should happen to me I must be sensible about it. Simply, it opens up how unspeakably awful it could be to have killed (outright) somebody through what was one's own fault.

I'm talking to you as though you were here. And you are here. Never has any one house been so filled by any one person. I have the feeling that you're 'away', as apart from 'gone'. This is your house, ours, and it's simply a matter of time till you're back again.

I so very much don't want to be poor-spirited about your going-away; it seems so ungrateful – to you, to God. But of course the thing is that I could collapse into the complete agony of being without you, of being again deprived of you, at any moment. I will not let myself feel that life is meaningless when we're not together. But as I know you know, it is hard not to.

---

[56] Paddy and Eddy Barry helped EB out at Bowen's Court.

[57] The old lady EB knocked over with her car.

[58] French: 'anything to reproach myself for'

I don't think I've ever lived in such a world of reality as in these last ten days. Every sound and colour, every shape of everything, seemed to be part of it, and to record it. These last ten days are not the past, they are a sort of eternity. Oh you beloved Charles, you beloved love. Let us neither of us forget, for a single moment, what reality feels like and eternity is.

I had (in Dublin, yesterday) a pleasant séance with my bank manager – it always is nice, he is so nice – then drove out to Corkagh and picked up Edie, and brought her into Dublin again for lunch. The Shelbourne (fraught for her with memories of the old days) is her favourite place, so we had lunch there. Very indigestible, very expensive. In the dining room we were met by Constantia Maxwell, accompanying the famous Mrs Cecil Woodham Smith, author of *Florence Nightingale* and *The Reason Why*. We joined up with those ladies to drink our coffee, to poor Edie's obvious reluctance. She (Edie) said, as she and I walked away from the Shelbourne to do some shopping, of hers: 'It's extraordinary what sort of people write books' – meaning Mrs Woodham Smith. When we had finished Edie's shopping we drove back out to Corkagh and had tea . . .

A fascinating thing about my Corkagh Colley relations – not only Edie but her daughters and daughter in law – their houses are pigsties (full of charm but pigsties) but their gardens immaculately kept. The entire Corkagh garden (surrounding the house) shows endless loving care: it has not a weed in it. Whereas, the rooms . . . except that vases of flowers are always fresh and beautifully done, rearing their heads above the slatternly ruin. Not that I am not, as you know, loving and always devoted to Corkagh.

So I shall not write any more now, you dearest and only. You know how I am, and what I am: God bless you and keep you. Yours, Elizabeth

17 May [Cologne]

Back 'home' again and rather whistling to keep my courage up, for what is one to do with this life? . . . Why did I come back and for what may I ask? I might have gone down to stay with Mary [Adlington]. It would have given her pleasure; and I might have stayed the weekend with B[59] and made something of it, if it hadn't been for the itch, if it hadn't been after Ireland. . . . I missed Sylvia when I was ill that night at Brooks's;[60] and when I was scared, she was the one I turned to for reassurance.

Bruree House, Bruree, Co Limerick. Saturday, 19th May 1956
My darling love . . . The awfulness of being torn apart is not knowing what you're doing, what you're at. I feel loneliness for you like a bruise all over. The beauty and happiness of our being together under the same roof is that it seems so natural – it's so against nature, being parted. I, like you, though, am still living in our world, having that feeling I have with you almost of identity, seeing the same things with the same eyes – whether it is large waves breaking on the coast of Clare or a vase of flowers in the middle of the library.

I'm writing upstairs in my big room at Bruree, the one you remember with the striped red-and-white huge sofa, the enormous bed, the wardrobe painted with panels of owls on a gold background. I like being here. I don't think I could have lived through this first weekend without you alone at B Court. The weather is still so beautiful, everything glowing, and it would hurt. At least here I feel very cosy, and everyone speaks of you constantly and with so much love.

. . . I went to bed very early last night, exhausted by a day of helping Eddy move his furniture into Cooleville. . . . This afternoon I am going with Stephen [Vernon] to the church, where he will be practicing hymns for tomorrow (Whitsunday) on the organ. Eddy has been parked with Jim [Egan] in whose house he has rather inconsiderately retired to bed with flu. Urssie has not got room for

59 Unidentified fräulein

60 His London club in St James's Street.

him, as 2 other people are also coming to stay. Poor Eddy, I think there's rather a feeling that he could just as well, by now, have started camping out in his own house – and I must say I rather wonder why he doesn't. But if he is going to have flu, perhaps it's as well he hasn't. He is by way of making the move into his new house next Thursday, accompanied by Miss Slattery, the cook . . .

Your Elizabeth

Bowen's Court, Friday, 25th May 1956

My darling . . . But I am worried that the skin itch has come on again, or rather not abated, and that you didn't feel well in London. I wish that even from the point of view of a Rest and Holiday you could have had longer here. You did seem better when you left – but it wasn't long enough. I want now again to hear how you are: feel like sending you what I considered to be Sylvia's masterpiece telegram to here: 'Darling are you fully well?'

. . . I feel more maimed and dazed by your not being here than I ever have any time before – and that is saying a good deal. I don't mind working, but somehow there's something ghostly about even the nice entertainments I take part in. I feel as though shot through one wing. Thank God, anyway, for that utter happiness – I keep reminding myself that's the way I must feel. But how can one not feel bad, feel lost, being torn apart.

Eddy has this morning departed to take up residence in his own house. And the awful thing is, I was glad to see him go. It was awful having him here just after you; the contrast was too great. And poor man he is so awful when he is ill – moaning and complaining and casting a gloom around. Otherwise he's such a good-mannered man: how it is that nobody's ever told him it's bad manners to make an awful depressing fuss, and get other people down, about one's own state of health?

. . . Think out our summer, my darling, won't you?

I love you –

Elizabeth

26 May

An uneasy feeling, a fear that the strength I have drawn from Ireland may leak away, that it may be a 'fairy tale'. I have just been reading the back entries in the diary and I am appalled by the misery they reveal. Why should anyone be as unhappy as the writer obviously is? Why does he not rebel? It's a terrifying picture and I wonder how much S[ylvia] has to do with it . . .

All the time is building up in me almost a fear of S, a belief that I could be happy without her.

Bowen's Court, Tuesday, 12 June 1956

Oh my darling. . . . I felt so near you, talking to you from Elizabeth's little Gothic Hampstead cottage drawing-room on Friday evening.[61] I wonder how we could live without the telephone – at least, there is the telephone. One of the horrors of your being the other side of the Atlantic was not having that. My love I'm sorry last week was bad, complications in the office, etc. I wonder what the complications were; obviously they're too complicated to write about. I wish nothing that was so (whatever it was) had been so. Oh if only we could look after each other – not that I could look after you in many of your spheres of activity, but you know what I mean. I wish I was the person you came home to in the evenings. How lovely it would be – every evening to hear you coming in at the door.

I have come back to Ireland to lovely weather – it was stinking in London: none of the June glamour; everyone blue-nosed and wrapped up in overcoats. I quite enjoyed London, in a mild way; it was nice having glimpses of friends, and everybody in spite of the weather was in a good mood. Or at any rate, everybody was very affectionate and kind to me, which naturally I consider a good

[61] EB stayed a night with the writer Elizabeth Jenkins at 8 Downshire Hill in Hampstead.

mood. Elizabeth Jenkins' dinner party was fun: she produced one of my favourite objects, a brilliant Jewish lawyer – he was, in fact, a judge.

... Last night the Blacks and I went to dinner with Eddy; a very harmonious evening, listening to some superb records on his superb gramophone. He is as happy as a bee in that house, really so happy he can hardly contain himself. I am so relieved it is all turning out well. The cook is a success, the mountains are a success, everything.

On Sunday, the evening of the day I got back [from] England, Egan, Eddy and I drove over the mountains to Ardmore, on the Co Waterford coast, and had drinks and dinner with Molly Keane. It was beautiful driving home again over the mountains, in the glassy half-darkness, with a new moon. The sort of evening for you and me.

This seems to be a deputation-receiving week for me. This morning a man who wants to acquire a Redundant Post Office House came and asked me to support his application. Later came a Mr Welsh who wants strings pulled with the Government in order that he may be appointed permanent Waste Water Inspector: he's only a temporary one now. Tomorrow there's to be a deputation form the Farahy Hurling Club – I simply cannot imagine what about. Who says that Paternalism is dead?

... Oh Charles I love you so much – Elizabeth

17 June

Sad, lonely, undemanding letter from E. The truth is that I am anaesthetized to this existence, even quite enjoy it. Someone said I look ten years younger. I am all right if I keep going – much more cheerful than this diary shows.

Bowen's Court, Thursday, 21st June 1956

My darling, your letter of Sunday 17th came this morning. You were angelic to write and tell me all those things I am always wanting to know (and feel so isolated and in a void when I don't know) about what you're doing, and are going to do. You do certainly work full time – oh my love, what a day-and-night life!

. . . My deputation-week (which I told you about in my longer letter) ended with a Sunday afternoon visit, last Sunday, from the Fermoy branch of the 'Trees for Ireland Society'. This society is for obvious reasons to be encouraged as they create (or purport to) public opinion about either not hacking down trees in this county, or growing more. About 24 very nice townspeople arrived in cars, about 3pm, and I took them for a long and fly-ridden walk around all the woods and plantations. The poor lady members tore their nylons to ribbons on the brambles, and I suspect that two or three of them sprained their ankles, but they were too enthusiastic to say a word. Afterwards, my lunch-party, Eddy and I and Jo Gibson (that dear nice American woman, friend of Egan's, who loved you and always asks after you) got into Jo's car and went off to explore a tiny lake called Lough Gur in Co Limerick, which I'd always wanted to see! It lies tucked away not far off the road one drives, to and fro, between here and Shannon. I long now to see it again with you. It's like a toy lake, surrounded by miniature scenery, rocks and ruins. It is full of swans.

I had spent the Saturday evening before at Eddy's house; he educated me by after dinner playing the entire opera *Tosca*[62] on his fine gramophone. I fancy *Tosca* is too emotional to be in good taste, but I did enjoy it.

Molly Keane (the only one of my girl friends from around here, except Norah Preece,[63] whom you haven't met) has been staying here for 3 days: she has just this minute gone. She was working at her new play that she is writing; I have been working away hard at

---

[62] By Giacomo Puccini, first performed 1900.

[63] Norah Preece, who lived at Byblox (an elegant 18th-century house, now demolished) in Doneraile, was close to both EB and Eddy S-W.

my Rome book. So we were quite a little literary colony of 2. In the evenings we went out to dinner. Darling Egan gave us a wonderful dinner last night, in his pansy little tiny dining-room: champagne and lobster. I came home, inevitably, with the most awful blown-up feeling . . .

Today, this afternoon, I am going out to tea in Mallow with 2 respectable local queers: Major Delacour and Colonel Wilson. They have a nice little Georgian house and are tremendous cat-lovers. In a minute I must go and put on tidy clothes: they like one to look very spick-and-span.

Beloved, I'm glad to have even possible dates for London (for you and me, I mean). That is the time which I am living for now, to the exclusion of everything. I wake up thinking, go to sleep thinking – '<u>When'?</u> I completely see your difficulty in steering between things, so don't think I am either worrying you or reproaching you. I
[Ends]

5 July

Telephoned E. It is really more satisfactory to write and get her letters – feel rather far from her, but not underneath.

Bowen's Court, Saturday, 7th July 1956

My darling . . .

My heavens, you know, you're a great man. I'm so proud of you. That terrific energy and drive. And making that speech in 3 languages. You do tremendously impress me – that sounds such a funny thing to say to someone one loves more than anything in the world, but it's true, too. You know it really is rather wonderful going on being impressed and fascinated by a person, as well as all the continuous tenderness and everything else of loving them. You know I'm too old and have lived too much myself to be impressed by the obvious or worldly or ostentatious things. It's your spirit and élan and ability and, well I don't know what else to call it except, again, drive – and as well as that, staying-power when things move more slowly and are dull – which are wonderful to me, my love.

One thing we have in common is being high-voltage. But my work though it can be exhausting isn't as wearing as yours must be, though you don't show it. As I know I've so often said, what kills me is having to deal with people. Brain concentration is another thing. You cope with both kinds of high pressure.

Well the Cecils finally did arrive yesterday, and are here and seem very happy and are very sweet. David in tremendous form. . . .

I'm having a week-end house party – that is, the Butlers, Noreen and Gilbert, are also arriving today, Saturday, in time for lunch and staying over till Monday. Noreen and David and Rachel [Cecil] are very old friends; they so often stayed here together in the days before the war. . . . So I'm rather looking forward to the little gathering. There will be tremendous parental conversations, I foresee. After tea today we're all going over to Annesgrove. Tomorrow night we're all going over to Sunday supper at Bruree. . . .

Eddy as I told you is away. He was in a great flap at being away while the Cecils were here, as he and David are old friends, enemies and (I think) cousins. He, Eddy, asked me to show the Cecils his house – which he was as miserable at going away and leaving, even for a fortnight, as somebody being reft from their bride. So yesterday I telephoned to the Cooleville servants and we went over. David says the house is exactly like Eddy's room at Eton, plus being like Mr Rochester's house in *Jane Eyre* – Thornyfield Hall, isn't it.[64] If you remember, that house had a very lush crimson-and-gold drawing-room, and Cooleville drawing room is like that. I'm not sure whether to tell Eddy David said this or not – the fact is David is fiendishly flippant and sardonic, but Eddy is so guileless, he never notices any 'edge' to a remark.

---

[64] Mr Rochester's house is Thornfield Hall.

Well my darling love I've got that dear nice West Halkin St flat again. . . . Let me know, when you know, approximately how much time in London you're going to have – I don't think I'll want to stay on there after you've gone back again . . .

Well now I must stop and go and put out glasses for my guests' pre-lunch drinks. It's quite a long time since more than 2 people simultaneously have been staying in this quiet old home, and it involves a certain amount of rushing around (domestically, I mean) still, it's nice. . . .

All my love, you dear love – Elizabeth

Bruree House, Sunday, 29th July 1956

My darling. . . . I keep on thinking 'last Sunday . . .' Here, there is sunshine now and then, but not warm, with the usual Co Limerick tearing gale. The rose-hedges round the terrace under my bed-room window are being battered to pieces . . .

My Friday letter was interrupted just when I was beginning to talk about Elizabeth, your niece.[65] Oh Charles I was so drawn to her, from the moment she came marching into the room. Oh what a character, what a clever girl! Somehow I had an immediate wish, longing, for her to be a person in my life. I don't think I have ever known a child – which after all virtually she is – impact on one so strongly. Perhaps it's because I'm – as I've said to you – in ways at a 12-year-old stage myself.[66]

. . . I long for her in one sense or another to get cracking. It seems to me, too, that she and you are born boon companions.

She's clearly at an age when she shrinks from any emotionality. The sad thing (considering, I mean) is, that I think you'd – at any rate just now – be better with her and better for her than Roley.

---

[65] Elizabeth, daughter of CR's brother Roland (Roley) and his wife Bunny, to whom CR was always very close.

[66] Elizabeth Ritchie was fourteen.

She'll be a handsome, attractive young woman, won't she. Better probably as a young woman than as a jeune fille. She was wearing a rather good green pinafore dress (over a light-yellow shirt) which suited her hair. Otherwise clearly not looking her best, partly because she was peeling from shipboard sunburn, partly because she had only just arisen from a bed of weeping, which left her dear little nose scarlet. Her way of sitting limply and longly in her chair, with her mouth ever so slightly open, reminded me of what you must have been slightly like in adolescence.

I am left wanting so much to sometime, somehow, see more of her.

Oh you darling beloved uncle! – not mine, alas. I must stop this letter now, too: it's church time.

I am sad from missing you. I do so love you. Elizabeth

Bowen's Court, Saturday, 3rd August 1956

My darling . . .

Yes, about Iris Murdoch,[67] and her visit. After all my apprehensions, which I told you of, I liked her very very much. She is an odd character, almost as odd as Eudora [Welty]. Anglo-Irish, of all things! An only child, and with highly-developed only-child traits. Fair-haired, with her hair in a roughish 'tulip' cut, rather thick-set, and at the first glance studentish-looking. Not elegant, but I like her for taking the trouble with her clothes that she clearly did while she was here. She is good-mannered. I think I was terrified of her partly because she is an Existentialist – I feared she might be gaunt, scornful, unaccommodating or bleak – on the contrary, she gets on well with people, was liked by the people she met here and expressed and showed a liking for them . . . She was in a rather

---

[67] Iris Murdoch (1919-1999), Dublin-born novelist and philosopher. Her first novel, *Under the Net*, was published in 1954, and her second in 1956. She wrote 26 novels in all, plus works of philosophy, plays and poetry.

distraught state while she was here – she said: I must say she did not most of the time show it – as she is shortly, in a month or so, going to marry a young man with whom she's been having an affair for some time; he's a New College don.[68] She seems to have a terror of marriage, for some reason, is obsessed by the idea that it will mean loss of identity. Over that I couldn't help her at all, as marriage has never struck me in that way. I think it's a point of view more usual in a man than in a woman – also the fact is that most women marry younger than she is doing, before they have begun to 'think'. She, I suppose, is about 35/37 – sometimes she seems younger than that, sometimes older. Also, as you know, she is a don, and she loves teaching: she is, I hear, a very brilliant teacher of philosophy – she has resigned her Fellowship[69] because of marrying, and is to give up her teaching at the end of a year. I said, 'Well, that will give you all the more time to write,' but that did not cheer her up. I've a feeling that only half her mind goes into her writing, and that she's frightened of the other half being left in a vacuum.

She really, deep down, is an intellectual, in the sense that I'm not. I can quite see that life is simpler for me than it is for her. Well anyway, I after all very much did enjoy her being here. I myself was in an abstracted, half-batty mood, unable to stop thinking about you, and aching for you. As you say, partings are sometimes a shock, like an amputation. It's as though one's whole being felt a kind of bewilderment and outrage, as after the hacking-off of a limb. If I had to have anybody in the house, Iris, herself abstracted and at any time, I should imagine, a bit odd, was the best person to have. I felt she either did not notice that I was not normal or else did notice and did not mind . . .

Edie, aunt, arrived to stay today. I drove to Limerick Junction

---

68 Later that year, Iris Murdoch married John Bayley, critic and scholar.

69 At St Anne's College, Oxford.

(that queer station where I met you in the dusk, last August) to take her off the train. She is in top form and I think very happy to be here. We got back here in time for a late lunch. This is the afternoon; she is unpacking – in your room, the Green Room, and by way of resting, though she sturdily protested she didn't need to. Shortly, we shall have tea. After that Eddy and a friend who is staying with him, Jack Rathbone (whom I haven't yet met) are coming over for a drink. Tomorrow night we are going over to dinner there, Cooleville.

I love you so much. Elizabeth

Kildare Street Club [Dublin]. Wednesday, 8th August 1956

My darling . . .

I was very glad to have the news of Roley and Elizabeth. To me those 3 do seem so like relations – I feel indeed more related to them than I do to most of my own family. I am so awfully glad that Elizabeth's crise began to be over . . .

It is lovely to hear the things Roley said about my looks. And that he thought I looked younger rather than older. Also that there was a good report on my looks from Norman and Jetty[70] – how sweet of them! I did feel 'in looks' those particular days, because I was still in an afterglow from our happiness together. I felt in a summer mood. Also it made me happy seeing Roley, and though in a different way, Norman and Jetty – Oh Charles, if I can't be more with you, I wish I could at least be more with your relatives and friends . . .

I am simply in Dublin for the day, to meet my new bank manager: he is very charming and I do hope will continue to be as reasonable in his attitude to my overdraft as he today seemed . . .

---

[70] Norman Robertson and his wife. He was Canadian High Commissioner in London at the time. The Roley Ritchies were passing through on a European tour.

Horse Show[71] is (as you know) going on, but wild horses won't get me near it. It's no fun going unless one goes in style, and I had not forethought enough to arrange that. So I am catching that 6.45 train home this evening. I left my car outside the station (Mallow) early this morning.

. . . I understand why you're low-spirited – perhaps you're out of that again by now, but I understand why you were low-spirited. My dear beautiful precious and lovely Charles –

Elizabeth

Bowen's Court, Thursday, 4th September 1956

My darling – I got your letter yesterday. October 7th approx. will be lovely: a week longer to wait but all the more heaven when it comes. And then we'll have Montreal to look forward to too. I note you'll be having your Degree[72] on Oct. 31st. The only day I can't be in Montreal is November 3rd, Saturday, as I promised to speak to the Bryn Mawr alumni, God help me, that evening. But I could fly to Montreal the following day, 4th. And perhaps as you'll be on holiday you could stay over Monday? However, we can talk of the plans for that side of the water when we meet here . . .

One advantage about your being here in early October is that my over-loving (of you) neighbours the Blacks and the Vernons will be away, so we shan't have to spend our few evenings going out to dinner. If the weather's fine, as it often is in October, it would be fun to do some more exploring of the country.

Oh my darling darling love. I'll be writing you a proper letter shortly.

Elizabeth

---

[71] Dublin Horse Show, the major social and equestrian event held every summer under the auspices of the Royal Dublin Society at Ballsbridge in Dublin.

[72] CR was awarded an Hon. D.CL (Doctorate in Civil Law) by his old University of King's College, Halifax, Nova Scotia.

Bowen's Court, Sunday morning, 16th September 1956
My darling . . .

This afternoon I am driving back again to Dublin, to broadcast this year's 'appeal' for Missions to Seamen. There is practically nothing about seamen I don't know now, after reading all the Society's hand-out leaflets. I never have done an Appeal before, and the idea scares me. I've also never before broadcast from Radio Eireann. I would very much rather stay here and stay in bed. As it is, I am staying tonight and tomorrow (Monday) night at Corkagh, and shall come back here, ALONE, on Tuesday.

The other person who is cracking up is poor Eddy, who has now had non-stop visitors, of a much more exacting kind than mine, for the last 7 weeks. I said, 'Why do you ask them all, you silly: naturally if you ask them they will all come streaming over, if only out of curiosity.' He said, 'I shall know better another year.' He dropped in by himself, looking quite worn, between seeing off one party on the Cork boat and going to pick up another at Shannon. And this violent social activity on his part has created rather a restless summer as, as you know, we all here take in one another's washing. I think the worst thing for him was Raymond M and Eardley Knollys arriving, like a couple of witches on broomsticks. However I noticed he had on the whole rather got them down; butter would hardly melt in their mouths. Raymond was all over me, full of compliments. But I'll never trust that little creature again . . .

It's horribly sad about Bill Patten. And in a way perhaps worse for Susan Mary.[73] Your description of them gave me an agonising flashback to the last year of Alan's life. One can know somebody is dying, and yet frantically hold out against the truth, like somebody

---

[73] William Patten, US diplomat, and the now widowed Susan Mary, author and socialite. In 1947, while married to Patten, she had a son, William Patten Jr, whose biological father was Duff Cooper. Susan Mary's second marriage (1960-1972) was to the journalist and political commentator Joseph Alsop.

holding a position in a war. Oh Charles, don't die. You won't ever ever die, will you. . . .

What a wearing summer this has been. The only realities in it have been May and July: every moment of our times here, then in London, I remember and shall always remember: everything else – I feel – I shall forget. . . .

All my love –

Elizabeth

22 September

I feel as if I had lived between Köln and Bonn all my life. It's so long, such a deep separation, since I have seen E. She says that she expects to forget everything that has happened this summer except the time we were together in May. I know life is sliding by for both of us. What I never knew before was the compensation of middle age – damn, the telephone rang and I have forgotten what the compensation of middle age IS.

15 October

Everything is changed. I have been to Ireland and come back. Being with E has been like a shift or displacement of the angle of vision. Her own vision or insight is so powerful that it alters the focus of mine. Those days at Bowen's Court in the unpredictable Irish weather, days of drifting, made one's will power seem an irrelevancy, one's programme of life something adolescent – tailored too small to fit real life . . . I came away different. Yet never has it been so hard, so frighteningly hard to make contact in words. We both felt it. In a long pause in a walk in the country she said, 'I have become more taciturn.' So had I. But the impotence to find words did not weaken the influence, or the love.

21 October

It was not all sad. There was even a morning when walking alone down the avenue at Bowen's Court I felt outrageously happy. There was our expedition into Cork together. But there was that last afternoon when under a still and leaden autumn sky we walked together by the deserted mill (the hiding-place of the IRA man in *The Last September*[74]) and stood together looking at the shallow, clear, dark flowing water of the Funcheon river and a sadness so final fell on us that it seemed a foreboding of an end. And that night she came to my room and pleaded for her life, our life. And I never said a word or put out a hand. Yet I was happy there . . .

All the way back on the plane . . . I was thinking that there must be some lessons that I can draw from this renewal, something that I can live by. Perhaps it was that I could not face the sadness of the enforced separation from what was so deeply natural, perhaps I feared more than ever – not that we might lose each other – but that there would be too little of us left after these many partings.

9 November [Ottawa]

Just now I am sitting on the side of my unmade bed in the Chateau [Laurier] waiting to put in a long-distance call to E at Bryn Mawr.[75] I am scared of some sort of frenzying snarl-up over getting in touch with her, which will make us miss each other in Montreal . . .

Later in the train just coming into Windsor Station Montreal to join E for the weekend. The deep, deep peace of the parlour car after those eternal planes. With a bit of luck all will go well this weekend and we won't run into everyone I know in Canada – but we'll need luck.

10 November [Montreal]

I've certainly never written this diary at a moment like this before and NO – there would be something indecent in doing so . . . I

---

[74] EB's second novel, published 1929, set during the 'Troubles' in a house based on Bowen's Court.

[75] EB was awarded the Lucy Martin Donnelly Fellowship at Bryn Mawr for the autumn term.

wonder if I shall get to sleep again tonight. There is something overstimulating about this place. It's the beginning of winter, the whip in the air and the contrast between that and the overheated hotel room. E and I walking on the mountain this a.m., or as it is now 5.30 of the next morning, I should say yesterday morning . . . and tomorrow I am gone, on the plane back to England and to Sylvia.

11 November

Yes, I feel as I knew I should feel, charmless, guilty and irritable. It's always the result. But what an odd sense of guilt to feel it for that[76] and not for the other.[77] But most of all in the lift yesterday I knew temptation. It came over me in a flash. I told myself that I was only playing the picture in my mind. But if the opportunity walked into the room now, would I have any mind with which to assess risks. Wouldn't there be another flash, like that earlier, dissolving my will with a power which was to me unexpected. Work and marriage with S and association with playing safe, or half-dead people like most of my acquaintance, have coated over a part of my nature so that I supposed it dead. But E has a miraculous and terrifying capacity to bring one to life, to awaken other desires and inspire belief in other possibilities in oneself.

13 November [Brown's Hotel, London]

There was something light-hearted about this time in Montreal. It was an escapade – very happy. But when we passed a poster advertising a meeting in the McGill University grounds on the subject 'Is man free or determined?', I asked E which she thought and she said grimly, 'I NOW think determined.' We agreed that a crisis suits

---

[76] The one-night stand.

[77] His relationship with EB. It is impossible to know when this stopped being fully physical.

Courtesy of Judith Robertson

Elizabeth opening the door of
2 Clarence Terrace, 1946

Courtesy of Judith Robertson

Charles Ritchie in the 1940s

By kind permission of Limerick Museum, Ireland

Bowen's Court

© Getty Images

Elizabeth in the walled garden at Bowen's Court

Courtesy of the Cecil Beaton Studio Archive at Sotheby's

Portrait of Elizabeth Bowen by Cecil Beaton, 1943

Courtesy of the late Audrey Fiennes for publication in Victoria Glendinning, Elizabeth Bowen: Portrait of a Writer (1977)

Alan Charles Cameron, Elizabeth's husband

By kind permission of Library and Archives Canada

Portrait of Charles Ritchie

Courtesy of Judith Robertson

Portrait of Charles's wife, Sylvia Ritchie

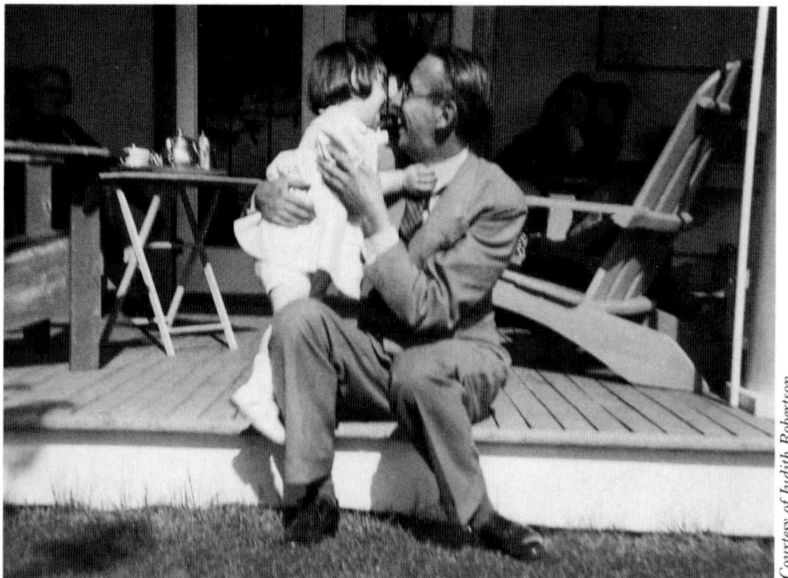

Courtesy of Judith Robertson

Charles Ritchie with his niece, Elizabeth Ritchie

Courtesy of Judith Robertson

Charles and Sylvia Ritchie (left) with Norman Robertson (right) and his wife, Jetty Robertson (centre)

By kind permission of Lady Rathdonnell

Parties at Bowen's Court in the 1950s
Top: left to right, Lady Ursula Vernon, Jim Egan, Mary Delamere, Elizabeth, Stephen Vernon, Iris Murdoch

By kind permission of Lady Rathdonnell

Left to right: Maurice Craig, Iris Murdoch (back to camera), Eddy Sackville-West, Elizabeth, Hubert Butler

Elizabeth and her students at Bryn Mawr College, Pennsylvania

Charles Ritchie with President John F Kennedy

One of the last pictures of Elizabeth Bowen

© Angus McBean

By kind permission of Library and Archives Canada

One of the last pictures of Charles Ritchie

us. Perhaps, but not THIS crisis – it's too embarrassing. I hate being in London at a time when so much is at stake and not being at one with the Londoners. I feel an outsider and I am haunted by memories of 1940 when I felt such a complete identity with London.[78]

Sunday, 18th November 1956, as from The Deanery [Bryn Mawr, Penn.]
My darling – you were good to write on your way through London. I'd hardly dared expect a letter so soon. I've inevitably felt desperately lonely for you, a passionate wish to go with you or follow you back to Europe . . .

That weekend at Montreal was a sort of salvation to me. I don't think it's ever meant so much to see you. Directly I saw you, directly you walked to that red-lit hotel cocktail bar, and I could look at you and touch you, I felt not only happy but safe and sane.

And from that moment a rebound into beautiful pure gay happiness. Something I shall never forget. Not that I ever do forget anything of ours, any time of ours. It was simply that this time Montreal and you and me in it seemed to burn into me with a particular sort of joy, as even it had never done before. It was such a triumph to be there – triumph over what I don't quite know.

I'm writing this in darling Gertrude Ely's house, between tea and supper. I came back here after giving a talk at Haverford – she swept me away from a Quaker tea party, for which I was grateful. She suggested that I and her house-party could amuse ourselves

---

[78] The Suez crisis: on Nov 5 British and French assault troops landed in Port Said with the intention of retaking the Suez Canal from Egypt. The governments of the US and Canada, Britain's natural allies, were appalled. In the United Nations, Lester Pearson, then Canada's Minister of External Affairs, pressed through a resolution to send a force to the area on the withdrawal of the British and French, while the USSR proposed that the UN give military assistance to Egypt. Canadian and British public opinion was divided. EB argued that one should back one's friends, whether they were right or wrong.

between tea and supper. So we instantly scattered like chaff before the wind or rabbits scattering to their burrows, as Gertrude seldom relaxes her grip on the situation for a single instant. Alice Biddle, that wonderful other character I told you about, is here too. It is so long since I used a pen and ink to write with (as apart from an ink-pencil) that I feel rather physically sticky writing with one – I'd really like to be writing you a long type-writer letter, or go back to the Deanery (which is quite near) and collect my usual ink-pencil, but Gertrude does not like anyone to elude her fascinating – and it is fascinating – grasp.[79]

Oh I wish you could have come here for a day and met all these characters, who are composing as it were a chapter in my life.

I've felt less bored here this last week – really I think last week-end (Montreal) revivified me. Also my time here will now be so soon over that a sense of distance is beginning to lend enchantment to the view, as though I were gone already – As I told you, I'll be at Hunt's House, Hopewell, NJ,[80] over the Thanksgiving weekend: back here on the evening of next Sunday, 25th, then off – having said my goodbyes to here – to Boston or rather Cambridge on Nov. 28th.

c/o May Sarton, 14 Wright St, Cambridge 38 for the night of the 28th, then, I'll be staying the night of Dec 3rd with her, also.

I'm going to Washington for 24 hours on Dec. 7th: I've been invited and suddenly thought I would . . .

I have seen quite a lot of the students, the dear girls, this week. And am very entertained by and fond of several of them. They're very funny, for one thing, quite often – I mean, witty.

---

79 Gertrude Ely and Alice Biddle, two aged *grandes dames* on the Bryn Mawr scene. Ely was active in international affairs, women's rights and civil rights. Biddle, a Southern Democrat, was one of the first 3 students to graduate from Oregon State University in 1870.

80 Home of Alan Collins, who ran the US branch of her literary agents, Curtis Brown.

Gertrude's house unlike most American houses is under-heated, and I'm beginning to sneeze. I should like a drink soon.

Goodnight, blessed beloved – Your E.

Bowen's Court, Tuesday, 18th December 1956. Evening

Dearest love, never more dear – this probably won't reach you till approximately Christmas Day. Have what you and I really would mean by a happy Christmas – just one gleam however momentary of joy in it, spiritual joy; and do also think of me. Otherwise, you must be giving yourself over to the party spirit. I guess all your many guests, the All One Big Family, will shoot through into another felicitous dimension in the course of the evening: I mean I'm certain you'll make them, at all events, happy. And I expect Barley A[81] will help: I'm glad she's going to be there; as you say, she enjoys anything there is, and that is a help. . . .

My travelling day had seemed very long. Actually I had not closed an eye since I said goodbye to Roley outside the Nova Scotia Hotel, Halifax (where I picked up the TCA. limousine to the airport) until I went to bed here in my own room 28 hours later. This gave me a queer hallucinated though happy feeling as though the time there had not yet come to an end – and in a sense I don't feel it ever will. It was uncanny, within the same 'day' (for a space of wakefulness does constitute that) to have been driving with Roley through the streets of Halifax, then driving in my own car from Shannon through Limerick city, through Kilmallock, through the mountains, through Kildorrery, and so back to here.

I think I'll begin by giving you an outline of what I, we, did, before I attempt to tell you (which I can't) even a little of what struck me or what I felt . . .

---

[81] Barley Alison, dynamic publisher at Weidenfeld & Nicolson, was spending Christmas with the Ritchies in Cologne. She later established her own imprint, The Alison Press, at Secker & Warburg.

There follows a long, almost hour by hour account of the weekend she spent with Charles's brother Roley, his wife, Bunny, and their daughter, Elizabeth, at 190 Inglis Street, Halifax, Nova Scotia, during which she met family friends and, for the first time, Charles's mother. This involvement in Charles's family life and the emotional link she made with his mother, who was very important to him, were also supremely important for her.

. . . Can you take in from the very boringness, the bareness, of this outline of the week-end how much it meant? The whole thing was like going into some extraordinary other dimension I've never been in before. I think really that ravishment is the only word. I'll have to wait till my next letter to write more, to tell you about all the extraordinary sensations of the place, the people. Nothing like this, that, the whole of it, has ever happened to me in my life before. But is the whole thing really a sort of crystallisation around my falling in love with your Mother? I can't forget her. The memory of her, and it's more than a memory, disturbs even in a curious way my senses. Her voice, her movements, the things she said and says are all burned into me.

How idiotic (anybody might say) to feel this way at my age. How amazing to be able to inspire it, and at such full force, at hers.

And I've only begun to tell you about so many other things, joys, amusement, romances of every kind, impressions. So I'll just have to go on and write you more, I mean, a second instalment of this letter . . .

On Friday I'm going over to the Vernons', to go to a Bruree Christmas Carol service and then spend the night. Jim Egan has been 3 times on the telephone. Tomorrow evening I'm dining with the Blacks. Christmas Eve I'm dining with the Vernons and spending the night. Christmas night I'm dining with the Blacks. St Stephen's Day I hope to be quiet. The night after, the Blacks, Molly Keane etc are coming to dinner to eat my turkey. The 28th I'm going out to dinner and going to the Hunt Ball, only I hope for a v limited time.

And meanwhile what about the PETROL SHORTAGE,[82] I'd like to know? Officially at present there's hardly a drop to be had, and petrol rationing on a very severe basis is to be introduced Jan 1st. Everybody says on the telephone, 'I can't very well explain on the telephone, darling, but I don't think you'll find you have to worry about that.'

I feel, in a dim way, that I should set a good example and not be seen using more petrol than there officially is. However, time will show . . .

Charles, my wanting to be with you has become still more unbearable. I'll await anything you can tell me about plans as soon as you can tell me. I won't – as you say not to – expect you before Jan. 10th. But you will not for GOD'S SAKE, will you if you can possibly prevent it, be more than a day or two after that? Even that seems such an awfully long time . . .

Oh my love, my love, my love. I feel a longing to write to you a whole book, not simply a letter. I could write you a book about any one hour, any one character, of last (the Halifax) week-end. But I'm tired, it's 11.30pm and I really must stop.

All my love, Charles, Charlie. Dear sweet one. A happy Christmas

Bowen's Court, 22nd December 1956

Dearest, I do not know what to call you. [*She is writing to Lilian Ritchie*] And it seems so silly that this Christmas of all Christmases I am not sending you, did not send you, any Christmas letter or any card. I should have left a letter for you before I left. But I felt all in a maze, in a way too happy, in a way too sad, to be able to write . . .

I don't feel so very far away, even here, now. I am always seeing you, and more than imagining I am in your house. I see everything

---

[82] A consequence of the Suez crisis.

there, everything in it, with the most startling clearness – piece by piece, the pieces of china, the roses on the chairs, the portraits on the walls – not only the painted portraits but the photographs. And I do also in spite of being there with you in spirit and imagination, often feel very homesick.

You will see that I am writing about <u>things</u> – objects, surroundings – because I can't possibly write about you, or what it is to me to know you, to have been in your presence.

I've written Bunny a letter, by this post, with more practical news. I expect perhaps she'll show it to you, if you'd care to know about the journey, or what's going on here, or anything. The house is surrounded by very deep mid-winter silence: no sound for hours together except the rooks muttering in the trees. My friends, I mean my friends who are my neighbours, have given me a very kind affectionate welcome back. There are to be a lot of Christmas parties. I went to a Christmas Carol service in one of the village churches yesterday, after dark.

A letter from Charles came the morning after I got back, and he rang up from Bonn yesterday morning. He hopes to be able to come here for a few days about Jan. 13th. So that will be something to look forward to. I had some bowls of hyacinth bulbs 'set' for Christmas; they won't now, clearly, be in flower by Christmas, but I'm rather glad as it looks now as though they would be out about when he's here.

I was unhappy that I wasn't able to send you any flowers. I know it could have been just a conventional thing to do, but it would have meant more than that.

Later I'll write a longer more coherent letter. I also have (<u>somewhere</u>!) some small, better photographs of this house. They give more impression of how it feels, as well as how it looks. But I must wait to look for them, and to write to you again, until the calm after Christmas. I shall be thinking of you on Christmas Day. And I shall think of the New Year as one in which I shall be seeing you again.

I can't begin to say thank you in the way I mean it: I shall just say thank you for those lovely gay parties, and for letting me meet your friends in your house. Please give my love, and remembrances, to Freda.[83]

Bless you. I do so love you.

Elizabeth

[83] Mrs Ritchie's companion.

1957

19 January [Cologne]

Back from B Court yesterday. In the plane on the way back I gave my forehead a convulsive slap at the thought that I might have left this book behind in my bedroom there. What a let-down – how anaphrodisiac – how dreary it would be for E to read (not that she would). . . .

I was v happy at B Court. One day of fine, cold weather succeeded another. When I woke up in my big airy bedroom[84] with the big old-fashioned windows looking up the slope of the park, I felt in a hurry to start the day. At night after dinner we sat in the dimly-lit library. The house goes on main electricity next month and E says that's the end of Celtic twilight and huddling over the embers. I wanted one more whisky to finish what we were saying before the evening was over. The days, as they say, were never long enough to say what I wanted to say and to hear what I wanted to hear. 'Race With Time', that is to be the name of her next book.[85]

---

[84] CR always insisted on his own bedroom, wherever he was, because he slept badly and liked to roam about at night.

[85] The next novel was in the event called *The Little Girls*. It was not published until 1964.

She says that she knew its title, but not yet what it is to be about. It is a 'star-shaped' plot with characters and events converging on a point in time. Perhaps it is in another way the Race with Time which gives the exciting but under-pressure feeling to these times with E. ... Our talk seemed always to be circling round the subject – which is perhaps Time – that we are getting older, that we see each other for a few days or at most a week, that months come in between, that in another five to ten years we must think of being finished or dying.

Something entirely different – I am filled with envious admiration for the way E fills her time – in the way we are both 'doing Time'. I think she herself said that a woman in a widow state goes back to the arts and crafts of her youth in attaching friends, and to her former gregariousness, not to be lonely. And E was at the beginning a careerist who combined people. She came to England without a friend, and only a few hard-up Anglo-Irish relations living in lodging houses, and made her circle; and now she has done it again in Ireland – as I have not done it in Germany. The incentive of course is greater if one is alone!

22 January

E and I have both in these two years become calm. The scenes between us here in this house and that day with the chauffeur B listening are not likely to begin again. That first year[86] was the last in which the panics of youth played a part. If the same things happened to me, they would meet a more marble surface – or would they? ... Suppose that E loved me less this time, felt she could do without me, that it was a faint bore my being there, that she mustn't for my sake show it. I don't believe anything of the kind. I believe we love each other equally. Is that possible? Yes. But it shows in different ways.

---

[86] Refers to his posting to Germany.

Bowen's Court, Tuesday, 29th January 1957
Dearest – your cuff-link was found (some days ago, actually) and I posted [it] off to you from Cork today . . .

Which made me think how I wish sometime when we're together we could buy two rings the same: one from me to you, one from you to me. They'd have to be plain rings such as a man (you) could wear without looking silly. But I'd just like the idea of exchanging rings, and having something of yours to wear, all the time and you something of mine. Do you think this idea very sentimental, silly? Does it sound faux? To me it wouldn't be so. The trouble is, I don't see how we'd ever find rings we could just buy and both walk out of the shop in, owing to your ridiculously slender fingers.

. . . This has been the most BEAUTIFUL day – Spring. Birds singing, and a sort of scented mildness in the air; snowdrops in the woods. Rather inappropriately, Edie and I went into Cork, me to see my Income Tax agents (the position is not quite so appalling as I had feared). She meanwhile pottered from shop to shop . . . Then I gave her lunch at the Imperial Hotel, an awful place I think – you and I have never been there and are not likely to, if I can help it – but more appropriate to Edie's generation, I think, than that Oyster Bar (up the alley) where you and I eat in Cork, as it does not necessitate a long, long wait for a table, sozzling away at the bar: she doesn't drink, apart from an occasional glass of white burgundy at meals. (One of the things I like about your mother and her generation in Halifax is that they do drink, if not to excess – this is no criticism of darling Edie!) . . .

I did so love your letter – and I mean love. You must not have apprehensions: I have them with regard to you, and your safety, horribly often; but you must not have them about me.

(Last time you had apprehensions, they brought in the Suez Crisis.) You have an apprehension heredity, just as I have a 'brooding' heredity – all the Bowens who went round the bend (and there were many of them) did so on account of continuous unchecked brooding. So my mother always warned me against it. I have seen (as you must, millions of times more) such absolutely bottomless apprehension in your mother's great beautiful disturbing eyes. If Roley doesn't fall out of an aeroplane and you don't die of that cyst under your arm in extreme poverty, it won't be her fault – if you know what I mean? . . .

What on earth is the matter with that unfortunate Sylvia's throat, that it doesn't clear up? I cannot imagine a worse fate for a dog than a hurting throat, so I'm sorry. But surely it's high time she thought of starting for Canada? I suppose she can't while she's bed-bound; but change of air (seriously) might do good.

I wrote a long letter to your mother about 4 days ago. Now I must walk down the avenue and post this. I love you. E.

Bowen's Court, Thursday, 7th February 1957
Darling, I have been thinking of you so specially much. That last letter of yours, written before lunch (sherry time here, as you said) in the office, in a break from sitting in the German parliament listening to the foreign affairs debate, brought you so particularly near . . .

Then, that ghastly storm with its holocaust of trees shook me and got me down. The day after, the day I wrote to you, was like looking at the results of a mass murder. A sort of vegetable Belsen. Torn-up trees, with their look of despair and ignominy, really rack my heart. I lost 63 for certain, plus I don't know how many more – fortunately, none of them 'show' from the house. They've all already been sold, at a good price (timber-buyers descend like vultures, after a storm), and the proceeds will put me slightly more out of the red, but I still don't like it. And as for poor Barry Black, awful things had been happening at Creagh Castle. His farm buildings, out behind the house, are fairly near the cliff overhanging the river as it is: a great row of trees blew down between the buildings and the edge of the cliff, and their roots have torn away chunks of the cliff, leaving a sort of cave under the buildings – which now look as though they would at any moment go toppling downward into the gorge also. At great personal risk we crept along and peered down into the havoc in the gorge. Poor Barry was looking as green as his tweed coat – your tweed, which increased my homesickness for you. He gave me a wonderful lunch – very much better food than when Jean keeps house. Why is [it] that men alone (even temporarily so, as in Barry's case) always do seem to have better food? The inimitable feminine touch imparted by dear ones always is, I do think, rather over-rated.

After I wrote that letter to you, at Creagh, I dashed back to Mallow to meet the Speaights[87] at the station – extremely late, as I realized. I found them patiently sheltering under an archway from the heavy rain. They were very nice about it.

Thursday February 7th 1957

Now they are here (as you probably gathered from my letter, I was not enthusiastic about the idea of having them), they are indeed very nice, quite amusing, entertain themselves by going for long walks, and are exceedingly easy in the house. Bobby Speaight is having a great success with his recently published Hilaire Belloc.[88] They habitually visit around a lot, so are perfect visitors. Tonight we are all going to dinner with Eddy; I leave them there to stay the night at Cooleville and Eddy is driving them on to their next destination, somewhere in north Co Tipperary, tomorrow.

The Butlers, Gilbert and Noreen, are coming the day after tomorrow, Saturday, for the weekend. And who do you think are coming on the 13th, for a night? The Berlins, Isaiah and Aline. That I do look forward to very much indeed. Shaya is lecturing in Belfast, then coming south. As you know, I took a tremendous shine to Aline when I was staying with them both in Oxford last April.

---

87 Robert Speaight (1904-1976) actor and author. A Roman Catholic convert, he made his name playing Becket in the first production of T.S. Eliot's *Murder in the Cathedral* (1935).

88 Hilaire Belloc (1870-1953), prolific author, poet, journalist and editor, prominent Roman Catholic, and a Liberal MP.

Then on the 15th I go trailing over to England.

My address from Feb. 16th, (Saturday) to 19, (Tuesday) will be c/o Miss Emma Smith, B.Sc.

Knuston Hall,

Irchester

Nr. Wellingborough – Northants.

Will you if you possibly can write to me there. As ELIZABETH BOWEN. It would save my life. This is an Adult Education course I'd promised to speak at. Knuston Hall is a former country house (hideous, from the photographs) taken over by the Northants Education Committee as a hostel for just these purposes. I shall have to bring an enormous bar with me. Two of the other speakers, I find to my horror, are to be American professors. Whatever I am doing this for, it is not money – love, I suppose. I have always had rather a love for Northants[89] and its educational problems since the 2 years Alan and I lived there, when we were first married. He was employed by the Northants Education Committee. . . .

. . . My telephone is OUT OF ORDER because of the storm – no hope of its being mended, they tell me smugly, for 2 days more. But if you telephoned, for instance in the morning of the 14th, Thursday, it should be mended. But perhaps you won't be able to?

And now my typewriter has gone out of order – the ribbon's slipped off the spool. I must hurry it down to Paddy Barry. I love you I love you, so very much. Elizabeth

4 March [Bowen's Court]

I can hear E typing her *Tatler* article in the bedroom next door. It must be ready by twelve; then we have our morning glass of sherry and unless it is snowing go to look for the ruins of a castle, or if the weather is too bad to a movie in Cork. E says: 'I could give a very

---

[89] 'Northants' is the abbreviation for Northamptonshire. EB and Alan Cameron's first married home, in 1923, was 73 Knights Lane, Kingthorpe, Northampton.

vivid description of the road past Headington where I used to walk every day, but who wants to read it unless something happened to me there.' She doesn't want to write a subjective autobiography. She wants to invent, or rather says it comes more naturally to her to invent.

This sadness is physical. I have had it before; but hoped never to have it, this kind of physical remorse, again. It appears there are to be no mercies in growing old.

11 March

I cannot describe the state I was in yesterday (can it have been only yesterday?) when I flew back from Ireland – the hallucinatory depression, the complete undermining of all confidence, the corroding guilt and sorrow. I never expected to feel all this again. E says that it is a 'natural' consequence of our parting, but it went much deeper than that. . . . She says she can't bear to think of me sealed away from life. I can't bear to think of that myself, and it is true; but if that last day is life, can I bear it? She says she feels it is some deficiency in her love which drove me to it, but isn't it some deficiency in me? No, this strain was too great. I cannot forgive myself for my impatience, my unlovingness, my dry irritability, my inability to accept. Yet I can entirely forgive myself. I understand and must never forget that all my cut and dried plans are the amusement of a bored man and bear no relation to reality. No, it was heart-breaking. How can I bear the memory of that last morning at the Shelbourne. How can I ever forget it. Surely I can't go on as I did before, yet I feel that is just what I will do; that the scales will form over my eyes, that merciful banality will set me off from life in my Cologne Nursing Home. Oh Elizabeth!

Bowen's Court, Monday, 11th March 1957

My dear love, I love you so much. These partings – nothing will get us around them, or through them or away from them without pain.

Without this ever-terrible sorrow, the crying out of our natures. And the greater our happiness, greater each time, the more the hours of parting hurt. Two creatures grown into each other the way we are, how can this not be so, I suppose. The thing to thank God for, I suppose, is that the end, the parting, doesn't hang over us until it's really upon us. Until then we have all time.

I believe why I can't bear to look at injured trees, torn up, is that they remind me of the Blow that strikes us and upheaves up, each time we have to part. It isn't 'an end', it's only a suspension. Yet even so each time it's a bewildering shock.

. . . I'm writing in the drawing room, an unusual place for me to be on Monday morning, but Mark Bence-Jones is coming over at about 11.30 because he wants me to help him go through the MS of his second novel.[90] He is a charge, poor boy! So I thought I'd better work with him in the drawing room, as Veronica's in the library.

Veronica[91] and I got back here about 7 o'clock yesterday evening, Sunday. About the time you and I so often came home after our expeditions. The same small moon was shining and the crows cawing. I found the enclosed telegram from that unfortunate Shaya on the chimney-piece. I'm a curious mixture of genuinely sorry and disappointed, and relieved. I don't at the moment want to make the slightest effort about anybody, just want to 'lose myself in my work' . . .

Oh, our beautiful dear perfect hours and days and nights. You dear perfect one. Your Elizabeth

---

[90] Mark Bence-Jones (1930-), whose family house is Glenville Park, Co Cork. He was to become known as a cultural and architectural historian of Anglo-Ireland and of the British Raj. His second novel *Paradise Escaped* was published in 1958. His first, *All a Nonsense*, was dedicated to Eddy S-W.

[91] Veronica Wedgwood

12 March

Hugo Charteris[92] said she [EB] looks like a man. Well, she has the 'bravery' of one and the generosity and intelligence, but how few men have much of these. 'Bravery' with the added meaning of Bravura is the attribute of some men – and women. It's a showing thing, but not at all the same as showing-off . . . What I am doing in this monologue is continuing the dialogue I would have had with E. Yet I can't bear to write her a letter. It is the transfer to an inadequate medium. Tonight she gets back to Bowen's Court with Veronica W. Tomorrow she has the Berlins coming and I am jealous of that. Yes I am, as she would be jealous if I had amusing people to stay who would break the circle of our intimacy, a kind of disloyalty.

Bowen's Court, Saturday, 16th March 1957

My darling, your two letters this morning! I loved what you said about the second (the evening) one being like your coming back into a room again and going on talking.

Yes this house is full of us, packed with us and the atmosphere of our days, which are not over. I feel far better now I'm alone. . . . I'm ashamed to have been so 'down' as I was when I wrote yesterday.[93] I think it partly was that I miss knowing what you are actually doing at every moment – that is the only 'separation'.

I've been working (at the Rome book) ALL day, and feel very very woolly, so I'd better stop. . . .

Light of my life, take care of yourself. You are so near me. In fact more than near: often I feel we are one person.

Your E.

---

[92] Novelist and translator (1922-1970). His autobiographical novel of 1957, *The Tide is Right,* was suppressed, and published posthumously with an introduction by Nicholas Mosley in 1991.

[93] This letter has not survived.

17 March

It is just a week since I left E that morning at the Shelbourne. I have been looking back at the pages of my diary about my time in Ireland. How sad and disturbed they sound, yet there was an intensification of feeling – no diminishing. To her I owe my present happiness, she is life to me. Yet by this I mean not happiness, but my capacity. That will do.

18 March

Reading Rebecca West, I feel the resemblance between her and E, which I think E would admit if she were here and I could ask her. I see now why I shrank from reading this book[94] at Bowen's Court and why I read it with such recognition now. There are parallels between them, and perhaps I understand now the quiet determination, overriding me, with which she pressed this book on me . . . She is [like] a relation, not only in the superficial things: the Anglo-Irish family, the 'Bohemian' phase, the return with bells to the tradition, but deeper with the class business, the argumentative politics, the family and at another level the more and more ingrained feeling for the supernatural – omens, portents. Imagine all that lurking below their acceptance of clever, rationalistic English contemporary ideas and this could also be E. 'You must always believe that life is as extraordinary as music says it is.'[95] This of course is what without knowing anything about music I believe; and if I fail to believe it, is death to me.

19 March

A sad letter from E, sad because for once (and it's so rare) her life illusion, which is a form of courage, seemed to have broken down.

---

[94] *The Fountain Overflows,* best-selling novel by Rebecca West (1892-1983), just published. The parallel between EB and RW is sound; but RW's imaginative world of omens and portents was darker and more threatening than EB's.

[95] This is what the mother tells her daughters in *The Fountain Overflows.*

I only hope to God that I didn't – apart from the pain of parting – cause this, didn't sadden her. I am sorry the Berlins didn't come. I think their being there would have plunged her back into social action, made her amused again by the worldly game.

Bowen's Court, Saturday, 23rd March 1957

My dearest – I got and loved your two postcards from Munich; they are so very beautiful, I am keeping them on the library chimney-piece . . .

I think it's partly a sort of loneliness of mind – as though a book one was completely absorbed in and utterly riveted to had suddenly (even though only temporarily) been snatched from one. I mean, our continuous talking, when we are together, is like that. And in a way what we talk about weaves itself into a story. What happens next? I am always wanting to know. Even small practical things, each other's quite passing preoccupations, are so interesting, exciting. And when we have to part, all those small stories are suspended. Also I miss knowing what is in your mind.

Do you know, one of the things I remember most, I mean dwell on most, about last time you were here was the end of the drive home from Kerry . . . It was the last part of the road coming into Mallow from the Killarney side, being sucked – as it almost felt like – on and on under that long tunnel of trees in the darkening twilight. You were talking about the little girls and girls of your childhood and late-adolescent days in Halifax, and the different kinds of feeling you had for them. Really it was a conversation about love, not in the abstract but as applied to people, the different kinds of love aroused by different kinds of people – and particularly the sharpness and bafflingness of that when one is young. The mood of the evening, with that faint taste of spring about it, and the curious compulsive smoothness of the car – I felt as though someone else, not me, were driving – all seemed to melt into what you were saying. And my love for you reached a pitch of anguish, almost, out of our very nearness and sheer happiness. Those particular miles of tree-road will always be yours. In a way I don't want to drive them again till you come back, though I suppose I shall . . .

Molly Keane has been staying here since Tuesday. We have both been working away like beavers, she in the Green Room (your room) at her play,[96] I in my study at my book. I don't know about her, but I think I've slightly overworked; I feel like a wrung-out rag this morning. She stipulated when she came 'no late nights', but we did inevitably go to dinner at Bruree [with the Vernons]; and the Blacks, who needed a holiday from their own cook – or at any rate, to give her one, I thought – came to dinner last night: so did Jim Egan, just back from his holiday in England . . . He is still on the wagon, till Lent is over, poor old boy, and therefore rather subdued.

Molly Keane is a fascinating little character and I'm fond of her. She's as clever as a bag of monkeys. But her cynicism and pessimism are terrifying. She makes me feel quite a blobby old idealistic sentimental optimist by contrast – almost like an American. Though equally if I'm long in the company of a sweetness-and-light merchant, I always find I react into violent cynicism, don't you? . . .

How is Sylvia since she came back?[97] I always wonder whether she ever varies or is always the same. This is not unkindness, merely the speculation one cannot but feel about any human being. Some things must make dents in her, surely, though I must say in my limited experience I have never seen anything do so . . .

---

[96] Molly Keane wrote plays under the name M.J. Farrell, in collaboration with John Perry. She could have been starting on *Dazzling Prospect*, produced in London at the Strand Theatre in 1961 and starring Margaret Rutherford.
[97] Sylvia had been in Canada.

Wouldn't it be lovely if you had a tape-recorder machine and could talk to me on it. But that would mean some outside person (I suppose) would have to read the tape off, and type what was on it. Oh Charles I feel so physically low and shivery: I think I'm on the verge of getting a ghastly cold. I shall go to bed very early tonight with 2 hot water bottles. I love you. Elizabeth.

Bowen's Court, Saturday, 4th May 1957
My darling – on Thursday I got your letter, written last Sunday – on the eve of what a week! I wonder how you've got through it, and whether apart from being exhausting it's been interesting? Well, it could hardly not be interesting[98] . . .

No I haven't read that Nabokov book you describe, and I do long to. The maddening thing is, I once could have: Raymond thoughtfully put it beside my bed once when I was staying at Long Crichel; but I didn't have time to read it while I was there, and he clearly didn't want it to leave the house. Everything I hear about it makes me want to read it. If you can get a copy – but then how can you possibly? – will you bring it over in your luggage when you come here? As you say I don't think there'd be a hope, owing to the watchful purity of this country, of getting it through the post[99]. . . .

Oh my love. Is it possible that the 17th is now one day less than a fortnight away?

The weather this week's been lovely. Garden full of tulips. On Tuesday Patrick Hennessy spent the day here and did some further

---

[98] L.B. Pearson, Canadian Minister for External Affairs, had visited Cologne, which involved CR in many meetings and functions. That year Pearson won the Nobel Peace Prize in recognition of his creation of the United Nations Emergency Force.
[99] Vladimir Nabokov's sensationally controversial novel *Lolita*, about a middle-aged man's sexual obsession with a pre-pubescent girl, was first published in English in 1955 by the Olympia Press in Paris, in an edition of 5,000 copies. CR owned one of these. *Lolita* was published in the UK in 1956 and in NY in 1958. It would most certainly have been seized by the Customs in Ireland, where the Board of Censors was ferociously active.

alterations to that portrait of me[100] . . . On Monday, May Sarton arrives, from Boston. . . .

How acute these waves of feeling, of extra feeling, of nearness to each other – I mean while we're apart – are. If I kept a diary, I could enter in it, as positively as any outside event, when they happen, what time of the day they happen. Different times of different days. Sometimes when I'm driving the car alone I feel you're in the car with me. Also so often when I'm in this room (the library, where I'm writing now). And the drawing room, in a different way, seems to be particularly <u>your</u> room. So many things in it have associations with you, a very great number you've actually given me – do you realise, you've almost furnished that room, apart from the actual chairs and tables? But also, you are near me in places with which you and I have no actual associations – sometimes, places in which I myself am for the first time. Last Sunday, for instance, when I was staying at Eddy's, we all went over to drinks with some neighbours of his who, though dull in themselves, have the most curious eerie beautiful garden – walking along beside a hedge in that, in the bright-green evening, I felt you beside me – almost, though you and I had no past in
[Ends]

Bowen's Court, Thursday, 23rd May 1957
My dear love – your 'arrived' telegram came. I've trusted and hoped you had a good journey, in the sense of a tolerable one: it made me so cross that you should have to rise up at <u>that</u> hour then have to spend 4 hours waiting at London airport. Oh Charles. I went quickly back into the house when the car drove off from here, so

[100] Patrick Hennessy (1915-1980), Cork-born painter of portraits and landscapes, painted EB in a formal evening dress standing against the Venetian window on the landing at Bowen's Court. The painting is in the permanent collection of the Crawford Art Gallery in Cork.

as not to watch the red tail-lights disappearing down the avenue. I felt like a murderess or an executioner rousing you from your sweet sleep at 3am. You <u>are</u> very sweet when you are asleep – though not only then. And I was terrified that not only the early start but the flying would bring your cold back and make it worse.[101]

I have that maimed, lost feeling, not knowing where to turn. I feel it's wrong to go on about it – a sort of ingratitude for all we've had. This struck-down longing for you is like a tax, and we must pay it. The parting itself hurt more even than last time (in Dublin) but the circumstances were less ghastly – weren't they? . . .

I didn't go to sleep again after you'd gone till nearly 8.30, when my breakfast tray came. I lay in a sort of daze, not unhappily or restlessly, thinking about you. Then after hours I heard dear Eddy Barry's sheeplike cough passing along the path under my bedroom window and realized that he and the car must be back again from Shannon . . .

God bless you and keep you, my darling love. Elizabeth

Bowen's Court, Saturday, 1st June 1957

Dearest – I woke up this morning in such a particular agony of loneliness for you. It was so beautiful with the early morning sun streaming though the house, and the house felt so EMPTY. A fortnight ago, you were here. Oh my love . . .

About grief there's a terrible kind of bruising dullness – or dull bruisingness.

Some part of me does die when you're away, there's no doubt. Only thinking of you – or feeling you very near, as I constantly do – brings me alive again and keeps as it were the blood running in my veins.

---

101 CR briefly feared that his cold was whooping cough. Later in his diaries he identified his 'health panics' as 'a substitution for a more deep-seated apparently incurable insecurity coming perhaps from a split life.'

This week-end, now, you'll be in Paris, or rather Chantilly.[102] I hope happy – as we were saying, reunions are rather a strain. Yet one in ten does come off, and is unexpectedly spontaneous and touching and enjoyable. So I hope this is being one. And I hope the weather is being as lovely as it is here. Here, really it's unbearably lovely.

It was I can't tell you what a joy to find that last letter of yours (the one written on the 27th) here waiting for me in the evening when I got back about 8pm, very tired from 'doing the tea' at the Hunt Fête at Annesgrove . . . We did have a funny day. Owing to the blazing weather, the Fête was really very like the one in *A World of Love.* However I, and the other willing assistants, saw nothing of it except the tea enclosure: about 500 streamed in for tea, and we were cantering about, non-stop, from 4 to 7. . . .

Tell me about Chantilly.

Talking of Paris, Eddy brought Nancy[103] to dinner here last night . . . Nancy was very amiable and friendly, and it was an enjoyable evening. Barry Black (Jean being away) and my cousin Walter Trench[104] and the Vernons also came. We were talking about notepaper (trying to say writing paper)[105] and Stephen said: 'I must

---

[102] CR was staying at Chantilly with Lady Diana Cooper. Duff Cooper died in 1954. He had been ennobled as the 1st Lord Norwich in 1952, but she refused to be known as Lady Norwich (because it rhymed with porridge) and remained Lady Diana Cooper.

[103] The writer Nancy Mitford, who lived in Paris. It was at Cooleville, on this visit or another, that she finished her novel *Don't Tell Alfred* (1960), in which the character Uncle Davey is based on Eddy S-W.

[104] Walter Trench and his wife Norah lived at Castle Oliver, a Victorian pile in Co Limerick, and bred pigs. Trench also had interests in Kenya.

[105] To say 'writing paper' was 'U' (for upper class), and to say 'notepaper' was 'non-U.' The terms were coined by the linguistic scholar Professor Alan S.C. Ross and picked up by Nancy Mitford, who published in 1954 an article in *Horizon* providing a glossary of U and non-U terms and usages. Her essay, with others, was reprinted in *Noblesse Oblige* (1956), causing amusement among the toffs and anxiety among the socially aspirational.

say, I think ours at Bruree is rather nice.' Where upon Eddy, with the greatest sweetness and amiability, leant across the table and said: 'Since you ask me, Stephen, I think the type of your headings is quite beastly.' This rankled for quite a long time with poor Stephen, and one can hardly wonder.

What a curious creature Nancy is. In a curious way, rather an underlying layer of pessimism and sadness. She was looking I thought v handsome, and I do always love and envy her clothes. I think it's her mouth which 'ages' her – it's not only so small, it has a strange drawn-in look, like an old person's, as though the teeth had sunk into the gums. She's the kind of character one would expect to have a big mouth. She was very nice about this house, more than conventionally so. She also said *A World of Love* had been a book she'd particularly cared for, and that she'd long been wanting to tell me so.

They are all coming here again on Monday, and then we are all going on to dinner at the Blacks'. Jean has shot up to Dublin and is buying a new dress, as I think she's terrified of the idea of Nancy . . . Your E.

Bowen's Court, Friday, 7th June 1957

Dearest love, your letter begun at Chantilly, finished at Bonn, came this morning. It was a lovely one, it gave me such an impression of Paris in the heat, Bonn shimmering in the lovely heat-haze . . . I can so imagine Diana's feeling about Chantilly: semi-nightmare, and yet a love <u>and</u> an attachment that she can't give up . . .

Oh WHY can I not be with you – in all these changing scenes of life – <u>by your side</u>? This is partly rhetorical, partly the most awful convulsive cry. We have so much the same vein of happiness, the same senses.

But we do have our life together. Timeless, continuous. We do. It's just that sometimes I cannot bear this thing of not being with you all the time . . .

Oh my love, you getting me a present in Paris. What a beautiful thing of you to do. And I shall count it as a birthday present, because the letter (yours, telling me about it, arrived this morning and today is my birthday. (This is not a reproach, as though I know when yours is, 23 September, I always get a black-out about it when it comes near the time.)

However that made it all the lovelier that a letter from you came. I woke up this morning feeling rather low, ill, shivery and filled with self-pity. Lonely. Then by the same post as brought your letter came an enormous birthday card from Alan's former secretary. Wasn't it touching of her? . . .

Also I've been burning the candle at both ends: there've been a lot of parties, as Deborah Devonshire and her Lismore house-party have also entered the fray.[106] It's very nice, but it does not go with obsessional hard work on the Rome book. Still I expect it does good – I mean, the parties. I tell you the person who's staying at Lismore and is very nice: Patrick Leigh-Fermor, who wrote that monastery book A Time for Quiet[107] (what did you think of the book, by the way?). He says he met me years ago – which I don't remember – at a lunch party of Cyril Connolly's, and I was smoking a cigar. I said that must have been Cyril's Second Empire fixation, always –

(Darling Jim Egan burst in: he has now gone again)

– trying to get me to impersonate George Sand[108]. . . .

I must go and put on my black linen dress (the one you liked).

I love you so very much. Elizabeth

---

[106] The Dukes of Devonshire, who live at Chatsworth in Derbyshire, own Lismore Castle in Co Waterford. Deborah, the Duchess, was Nancy Mitford's youngest sister.

[107] The title is *A Time to Keep Silence* (1957) by Patrick (Paddy) Leigh Fermor, (1915-), travel-writer, scholar, and former distinguished soldier.

[108] EB's appearance elicited comparison with the appearance of two nineteenth-century women novelists with masculine pseudonyms, George Sand and George Eliot.

Bowen's Court [nd, but probably July 1957]

My dear love – I had your telegram . . . I deliberately haven't written for 2 days because I couldn't: I cling to the idea of your presence, and the sight of a sheet of paper seems to drive in the fact (which I keep running away from) that you're not 'here'! What was lovely at Shannon was that no shade of parting seemed to fall on us till the last moment: it was so gay there, having lunch in the sun. When the realization that you were going DID come, I had to run away, as you saw . . .

. . . I suppose there are few real actual marriages, even the best and closest, which are anything like what we have come to have. That is why partings are bearable. If there were an unbearable parting from you the unbearableness would be so great that I cannot believe it would not kill me . . .

Practical question: when I find that cigarette case (in a shop) that I want to give you, shall I put your name 'Charles from Elizabeth' in it, or not? I suppose, under the circumstances probably not? It makes all the difference to me having your 'Elizabeth from Charles' in the cigarette case you gave me; but then there's all the difference – I'm simply a widow and you are an Ambassador. You see my point. Will you let me know? I don't want to give you anything you can't use because it might under some circumstances be embarrassing.

What about if I simply had 'Charles', in my handwriting, written on the inside? Let me know – because if I can get the cigarette case in time I might have it posted for you to pick up at Canada House, London.

. . . All my love (which you know you have). Elizabeth

19 July

Back from Bowen's Court. E was – what shall I say – I was very happy. She moved me by her gentleness with me, and her happiness in having me there . . . This time there was no sense of strain, but a domestic home-coming feeling. Only her acceptance of semi-defeat, her lack of scenes or outbreaks of unresigned alarming temperament made me wonder once or twice whether she loved me less. I remember her saying some time ago, 'When I become perfectly easy, that will be that I don't love you', yet I don't believe this for a moment. She moved me when she said, 'Forgive me if I am brassy or dreary. It's because you are going today and I don't want to think of it.' Imagine that at her age I should have to fear that she might be starting something else . . . Goronwy [Rees] called her a Welsh witch and she said, 'All right, if I am a witch, I'll put a curse on you.'

Bowen's Court, Thursday, 25th July 1957
Dearest love – it did me so much good having your letter: really I have been horribly unbearably lonely for you since you went away . . .

I have been very busy. A little too much so, rushing to finish that brain-cracking 4,000 word article for USA *Holiday* magazine, plus a number of people in and out of the house . . . I must get over this neurosis about people POPPING IN. Audrey helped me cope with the professor:[109] she said afterwards she could see I was furious with the poor man, but she was certain it passed unobserved by him. And I'm glad it did. But I think the Irish intelligentsia are insensitive. I think also they have a fantasy about 'the big houses' – that we ladies in them sit all day fanning ourselves like Southern Belles, longing for conversation and company . . .

On Monday I worked all day at that article for America, which I finally finished, thank God, the day after. (It's worth 1,000 dollars to me, if all goes well.) . . .

Eddy is staying here for two nights. He said the worst of having Cooleville was that he never stayed at Bowen's Court – I think he has been rather low lately and wanted a change. It seems a good

---

[109] Myles Dillon, senior professor in the School of Celtic Studies at the Dublin Institute of Advanced Studies.

plan having him while Audrey's here, as for a long time they've always got on well . . .

I think one of Eddy's reasons for depression is having to grow this beard and the other that his sister's visit ended by getting him down. (They both looked so cosy that evening we were having drinks over there, didn't they.) He says Diana[110] resents him and keeps pointing out to him what horrible lives other people have, in a reproachful way. And he has, I think, some obscure feeling of guilt or self-reproach about her. He says all the time they were together her nose bled, bled, bled, and that even when it was not bleeding she sat there gazing at him in total silence. Directly there was company, her nose immediately stopped bleeding and she brightened up.[111] In that case, considering how sociable he normally is himself, I can't think why he didn't arrange more company for her. But he had got it into his head that she must be kept almost entirely incommunicado, or she might die . . .

Well, that's what life has been and is being like.

Typing is good, just for running on. But somehow I'm shy of typing how much I love you – You do know; I'm certain you do know. Take care of your precious self. All all my love – Elizabeth[112]

Bowen's Court, Saturday, 27th July 1957

My dearest love, I got your letter yesterday morning, with the news that you are very probably going to London.[113] (And have noted the fact that this is still secret.) Oh I do hope and pray that it comes

---

[110] Eddy's younger sister, divorced from Lord Romilly, in 1951 became the third wife of Sir Douglas Hall Bt, who died in 1962.

[111] Both Eddy S-W and his sister Diana suffered from hereditary telangiectasia, a disorder of the veins. Symptoms can include painful skin eruptions (which is why Eddy had grown a beard, so as to avoid shaving), and nose-bleeds.

[112] This last paragraph is appended in handwriting to a type-written letter. The vast majority of EB's letters to CR were handwritten.

[113] For a conference.

off. I expect the work will half kill you, but I know it's what you like. Something really to get your teeth into . . .

If you do go [to] London, does Sylvia go with you? I'd like to know this because of telephoning. It would be nice if you could ever put through a late-night call: as you know the telephone's by my bed here and we now have the 24 hour service.

I won't build any castles in the air about seeing you (in August) but as you know I could always get to any airport to meet you if you ever did find you could take a Sunday off.

Oh Charles, Charles, Charles.

Audrey and I are now going out to dinner with some RC's. RCs in this country always have rather over-rich food, rather egg-y mayonnaise, etc.

Forgive the mess at the top of the sheet: it's glue.

. . . I keep on and on missing you, tormentingly. What are you doing <u>this</u> Saturday afternoon, I wonder?

All my love Elizabeth

Bowen's Court, Saturday, 17th August 1957

My darling, it was lovely talking to you – at last! I'd been maddened by just missing you on the telephone before. What a week you have been having. It makes such a difference knowing, since last Sunday, more or less the outline and plan that your London days have. And this week to come, with you in the chair, it will be even more exciting. Oh thank heavens I saw you; it's left me feeling so near.[114]

I do hope Sylvia won't overstay the weekend by too many days. Not that she's doing any harm, but it sounds so futile, as well as being slightly one thing more for you to cope with when at high pressure anyway. Let me know whether she goes or stays . . .

Oh darling darling darling, I love you in the most inarticulate way. I hope I did not say too much on the Canada House telephone;

---

[114] CR flew to Dublin and back within a day, to see her.

I hadn't realized till towards the end of our conversation that you were there.

It's Saturday afternoon, after a lunch party – how I wish I were again driving up to Dublin to meet you, as I was this time last week. The lunch party consisted of Eddy's three week-end guests, a fascinating Jesuit called Father Corry and a married couple whose name I've forgotten, and Barry Black, Aunt Edie and Miss Hawes.[115] Edie spent the morning doing the flowers all over the house and has done it beautifully. Miss Hawes is very speechless in general company, but I think enjoys herself.

Eddy is I think cheering up, but was very overwrought when he came to dinner with me last Tuesday. He suddenly burst out into a rush of talk which was like somebody verbally bursting into tears, saying he felt in such despair about himself and he said he kept feeling his whole life as something lessening and failing and running down. Largely I think it's his health, this awful constant pain in his tummy, some sort of lesion he thinks. I said was it because he didn't after all like Cooleville, and he said oh no he loved it, it wasn't that. He said at any rate thank God he had this enormous power of enjoyment, and so often does enjoy himself – he said however that there's an immense gulf between enjoyment and happiness, which I suppose there is. Or is there, inevitably? When I'm with you I both enjoy myself and am happy.

However I think the outburst did him good, as he then cheered up and was funny about the inevitable Vernons – à propos of the evening he and I had spent with them at Kinsale. I think if anyone pushes Stephen off that pier, it will in the end be Eddy. I can imagine him saying, 'Oh dear, I'm afraid I've done rather an unkind thing; I can't think what got into me!'

On Thursday I drove over to Ardmore, taking Miss Hawes, to spend the day with Molly Keane and the children . . . They'd all

---

115 The former secretary of Alan Cameron.

been the night before to the Blarney ball, and the boys and young men who'd been in Sally's party were still straying dazedly but happily around the house, or going swimming to wake themselves up properly. It was my dear Sally's first grown-up ball (she's just had her seventeenth birthday) and I really think she had had a dream-like carnet de bal[116] time.

Molly's younger child Virginia, aged 11, was walking about looking white with contempt and boredom and fury at being out of it. She sat looking distantly out of the window at the sea, like a disillusioned woman of forty.

Yesterday my old friend Mary Pakenham, who I hadn't seen for nearly 20 years, came to lunch, with her 2 very nice children – George 17, Alice 16 . . . Her name's now Mary Clive: it was she who (though I didn't know it till later) wrote that book I liked so much, Christmas Among the Savages.[117]

It's been rather Young People's Week, as you can see, one way and another. I rather yearned after the Clive children, George and Alice – if I had had children I'd have liked them to have been exactly like that . . .

All my love, my love Elizabeth

1 September[118]

The only thing that runs in my mind to sadden me is that I can be happy away from E, and she apparently away from me is happy. I wonder if we love each other less or are getting more tranquil. I am happy too at this time with S, and we are cheerful and gay together as we used to be.

---

[116] At formal dances, each girl had a *carnet de bal*, a dance-card, in which young men wrote their names, booking dances with her. EB meant that Sally danced every dance.
[117] Lady Mary Clive (1907-), née Pakenham, journalist, memoirist and biographer, daughter of the 5th Earl of Longford. She lost her husband Meysey Clive in the war. Her book for children *Christmas with the Savages* [*sic*] was published in 1955.
[118] CR was still in London, returning to Germany at weekends.

Bowen's Court, 4th September 1957

. . . The only thing halting and haunting me – inevitably – is the fear of your having to go further away; the terror of your being out of Europe. The wonderfulness of this last year, of seeing you even comparatively often, has made the space between times worse, and driven into me the fact that I positively and literally could not live without you. There have been times – and we've survived them – when our meetings have had to be 6, 8 months, sometimes almost a year, apart. I should find it – we both should find it – terribly hard to go back to those times again, after what we've had. However. No use meeting trouble half way. We shall have to see. I still do want you, soon, to be out of Germany.

My cousin Hubert Butler is here for 2 days. He's a nice gentle creature, a trifle donnish. He has recently – that is in the last year – visited Russia and red China. The latter obviously rather bored him, but he has a (non-political) passion for Russia, where in the 1930's he succeeded in spending a considerable time – chiefly in Petrograd. He speaks the language. This time, he says, he wandered around seeking for his former friends, but they all seemed to have been liquidated[119] . . .

Good night, beautiful darling

Elizabeth

Bowen's Court, Friday, 13th September 1957

[*Parts of this letter burnt away, hence incomplete lines.*]

My dearest – I remember how you've always hated a Friday that also was the 13th. . . .

---

[119] Hubert Butler (1900-1990), who with his wife Peggy, sister of the actor-manager Tyrone Guthrie, lived in the family home Maidenhall, Bennettsbridge, in Co Kilkenny, was a farmer, a Russian scholar, a translator, a historian and a distinguished essayist. He did not publish in book form until 1972. His best-known book was to be about Yugoslavia, *Escape from the Anthill* (1985). He was the brother of Gilbert Butler who was married to EB's first cousin Noreen Colley. Both the Colleys and the Bowens were connected with the Butlers by marriage.

I expect
the conference
It's hard not to
I wonder whether all situations
Perhaps better left undiscussed.
life (in personal life) have I ever known anything that was not still further complicated by attempts to talk it out. Is it possibly so with world affairs? It seems to me no one will keep to promises – in a big issue – so why extract them? Or better say, no one will keep to agreements . . .

I am getting worried about my relations with Eddy. He is very fond of me and has pointed that out. Till he said so, I never realized he was. He is not making any trouble, in fact is being very sweet and considerate, but I don't want him getting into a state. Leslie Hartley is coming to stay with him next week, which is a good thing as Leslie's such a nice comfortable old buffer, a tension-lowerer. There's nothing to worry about. I remember your saying you thought Eddy had more feeling for me than I realized, and I see now you were right.

. . . You must see why I am wishing so distractedly that you were here.

All my love, my dear love, Elizabeth

17 September

I have been disturbed – frightened – by E's letter about Eddy. I do hope I may be spared that confrontation – which I did [?not] spare her. If he wanted to marry her – no, what I dread is that she might want to marry him – security, that's it, and a title.[120] How could I

[120] Eddy Sackville-West was heir to the Barony of Sackville, to which he succeeded as the 5th Lord Sackville in 1962. CR does not seem to consider that Eddy's homosexuality was any bar to a possible marriage. Norah Preece, a friend in common, was told by both Eddy and EB that the other had proposed marriage, and how embarrassing it was. All one can say is that the idea of a companionate marriage seems to have been

deny that it would be the 'ideal solution' for her, remove the strain – the financial one – and there he is installed in the neighbourhood. Have I been a fool all the time? She imported him, she installed him; she sees him every day and every night. . . . If she married him, I should know what she knew when I married, and should not 'behave' half so well. It would be justice all right, if that means anything. Mind you, I don't think he intends to. Though what he intends matters much less than what she intends. If she put her will and her witchcraft to it, could his little sense of preservation stand up to it? . . . At least it has made me understand a little, and for the first time, what she has been through over my marriage. At the very thought of her marrying Eddy, the ground cracks under me. I think I should fight it selfishly – unless that way I thought I should lose her for good, in which case I might do what she did, and we should lose each other by inches – aren't we already?

20 September

Does the constraint that I had noticed between us mean that she has ceased to love me, but won't admit it to me or to herself? Does she cling to this love, to the idea of it, as a lifeline; but with half her nature think of it as a 'fairy tale', a word she once used about it. In her last letter, writing about 'disarmament' but thinking of personal relations, she wrote of how fatal it was to 'talk things out'. So she must have been thinking of doing so. I dread her letter in case it may break into that note of brutal candour which lies behind her flattering loving kindness. I cannot do without her – nor she without me.

30 September [New York]

I seem to have known nothing about coming here when I wrote that last entry, and yet I feel as if I had known for weeks. In between there

---

in the air. Michael De-la-Noye in his biography *Eddy Sackville-West* (1988) was, however, sceptical, chiefly on the grounds that Eddy, a devout RC convert, would never have married a Protestant.

has been B Court, so short and so happy. And E says she cannot give me up and so can't marry Ed. But now I am on the disarmament delegation to the UN I can't write about Bowen's Court. I feel more assured of her love than ever. It was beautiful there.

Bowen's Court, Monday, 30th September 1957

My darling. . . .

Oh you were, and are, so beloved – Utterly. The joy and ease of your just walking back, as though you'd never been away, into this always-waiting-for-you house. It's as though the whole place breathed a deep sigh, of satisfaction and of the end of a tension, when you take up life in it again.

Well, what sort of a beehive are you in now, I wonder, my beautiful, valuable and distinguished one? I realize it won't be in your power to write long letters; difficult, I quite realize, to write any, but send me just half-sheets with clues from which I can imagine the rest. I know so much of the circumstances, from what you've predicted and from your accounts of other times that I can quite easily piece the picture together when you just give me one or two clues . . .

Yesterday's (Sunday's) social programme ran through smoothly, as planned. To begin with I thought of you in the church, where you'd been with me when I arranged the flowers. Then the boys called for me about 12 noon, and we set off to motor to lunch at Blarney . . . Darling Leslie [Hartley], left alone with me for a moment, spoke of you with great and I felt genuine enthusiasm and love. Eddy confined himself to saying, 'I thought Charles looking very well,' in a rather persecuted voice. When we got to Blarney, Eddy insisted on poor Leslie's kissing the Blarney Stone, which involves hanging upside down at a great height. Leslie returned to the perpendicular quite pale, and said he had been through a terrible period of insensibility. 'I think, I just brushed the stone with my lips,' he said. Myself I think it nearly killed him.

Oh Charles I must go to bed. I've got a cold coming on, and I'm ghastly lonely. Oh how I hate the Atlantic. I would not if I were in New York. It seems so idiotic my not being there, <u>this</u> year of all years!

Can you read this, I wonder – my love, my <u>love?</u> Elizabeth

Bowen's Court, Wednesday, 16th October 1957

My darling . . .

What a harassing time you are having. Oh Charles, if it <u>is</u> to be NY and the UN, we'll still make out, somehow. I feel, myself, very agitated, I must say – somewhat trembly. It could I agree be worse – much much <u>much</u> worse. It's only that damned Atlantic. I am as you know so often in New York, and could be there often-er. I love it. Only it's the question of an interior, when I do get there. Really we must have some place of peace and calm – we've grown so much into the way of having one it would be dreadful to do without one. But we will manage.

How I wish you could <u>live</u> <u>alone</u>, for a bit. I do so by now long for the place we are in to be either your home or mine.

Oh darling, don't be distressed; don't be worried. If only we could be together and talk.

What I do long to know is, when you're likely to be coming. . . .

How agitated my handwriting seems. I <u>am</u> agitated, I can't help it.

Today I drive to Corkagh via the Butlers in Kilkenny. I'm travelling to England by sea on Thursday/Friday night.

At the moment I wonder if I ever <u>shall</u> get to Italy, as I seem to have lost my passport!

I long for news of your mother. Write to me as <u>soon as you can</u>, to the [Hotel] Inghilterra.

Oh Charles I love you so much.

Your Elizabeth

21 October

[*M, the unidentified woman Charles had known in Paris, was also in New York, and the affair was picked up again.*]

Is all this disloyalty to E? The word disloyalty doesn't belong here – or does it? I don't think so.

Hotel Vesuvius, Naples. [nd] October 1957

My darling . . .

You will be hearing from some great New York friends of mine, Kirk and Constance Askew. I had lunch with them in London on the other day, and they are on their way back (should be in NY again in early November). Kirk wants very much to get in touch with you: he will either write or telephone. Do manage to see them if you possibly can. They play a great part in my life, and are likely in the future to play a larger.

Kirk Askew owns Durlacher's Art Gallery, on 59th Street. They have asked me to stay with them (in their spacious 5th Avenue apartment) for as long as I like, this coming February.

Charles, one thing we – you – must be realistic about: I shall never be able to have a NY apartment. To earn (while there) enough to pay for one would run me ragged. I'm not allowed (under British currency restrictions) to 'touch' my USA book royalties. Therefore any spending-money I have in that country has to be made on the spot. Would you really care for the off-time company of a practically full-time female lecturer? I doubt it. It would be no kindness to you to kill myself (to all intents and purposes).

The point of this is, if we are to have an interior you'll have to provide it. It would be nice if your home were sometimes your own. Otherwise, you'll have to (very considerably) help me to pay the rent of where ever I am. How, God knows. But do face that.

Naples, which I am madly enjoying in one way, also inevitably makes me feel sad. This place was stolen from us. And for the same reason, I'm leaving the Blacks to go on to Positano, possibly Amalfi, and myself going back to Rome . . .

Oh my dear love, more than ever, ever, do take care of yourself. As I said in my cable, I am thinking of you at every turn.

Your E.

29 October

Oh I am at home nowhere now, except at Bowen's Court – and is that an illusion? At any rate I feel at home there. E's letter today about money upset me and came at the wrong moment, on the same day as M's. I suppose my letter on her being in NY had irritated her by its vague references, and she didn't see that I was genteelly hinting at what she felt she would brutally, clearly put she thought of as the 'silly' love. I'll tell him. And I, when I think of this, get quite angry. It's a thing that could be corrected with a few words if we were together, but je n'aime pas qu'on me parle de cette façon et surtout sur ce ton,[121] and then she doesn't allow for or know this other source of confidence. Anyway there it is, there was asperity in her letter, partly because her pride is involved in a delicate matter. I think that is what made for the failure in tact. I know it is, and my reaction is complicated by this other thing. Yet I never doubt that she loves me or I her. Oh what am I up to? And S. What do I feel?

Rome, Thursday, 31st October 1957

My darling . . .

Oh dear, dear, dear, if only you weren't at the far side of that wide sea. A week seems so long, even to have to wait to get your letter; how long do I have to wait to see you? I suppose you don't know at all yet when you'll be coming back, to pack up your things in Germany? I know you will see me as soon as you can, so I won't fuss.

I wonder so much how your mother is. This evening is my last evening in Rome. I sat on a terrace of the Pincio gardens watching the sun go down with tears, largely of enjoyable sentiment, not sorrow, pouring down my face. But this great place is eternal: always here to come back to. I am not so afraid of leaving it now. It is so reassuring to come back – to have more rather than less than one had remembered.

---

[121] French: 'I don't like to be talked to like that, and certainly not in that tone of voice.'

And Rome: to me, my dear love, a symbol of us.[122]

I've been so magically happy here, on my own, these last five days. . . .

Good night, good night
Your E.

1 November

I worry over E, feeling this growing sorrow at our separation. I want to come to rest in Cologne. It's all too complicated, and all my own doing.

Hotel France and Choiseul, Paris. Wednesday, 6 November 1957

Dear Beloved,

Here I am in Paris, in transit . . .

I must say, it is mad fun doing this entire drive, by road, from Rome to London.[123] I'd never before, for instance, crossed the Italian-French frontier, which we did at Ventimiglia. Finding oneself, within ½ hour, torn from the heart of one kind of civilization and plunged (as one immediately feels one is) into the middle of another. Oh yes, I had crossed that border years and years ago, when I was 21 and spending that awful winter at Bordighera, but I was too stupid and too unhappy to notice. Unhappy partly because I was bored, partly because I was wondering how, and when, and indeed partially why, to break off my engagement to that young man I told you about, John Anderson.[124]

---

[122] The last sentences of EB's *A Time in Rome* were to be: 'My darling, my darling, my darling. Here we have no abiding city.' She did not dedicate the book to CR, and 'my darling' remained unexplained, almost (apparently) generic.

[123] She was travelling back with Jean and Barry Black.

[124] This engagement was in 1921, during the period evoked in EB's *The Last September.* John Anderson was a young lieutenant in the British Army, stationed near Bowen's Court. The engagement was broken off after John Anderson visited her in Bordighera when she was on holiday with Aunt Edie. Cousin Audrey visited too – and took home with her EB's engagement ring, to post back to John Anderson.

This time, I appreciated the whole drama, and contrast, very much . . .

And oh the beauty of those towns, first in Provence, then Burgundy. The little Burgundy towns in the sunshine looked like plates of fruit, peaches and yellow plums, all set around with their alleys of yellowing trees, and with burning scarlet woods in the distance . . . I wondered why you and I could not together pull out from the world's battle and live en retraite in a small kind house in a small kind town in Burgundy. That is a part of France one could truly love.

Paris today is NOT sunny, not at all lovable, poor thing. In fact looking its worst, I'm sorry to tell you, grey and tinny, humid with patches of wintry rain, gnawed by icy winds. It is awful, driving from south to north, out of the summer, into the winter. To add to which, and can you wonder, I unspeakably miss you here at every turning, every corner . . .

I've been thinking of you in a dreaming way all these long driving days along the roads. All my love, E.

7 Linton Rd., Oxford.[125] *Thursday, 14th November, 1957*

My darling – I loved getting your telegram, indeed telegrams, in Oxford; and I hope you'll have got the one I sent off yesterday from Headington (so near my dear little former home[126]) while I was staying with the Berlins. It does make me so happy to think of you (at this moment of writing, that is) in Halifax, and with them all. Obviously selfishly at any moment I'd prefer you to be here; 'here' being with me where ever I am. But Halifax seems next best; such an always vivid and forever dear scene to me . . .

It really is being heaven here, I mean in Oxford. This is such

---

[125] Probably a guest house.

[126] For ten years from 1925, EB and Alan Cameron lived at Waldencote, a cottage converted from the coachhouse of Old Headington House.

a good time of year, anyway, with everybody in good form. Maurice [Bowra] was sweet (a peculiar adjective to apply to him, but he was) and I had a very both cosy and brilliantly entertaining time with the Berlins. Of Aline Berlin I grow fonder and fonder. I saw Miriam [Rothschild] there, among other people; looking very handsome in a scarlet taffeta coat, though with as usual a terrible black pair of Queen Mary shoes.

How I love this place, Oxford always seems to me to be a success in the sense that London (these days) is not. It's becoming considerably more mondaine, though without loss of intellectual height. One of the topics exercising everybody is, is David to be Warden of New College (the old Warden is on the point of retiring). The Wardenship seems very likely to be offered to David; the real point is, does he want to take it? I can see his mind, his powers of decision, whirring round and round, at times feverishly – rather as yours would in like circumstances . . . Shaya says, David always is driven into hysteria by any form of ganging-up opposition, and Head-of-House baiting becomes a more and more popular occupation with Senior Common Rooms.[127]

. . . Goodbye for now my beloved beloved love. You'll be writing a line, soon, to B Court won't you? Elizabeth

Charles was appointed Canadian Ambassador and Permanent Representative to the United Nations in New York. He was to take up the position in January 1958.

20 November[128]

And E, that thought gives me pause and a sense of guilt and fear. The prospect of our separation, fear that this time it might be a real separation. I love her. And S? What of her? How has she felt?

---

[127] Lord David Cecil did not become the Warden of New College.

[128] Written while flying between New York and Cologne.

Have I dealt lovingly with her? Oh I don't want to come crashing down on that plane, but apart from fear, might it not solve the insoluble state of my life? If I saw the future full of pain and old age and the death of those I love, or a change in E's love, of making S different, harming her, would it not be better to call it a day. It's been a full one, and this last happiness[129] has in a way completed it. Yet of course I don't want to die.

Bowen's Court, Friday, 20th December 1957

Oh my darling child – I don't know why I should call you that, except that I do love you so much – the beautiful and QUITE PERFECT bag has arrived from Paris. Flawless, through the post and (as you want to know) not a cent of duty to pay. I don't know when the sheer opening of a parcel has given me so much excitement and joy and pleasure. Dear love, it's more even than elegant; it's so beautiful. And though it's presumptuous to say in the same breath that anything so elegant is my style, it so much is – I mean, so much what I love and feel a sort of inspired companionship with, from the first glance. All of which you saw. The seal of its loveliness is your having chosen it.

The red stone clasps, and the sensible as well as so stylish cord handles. I wonder what French genius thought that one up, because it really did need thinking up. Because the Achilles heel of a suede bag is when it has suede handles; those tend to get rubbed-looking quite early on, which gives the whole of the rest of the bag a slight shabby look. Whereas, with cord handles . . . Every time I take that bag to a party, I shall feel in the tactile sense that you're coming too. I don't think anything, I mean any object, you could have given me could have made me more happy.

---

[129] With the unidentified M.

God grant, you and that bag and I will have happy hours, à trois, in New York.

Do you from Germany see that
[Ends]

Bowen's Court, Monday evening, 30th December 1957
Dearest love – I keep thinking about you, with odd almost hallucinated nearness and clearness, and at the same time with a sort of stress and anxiety. It was a great relief to hear your voice . . .

But I can't help feeling that though you got over the flu itself there's a horrible aftermath, and this you couldn't have been hit by at a worse time.

It does anyhow give one a sort of psychic distress. I think any departure,[130] any upheaval. Rationally one may be in the main glad to be leaving a place, and yet it's as though, when the thing comes to a point, imperfectly loved places (like, I suppose imperfectly loved people) revenged themselves in some way on one's nature . . .

So, I feel, as though I were you, a sort of distress at your 'going away'. Charles, I am being gnawed as never before by the aching hopeless wish that we were married. I mean, actually married: in a sense, as I said in another letter, I could not feel closer to you, if we were, than I already do. But I long to be practically with you, and never more than at this juncture. (For one thing, I long to be near you when you're ill – not that I should be the slightest good, but I long to be under the same roof.) I long to be taking off with you into this new phase of life. The maddening thing is, I could have been some good to you in New York.

Oh well. The whole thing only bases on my increasing, insatiable loneliness for you, I suppose. I am terrified of this loneliness

[130] CR was leaving Germany to take up his new post in New York.

becoming a sort of dementia, equivalent to a breakdown, sending me battering round and round the rooms of this house, knocking myself against the furniture – like some unfortunate bird that has got indoors (they're always coming indoors in winter here) and proceeded to entirely lose its head.

One ought not to write letters late at night.

Christmas was fun; I mean, it went well . . . My own Saturday 28th evening party (I wrote to you just on the eve of it, I think) was slightly more fraught with dynamite: Urssie (Vernon), who as you know loathes Jean (Black), whether for jealousy reasons or what I don't know, arrived in an unmistakably fighting mood – footless and dizzy with drink, exquisitely beautiful in black chiffon, naked shoulders and diamonds. A real dog-fight broke out about halfway through the turkey, involving the unfortunate Dudley Colley,[131] who was <u>bouche béante</u>.[132] I, with the frigidity of an infuriated Edwardian hostess, continued conducting a highly conventional conversation at my end of the table. I will <u>not</u> have rows at meals. Actually I think all combatants rather enjoyed themselves . . .

On Sunday afternoon (yesterday) I had a sardine party for teenagers. They were all rather sweet. After a large tea in the hall, with crackers, they disappeared (as ordered) into the depths of the house to play sardines, in the dark. At intervals there were bumps, slatherings and screams, and they all finally emerged looking rather sexy. We grown-ups (6 or 8 of us) meanwhile sat and boozed in the drawing room. It was fun.

. . . I wish one <u>could</u> telephone late at night. I love you. I hope you are sleeping well.

Elizabeth

---

[131] EB's cousin, son of Aunt Edie.

[132] French: open-mouthed.

1958

Bowen's Court, Tuesday, 21st January, 1958
Dearest love – I got your heavenly letter written on the Queen Mary this morning . . .

My beautiful, it makes me so happy to know you like the cigarette case, and to imagine it on your darling person, and being handled by you.

Last night I got snowed up here with the piano tuner, which sounds like an Aldwych farce. The blizzard came on while he was tuning the piano, and the poor creature had only a bike on which to travel the 13 miles on to Mallow. My heart sank at the idea of having him here for the night. I piled him and the bike into the car and we set off to drive to Mallow, but the roads were impossible. There were no maids in the house and no food – as I was supposed to be going out to dinner that night, but of course snow stopped that too. So Mr Speechley and I had a cultural evening. He was really far from bad, the poor little thing (except for looking like Raymond Mortimer). He pedalled bravely off on his bike early this morning.

Eddy returned at the end of last week, and I spent the week-end at Cooleville. He has had the flu 4 times and is now in the nervous breakdown stage of convalescence. Actually he was quite gay during the weekend; we went out to drinks with some neighbours of his and he drank enough whisky to float a battleship, but on Monday morning, when I went to say goodbye, I found he'd retired to his bed again and was lying with his beard in the air like a dead Assyrian. I said, 'Oh dear, how do you feel?' and he replied, 'Utterly wretched, utterly black!' I felt rather a pig driving away and leaving him, but I had an amount of things to do at home. He sounded a bit brighter on the telephone next day.

Oh bother this pen-pencil is giving out, and it's the only thing to [Ends]

Bowen's Court, Wednesday, 29th January 1958
Dearest – I've had your first New York letter, on the Mayfair [Hotel] paper. Oh what a lot you've plunged into and forthwith! All that new set of machinery to be set whirring. So many things I wonder, what your new staff (or secretariat or whatever one calls it) is like, and like to work with; what your office is like. And being plunged immediately into a meeting of the Security Council . . .

Thank God for Feb. 17th (less than 3 weeks to go now) and the chance to talk.

I suppose you have not yet found an apartment – no, how could you. Yes, I imagine the Mayfair must cost the earth: one could hardly be in a more expensive place. I do trust the Canadian Govt is paying? Wouldn't it be an economy if Sylvia went to Ottawa? Except that it would be nicer if she were in Ottawa later, while I'm in New York.

My life goes on as usual. Last week there was that complete seal-up of snow then ice – it was really rather peaceful, bringing all social life to a halt because the roads couldn't be travelled. I worked intensively at my Rome book. I'm reading a tremendous amount of Roman history, which does fascinate me: one book after another I can't put down. Why I ever read anything but history, particularly Ancient history, I can't think. I think it's its slightly abstract quality (due to distance of time) plus the almost utter absence of personality-interest which I like so much – this may sound rather perverse.

Now is the age when I should like to go to a university and really study. (I felt a solid resistance to the idea when I was student-age.) I've a theory that – at any rate to some natures, for one mine – only having had experience makes learning acceptable. When one's older, so many things become comprehensible. It's really only quite late in life that I've begun to have a desire for knowledge.

. . . Poor Eddy has been prostrate with either a fifth go of flu or a renewed onset of convalescence, including all sorts of horrors such as trembling-fits. However he is reviving now. Jean and I drove over to dinner with him the other night; when we were leaving she somehow in the dark drove her Jaguar across that immaculate Cooleville front lawn: the Jaguar bogged right down (it was a wet night) and we had to go and wake up Eddy's head man, who towed the Jaguar off the lawn with a tractor. A tremendous to-do, as you can imagine: poor Jean most upset, protesting 'I wasn't drunk!' I don't think she was.

I'm so bored without you, apart from everything else. Without you, life's like being in a half-lit room. . . . Elizabeth

17 February

Thank God E gets here tomorrow, though she is unlikely to make me more contented with my lot. Still, her coming has never been more necessary – never have I felt more strongly how unendurable my life would be without her.

2 March

E and I went to the Three Penny Opera[133] together the last night she was here, before she left for the women's college at Wisconsin where she will stay a month.[134] We were both fascinated by Captain

---

[133] *The Threepenny Opera*, adapted from John Gay's *The Beggar's Opera* (1728) by dramatist Bertolt Brecht and composer Kurt Weill, was first performed in Berlin in 1928. The production EB and CR saw was at the off-Broadway Theater de Lys.

[134] As writer in residence.

Macheath – the shape of his head, the angle of his bowler hat, the cut of his cynicism.[135] E said I was like him – especially when the 2 doxies were fighting over him and his voice went shrill with exasperation. The 3penny Opera was the thing for us – for both of us. We loved the scarifying Berlin-New York mixture, like some new potent drink served raw 'on the rocks'. E's being here has taken away the boredom. I become like a character in one of her stories – a romantic character observed with love and brought to liveliness by absurdities and vices. Only what is bourgeois life is excluded from this personage, and so of course my marriage is excluded. This is Sunday morning come round again and she has gone. I shall live on the stimulus for a few days or weeks and it will begin to fade, and I shall need restlessly my E.

Madison, Wisconsin. Monday, 3rd March 1958
My darling – I'm going to type this, as it takes up less room. It meant everything hearing your voice this morning (I hope I didn't upset Miss Brewer[136]) I was having one of my rather 'dark and cheerless is the morn, etc'[137] feelings. In future I'll leave you to telephone me; not out of economy but because I think it possibly more tactful to your office . . .

I think there could have been nothing more beautiful than those ten days – no, near fortnight – with beloved New York all as it were lit up for us. As I said to you on the telephone this morning, I am now reliving and living on every moment, so much so that I hardly yet see or feel this weird place I'm now in. I feel like someone not only under a spell but within a spell. Only one thing could have made the time more perfect, but in one way I'm beginning to learn

---

[135] Macheath was played by Jerry Orbach.

[136] CR's secretary

[137] From 'Morning Hymn' by Charles Wesley, 258 in the *English Hymnal*, familiar to both EB and CR.

the wisdom of love – if one knows a thing to be temporarily impossible, one lets other kinds of happiness together loom all the larger, and for the time compose a life in themselves. Besides being genuinely happy and cosy staying with the Askews,[138] I know it was the sensible thing to do, going there. When you've been longer in New York, we'll somehow find ourselves some sort of home life. Meanwhile, everything was so beautiful – that morning walking in the sun and scraps of snow in the Cloisters park, and coming down Montreal-like to drinks and lunch in that cosy sunny-feeling St. Moritz, all those 6 o'clock drinks in the Mayfair bar, the Sunday movie, our last heavenly evening, everything . . .

Well . . . I'm beginning to like this place better since I talked to you this morning. Having to totter down to breakfast in the cafeteria, with my eyes all still bunged up, will remain a snag – but mercifully the cafeteria is all but empty, only 4 or 5 students, glum as I am myself, crouched at the self-service tables in that vast space with glass sides overlooking that bloody frozen-and-snowed-over lake. My nightmare was that the place would be packed out, and that I'd have to join some table of clear-eyed, eager, chattery students, and be jolly with them at 7.30am. As it is, I suppose most students eat in their dormitories; only my fellow-unsociables breakfast here. The only trials are the vast slabs of suppurating buttered toast: there seemed no plain dry toast to be had. Tomorrow I must ask the girl if she can't extract some toast for the toaster for me before it has been finally processed. What I really prefer is Melba toast, but one can't hope for that in a State university, I expect.

I had lunch today at the University Faculty club, which I've very kindly been made a member of. My host said it was comparatively empty in the evenings (it was packed at lunch) so I think I shall probably dine there, when not being entertained. If I kept on being

---

[138] At 563 Park Avenue

surrounded by students I should go mad, much as I like young people. My host was a nice New Englander, Robert [K.] Presson, an Elizabethan specialist. He also showed me where there was a bar, next to the Lutheran church. He also very kindly showed me round cogent parts of this place, including the University Library which is a jolly good one, with a good Rome section, and got me a card so's I can get books out.

I have never seen so many appalling buildings as there are on this campus. I would have thought it impossible that there could be so many varieties of perverted architecture in the world, or at any rate all in the same place – mock-baroque, mock-gothic, mock-romanesque, mock-jacobean. Yet somehow when one gets over one's first horror the effect is beguiling and bold and artless. And the town of Madison itself is rather fun: obviously extremely prosperous and full of amusing shops – student vanity shops, excellent bookshops, perfumeries, bars, restaurants (really no need to eat on the University premises at all). . . . All I haven't begun to do yet is any work – I mean any connected with my employment here. However they all say there is no hurry, and that for these first few days it is just nice having me around . . .

I must stop now. I can't bear not being with you, beloved love. Your E.

Will you please tell me, point blank, what I should address my letters to you as? I feel C. Ritchie Esq is insufficient.

Madison, Wisconsin. Monday morning, 10th March 1958
My love – it was a lovely feeling of Sunday, hearing your voice yesterday morning. It made me feel so near you all day – I mean in the near up actual sense of knowing what you were doing. And it's such heaven my knowing Halifax and being able to visualize Inglis Street (so uncannily clearly, as though I were there myself) and those two houses, your mother's, Roley's, and you walking in and out of them . . .

When and if I cannot be with you, I am as happy here as anywhere else. It's a bouncy exhilarating existence, and the vast size of the place and the thousands of streaming figures in constant motion are un-claustrophobic. There's a strange blend of extreme friendliness and total incuriosity which suits me. I do see the point of the Middle West. I have been several times enough to acclimatize. Its complete self-centredness and self-sufficiency, its immense remoteness in space and ideas from anywhere else is the outstanding thing. The east (New York, etc) and Europe seem equally far away. These seem to me the only kinds of Americans I have ever met who don't have inferiority complexes, whose faces one is not in some subtle way always having to try to save for them.

The university itself is a Pentecostal mixture of races. The students I work with in my 3 classes are of extremely various kinds. They are good-humoured and good-looking, but chiefly I'm glad to say, as that's to the point, clever: quick on the uptake. Their standard in writing varies: what strikes me most is that it's unimitative, for the reason that I don't think they read much. Their work makes me realize that writing is always a form of egotism – all that varies is, to what degree. But having opted for this particular outlet for their egotism they are set on doing what they do as well as possible – so are out for criticism, and always ready to take their work back and re-cast it on other lines. Sex, in most cases, is the main theme.

The leading bright boy, or at any rate the most pushing, is inevitably a Jew – Mr Marshall Berland.[139] I must say I do see why Jews get themselves hated – always there slightly before anyone else. Mr Berland has adopted me into a sort of Deified Aunt relationship which I hope won't become rather overpowering – he is

---

139 Marshall Berland was the future author of *Cooking Without a Kitchen* (1978). He became and remained a devoted friend to both EB and CR.

always streaking round a corner, wherever I am, in his enormous turquoise-blue car. He's very bright-plumaged, not unlike a junior, Semitic edition of Stephen Tennant – only not a queer, I think. He took me for a tremendous drive yesterday, Sunday afternoon – trickling around Madison city looking at varieties of architecture and out into the surprisingly pretty countryside of small hills, woods and lakes.

Many of the Faculty (as so often) come from the east [coast]. They are a very good lot, it seems to me. In fact, this is quite a university. My two chums so far are 2 New Englanders called Mr Presson and Mr Forker,[140] who like going out drinking and going to the movies: we have had several pleasant evenings around the town. . . .

It would be a nightmare if I did not see you on April 2nd. Largely the reason why I'm happy here is that it's simply an interim before seeing you again.

All my love, my love. Oh how I wish you could suddenly be here. Your E.

University of Wisconsin. Tuesday, 18th March 1958
My darling . . .

Yes, I am enjoying myself. I like the people and the scurry and bustle. I feel at times as though I were living inside a book on a subject I wouldn't normally read – or for that matter, sitting in at a non-stop movie, not a particularly good one but one which is animated and absorbing, so that one is never bored. And I get so fond of so many of these creatures. And I enjoy working with people, if chiefly because I so very seldom do. I know I wouldn't like it permanently to work with people, but in a snatch like this it makes a change and a break.

---

140 Charles R. Forker, then a young instructor at the university, was, like Robert K. Presson, an Elizabethan specialist.

My 3 composition classes are proceeding along their normal course, quite briskly, on the usual variation of sex themes occasionally varied by violent and lurid deaths. There are one or two quite considerable operators in each class, who have the effect of keeping the others turning over . . .

Campus life is becoming extremely gay, drinking and dinner parties, etc; also long drives around the country, which actually is very pretty, in places outright beautiful, in an odd way. The parties have to take place off the campus, as alcohol is not allowed on the campus – perfectly rightly, I say benevolently, as there are unstinted means of drinking it elsewhere. I have now got those two big public lectures I had to give, which were the only things which were hanging over me, off my chest: they went quite well. I must say I also am working very hard.

I must stop. I've got to do Television. . . .

Dear, beautiful – you'll take care of yourself? Your E.

Boston Airport Sunday morning, 27th April 1958

My dearest love,

I was so glad you rang up again, yesterday evening. Your beloved voice. I hope I didn't sound too shook and sad; I did feel it. So long as I've been with your Mother and Roley, apartness from you has been bearable; but now . . . I am so endlessly glad I went to Halifax; I was even happier there than the time before, which as you know is saying much. No loss of illusion, rather an increase in one. She more fascinating and dear to me than ever; and as for Roley I feel in an odd way that he's the nearest thing to a brother (a romantic brother) I've ever had. I think I've told you I felt this before, but I felt it more strongly than ever this time . . .

Dear love, what an assignment you have ahead of you, this coming week! I feel absolutely confident that you'll not only show your mettle but make history. Oh if I could only be there, could only be there. You're already right into your stride, and you won't look back. I'm so awfully glad (now) that you're where you are; you are absolutely the right man in the right place.[141]

As soon as I get home I am going to write you a long detailed letter (like I did before) about every moment I spent in Halifax. It's obviously impossible to write a long 'story' letter from this inferno airport: I need time, space and a typewriter. I will then tell you EVERYTHING.

I haven't really got over saying goodbye to you. I don't think I felt anything except stunned. I stood for a moment . . . watching your back view walking away through the rain, towards that steam rising out of the manholes at the corner of Park Ave, and thought, we're now beginning to share the thing we have to share when we're apart: loneliness. Your figure looks heartbreakingly lonely; and as I went down to put my latchkey into the door, I thought 'What becomes of me, now?'

11 Tomorrow

That New York time was – is – one of the happiest times of our life. Wasn't it. Day after day, moment after moment. Oh my most beautiful Charles. In a queer way I can still hardly bear to write about it, as though writing about it put it in 'the past'.

. . . I'm glad in a way you're having so much to DO. I won't expect long letters while this high pressure goes on; just from time to time write me a half sheet? If only I could hear your voice.

Dear loved love, my bright and beautiful; bless you. Your Elizabeth

Bowen's Court, 1st May 1958

Dearest love. . . . Here I am, back. Everything very springlike, though spring as this country goes is late. The woods are in a sort of a green mist, with only here or there a chestnut or something in full leaf.

---

[141] On 2 May, CR took over the presidency of the Security Council of the UN.

That great pink cherry, at the top of the bank over the side lawn, is in glorious flower. The white seats on the steps have been repainted, and the lawns new-mown, so there's a smell of cut grass. Weather's fine, sunny and warm. In fact every prospect pleases, and this is a darling place. If only I wasn't feeling so bloody LONELY.

Well, Halifax. I hardly know where to begin, so much is there to tell. . . .

There follows, as after Elizabeth's previous visit to Charles's family in Nova Scotia, a very long, gossipy, blow-by-blow saga of a sociable three days with Roley and Bunny and their daughter Elizabeth in Halifax, at 141 Inglis Street, and of spending time with Lilian Ritchie up the road at 190 Inglis Street. There was implicit denigration of Sylvia in EB's emphasis on how wonderfully well she got on with them all, especially with CR's mother.

My dear love, this will be a lot for you to read in the middle of your busy onerous life. If only I could speak it all, instead of writing. If only . . . Take care of yourself, take care of yourself. As you know, you are life to me; nothing else is.

Your E.

Kildare Street Club, Dublin. Wednesday, 14th May 1958

Dearest love – yesterday I got your letter of the 8th. . . . You were right to have an 'impression' of me opening that letter – I ran through to the back hall, the instant I got back to B Court, to see if there was anything from you; my heart gave a thump of pleasure when I saw the envelope, and then (rather like a wild beast tearing back into the jungle with its prey) ran into the library and, standing with my back to the fire, in a patch of sunshine – which intervened between showers of rain – tore open the beloved envelope. Do you know, my fingers still tremble when I do – and this after 17 years – in fact rather more after 17 years; indeed slightly more each year. Though also in a way I hate lacerating (as one does an envelope) anything you've touched.

You will send me those 2 profiles, won't you: the NY Herald Tribune one and the Time one. Indeed I hope you already have. I looked hopefully at the post this morning, to see if there was a big envelope, but there wasn't. Promise you won't fail to send them.

Well you are going to have a jolly tense time, my dear dear President, in the Security Council in the near future, with the Near East. Lebanon. And this Algiers news is most peculiar. I wonder what more will have happened by the time you get this. You said you thought the Arabs would start blowing up in May.[142]

It all seems a far cry from dear dim Dublin on a wet Wednesday. I'm up here (by train) for the day; largely for the purpose of paying one of my periodic pacifying calls on my bank manager. Having got that over I'm now feeling rather relaxed and cosy, but also rendered so sleepy by the rain that I've simply retreated into my (this) club, where I shall remain till it's time to go to Kingsbridge station and catch the 6.45pm train home . . .

The bright green May hedges in the country give me awful pangs. For the last two Mays – do you realise? – you have been here: I mean, at B Court. I am so awfully horribly lonely for you. I don't think I have ever missed you so much before.

I'll write again very soon, my dear, dear love Your E.

Bowen's Court, Friday, 23rd May 1958

Dearest. . . .

Tell me how you are, tell me how you are. I do feel so worried and anxious and lonely, Charles.

I wish you could come over here, in June, after your presidency ends, and do nothing more ambitious than just sleep, and in our car trickle gently and aimlessly round this green country . . .

---

[142] From 1954, there had been a guerrilla war between the Algerian FLN and the French authorities, who in 1958 were inclining towards negotiation. By insisting that Algeria must remain French (*Algérie Française*), the settlers and army in Algeria contributed to the downfall of the Fourth Republic in France that May.

I long to talk to you about Diana's book[143] . . . It really is amazingly satisfactory. It seems so much the perfect Diana style that I wonder whether Diana could have achieved it for herself. Unless one is habitually a writer (in the sense that I am) I've a feeling that in writing a book about oneself which should be expressive, one would require to have a style designed for one, as it were at once created and tailored for one – in the sense that a great dress house creates clothes <u>for</u> a particular person . . .

The only thing I thought a cracking mistake was the reproduction of all those letters between her and Duff, pre-marriage. Not that they were too intimate – in a queer unnerving way they were quite the contrary. They were like two people sweating blood to give a situation (or rather, a relationship) an immense build-up – for the benefit of each other. Surely people who are immensely in love and immensely <u>liés</u>,[144] and who have spent immeasurable time together, are more <u>taciturn</u>? I mean, I would have expected there to be a secret vocabulary, innumerable terms of reference, which made it unnecessary for anything to be <u>gone on about</u>, or described, or explained? One would somehow expect letters between people who are very intimate, very much at one in their associations and memories, to be almost unintelligible to the outside world – because of being written so much in words of private reference that it amounted to a code. It's enough, usually, to say: 'I had lunch in that place where there is a canary' – but with Duff or Diana, the return to any place associated with the dear one occasioned pages of descriptive, do-you-remember prose. . . .[145]

I love you, and want you and miss you so unbearably much.

Your E.

---

[143] The first of Lady Diana Cooper's three volumes of memoirs, *The Rainbow Comes and Goes*. CR, as a close friend, had read the book in manuscript.

[144] French: bonded, close.

[145] This is a curious paragraph in view of the nature of her own letters to CR.

Bowen's Court, Monday, 16th June 1958
My darling love – I got your 'good journey' cable. I'm not now actually going to Rome[146] till Friday next, 20th, as I have got to wait to cope with a Holiday magazine photographer who is arriving at Shannon on Wednesday. I wrote an article for Holiday about B Court, do you remember, and they are of all times sending the photographer, to do the illustrations, of all times now! It seems best to get it over, and I've managed to change my Pan-Am air reservations.

This is written in Cork general post office, standing up. I've come in for the rather depressing purpose of selling a good deal of silver, and some pieces of good jewellery I unearthed. I am having the most unspeakable dreary financial crisis.

Can you possibly send me a hundred dollars? No use beating about the bush and saying I hate asking you: obviously I do; but would be a help. Will you send the cheque to the Rome address and I'll post it back to my Dublin bank. Everything will be all right when I've got the Rome book done . . .

One way and another, this is an awful summer. I live on thinking about you.

Your E.

18 June
I don't even write to my M[other]. As for E, I feel further from her than ever before in my life. Another visit to NY and meeting on those terms will separate me from her more thoroughly than if I never saw her. I fear the transition from love to friendship which I used to hope for. I dread her losing me – for myself, I dread it. She was perhaps right when she said ironically could I not do that 'bold thing' and take a plane and go to visit her in Ireland. Nothing stops me but conventionality and Syl, that passive power. Why else am I

[146] To do more research for *A Time in Rome.*

spending a week with the S's[147] in July rather than at B Court. No, all I care about is my health and my job – it's not true, E my love.

Villa Aurelia Rome. 23rd June 1958
My dearest – Your letter with the cheque came today. Very fast! This was twice what I asked if you could send me. You are very good – and I only desperately hope it isn't too great an embarrassment to your own finances. For the present, I shall take it as a present: I have a reasonable hope that I'll be able to make you an equivalent present back in the course of the autumn. Thank you, darling. I won't waste paper telling you how I fell into my present melancholy state, but I'll tell you later.

One fact I'm facing: I can't go on carrying Bowen's Court. I'll have to get out of it somehow. And I'm not sure that it really would break my heart if I did. Its virtue to me these last years (while you've been in Europe) has consisted in its being our home. Lately, since I've come back from New York, the house has become one great barrack of anxiety.

Here is lovely. I'd never been in Rome in June before. It's hot but not too hot; really not hotter than an English or Irish June, when it goes all out, can be. All the oleanders are in flower, and the town is bright yellow in the sunshine – at sunset, looked down at from one of the high-up terraces of this villa, it all turns treble-yellow, liquid gold. This Villa Aurelia is delightful – not architecturally beautiful, but spacious and with mirror-like marble floors. It's rather like staying in an Embassy. Heavenly Italian servants – how good they are! The Robertses[148] are sweet – I forget if I ever described them to you? They became great friends of mine that winter I was in Rome . . .

You see, if you were here – if you were here –

---

147 Sylvia's brother Peter, his wife Fran, and their son Jamie.

148 Laurence and Isabel Roberts: he was director of the American Academy in Rome, where EB had previously done a spell as writer in residence.

It's nice drinking before-dinner vodka on ice on a terrace lit only by candles, packed with white oleanders. I keep watching the illuminated drawing room window, as people come stepping through it out on to the terrace, as though you were going to be the next to be seen in silhouette.

Now I'm here, I'll be writing you many letters . . .

Goodbye for now, only for now – darling love. Your E.

Villa Aurelia, Rome. Thursday, 25th June 1958

My darling . . .

Charles, I say this seriously: you and I must, please, have a spell of time in Rome together before one or the other of us dies. I often have the queerest sensation, when I am here, that you and I are breathing the same air, seeing the same scenes. And so many men I see walking about Rome are (as I often told you) just slightly like you – the same high forehead, carriage of the head, cut of the jib, even sometimes the same quick walk. But instead of this being a happy hallucination, I should like it one day to be reality.[149]

I'm leading a very gay, amusing, glamorous, sumptuous life. As I said the other day to Isabel Roberts, 'This is what I hoped life was going to be like, when I was eighteen!' Floods of exquisite people, everybody so nice to me. A Frenchman said the other day, 'This June Rome, we call "the Rome of the terraces"'. One charm I find about the parties, is that nobody gets drunk – unlike much of America and indeed my dear little set in Ireland. The atmosphere is romantically flirtatious but not sexy.

The French ambassador – which I had forgotten – is Nancy's 'Colonel'.[150] He is having a high old time rattling around in the

---

[149] They never did have 'a time in Rome' together.

[150] Colonel Gaston Palewski, with whom Nancy Mitford had an affair in London during the war, afterwards moving to Paris to be near him. The affair became one-sided and gradually petered out; in 1969 he married someone else.

Farnese palace, rearranging it, digging out fascinating objets which had been put away, and adding things of his own. (He had rather a flair for objets and pictures when he was in Paris, do you remember.) I imagine he's being rather universally amorous, too, as the Farnese is now known, in Rome, as l'Embrassade Française.[151]

I am feeling a little scared of Saturday night, when I shall have to go all alone to an enormous dinner party at the American Embassy, followed by that Origo ball I told you about. Alone, because the Roberts have got to make an emergency over-night dash to Naples. I felt like crying off the dinner and the ball, but I think it would be thought – and, indeed, be – rather muffish of me if I did. I shall wear that evening dress I bought in New York, buy some long gloves and elegant evening sandals here, and try to feel as un-shy as I should at my age! But really after my life mousing around in Co.Cork, all this is rather a change, you know. To you – my beloved and beautiful Ambassador – it would be an average existence . . .

Oh my dear one . . . How can I ever be unhappy, with you to think of? Your E.

3 July

E writes that B Court has become for her a Barrack of Anxiety and that she has to face the fact that she can't keep it up. She had only done so because it might be OUR home. I am distressed but what can I expect? Why should she? The question is whether I can contribute money to keep it going. The trouble is that it IS my home, but that I get the pleasure of it at her expense in money and worry. If we were married in reality it would be different of course. E could contribute to its upkeep. Certain things are catching up with me – one is that I may do E harm. I can't believe it though. I want her to keep B Court – well, the answer is to offer a $1000 pa for

---

[151] The sixteenth-century Palazzo Farnese houses the French Embassy in Rome.

the purpose. It might do the trick. But does she want it? And have I got it?

6 July

I spent last weekend at the Collins at Hunt's House, Hopewall NJ.[152] E has so often written to me from there and has described the house and people, so that I feel as if I were picking up a book in the middle and had read the earlier part before. Catherine [Collins] was cutting back the syringa bush by the drive when I came up to her and began to talk about E. 'She is the YOUNGEST person', she said. Yes she is, and I began to try to remember when this first struck me about E. It is since she has got older only. Yet it's what I thought when I first saw her body. How many years ago – yes 17 years it must be. Is this power of enjoyment, this immediate responsiveness anything to do with being a writer? Is her art the secret of her strength? No, that sounds absurdly portentous.

Bowen's Court, Saturday, 5th July 1958

My beautiful . . .

It's most fascinating imagining you at Hunt's House. Quite uncanny. If you telephone, you'll see the telephone in the coat-closet in which I've so often sat talking to you. I've never been at HH in summer: to me it's a winter or spring house. I hope there won't be too much of a CROWD. I wonder if you'll see that queer little cemetery, just a stone's throw from the house – I am very fond of it. I have so often wandered about in it, looking at the old gravestones and thinking about you. Not that there's any connection between you and ancient gravestones, but that place is a queer, semi-haunted, seductive place in which to think . . .

I wept, leaving Rome. It was a most beautiful evening. My departure hour was around sunset, with those little hill-towns one

---

[152] Home of Alan Collins, head of Curtis Brown, EB's NY literary agents.

sees from the airport powdered over the mountains like pink sugar.

You're right: that fortnight has done me all the good in the world. Nothing, in a summer in which I've got so tense through not being able to see you, could have been more ideal. It was at once a reviver and a balm.

When do you go to Halifax? Your mother (in her letter-before-last) said July 15th. I had another letter from her a few days ago, with press-cuttings about beloved Elizabeth (your niece) and her tremendous examination triumphs. There was a charming, romantic photograph of Elizabeth in her white graduation dress. You know, you are an exceptional family, you Ritchies!

. . . I hope you know the joy your letters give me? They are my life line. I'll write at greater length in a day or two. E.

Bowen's Court, Monday, 21st July 1958

It was like an answer to prayer hearing your voice on the telephone on Friday evening. I shall never be able to tell you how it felt. It was the end of what had somehow been an unusually awful day; and I felt at snapping-point. Oh my darling darling love, what a lot you mean, and what strength and reassurance your love has the power to give me . . .

You've strengthened me, cheered me and cleared my mind over this decision I've had to take. Yes, I'm giving up Bowen's Court. I'll take the first step, in writing to my young cousin Charles Bowen, now in Nyasaland. He, as you know, is my heir, and I always had told him I'd like to make the place over to him while I was still alive. I've now told him that unless he can take it over, and that almost at once, I shall have to sell it. I've also told him not to feel badly if his answer about the takeover has to be 'no'. I'm not prepared to sacrifice the remainder of my life to this dear place, and I want him to see I don't feel he 'should' do anything that wouldn't be good for his future. I think he could make a go of the place; but ideally he should have had 3-5 years more in Nyasaland, to make some more money first.

In a way, do you know, I shall be not so upset if he says 'No'.[153] I dread a making-over of property leading to any form of family friction. I shouldn't mind if a religious order bought this place and it became a monastery or a convent. I should feel God had moved in (if in RC form) and I'd prefer that to the house's being inhabited by mean people. However, one must just wait and see.

No news, particularly. Edie Colley left on Saturday; I am working very hard at the Rome book and leading the usual minor social life. Oh Charles, I am getting bored here, and that's a fact. I suppose it's the effect of hardening my heart: when one can no longer afford to support an illusion, one rather welcomes seeing it break down – or perhaps rather, in this case, run down.

So long as we have each other.

All my love Your E.

27 July

E writes that she must sell B Court. I feel as if my home was going – the other home I have had since The Bower[154] sold. I would willingly pay money to keep B Court going, but my practical worldly instinct tells me that would not be a good idea. One lump sum won't save it, paying year after year would be gênant[155] for E, and at any moment if I had to stop the same problem would be there. Besides, I think she wants to get out of it – out of her life there. What is driving her away? Is it only financial or is there something else – to do with Eddy? Some complication she has got into? Is it the pull of Rome – I mean the city, not – at any rate, yet – the religion? I know the money question is real enough. I just wondered if there was anything additional. Does she know how much this will

---

153 He did say 'No.'

154 The Bower was the Ritchie family home in Halifax, sold when CR was a young man, its semi-rural surroundings almost immediately covered by building developments.

155 French: awkward, embarrassing

hurt when the time comes? She writes, 'I am getting bored here and that's a fact. I suppose it's the effect of hardening my heart – when one can no longer afford to support an illusion, one rather welcomes seeing it break down – or perhaps rather, in this case, run down', and again she speaks of her life of 'ambiguous futility'. I for my side have been these last days sunk in summer New York.[156]

Bowen's Court, Tuesday, 2nd September 1958
My darling – your letters have given me such a tremendous idea what you are doing, and sense of your life . . .

Now, at this moment, you'll be at Halifax. I take it you've gone there without Sylvia – after all, nicer for all. I sent you a telegram this morning. It seems a long time since I wrote; it's been not easy, with Audrey in the house (no fault of hers). Any time I've had, I've been working at the Rome book – my only chance of solvency is to get it finished. My finances are being a nightmare; the continuous kind of worry that drains the ordinary happiness out of everything (except you). However, I shall see daylight sooner or later, I expect. The sadness (and that is an understatement) of giving up this house will at least be compensated for more peace of mind. [*sic*] Wasn't it the Stoics who defined happiness as 'freedom from pain'? At the moment that's all I ask for.

And all I hold to is, seeing you in October. . . .
[Ends]

Bowen's Court, 23rd September 1958
Dearest, it was wonderful to see your handwriting again . . . And THANK you, my darling, for the cheque. A 1,0000 [*sic*] times. I feel

---

[156] Lack of money was, overwhelmingly, the determining factor. But the 'illusion' she could no longer support was that CR would one day come and share life with her at Bowen's Court, and 'ambiguous futility' was her bleak assessment of her situation. This was hard for CR to acknowledge to himself. There was no 'additional' factor.

awful letting you send it, specially such an enormous one as that. More than a hundred pounds. It is a tremendous help, at this juncture, as I'm so awfully anxious to clear things off. This must, please understand, darling, only be a loan: with any luck I'll be able to give it back to you in the course of the autumn, and I hope, even, earlier rather than later. Meanwhile I do pray you haven't run yourself short, with everything so infernally expensive? I should feel ghastly if I thought you had . . .

Oh Charles, my dear love, you are good. I am beginning to get out of the wood (financial). All sorts of kindly suggestion are being offered me, about my future. It now sounds just possible I may sell the land and keep the house, putting some of the money I would get from the land into reconstructing the house slightly, so's it could be run on a whole lot cheaper basis. I could de-rate, I mean have the rates considerably reduced, apparently, if I moved out of and emptied the top floor and the basement floor. That would mean making a small upstairs kitchen. In fact, if everything could be worked out, and reorganized (and paid for) I might be considerably cosier than I am now. It would be like living in a much smaller house carved out, as it were, from the middle of Bowen's Court. And I could concentrate the more pleasing of my belongings in the far fewer rooms – at present, the sensation of all these indoor great open spaces, many of them running to rack and ruin, has been among the things which have been getting me down . . . I shan't, however, embark on any of this for quite a bit of time. My immediate idea is to put the house on half-commission, in fact quarter-commission, and shut it up, with a caretaker, for the next 6 months or so. At present, wherever I am, B Court and what it keeps costing (at the present rate) is on my mind.

I must always have a home, because WE MUST have a home. As has been pointed out to me, this house, qua building, would be difficult to sell (though land's always easy to sell). So why (they say) go to the expense of establishing myself elsewhere, when possibly this house might have to be left to rot (unbearable thought). Anyway, I shan't have to take any final decision before I see you. It will mean, as you can imagine, the world to me to talk things over with you. You see, apart from the world of love I have for you, you are my greatest friend. Yours is the judgement to which I attach most, and I perpetually find myself needing your advice . . .

I'm reading that novel extracted from Russia, that there's been so much talk about – Boris Pasternak's *Doctor Zhivago.* Shaya, who's been much concerned in its fortunes, sent it to me.

I must stop, or we shall arrive late for tea at Eddy's: a fine to-do would be involved! . . .

All my love, all, dear blessed one. Your E.

Elizabeth closed up Bowen's Court and went to New York for eight months, writing for American magazines to make money. Her friends and relations in Ireland believed she was having a nervous breakdown on her feet, and they may have been right – she communicated with them hardly at all, and bills and wages at Bowen's Court were left unpaid.

Charles Ritchie was still in New York, at the United Nations. Sylvia was with him.

7 November

E arrives tomorrow. . . . I must try to keep off the drink while she is here, otherwise I'll wreck everything.

9 November

No this is definitely not so good – not good at all. I knew it wouldn't be. Oh Hell – damnation oh balls-aching oh Damn Blast and eternal fucking Hell. This is unbelievably boring. However she is here, that's the point and worth it all. She says, 'I would like to die or live in a different way.' She looks less well, thinner, tired, cheerful – and it is all right – at first I thought not, but it IS.

14 November

Dinner – it doesn't quite bear thinking of – it would be fine if there hadn't been so much before, if one or the other of us didn't notice the difference, as we both pretend not to do. E has a look of feverishness and her cheerfulness doesn't seem solid.

7 December

Dined with E last night. Impossible to put down the mixed feelings – better not to try. Is this the wreckage of love? Or is it love? Once I was frightened of her clinical eye, now I am even more frightened of my own. I have for years known that if I was incapable of loving her it would be because my power of feeling was gone. We fear old age and drink, we harbour resentments. We know that the best is gone, we are intertwined. I am at an age when I am frightened of age and have a merciless eye for the things that are in store for me. She is indestructible. Thank God I can telephone her now and find her in the same city. Yes I am frightened of what we could do to each other, if we were without charity.

21 December [Halifax, Nova Scotia]

All this time I have been in undercover, underground dialogue with E. It came to the surface today as I read her Rome book [typescript]. This is the mind and the being with whom I wrestle in Love's queer civil war. No – the wrestle is not with her mind and being which I love, but with her will – with the pressure she is beginning remorselessly to apply to me. She talks of the 'slow burn' of her resentment. I feel that, mixed with love towards her. I want her to be unselfish and let me be selfish. I can hear M[other] fussing on the telephone – or not fussing, intelligently planning. I see in E too, and perhaps in myself, as old age approaches,[157] this restless exercise of the will, the impatience to make plans into realities and hurry on.

---

[157] He was 52.

part three

1959-1973

1959

Charles Ritchie preserved none of Elizabeth Bowen's letters to him between early October 1958 and 1 August 1959, a period which was, for her, one of deep distress, and anxiety about the future.

17 January [New York]

Chastened, that's what I am, and I had it coming to me. I am no more good to the girls young or old. . . . I am off to Mexico day after tomorrow – quite why I can hardly remember. E and I both realize that we had in that scene gone too far – come to the very edge of the end. We sheered away from it in horror. We have both by the same reaction slammed down the lid on that exploration of pain and resentment. We are to be on the surface and stay there. We both leave on almost the same day for our 'holiday'.

18 January

E and I went to El Morocco.[1] It was like the second or third time we met and went dancing at the 400. She loves dancing, and I take

[1] El Morocco, nightspot at 1036 Second Avenue, New York. The 400 in London was a nightclub off Leicester Square.

her very seldom – hardly ever. She says that I have changed more in this last year than since she knew me – got older, more respectable – that she is younger than I. She thinks this change may be due to the daily commerce of the UN and she may be right.

27 January [Mexico]

I could manage my NY life if it wasn't for E, and perhaps she could manage hers better if it wasn't for me. Living in NY is for me a game, complicated, requiring self-discipline of a kind if it's to be played successfully or even enjoyed . . . But the game blows up in my face once it's a matter of E and myself. Oh, how she fills my mind and imagination, infects me by her despair, and in her absence how impossible it is to forget her. 'She is a witch but a good witch', R[oley] said. I sometimes almost believe it and that it is a case of 'Possession'. And the peace of this release from pressure, this temporary let-up from emotion, and this happy easy being together with S[ylvia].

5 February [New York]

This wild wind, after the spring-like day when E and I walked in the Park . . . We talked too – we dared to, for the first time in weeks.

16 February

[*Charles has been absorbed by a new love affair*]

Of course E has found me dreary, and S too – a crabby sad old man. A happy guilty day, full of betrayals – oh God I thank you. I know it sounds in bad taste to thank God for such unconventional blessings. I had lunch with E in a dark restaurant. She had just come in from writing the last chapters of the Rome book and was in that extraordinary state of natural fascination. She says she thinks I have become a queer at 50 and that I am in love with NAR[2] as we telephone each other twice a day every day.

---

[2] Norman Robertson, then Under-Secretary for External Affairs in Ottawa.

10 March

E says that three manhattans[3] make me quite crazy. I think she is right. She drank four tonight, just quietly, prior to going out to dinner with a girlfriend of hers. But there, her drinking – which has certainly grown to quite some proportions – is the aftermath of strain, of doing positive work. She hardly notices what she is putting away. . . . She was suddenly hurt and resentful at not having been asked by Stephen Spender to contribute to those tributes to Rose Macaulay.[4] Instantly I felt the outrage of this – like Roley being, perhaps, passed over for this judgeship. That is a real sign of love, that sense of non-appreciation by others of those one loves. I'll never forgive Stephen Spender for that . . . She wanted to know if I would go with her to Tennessee Williams's play about an aging actress attempting to keep the flames of love alight with a younger boy-friend[5] OR to an ice-hockey match. I think the latter is more suitable to us. How can one alternate between love and the desire to denigrate that love, as I do with her. Once – no, never – once, I was going to say, it was pure love. But only when we were apart. Together the irritant has always operated, irrespective of age, and after each outrage the bond has become more unbreakable. Hell, that's the result of four manhattans. Now I'll go to bed.

16 March

I still don't know what I should do with these damned diaries. At least I do know – destroy them. Perhaps the Bank will be bombed with them in it. What bothers me is not only what is in them, but

---

[3] A cocktail, whisky and vermouth

[4] The writer Rose Macaulay, an early supporter of EB and her writing, died 30 Oct 1958 aged 77. The magazine *Encounter*, of which Stephen Spender was co-editor, carried a tribute 'The Pleasures of Knowing Rose Macaulay' in the March 1959 issue, with contributions from various authors.

[5] Tennessee Williams's *Sweet Bird of Youth*, starring Paul Newman and Geraldine Page, premiered at the Martin Beck Theatre in NY on 10 March.

what is left out: my love for Sylvia and my life with her, my thoughts every day about my mother and Roley, not to mention my work which takes up so much of my waking time.

23 May [or 24?]

Reading Elizabeth Jenkins's 'Queen Elizabeth'.[6] E has been reading it too and is fascinated by the picture of this 'one-idea'ed' woman, in whom she sees something of herself. She was ranting the other day against the sorrows, not of the very rich, but of the moderately rich. 'Fortnum and Mason sorrows', she calls them – as to whether the new curtains are double silk lined, or a new kind of morning glory can be got from the seed catalogue. What a fool I was to leave her to go to the country this weekend. We could have had lunch at the Plaza Bar and walked in the Park.

What about the prospect of going to England in the summer? Perhaps I might take a shot at it, but it immediately brings up the problem of how much of my short time should I spend in Ireland? What will Sylvia do in the meantime? Is it really worth all the scenes and schemes involved? I am getting old and tired of concealment, and intrigue, which once amused me, now worries me.

. . . I miss my E down in the country, and how much more shall I miss her in a month's time when she goes reluctantly back to Ireland. If we do not love each other in the romantic way of before, there we are still and always (?) embarked in the same ship. Separation is hard to tolerate.

28 June

Marshall to lunch with me at L'Aiglon.[7] I had a hangover which helped. He talked of E. He loves and reveres her as I did once.

---

[6] *Elizabeth the Great*, published by Victor Gollancz in 1958.

[7] Marshall Berland was EB's former student at the University of Wisconsin. L'Aiglon was a smart restaurant on E 55th Street, NY.

I mean in the same way for her goodness, intelligence, and generosity of heart. He memorizes passages from her books and is in love with her. Twenty years later she is still able to mould and to inspire another young nature. I told him that even when she was gone and however long he lived, her quickening influence would still work on his imagination. He seemed so like myself when young.

151 Old Church St., Chelsea SW3. Saturday, 1st August 1959

My dearest love,

. . . I was glad you didn't ring up; I don't think we could either of us have borne it. It was so queer being in that apartment, those last hours, with our 'black hole'[8] just round the corner, on P[ar]k Avenue, one block away. Now, you'll so soon be living on Pk Av. Do go into the 'black hole' occasionally and have a drink for both of us – though of course that would be silly with your own (home) drinks so nearby. But, do.

. . . Marshall B saw me off. I wouldn't let him come further than the airport bus terminal (I mean in New York). He was very sad, poor child; it went to my heart so much that I nearly cried.

The journey was easy though uncomfortable. It took longer than I'd realized; I didn't get to the house (151) till 5 o'clock on Friday, (yesterday) afternoon. I took a cracking big sleeping pill and rolled into bed. BOAC,[9] which I was flying on, don't seem to air-condition their planes, and this one was a furnace. The more height we made, the hotter it seemed to get. And I must tell you the British, which most of the passengers were, are very smelly. I noticed it at once. Do you remember how several times in New York I said how tremendously smelly a London crowd would be, in anything like that heat? On my BOAC plane this proved true – even

---

[8] Probably the subterranean bar at L'Aiglon.

[9] British Overseas Airways Corporation, the British long-haul state airline until merged with British European Airways (BEA) in 1971 to form British Airways (BA).

though the passengers were quite good-class. A pretty little redhead next to me stank like a badger. So in spite of sleeping pills I didn't sleep much, and was but glad to be off the plane at London airport!

I think I told you, my two hostesses[10] here are away, till next Wednesday. So I have this very pretty spacious house, and garden, all to myself. Today I immediately unpacked my typewriter and started typing away at the 'Christmas' story I began in Connecticut and had hoped to finish in New York. I've hardly had time to realise yet that I've left NY. I feel I'm simply in some other part of it. My way of life, typing away and eating things out of the icebox continues so much the same. I still feel distinctly sleepy and tired.

Sunday

. . . I am going on with this letter where I left off yesterday – in a wicker chaise longue in the garden. It's fun having the garden.

Charles, I can't tell you how lovely London is looking. It's completely knocked me flat – I've fallen in love with it all over again! Glittering fresh paint, of every possible pretty colour, endless striped awning, trees everywhere (I [had] forgotten how many trees!) and most of all FLOWERS, liberally all over the place – in window-boxes, along in front of the houses. And the whole place looks as clean as a new pin, and as fresh as the month of May – not, as I'd expected, the frowstiness of August. I speak chiefly, of course, of SW3, which so far I've barely been outside of. In the evenings I walk about the roads and streets in a dream, dining at one or another small restaurant – there are now masses of them all along Kings Rd and Fulham Rd, quite a number of them quite elegant – charming on these warm evenings, with the doors standing open. I'm surprised to find how many people there are 'in town' – I mean, considering this is August Bank Holiday. I cannot imagine a lovelier place for you and me to be. Imagine if we had this house all to ourselves – you and

[10] Helen Arbuthnot and her woman friend.

me, sitting in this garden and walking in these pretty streets, past these enviable and fleuries little houses, in the evening.

What's come over London (in the favourable sense!) I can't imagine. I suppose actually this change for the better's been going on for a long time. Really, now it's very much more attractive, pretty, stylish and gay-feeling than ever it was before the war (I mean in the 1930's). And really a lot of nice-looking people around. Sooner or later, do you know, I would awfully like to come back and again live here. It's being so different from what it was would make living here like starting life all over again – Oh it would, now, be such a perfect city for you and me . . .

Tuesday

Your beloved letter came this morning: still no address to write to. . . . This morning I had a nice drink with Spencer [Curtis Brown] in the Ritz bar. Then my cousin Hubert B[utler] who's in London came for a drink here: we sat here in the garden.

Thursday

Just had your telegram: oh my beautiful. . . .

This week-end I'm going to stay with my friends the Ryans. I don't think you knew them? Rachel's a great chum of mine; he is A.P. Ryan, on the Times – a rather nice and amusing though Balliol-y[11] character. After that I return here till Friday of next week. I am then going for a fortnight to Stratford-on-Avon, where I've been offered a flat: rather fun. I shall be staying with various friends, but want to have Stratford as a base, to keep my typewriter in. Go on writing to here, my love, till I definitely confirm Stratford and send you the address. I'm so much enjoying London, and being so gay, that I'm quite sorry to leave, but feel I ought to have some country air – as you said.

---

[11] A.P. Ryan (1900-1972) joined *The Times* in 1947 and was assistant editor and literary editor until 1968. Men from Balliol College, Oxford, were stereotyped as being formidably clever, and politically left-wing.

Beloved Urssie V is to be in London next week. I'm awfully glad; I realise I long to see her. We meet for dinner next Wednesday (12th) at Quaglino's,[12] imagine us.

Are you well, oh Charles? I am except that it does make me feel ill and uneasy and lost, being separated from you. I'm so awfully glad you went to Wolfville, and that your mother was better while you were there.

Oh my love – Your E.

Monk's House, Suffolk. Sunday, 16th August 1959
Darling Charles . . . As you'll have gathered from my telegram it 'unsettles' me desperately thinking of you back in New York again, and my not being there. The few ghastly days – and mercifully they were few – in which I was in New York when you weren't there (I mean, just before I left) were as bad to me as these ones: you in New York, me not there. However I feel this too much to 'go on about it' – it's no good letting too much distress come into a letter, we must get through these next months as best we can. In a way, once 'a parting' is behind one a meeting comes nearer . . . Goodness, we're half through August! On the assumption – which in fact is more than assumption, it's what my life is based on – that we are together again in January, there are now only 4 whole months – Sept, Oct, Nov, Dec – to be lived through till I set eyes on you . . .

You are beloved to offer me 'help out' money – that is, immediate current expense money – if I need it. Actually I don't think I shall; or at least at the moment it certainly doesn't seem so. My current account (bank) is in a quite healthy state; the overdraft is 'sealed up' in a different account; and it's that, I gather, that my 'helpers'[13] are going to pay off for me – me gradually, under an

---

[12] On Bury Street, St James's, SW1.

[13] The Vernons and the Blacks, and probably the Butlers.

arrangement to be worked out by an auditor (at my wish) to pay them, gradually, back. Edmund Carroll, my solicitor in Ireland, has two thousand pounds of mine from the sale of trees, with which he is clearing up Bowen's Court back accounts and paying the current wages and expenses. Over the matter of the sale of the house, my cousin Gilbert Butler is being extremely helpful.

Of course, as you know, my whole wish is to get the whole cable cut.

My literary future seems rather good. My London publishers[14] v enthusiastic about the Rome book; I spent a nice long day with them planning various things about its production, and the various things about how it's to be 'handled'. I also realise I've got another book (in existence) ready to come out a year after the Rome book – i.e. a collection of essays, prefaces, etc,[15] which will be on the lines of *Collected Impressions*, if you remember those.

Besides it's being pleasant to be in England now, it's v good policy, I realized. It was time I 'showed', and I'm awfully touched by the tremendous welcome back everybody has given me. In a way, the idea of being a 'career woman', and having my finger in a number of pies again – indeed, probably, rather more pies than formerly – rather fascinates me. I like this new, rather flashy, robber-baronish, up-and-coming England, and feel well able for it. I think really I had become panicked by the decay and depression and dishevelment of those immediately post-war years in London: my one idea was to barricade myself into Bowen's Court as far as possible from the hideous scene. But now the scene has changed, or is at least very rapidly changing.

I don't, all the same, regard those B Court years as a mistake. In many ways they were worth a lot to me. The long and the short of it is, it was worth trying.

---

[14] Longmans

[15] *Afterthought*, 1962, published in USA as part of *Seven Winters and Afterthoughts.*

I wish there were likely to be any way you could be in London for a term of years – other than as High Commissioner. Do you know what I mean? A way like you are in New York: highly concentratedly busy at something important, but free-ish, 'out of hours'. By hook or by crook, by any means, it would be lovely if you and I were setting out on a London spell again, about 1½ or 2 years hence. I've learned so much in New York about making out that I think I could sustain a small but I hope pleasing London apartment not too expensively, and successfully – that is, if I had (as it is to be hoped that, by that time, I shall have) no other liabilities of any kind elsewhere.

It continues to be amusing comparing London with New York, [and] England (what I've seen of it) with the US such as I this summer saw. In a way, I'm living much the same kind of life. It's amusing going from a series of US weekends and visits with English ones – your and my endless inexhaustible interest in moeurs, and to a point anthropology. Last week-end with Patrick and Rachel Ryan in their Elizabethan home in Surrey (Belchworth, a countrified pretty part) was fun – village ladies, WI[16] type, to Saturday afternoon tea: we play treasure hunt and other games in the garden. We drank tremendously: Patrick's a host with an ever-open bar.

This week-end I'm with Spencer CB[17] in his exquisite Elizabethan home in Suffolk. The floors heave and ripple with age, the windows have leaded diamond panes. I'd hate to live in a house of this age (400 years, I suppose) but for two days it's fun. Angus Wilson[18] lives here and came to dinner last night; he's a gay little thing. This evening we're going over to him for drinks . . .

All my love Your E.

---

[16] Women's Institute

[17] Spencer Curtis Brown

[18] Angus Wilson (1913-1991), author of novels, short stories and literary essays, lived in Bradfield St George, Suffolk, with his partner Anthony (Tony) Garrett.

151 Old Church St, SW3. Wednesday, 19th August 1959
My darling . . .

Today I am going to Stratford-on-Avon. My address (which I'll also cable you) will be c/o Mme Zajdler, 19 College Street. I've taken the flat there for 2 weeks, but don't think I'll stay all that time – probably till about August 28th. I'll cable again when I again change address. I do want to get a lot of work done while I'm there, and finally clear off the commissioned jobs which represent my great money-making pay, and get back to 'writing'. I've conceived a great London 'piece' – this peculiar 'vision' of London I've had, these last 2 weeks, which I want to call 'Like Nothing So Far', or 'Like No Other' – or something like that. It might possibly do for the New Yorker. (By the way, have you read Thurber's *The Years With Ross*[19]? It really is fascinating.) . . .

I went up to Hampstead yesterday afternoon to see Elizabeth Jenkins and congratulate her on *Elizabeth the Great.* She was looking well and pretty, and has painted her house pale pink outside on the proceeds. All that part of St John's Wood on the Finchley Road route to Hampstead is completely gone – rather elegant pale yellow brick blocks of flats rising out of the gardens of what used to be those Gothic cottages ornés. In fact all that NW part of London, beyond Lords Cricket Ground, now looks very continental. I wondered if I [would] like to live there, but I don't think so – I'd rather have a stab at SW, next time.

Goodbye for now, dearest dearest love, Your E.

19 College St., Stratford-upon-Avon. Sunday, 23rd August 1959
My darling. . . . Now you'll be in the new apartment.[20] You will like those high, large rooms, I can quite see; and the space – I mean, having more opportunity to call your soul your own. I'm awfully

---

[19] James Thurber, published 1957.
[20] On Park Avenue

glad I saw that apartment; I should feel frustrated if I couldn't imagine where you were living.

And oh what fun we'd have if you were at Stratford-on-A. Strictly, you and I here together would I think feel slightly cribbed, cabined and confined, for long, but for a day or two it would be fun to potter around. I don't think I ever told you how I came to come here – no wonder you are somewhat surprised! I have a girl friend who lives here called Zoe Zajdler (Irish married to a Pole, or rather was) who I knew by repute to have a rather charming small house here with a flat to let at the top. Normally John Gielgud[21] and very high-class chums of his stay here. I investigated when I first got to London and found the flat was temporarily empty and that she'd be glad to have me. . . The object of the operation was to get some work done, which I certainly have (various things commissioned in New York, which I still had to clear up) and this has been an excellent place for that –

Monday morning

– at that point, 6pm Sunday evening, I broke off and went to 6.30 'evening church'. It's a service I'm much given to because I love the hymns, and I thought it would be pleasant to go to it at Stratford-upon-A church, which as you may remember is a great perpendicular church of heavenly beauty, overlooking the Avon. Mellifluous peals-upon-peals of bells tempted me (not that one ought to refer to a revival of the church-going instinct in that way, I suppose). I then went for a long and beautiful walk along the Avon in the sunset, thinking about you, and stopped for supper in a small hotel called The Arden. One would clearly go raving mad if one stayed in this place for long, or lived here, but as a 10-day interlude it's extremely charming – that is, in the beautiful shimmering late-August weather, which makes all the old brickwork, garden walls etc, look like ripened apricots. . . . I suppose this for

---

[21] Sir John Gielgud (1904-2000), leading English actor.

me is a substitute for being in a small French town in Burgundy or somewhere – which I'd prefer. And yet the curious religious feeling about Shakespeare that's in the air everywhere here is moving. One feels the sweatiest tourist climbing in or out of a charabanc is conscious of Him – He pervades the place as the Love of God ought to pervade our hearts.

Jean Black is coming to see me here, next Friday (28th). She's flying from Dublin to Birmingham, which is apparently about 20 miles from here, picking up a car in Birmingham and driving over. I've got her a room in Zoe's house for the night. It will be nice seeing her, the dear handsome thing! I got a slightly furious letter from Noreen (Butler) saying that as all my friends seemed to be rushing over to see me, meaning Urssie, then Jean, why shouldn't she too? She may come with Jean, but I think it might be a better idea if she came separately. It's very sweet of them all.[22] I have to go back to London on the 30th, as I'm recording a broadcast at the BBC the following day.

Zoe has just come in with the news that I've been offered free seats for any of the plays here, any night – which I am v pleased about. I'd imagined it would be impossible to get into the Shakespeare theatre as everything's booked up about a year ahead to Americans etc. I'd been prowling rather wistfully past the theatre in the evenings. I think Zoe's been working on somebody influential; it is good of her! . . . I shall see among other things this *King Lear* there's been so much talk about with Charles Laughton (of all people) in the role. I don't like what I hear of his playing it, but it will be interesting.[23]

---

[22] The truth was that EB's friends and relations were concerned about her state of mind. She was, as she says in her letters, drifting – functionally homeless and, until Bowen's Court was sold, in financial difficulties.

[23] In failing health, Charles Laughton (1899-1962) not only played King Lear, but also Bottom in *A Midsummer Night's Dream* in the 1959 season at Stratford. Neither performance was well received by the critics.

. . . Amputation is the word. I've got the strangest feeling of simply drifting through time, with a sort of indifference, for these next few months. I feel only 2-dimensional, like a (large) paper doll.

All my love, beloved. E.

19 College Street, Stratford-upon-Avon. Thursday, 27th August 1959
Dearest – my dear accident-prone love, it is a nightmare that you should have hurt yourself AGAIN. Apart from anything else, if all the sheer pain you have suffered within these last few years were laid end-to-end . . . What you did to the bone in your foot this time must have been unspeakable agony. I can't bear to think of how much it must have hurt, and probably still does. Your mother told me (though you never did) how the pain after the fall in Halifax, last summer, caused you dreadful sleepless nights and frayed your nerves.

What does make these things happen? It rather terrifies me that accidents should recur the way they do. You don't think they're abortive unconscious suicide attempts? . . .

I'm eating out my heart at not being in New York – no other word for it. Coming here, England, was a good thing, in fact a necessary thing to do, which is paying back all round in view of a) the Rome book business and b) the Ireland business. Re Ireland I've been having an immense correspondence with my lawyer Edmund Carroll, who's in charge of everything including the sale of Bowen's Court (he tells me he's had some enquiries after it already). I'm beginning to wonder whether it will be necessary for me to go to Ireland (immediately) after all: everything now sounds to be under good control, and all my good helpers who are helping me are coming over here. I shall have to go when anything definite comes up about the sale of the house, naturally. . .

I've done well spending time with the London publishers, Longmans, as they are now whipping themselves up into a great state of excitement about *A Time in Rome.* I have letters from them about one detail or another almost daily. I think it's well to fan the flames – I mean, of their enthusiasm.

Mr. [John] Guest, the man in Longmans who is chiefly dealing with the book, described me to a mutual friend as looking 'frail, but enchanting'. I think that's rather a good note to strike, don't you? I had no idea I had. But I have been told once too often that I'm 'as strong as a horse'. Next time anybody tries that on again, if they ever do, I shall say: 'What kind of horse do you mean?' I don't aspire to be like a race-horse, but I think I am quite like a hunter. But a cart-horse – no.

This evening-after-evening of Shakespeare theatre-going is being very great fun. Also the place is becoming very social . . . nicest of all, David arrived last night, in time for the play (*All's Well that Ends Well*). He gave a lecture on Shakespearean Tragedy this morning (at 10am!) and then I spent the morning with him, pottering about. It has been very nice running into him, and Leslie [Hartley]. They both were very consoling about Bowen's Court and said they were sure I was doing the right thing.

David seemed in rather a frenzy about his life. He says he's got a 'block' about the book he's supposed to be writing – the Max Beerbohm biography.[24] (I think it's such a boring subject; I wonder indeed whether it may not be repressed boredom that's caused the block.) He also I think is in rather a state about his relation with his two sons – 'Other people', he gloomily said, 'seem to me less fond of their children than I am of mine, but far better with them!' Having children is not all jam, he says.

. . . Feeling runs very high about – that is, for and against, the productions here. I must say, I enjoyed *Midsummer Night's Dream* – though the fairies, including Auberon [*sic* for Oberon] and Titania seemed more like a run-down Elizabethan county family which had taken to the woods, plus tow-headed idiot children and mad retainers. I liked the battle scenes and the rag-in-the-mess scene in

---

[24] *Max*, David Cecil's biography of Max Beerbohm, was published in 1964.

Othello. [Paul] Robeson played the part nobly though perhaps a shade too much as the dumb nigger. But oh the words! About love particularly. How lately have you read the play? I hadn't, for ages. I'm going to buy a copy here in town. Last night we had Dame Edith E[vans] sweeping about as a French chatelaine in *All's Well that Ends Well* (in modern dress – I thought, v effective: a Tony Guthrie[25] production). Tonight, *Lear*, with Charles Laughton . . .

Please write as soon as you can, tell me how you are. Your E.

151 Old Church St, SW3. Wednesday, 2nd Sept. 1959

My darling. . . .

Your telegram came when Jean was with me, and I gave her your 'love' message; she was v pleased. It was lovely seeing her, and her visit was a great success: she arrived (in the car she'd picked up in Birmingham) mid-morning on Friday and stayed the night in a room I'd got her at 19 College St; we had Saturday together, then she left about 5.30 on Saturday evening and drove back to Birmingham, where she handed back the car and caught a late-evening plane back to Dublin. It was sweet of her to come over. . .

Thanks to her, and letters from Edmund Carroll (my Fermoy lawyer) I am now 'in the picture' over Irish affairs. Carroll writes me that he has offers for the B Court property; he thinks he should get ten thousand pounds or possibly twelve for it. Meanwhile, he, Jean and all my helpers and well-wishers feel it much better I should not come to Ireland till the sale is through. Partly I think they think I'd find the situation trying (which I would, naturally, but I was perfectly prepared to face up to it if necessary), also, I wouldn't wonder if they had a secret fear of my being 'got at' by somebody wishing to pay a lesser price in the course of the bargaining.

---

[25] Tyrone Guthrie (1900-1971), Anglo-Irish theatre and opera director, instrumental in founding the Stratford (Ontario) Shakespeare Festival, knighted 1961. His sister Peggy was married to EB's cousin Hubert Butler.

So I'm <u>not</u> going to Ireland; not, that is, before I go to Rome. Jean suggests my going to stay with her and Barry at Creagh Castle after Christmas, between my leaving Rome and returning to New York. I could then go through the contents of the house (B Court) etc. I should like to do it that way v much, if it all works out. The trying part of saying goodbye to B Court would be made much less by the fact that the moment it was all over, I could be into a plane (for New York) at Shannon, and back to YOU.

. . . Oh, last night I saw the most WONDERFUL television version of *The House in Paris.* It was produced by the very intelligent man, Julian Amyes, who had written the script, and I thought it one of the best pieces of television I'd ever seen – both dramatically and aesthetically. It's unbearable to me that you can't see it. The casting was a matter of genius – the man Max and the boy Leopold were both formidable. The love scenes were so moving I nearly burst into tears – and I must say that the language sounded very grand. And I thought it marvellous how they'd kept both the tension and the atmosphere of the story. The little girl who played Henrietta was very 'right', too. Oh how I wish they could, now, make a film of the thing with exactly that same cast. I've always thought – and you do, too, don't you? – that *The H in P* was much the most screenworthy of my novels.[26]

A very tantalizing invitation from the Berlins to go out and stay with them and Stuart Hampshire in a villa they've got at Portofino. Tantalising because the dates won't fit and I <u>can't</u> go – have just sadly telegraphed them to that effect . . . Otherwise, as a stop on the journey to Rome,[27] it would have been ideal and, as I'm not going to Ireland, I <u>shall</u> have time to fill in. But I'm not checking

---

[26] The BBC's adaptation of EB's *The House in Paris* (published 1935), co-written and produced by Julian Amyes (1917-1992), was transmitted on 1 Sept 1959 with Trader Faulkner playing Max, Jeremy Ward playing Leopold, and Ingrid Sylvester playing Henrietta.

[27] EB was going as writer in residence to the American Academy in Rome.

in in Rome till Sept. 29th or 30th, and pottering about Italy on my own from the 19th to the end of Sept. would though a heavenly thing to do, be expensive. And there really are masses of things I might as well do, and indeed ought to do, in England while I am here, as I shan't be here for some time again.

... Oh Charles, now we're into September it's one month less, till next Jan. Where ever I go where ever I turn, I think of you. All my love, Your E.

Bailey's Hotel, Gloucester Rd., SW7. 10th September 1959
My darling...

The heat-wave goes on and on, making all England look blonde and curious; every where there are masses of roses; everybody looks sun-tanned and amiable.

Bailey's is a great success: I work (write) by day and am out in the evenings, so don't see much of the hotel, but what I see I do like. I'm sure it's been in your life, at one time or another? It seems to have been in almost everyone's. It's not in many ways unlike the Grosvenor, in New York: comfortable rooms and nice old-fashioned servants. Alas, no bathroom of one's own: what a bore that is! Architecturally, also, Bailey's is not so unlike the Shelbourne, Dublin. I'm getting so fond of this part of London – more and more do I think I'd like to 'settle' somewhere in this neighbourhood, when, about one and a half years hence or so, I do have a flat. Funny how from having been so dowdy Kensington's now getting so chic and streamlined: in fact parts of it are now as pretty as a picture; and of course a great charm are all these bowery trees.

I had dinner with darling Leslie 2 nights ago; he asked after you with great affection. Have been to various places of entertainment, including the play of the *The Aspern Papers*:[28] very good, only

---

[28] Novella by Henry James, adapted for the stage by Michael Redgrave, at the Queen's Theatre, with Flora Robson, Michael Redgrave and Beatrix Lehmann.

that I slept through part of it. It really does take Shakespeare to keep me awake these days.

Tonight I'm being given a sort of celebrity interview, in the series called 'Speaking Frankly' [*sic*] by the BBC.[29] Very gratifying. At least, they record it this evening; I don't know when it goes on the air; I should think probably while I'm in Rome. It begins with a dinner party – I must go and have a bath and dress.

I'll be here till next Wednesday, 16 Sept: after that I'm going to stay with David at Oxford and one or two other visits. . . .

I sometimes have an obsession that you're in London and that I shall

[Ends]

As from Bailey's Hotel, Gloucester Rd, SW7. Thursday, 30th September 1959

My dear darling – though I head this 'Bailey's', I'm actually, at this moment (till tomorrow) in the country . . . I start for Rome, by boat and train next Thursday, 8th October. I'm due to arrive there in the early afternoon of Friday 9th. I'm deliberately making a train journey; a Continental one is always to me such a treat, and I seem to have done so much flying lately and have got so bored with it – one of the things in life I do hate is bumping about in the air over the Alps. So I am going luxuriously, 1st class. The American Academy is paying for my ticket, and as even luxury train travel costs less, I find, than an air journey, they ought to thank me.

My address in Rome will be
c/o The American Academy in Rome,
Via Angelo Masina 5
Rome
Cables: AMACADMY, Rome

---

[29] The series *Frankly Speaking* was on the Home Service.

. . . It's perfectly all right to write to me at the Academy as 'Mrs. Cameron', as they'll be warned that I have two names. Actually, I shall be first staying with the Robertses, at the Villa Aurelia, then moving into my villino[30] in the Villa Aurelia garden, but I feel it would probably be more 'regular' of me to use the Academy address – the one I've given you.

. . . My secular retreat here in the country, to clear up things (bits of writing I've got to deliver, and letters) before starting for Rome has been really very enjoyable, in a bizarre way. I have, incidentally, got quite a lot done. At a short distance away from me are my two girl friends, Rachel Ryan and Sylvia Luling,[31] with one or other of whom I drink, spend the evenings or go to the movies in Reigate. The actual place I'm staying in is a perfect English Charles Addams piece: a large neo-Elizabethan country house, called Hartsfield Manor, converted into a residential hotel. It has – which slightly shook me to discover, on my arrival – not only no bar but no licence; however I've now laid in some drink, and there are various inns and bars quite near. The hotel largely is 'resided in' by old ladies who can no longer maintain their homes (owing to servant shortage). I seem to be almost the only transient, and, from what I see, am by some years junior to any other 'inmate'. However, as I spend all the time in my very comfortable room, writing, that doesn't matter . . . When you and I are, again, in London, we'll take an electric train out to here (that is, as far as Reigate) and wander about among these dales, woods, groves and streams.

I'm quite sorry to be going back to London tomorrow. Next week-end, that is, Saturday, I'm going to stay the weekend with Cyril Connolly. . . . I must discover whom he's living with now, before I

---

[30] Little house, cottage.

[31] Luling was the married name of Sylvia Thompson (1902-1968), novelist, best-known for *The Hounds of Spring* (1926).

get there. – I don't know whether he's again settled down with Barbara since George Weidenfeld traded her back to him.[32]

. . . One of the first things I am going to do in Rome is to buy the evening dress you have given me. I have been told of a very good place to go. I have also finally succeeded in taking your/my darling shagreen cigarette case back to its birthplace, Asprey's.[33] They've promised to have it mended for me by the time I start for Rome.

Goodbye for now, dear love. All my love. Your E.

American Academy, Rome. Wednesday, 21st October 1959

Well, my darling love. . . .

I am glad you like my Collected Stories.[34] There were one or two misprints, both in the preface and in the stories themselves, that I expect you spotted. Yes, I do think 'Ivy Gripped the Steps' is a fascinating tale: it's one of my favourite things of anything I've ever written – in fact I think it's so good that it doesn't seem to me as though I ever wrote it. And another story I thought came back well was 'No.16', about the decaying author in the decaying house in St John's Wood. It didn't seem to me so moving when I first wrote it; possibly I was more heartless then (some time towards the end of the 1930's). When I re-read it, as I did only the other day, it rather brought tears to my eyes.

Also, when we got back to Rome, there was a letter from Howard Moss,[35] dated October 17th, saying you and he were lunching together next day – did you, I wonder? He is dithering as to whether

---

[32] Barbara Skelton married Cyril Connolly in 1950. He divorced her in 1956 citing the publisher George Weidenfeld as co-respondent. She married Weidenfeld in 1956, and he divorced her in 1961 citing Cyril Connolly as co-respondent.

[33] Upscale shop in Bond Street.

[34] *Stories by Elizabeth Bowen*, New York: Vintage Books, 1959.

[35] Howard Moss (1922-1987), American poet, dramatist and critic, poetry editor of *The New Yorker*.

to come to Rome, and what is clearly in his dear neurotic mind is that he wants me to take care and charge of him if he does – which, much as I love him, I don't want to or intend to. Going on and on reading this wonderful George Painter book about Proust,[36] which I hope you'll get hold of when you have an instant's breathing space, if ever, has given me a sort of terror of the neurotic set-up and how infectious it is, and what a formidable area of compulsions it creates. You and I are not neurotics, why I don't know. Highly nervous and highly organized, yes; but not more. I really am just as glad.

You'll have had by now I expect my very scatty letter, posted in Urbino. That trip was I think the most visually beautiful ten days, almost, that I've spent in my life – I mean, the continuous dazzling, unwinding countryside, golden with light and yellow trees, and lush with vast bunches of grapes hanging on the vines ready for the vintage, and paintings and frescoes, and wonderful honey-coloured buildings and peachy ancient brick little towns (Urbino was the <u>most</u> heavenly, I think). I think so often of something you said as to which we're the same – that one's most genuine, spontaneous religious feeling is one of gratitude. Really such things do make one's heart swell with love of God, for having caused such things to be, and for having given to human beings, artists and builders, the power to conceive them and the power to make them. At the same time, that trip was extremely tiring – in fact more so, it put one into a peculiar other dimension, a sort of punch-drunk dizziness, out beyond and at the other, far side of ordinary fatigue.

In Florence my feet blew up, I mean swelled up, violently and agonizingly, like they did that time in New York, so I spent most of one of the two days we had there lying on my bed, incapable [of] being vertical enough to write to you, which was what I'd been

---

[36] The first of two volumes of George Painter's biography of Marcel Proust was published in 1959.

hoping and intending to do in Florence. After that I was QUITE ALL RIGHT, and have been so since. In fact I got a sort of second wind for the second half of the trip, which I think I really enjoyed more than the first.

I tell you one small Italian city I'd gladly settle myself into for a term of time, and that is, Lucca. There's something gay and elegant and Stendhalian[37] about it, with its trees and gardens. It has at least the air of having amenities, such as one more often finds in a small French town, though it probably hasn't. But poor unfortunate Florence is really hellish – don't you think, apart from its divine contents? Pallid, low-pressure, dusty and boring – combined with what under the circumstances is unforgivable, a chaos and noisiness which beats Madrid's. As you know, I'm not really as hypersensitive to noise as many people, but somehow in Florence it infuriates me, because really I can't see what it's all in aid of – such a hullabaloo to be constantly raised and caused by so dull a town . . . All the same I'm nagged by regrets at the things I missed, such as Donatello,[38] owing to my mixture of ill-temper and sore feet; and I think that in spite of all I'll take myself back to Florence, all on my own, for 2 days, and see properly the things there I do so really enjoy and love, taking taxis from one point to another so as not to be trampled on by the witless natives, and spending all the intervening hours either drinking or lying on my bed: a technique I successfully adopted in Madrid . . .

Now we're back in Rome,[39] I've moved into my own villino in the gardens of the Via Aurelia. What a perfect place this villino

---

[37] Stendhal was the pen-name of author Marie-Henri Beyle (1783-1842), whose writing combines psychological shrewdness with an ecstatic sensibility – particularly in regard to Italy, which is probably what EB was thinking of.

[38] Donatello's statue of David, to which CR had compared EB's naked body when they were first lovers, is in the Bargello in Florence.

[39] She had been travelling in a group with the Robertses, their young sons, and another friend.

would be for you and me does not bear thinking of; to think how happy we could be sitting about in it if you were here breaks my heart. There's a rather big living-room, with a big comfortable sofa and armchairs, an open fireplace in which one can have a wood fire, and a lot of lamps. The room, like the bedroom next door to it, opens on to a terrace, below which there's a view of Rome, glittering through trees. There's an inlaid writing-table, at which I'm writing this – I couldn't think what this table reminded me of, then I remembered, it's very like one which used to be in your apartment in the Bd St Germain, when I stayed with you there, when I used to sit typing away at the later chapters of *The Heat of the Day*. (I always have a feeling that I damaged that Paris writing-table, which was pretty decrepit anyhow, and that you probably had to pay large sums for it.) In this villino's also a nice large bathroom, and a well-equipped small kitchen, in which I have no intention of cooking, but it contains a capacious ice-box with many ice-drawers. A very nice rather hoary maid called Assunta comes in to bring my breakfast and clean the place. I go over and have meals in the main Academy building when I'm not out for meals or down in Rome . . .

The darling Blacks are passing through Rome, staying two nights, next Monday. After that I am going off on another short (I am assured) safari, this time to the coast and interior south of Naples. . . .

This letter lacks 2 chapters, with which I'll begin my next: my week-end with Cyril in Sussex, and my day in Old Headington with the Berlins, from which has arisen a rather interesting suggestion as to a possible future home for me. I shall be longing to know what you think of the idea, so I don't want to sketch it out in a hurry. . . .

Your E.

American Academy in Rome. Tuesday, 3rd November 1959
My darling – I posted a letter from Ravello. . . . I was v happy in finding that letter from you – the one in which you speak of walking in Central Park before breakfast – when we got back from our tour South, at the end of last week. We were dislodged sooner than had been planned, by vast almost continuous bursts of operatic rain, together with a quite continuous roaring gale. . . .

The great gale had started the day before, just when we were whizzing over that cultivated plain towards Paestum. I remember your feeling about those Paestum temples, and I share it. Though one has been expecting them, they come into view so suddenly, like an apparition – or so I found. Somehow they looked almost sinister, in their honey-yellow, under that day's rapidly darkening sky, with the wind almost visibly shrieking through them. . . .

I had expected the temples to be higher and more slender: their heavy, primitive almost dumpiness surprised me (though I must have seen photographs of them: in fact I think you sent me a picture postcard). I also expected to see the sea lapping up almost against their bases . . . I do think it's been a mistake, digging up those fearfully lumpy remains of the original Greek city – had they done that when you were there? – instead of leaving the temples to stand, as they stood so long, simply in a great undisturbed sea of grass.[40]

I am far from fascinated by everything the Greeks did, simply I suppose because there's always such a racket about them (a racket sponsored, I always privately think, by queers and Germans). I get sick of being told how fearfully superior the Greeks were to the dear old Romans. Everything that the Romans did, one is always

---

[40] Paestum on the Gulf of Salerno was a Graeco-Roman city, abandoned in the mediaeval period and 'rediscovered' in the 18th century. The 3 Doric temples date from the 6th century BC. The excavations regretted by EB were begun in the first decade of the 20th century.

told, 'was merely a coarsened and grossened version of the Greek'. All the same, the Romans did get around to building the most exquisite fragile temples, like spun sugar – and another thing, they really could paint like angels, lyrically and wittily, as those heavenly things in the Naples museum and elsewhere show. Whether the Greeks did I don't know, as nobody's ever told me and I've never been to Greece. However, enough about the Ancient World.

Talking of the Ancient World, have you yet got Mary McCarthy's book on Florence? It's out, I hear . . .

A book I have just bought is Harold Acton's *The Bourbons of Naples*. I'm in the mood for reading anything about Naples (which does not mean I'm unfaithful to Rome). Anyway, it's a most absorbing book, in its own right, once one gets past his rather bothering 1920-aesthete style. He was here in Rome the other day: a nice though slightly bothering creature, like his own style.[41] Before that, all through those travels in the south, I was reading Iris Origo's *The Last Attachment*[42] [about] Byron and La Guiccioli. . . . It was so odd, lying on my bed in a succession of hotel rooms, shaken into another dimension by those drives through storms, with, first in Salerno then in Naples, the sea roaring and banging about outside, and one's bedroom shutters demoniacally rattling on their hooks. A Byronic atmosphere to read about Byron in, one might say . . .

A more cheerful diversion has been seeing that divine Hitchcock film you told me about, *North by Northwest*. I'd been on the look out for it ever since you told me about it – the Plaza Oak Bar, the murder in the Delegates' Lounge, etc – but it hadn't yet come to London when I left. The only slight snag was, I had to see the Italian version

---

41 Harold Acton (1904-1994), *The Bourbons of Naples 1734-1825* (1957). Acton was a gay English writer, historian and connoisseur whose great house, La Pietra in Florence, was for decades a focus of Anglo-Italian society. He was knighted in 1974.

42 The author Iris Origo (1902-1988), an acquaintance of EB, lived in Italy at La Foce near Montepulciano. *The Last Attachment*, about Byron's love affair with Countess Theresa Guiccioli, was published in 1949.

– ie, dialogue dubbed into Italian. This, as you can imagine, was annoying. . . . From the purely Boys Own Paper form of excitement point of view, I don't think I've seen any film which excited me so much since I was about 10: I was perpetually stuffing both fists into my mouth, biting on them, and swaying to and fro uttering moans and shrieks, as more and more things happened to Cary Grant and that heavenly girl.[43] Incidentally I thought their love-making scene in the train, with the train to Chicago tearing along that track by the Hudson in the deepening dusk, very very beautifully erotic, did not you? I suppose partly because I have got a love of touching the nape of the beloved's neck, or of having the nape of my neck touched . . .

Goodnight, and goodbye for now, my dear dear beloved. Your E.

American Academy in Rome. Wednesday, 11th November 1959
My darling love – getting your signe de vie letter, 2 days ago, made me feel you must have written it out of some 'psychic wave' – never have I needed a letter more, and just that letter. I had, for a few days back (one having been, probably, the day on which you wrote it) been feeling inexplicably low and sad – saturated by a sort of feeling of permanent loneliness for you. I mean by permanent, ever-recurrent. That state of loneliness, almost like a climate or a sad terrain, which again and again settles down on me when we have been for any length of time apart. It's more than a wanting to talk to you, or conscious missing (or lack) of the joy of your company – it really is a sort of malady of the soul. I dread this 'illness' like a person subject to a particular illness dreads its returns.

We feel the same, I know . . . You know, I think Naples is inhabited by some poltergeist. Though I'm always fascinated by the place (in a way, it's an even more fascinating fascination than that

[43] That heavenly girl was Eve Marie Saint.

of Rome) it also rattles me, or disturbs me – so much so that the effect lasts for some time after I have left it. (What does the 'See Naples and die' saying really mean, I wonder? One's always told that above all it does not mean what it appears to – but that's not much help.[44]) I feel I die, in some queer way, each time I go to Naples: yet, I never fail to seize any opportunity to go back. Also, I know reading that *Last Attachment* book upset me. Or at least, it harrowed me unbearably.

My existence here is so enjoyable and easy and taken-care-of. Ironically, it is sometimes when one is most circumstantially 'happy' that one feels sad. One's defences are down; feeling, therefore, comes storming in . . .

Goodbye for a day or two, dear dear Charles. Your E.

American Academy in Rome. Wednesday night, 18th November 1959
My darling, I had yesterday, your letter about the whirl; it made me laugh so much – I mean, the day-and-night non-stop, and the 'what exactly is this all about?' feeling.

You will be extremely tired when it's over: while it's on I suppose one simply does keep spinning the way a top does. I hope really it isn't taking a lot out of you? It's brilliant what you say about diplomats generating something by sheer force of being together.[45]

As you say, there would be NO time for us – I mean, if I have to be away, this is the best time . . .

Oh Charles, I've started my new novel.[46] That is, I'm roughing out the first chapter: it's so much in my head, and I don't want to

---

[44] The saying in Italian is 'Vedi Napoli e poi muori': 'See Naples and then die,' the implication being that once you have seen Naples, nothing you might see afterwards could ever match its wonders.

[45] CR was dealing with visits of Howard Green, new and very active Secretary of State for External Affairs, who came to lead the Canadian delegation in person for certain UN meetings.

[46] This was to be *The Little Girls* (1964).

forget it. I've gone on working and working at it tonight. I must go to bed now. I think, sometimes, that I think about you more, now, than I have ever. In the rather weird Rome of this time of year, I feel so near you. I love you so much. Elizabeth

[*Fragment of letter from Rome, autumn 1959*]

. . . This Canadian novel I've just finished reading really is heaven. It's got wonderful pieces in it about Canadian-Victorian architecture. But also the characters, the setting and the whole set-up are I think so awfully good.

The author's Robertson Davies. The book's called *Leaven of Malice*. It's published in England by Chatto and Windus. I think you, my dear Ambassador, ought to encourage this man. Will you get one of your slaves to order the book, then read it. Then, if you think as well of it as I do, give it a bit of shop-window by leaving it around on one of your drawing-room tables. Who is he, I wonder? It's the only Canadian great work I've ever read that was at all flippant. And yet in a 20th century way he's Trollopian too, only not so long-winded. He writes about a city he calls Salterton (oldish, with a cathedral and university) much as Trollope writes about Barchester. And yet in a way he sometimes, too, reminds me of you talking about Canada.[47]

. . . All my love Elizabeth

---

47 Robertson Davies (1913-1995) much-honoured Canadian author, playwright, critic and academic, was already established on the literary scene in the 1950s. *Leaven of Malice* (1954) was the second novel in his Salterton Trilogy, and won the Stephen Leacock Award for Humour. In 1986 his *What's Bred in the Bone* was shortlisted for the Booker Prize for Fiction.

American Academy in Rome. Wednesday, 2nd December 1959
My darling . . .

I feel more and more drawn to that Old Headington flat, I must say.[48] It's an odd but attractive interior, and I like the surroundings. It would have a small but capable of being made comfortable spare-room; so you could stay with me – we should once again have a roof over our heads. I really have always at the bottom of my heart wanted to go back to Oxford; but in a way I wanted to be asked back; and the offer of this flat, together with Isaiah's determination to get me into it, acts on me like a sort of invitation. I know I really do like, and in a way need, the company of savants, the atmosphere of learning. What are described as 'writers and creative people' mean singularly little to me: I suppose the fact is I am not impressed by and have little respect for anybody who does anything I can do myself.

But there's another thing to it. I sometimes wonder whether even you, knowing me as well as you do, really realise my horror of my state as a femme seule (legal definition). It seems to me abnormal, it fills me with a sense of ghastly injury, that I should have to organize my own life. It seems abnormal that any woman should have to do so . . . Look at my life since Alan died – when I'm not with you I simply go drifting from one orbit of influence to another. It's all very well for me to complain of 'possessive' friends – I invite possessiveness, I can quite see. I am slightly independent in my mind, that is, in my intellectual part – but quite outstandingly the reverse in disposition and temperament. In a way, I am like Elizabeth I – run, as she was, by a succession of different people. She was a marvellous actress, giving the full interpretation to the

---

48 The flat suggested by the Berlins as EB's new home was on the first floor of White Lodge, a house belonging to the Berlins and next to where they lived at Old Headington House, the two linked by a door in the garden wall. White Lodge faces on to Osler Road. From the back, EB could see Waldencote, the coach-house cottage where she and Alan had lived for ten years until 1935.

role given to her to play. But somebody else jolly well had to write the play. In a smaller, alas very much smaller way, I am like that. People make a mistake when they identify the performance I give with my real being.

The long and the short of it is that since I am forced – doomed, I sometimes feel – to what is called 'make my own life', it is simply a question of into what zone of influence I move next. In Oxford at least I know what I'm in for. The crippling thing, the thing that is slowly breaking my heart is your and my not being continuously together. If we were, my hopeless sense of dilemma would be banished . . .

All my love, Your E.

The sale of Bowen's Court went through at the end of 1959, while Elizabeth was in Italy.

American Academy, Rome. Tuesday, 8th December 1959
My darling, when you opened this letter a piece of satin probably fell out of it – do make a dive and retrieve it, even if the scene is in the middle of the UN General Assembly, at a tense moment. This is the stuff of the beautiful Roman evening dress you have given me, which I have finally found . . .

I collected the beautiful garment yesterday, and shall be wearing it at a dinner party this evening. It cost more than a bit less than the sum – the $200 that you – you dear and generous beloved – gave me to spend. So I shall be putting the difference into a pair of shoes dyed to match, and yet one more of these beautiful and I think breath-taking Roman 'costume jewellery' necklaces – which, I notice, even the richest of the aristocracy or more nearly aristocratic of the rich wear in the evenings, when in grande tenue, in preference to any family diamonds they may or may not possess.

Out of my own money, which is rapidly accumulating here, I also propose to buy an evening bag worthy to carry with this outfit – probably gold mesh.

The trouble is, all this is going to be out of the picture in dowdy New York. Having spent far more than you should in giving me the dress, I don't want you to again ruin yourself by transporting me to places worthy to wear it . . . You know, Kirk [Askew] is right; New York, looked back upon a whole, is dowdy. He says this is the fault of the Eisenhower-Republic[an] regime. Whether or not, London when I got back to it, even at the beginning of August when 'everybody' might have been taken to be out of town, was by contrast a modern Babylon, with wonderful-looking creatures wandering dazedly, slipshod, through the arrogant-looking sunny streets. Yes, from the prestige point of view – and what other matters? – the British Empire has begun again: there's no doubt of it . . .

By the way, please don't speak of any future housing plans of mine to any member of your family, whether Sylvia or your Halifax relations. By all means tell anybody who's interested that Bowen's Court is now sold and a thing of the past. Beyond that, just say that, beyond the fact that I shall be arriving back in New York in the third week in January, my future plans are on the knees of the gods.

No, since you ask me, I'm far from well, thank you, darling. Possibly in part this revolting weather; not I think really that altogether. I'm what Edwardians used to describe as 'very run down'. The fact is, I suppose, that for these last years I have been doping myself with non-stop hard work. The effect of this luxurious, taken-care-of holiday has been, to allow me time to ask myself how I am. However, I hope at least to live long enough to wear this heavenly dress – for which, 100,000,000 times, thank you.

Your loving E.

Poem by EB, enclosed in the letter following:

First Fine Day

(20th December, 1959)

Golden Rome
Is home again
Out of banishment,
Into which it was sent
By its hater and slater
The vain rain.

Dredged, drenched, dead
It was. Enemies' smiles were fed.
Smirched, smeared, smacked
It lay, day on into day.
There lay I too.
All dismay had hold.
Where is Rome gone?
Nothing shone. Where is God?

Golden Rome
Sails home again.
As it was? No,
More resplendent, innocent and forgiven,
More near Heaven.

So perish all traitors, haters
And the vain rain.

EB

American Academy in Rome. 21st December 1959
My darling, I realise this can't reach you till after Christmas. For the day itself I'll send you a telegram, and you'll be thinking of me, oh my love, won't you? As I of you. Christmas has seldom been a time together of ours, except I remember one Christmas morning in London when we stood and looked at a Christmas tree in the

Ritz. But after all it's a human season, and you and I are human, as well as everything else . . .

I've been losing my grip rather. . . . The weather has been beastly. Yesterday however blazed out into a perfect day; and I was so moved that I wrote the first poem I have written for 40 years.

. . . On the 6th and 7th [Jan 1960] I ought to be going to Ireland; probably to Urssie's. I'll let you know. Bless you, my beloved love, for your letter; its warmingness and reassurance and understanding. I shall feel happier when this surgical business of detaching myself from Bowen's Court, in mid-January, is over. The prospect of it has made my feet swell up, but no doubt they will soon go down again.

. . . Give my love to your mother. Oh, the preliminary copy of the *A Time in Rome* book arrived, today. I wonder how soon they'll be sending yours . . . I love you, I love you. Your E.

1960

Charles Ritchie kept no letters from Elizabeth Bowen written between December 1959 and November 1960.

29 January [New York]

E arrives or has arrived. I will be telephoning her in an hour.

4 February

I am in a diary-despising mood today and want only to burn the lot. E gave me such a feeling of her pathos last night at that party and afterwards. How I wish she could bring off some fortunate coup, if they would make a hugely successful play and movie out of one of her books, if she could come into money in a big way. But Billy Buchan, typically, is the first to put it to me into words. 'She isn't a very fashionable writer just now.' I can see why she isn't in the taste of the times, the more so because she was so very much in the taste of twenty years ago. Then these people saying to her, 'So we hear that you have had to sell your Irish castle.' That Eddy business went deep.[49] Then Billy said of her writing, 'If she got really angry she could surprise them all.'

---

[49] CR was referring either to the fact that Eddy Sackville-West took umbrage when EB sold Bowen's Court without even telling him, or to their previous tentative entanglement. EB, in 1960, had not contacted Eddy for more than a year.

7 February
E left yesterday for Vassar, leaving me with a saddened and loving feeling of her defeat and exhaustion. It was a languid day of early spring or late autumn. We went to *Black Orpheus*,[50] but the carnival scenes made us both feel queasy – the jigging dances and repetitive tunes, and a shared hatred of carnivals – so we had to leave and totter down Park Avenue and into a plush bar where they gave us tea with a jigger of rum in it. E is up the Hudson at Poughkeepsie having taken on a seminar at Vassar, which she is looking forward to with alarm and despondency.

22 April
E plainly loves the adulation of the girls at Vassar – the frieze of young creatures drifting across the campus, the girls going to collect their letters like going to collect eggs on the farm, and a girl coming back reading hers as she walked and smiling to herself. The whole place threaded with stories. I wish ER[51] could know E at this stage, if E doesn't have too many girls in her life already. I think E an immensely potent witch.

14 May
E says, 'Yes, hang on to the diaries.' She would like to prune them for publication.

In April there had been a two-day auction in Cork of the contents of Bowen's Court – the accumulation of many Bowen lifetimes. Now, Elizabeth learned from her artist friend Derek Hill,[52] whom she had asked to paint a picture

---

50 Award-winning 1959 French film, made in Brazil and famous for its bossa nova soundtrack.

51 Elizabeth Ritchie

52 Derek Hill (1916-2000), English portrait and landscape painter who became an honorary Irish citizen and donated his house St Columb's, near Letterkenny in Co Donegal, to the Irish state. From the 1950s he also shared the weekend house at Long Crichel in Dorset with Raymond Mortimer, Eddy Sackville-West and others.

of Bowen's Court to hang in her English home, that the roof had already been taken off by the new owner, Cornelius O'Keefe. He had only wanted the property for the timber, which was felled, and the land. By the end of the summer, the whole great house had been demolished. It was, Elizabeth said, 'a clean end.'

16 July

E is ill with virus pneumonia in St Luke's Hospital.[53] I think she, certainly I, feared something worse from the doctor's first obscure utterances. I feared cancer of the lungs. Today her temperature is down and she says that if she were one of those people who broke out of hospital, she feels well enough to do it. This is nonsense. She might have died in the days before penicillin.

18 July

I shall go out to the hospital to see the poor darling. She is so hot – such weather to have a fever. She keeps pounding her pillows, pummelling them and putting them first behind her head, then in the small of her back. Although full of tranquillizers, she seems far from tranquil; and it is all so expensive – forty dollars a day for her room . . . She seems to be able to do anything she likes except have two 'snipes'[54] of champagne, which she keeps asking for.

Elizabeth recovered from her illness and returned to Ireland.

13 August [Halifax]

I heard from E today, from Kinsale where she is staying with Urssie.[55] She sounds cross. It irritates her that I should be in the family party. She has taken against my family.

---

[53] In Newburgh, near Poughkeepsie.

[54] Small (20cl) bottles

[55] EB was with the Vernons in Co Cork.

31 August [New York]
Letter from E. She sounds demoralised and sad, and if I were not anaesthetized in this peculiar way my heart would ache for her.

10 September
I have been reading O. Henry's short stories and Edgar Allan Poe's and Chekov's. I took them over from E when she left and am giving myself her course in the short story. Those lucky girls at Vassar who took her course. She never talks to me nowadays about such things. Her letters are loving and natural, but she doesn't tell me much about people and circumstances and they seem written in a hurry.[56]

16 October
Let me see, when did the pressure of the Assembly relax? Only the day before yesterday, and already I am back where I was and always will be. There is no doubt that I have madly enjoyed the UN this time. E as always with me was the first to know, before I did, how much I was enjoying myself in that Hell's kitchen.[57]

Lewes,[58] Wednesday, 2nd November 1960
My darling, I sent you off a telegram from Thame last Saturday afternoon, wanting you to know that the major part of the Major Operation of getting into the Headington flat had been accomplished. Oh I did so want to sit down and have a tremendous drink with you, that evening. I imagined how if you had been in reach, and could have been there, we would have pottered about among the stacked-up furniture, glasses in our hands, picking our way

---

56 He did not keep these letters.
57 The General Assembly of the UN had been much occupied by events in the Congo.
58 In Lewes, Sussex, EB stayed with Beatrice (known as 'B') Curtis Brown, aka B Horton, sister of her literary agent. She had many 'girl-friends' of a certain age, mainly in Sussex and Kent, some of them emotionally linked, whom she met frequently. CR was not told much about this aspect of her social life.

among the books and *objets* strewing the floors, in the cosy autumn dusk. As it was, I drank alone (having already laid in a small bar) and said a solemn prayer, of the 'Bless this house' kind.

Not that the flat is by any means yet habitable – the carpenters making some of the built-in furniture (kitchen cupboards, etc) are still hammering away, with the decorators squeezing their way between them, applying licks of paint here and there. None of the wallpapers have been 'hung' yet, and when it will be possible to have the carpets laid, I have no idea. Nevertheless I intend to take up residence in the flat on Tuesday next, November 8th. So, the next letter you write after you get this CAN be addressed to – White Lodge, Old Headington, Oxford.

It will be a very exciting moment when the first of your beloved letters to arrive at White Lodge, arrives. I mean, when I pick up one of your blue envelopes from the floor in the little entrance-hall. (There is no internal letter-box: letters dropped through the letter-flap drop on to the doormat.)

It seems a long time since I wrote – how long? I really have been dazed, mazed and dotty with tiredness over all this organization. This is the first house-move I've ever done single-handed, and it requires still more concentration than writing a book.

It's been a great thing to be staying in the nice, comfortable Golden Cross Hotel.[59] I have simply tottered down there every evening in a state of stupor, drunk an enormous amount and reeled off to bed at about 9. My feet started blowing up again, rather to my alarm and depression, but have now subsided. Friends have also been very kind about taking me out to meals and drinks. David [Cecil] took me out in the car to various antique shops in Dorchester, Wallingford, etc to look for various odds and ends I wanted . . .

---

[59] In Oxford, on the High Street

The last letter I had from you . . . was the one in which you said how sickening and ghastly and quite un-funny it was when the Russians screamed and made scenes like that, and banged their shoes on the tables. I can quite imagine F. Boland when the gavel broke.[60]

Things like that must be like the whole surface of life cracking. I mean, it's the sort of thing one never expected to live to see. Curious it is, the difference between what is bizarre-frightening and what is horrifying. For instance, I never found air-raids horrifying. (V-1s,[61] as you may remember, I did.) In the middle of an 'ordinary' air-raid, however heavy, I remember wondering, 'Why is this terrifying but not horrifying?'

I think the horror is, the sense of fumes of evil when people lose control.

. . . My beloved Charles, goodbye for now. All my love. Your E.

Golden Cross Hotel, Sunday, 6th November 1960

My darling – 2 days ago I got your letter written last Sunday: on the day at home when you were turning this disarmament thing, from the Canadian side, over in your mind. It was wonderful, that sort of burst-out of your thoughts – I mean, exactly as if we were meeting for a drink in the Black Hole or somewhere, and you came in and flung your beautiful self into the seat beside me, or opposite me across the table, and began to talk. What a terrific and increasing amount is weighing on you – I mean, problem piled on problem . . .

---

60 The Americans refused a meeting between President Eisenhower and Khrushchev, after what CR in *Diplomatic Passport* called 'wholesale insults hurled at them [in the General Assembly] by Khrushchev, whose behaviour is becoming more and more Hitlerian.' Frederick Boland, Irish ambassador to the United Nations, was currently president of the Assembly.

61 V-1s, known as 'flying bombs,' were German guided missiles deployed against Britain and other Allied cities, 1944-45.

I cannot tell you how I respect your power of judgement. You're like me in being impulsive in your personal life; but in all this heated world of the UN you stand out as temperate, wise and patient, with what I suppose is most important of all, the power of comprehension, of taking in factors and issues, reflecting on them, reflecting on their balance against each other . . .

Oh I'm so glad you're reading those Flaubert letters.[62] What an extraordinary feeling one has towards him: identification, almost. The feeling of identification one has in love. To me he (in the letters) is the only person who transcribes the actual SENSATION of writing – I mean, of being in the grip of it, of being 'at it'. The feeling that everything else is an unreality. I love that letter beginning, 'I rode in the woods today . . .' after he'd just done the original seduction scene in Bovary. White heat, going on burning after the actual MS has been put away (till tomorrow). The engine of a powerful racing car still racing, though the car has pulled up to a temporary stop.

And one of the grand things is, that the letters, I mean what he says in them, are at once the core of writing and yet applicable to anything (almost) else that one does with passion: a passion at once of mind and senses and soul.

He's one of the few people I wish I had known. And yet I do know him: probably it's best this way, the way it is.

I don't think I could ever love to the full anybody who hadn't got the Flaubertian quality about them. You have.

Did I tell you how once late at night in the library at Bowen's Court, I was alone working away at that writing table off in that corner by the window, and I thought he was away off behind my back, sitting in one of those corduroy chairs by the fire, in the half-dark

[62] In 1960, they could have read either the *George Sand-Gustave Flaubert Letters* trs. A.L. McKenzie (1921) or more likely Flaubert's *Selected Letters* ed. Francis Steegmuller (1953).

room (that was before we had electric light and the only lamp, oil lamp was by me on the writing table). I must say, a frisson ran down my spine. And yet when I finally turned round and he wasn't there, with his beautiful heavy fair moustache, I was disappointed.

I must now stop. Lunch-time. I'm going up to the flat this afternoon to polish up some of my poor smeary furniture.

I love you so much, I love you so much. Your E.

1961

Elizabeth is in New York again. Charles has heard that his mother's heart is very weak.

28 January

Oh well, everything rusts out; it breaks or goes away, or slowly dies like my love for E. But my mother, life will shrink without her. Does anyone love me as I love her? . . . E is coming in to hear her script on the TV. She seems cheerful this time. We had a lovely lunch and movie yesterday. There isn't much more to say, except that I shouldn't say my love for her has died, that's not true; it's alive underneath.

30 January

Last night we had a gloomy little gathering to hear E's script on the TV. It was Ireland 'The Smile and the Tear', and the Irish Ambassador was here. They didn't use her script at all. She sat on the sofa drinking martinis and saying at frequent intervals in a sepulchral-furious voice, 'I didn't write that, I didn't write that', and finally announced that she was going to use the money she had earned for the script to sue the CBS.[63]

---

[63] Columbia Broadcasting System

16 February

E was still here, so I had a drink or two with her and wondered why I was not asked to lunch. We walked arm in arm in the dirty street amid the uncollected snow under the beginnings of a spring sky. I felt happy and normal that we were together again and began to feel how short a time she is to be here and how little we are together, a panicky feeling.

24 February

E is away at the Deanery, Bryn Mawr and I miss her. This is a rehearsal for her being really away when she goes back to England next week, if she goes. She said to me, 'If you start "trying to be good", it's still not too late after twenty years for me to break off. Being religious is all right, but "trying to be good" is too unattractive and would really come between us.' That's how she started off when we hadn't seen each other for more than a day or two. I have since profited by her advice and things are going much better.

Lunch. Where, now? Oh yes, with E, off whisky and sardine sandwiches at her hotel apartment. Twenty years ago I used to lunch with her off sardine sandwiches at Clarence Terrace in the early, early days when she lay stretched on that hard narrow Regency sofa in the little upstairs drawing-room. Outside the long windows trees moved, light cast reflections on the shining comfortless parquet. Elsie[64] used to say, 'When I go to Heaven perhaps I'll know what E and C talked about.' Well, what do we talk about? There is a change. It's less about ourselves, 'ideas', it's less imaginative, less 'interesting' and more about the people we saw last night at dinner and plans for our next meeting and me talking about the UN. Rather a lot of the latter from E's point of view I should fear.

---

[64] Sylvia's Aunt Elsie, Mrs W.H. Rowley

Anyway it's altogether more middle-aged talk or married talk. But still it sets me free.

12 March

I walked round Central Park in the windy bright March weather missing E. She left for England only the day before yesterday. To the end I gave her no present except that miserable cheap cigarette box, and then I couldn't even say goodbye to her because Eudora Welty and Marshall [Berland] came earlier to the Black Hole of a bar than we expected. She has been the E I first knew and loved. It has been happy and unclouded. E is sixty-one this year. We have waited everything out and would be lost without each other. Things lose a dimension when she is not here. It is easier practically without her. A tension has lifted from this house.

28 March

I have clumsily, cruelly hurt Sylvia tonight over this trip to Oxford which I claim as a sort of right, though it's one I could forego. But it makes me frantic, to be made to feel guilty. It's like Bonn again. Now that I will not endure again.

Charles's mother had a stroke and he went to be with her.

8 April [Halifax]

Also all this smell of death and decay makes me long for sex. So does the prospect of an emotionally over-stimulating 'holiday' with E. The only thing that could restore me would be fucking, after so much sympathy, distress and consideration. And E is as exhausting to me as my M[other]. I read about the English Augustan age and envy them their lack of pity, their complete ignorance of the anatomy of sympathy, their contempt for the feelings of others. Damn this thin-skinnedness.

17 April [New York]

Do I want to go to England at all? . . . Perhaps when I get started I shall be glad to be going. I haven't been back for how long? More than three years, nearer four. And what does London mean to me now – a visit to my tailor's? . . . The truth is I prefer New York and the UN job to anything, and I am happier here than anywhere else. And although I love E, I am not at all sure that it isn't easier without her here. . . . If I am happy here, why go to England? And Sylvia looks twenty-eight today. So Sylvia said, when I told her about looking twenty-eight, 'It's happy, happy marriage.' And without irony. And it is a happy marriage, partly because she has willed it to be so.

30 April [Headington, Oxford]

Even Oxford the first day I was there seemed to have come 'unstuck' for me. E said, 'Give it time.' She was right, and how much time shall I give it? Shall I stretch it out for three weeks, why not? Well, there are a lot of things I don't want to do here. Chief among them is going to stay with Mary [Adlington], which I dread. Also I don't want to be long in London staying at Brooks's and eating expensive, indigestible meals in restaurants, and 'looking up' Moyra. This time in Oxford is the point of the visit. Yesterday E and I walked in Christ Church Meadows and Magdalen. It was more like a summer than a spring day.

11 May [New York]

Now it's night; the night before last, E and I sat on the window-seat of The Compleat Angler at Marlow and looked out on a terrace. It was a musical comedy set of a Thames-side prettiness with its theatrical pink tulips and white garden furniture. That was on the way to the airport, the last of our little expeditions . . . I had written off the beauty of England, forgotten its pull and its power, become unfaithful to my love. But each day of shower and sun, and each morning walking to lawns and great chestnuts, each walk through field or cloister, each trip on the No 2 bus into Oxford, revived the power of the spell. And the Oxford talk and the London talk of the UN, Maurice Bowra, David Cecil, Stuart Hampshire, Isaiah Berlin, Diana [Cooper], Barley [Alison], not to speak of E herself. It's a heady brew from which platitude is totally excluded. A brew compounded of kindliness in the mixture, but it is tinged by sensibility and never diluted by discretion.

11 June

I time my writing by my hour-glass which E gave me . . . I'll telephone her tomorrow from the United Nations. If I was rich and free I would take a jet and spend next weekend with her in Oxford. But I am even less free than I am rich. I have told her that I shall never forgive her if she dies. But yes, she is the same age as the century. She had better come over in October. I shall go back now to England every spring whatever happens. I take her continued life for granted as much or as little as I take my own for granted. I look back with horror on those few spring months in New York in 1959 when I saw her from the outside for the first time in twenty years, when I was sane enough or mad enough to doubt her and myself. Now nothing, I believe, except death or the ghastly attrition of old age can touch us, and when either happen I shall be finished whether I know it or not.

No letters from Elizabeth to Charles between November 1960 and August 1961 have survived.

'Adriatiki', Saturday, 26th August 1961[65]

My dearest,

Now we have left the Adriatic and entered the Ionian Sea, which is surrounded by scenery and far more agreeable. We embarked at

---

65 EB was on a Hellenic cruise.

Venice on Thursday, had the most appalling (I mean boring) 'day at sea' yesterday, Friday, but this morning everything is beginning to be mad fun.

Yesterday during the 'day at sea' I was too depressed to write to you: I did nothing but think, 'Why did I get myself into this hell's cauldron?' I loathe the sea, I detest being on a ship, and I don't like people . . . So I locked myself into my cabin and read Greek history. (We had 4 lectures, all rather good ones, to stimulate our Hellenic sensations and cheer us up.) Maurice [Bowra] joins us today; we are to meet him (very appropriately) at Delphi, this afternoon. So far the unchallenged star has been Sir Mortimer Wheeler,[66] who gives wonderfully disloyal lectures sabotaging the Ancient Greeks – and cracking up the dear unappreciated Romans. Which pleases me, but annoys most of my fellow-travellers.

But last night there was a wonderful full moon; and I leaned over the rail of the top deck of the 'Adriatiki', weeping gently into the Adriatic. For there suddenly was something poetic and exciting about this small ship forging along to Greece, with its crew of souls. I need not say that I thought of you, and that that was partly why I wept.

. . . All my love, dear love. Your E.

28 August

I am alone in the [Park Avenue] apartment. I feel panic that makes my hand shake. I watch with sick fear the sand running through the narrow neck of the hour-glass. The whisky in my mouth tastes like grass. Oh this endless summer, these stagnant days . . . I am as much alone as I was in those last guilt-laden months on the Boulevard St Germain, before I was married. Yet I am not even sure that I want reassurance, or that normality will not be worse than

---

[66] Sir Mortimer Wheeler (1880-1976), knighted 1952, academic archaeologist and author who had great popular success on television.

this hag-ridden solitude. Sylvia comes back the day after tomorrow. D [girlfriend] comes the same day. This is a fatality which only needs one more to become comic.

White Lodge, 21st September 1961

My darling – the last letter I wrote was sent off on the morning of the Monday on which I, in the evening, heard of Hammarskjold's death.[67] Apart from the unbelievable shock and sadness (it seemed at the time, and still seems sometimes, like something in a horrible clear but incredible dream) I have not ceased to feel sad for you, and to think of you. Such a shock and blow to you, through the affections, and such pain, and loss. He had come to seem to me to be one of the people who was reallest in your life.

I see him with such distinctness – from the lunch when I talked so much with him, at your flat. The unexpected brilliance of his colouring – the golden crest of hair and the brilliance of those light-coloured but not 'light' eyes. And the animation of his face.

. . . My love, and great sympathy, dear love – Your E.

White Lodge, Sunday, 19th November 1961 [After a visit to New York, followed by a visit to Ottawa]

Oh my darling love, already it is almost a week since I have seen you. . . . That last day in New York (the day we'd agreed it would be no good trying to meet) was awful. I mean, still being in New York, yet knowing I should not be seeing you not only that day but for who knows how long. In a way, my being at the Askews made it worse – because I associated being there generally, with the beginning of my visits.

---

[67] Dag Hammarskjöld (1905-1961), Swedish economist and diplomat, charismatic Secretary-General of the United Nations. On a peacemaking mission in the Congo, the plane in which he was travelling crashed during the night of 17-18 September 1961. CR liked and admired him greatly.

As I told you, I had the most horrible hour of crying, that Tuesday morning. I could not wait to get out of the town. Going to that party at Princeton, on Tuesday night, was a good plan.

How absolutely lovely our Monday night, out round the town, was, wasn't it. Not only the way to spend a 'last evening', but lovely in itself. We always are so happy at the El Morocco; I love its queer other-dimension feeling, a sort of at once restful and light-as-air feeling. Almost a disembodied one. And the heavenliness of dancing. I do HOPE, though, you weren't tired next morning?

I could not live if it weren't for these times of seeing you. Dear New York – dear for being so easy to move into. It is agonizing to me, I mean agonizing, not to be there now, there still.

I'm going on with the rest of this letter in type, because that takes up less room, and there's so much to tell about Ottawa.

The first day when I arrived Wednesday, midday, the place was in blazing sunshine, of a peculiar quality which made it seem a little uncanny. Bunny[68] and I had lunch, then she drove me into the centre of the city. Parts of it were so much what I'd imagined (particularly the part round the East Block[69]) that it seemed ghostly, like the projection of some dream I'd had. There seemed to be too much space – so much space that quite a lot of it ceased to mean anything and became vacuum. I thought, a city with so much space already around it should be more crowded together . . .

The second day (Thursday) was quite different: mistiness, and a very heavy frost . . . suddenly it became stylish, mysterious and romantic, full of all the atmosphere which the day before (in that to me rather anaphrodisiac sunshine) it had seemed to lack. Bunny, taking me a wonderful drive along the canal – a part of the place I remember your saying you had a fondness for, and I don't wonder

---

68 EB was staying in Ottawa (her first visit to the Canadian capital) with Roland and Bunny Ritchie. He was, from 1959, a Judge of the Supreme Court of Canada.

69 The East Block of the Canadian Parliamentary Precinct was the home of the Department of External Affairs, where CR would have had his office.

– and out into that sort of uphill park with the arboretum, the Experimental Farm[70] – kept lamenting the change in the weather (disappearance of sunshine) and I couldn't convince her as to what an improvement I thought it was . . .

What we did. Arrived at R's and B's house, from the airport, in time for lunch on Wednesday. I think that house is just heaven. Was happy there from the moment I entered. It just suits them. The exterior isn't its strong point, I quite agree. The whole of that Rockcliffe residential area is very cosy, isn't it, and has charm.[71]

Roley had left a message saying I could if I wished (which I of course did) come into the Supreme Court and listen to a Lady Chatterley session.[72] So we whizzed in after lunch. Joined Roley upstairs in his elegant room, and he handed me over to a v nice Mr Campbell, who found a seat for me in the body of the Court and sat beside me. I rather drowsed through the Lady C session (never tell anybody) but the mise en scène was so impressive and fascinating. When it was over, Roley gave me tea in his room, then showed me the building, all those portraits of judges . . .

That evening, after dinner we were just on the point of starting round to Alison's and George's[73] when, in walked Norman, and Elizabeth Ritchie. They had met on the doorstep – she on her way from the Montreal train she had unexpectedly jumped, he prowling across the street to see if we would come in for a drink. So he and Jetty came with us to Alison's, instead. So did Elizabeth

---

[70] Canadian Ministry of Agriculture's Central Experimental Farm on south-west edge of the city, founded 1920s.

[71] Rockliffe Park on the southern banks of the Ottawa River was then a pleasant residential neighbourhood of Ottawa, before the arrival of embassies and mansions.

[72] The issue in Canada as elsewhere was whether D.H. Lawrence's *Lady Chatterley's Lover* was an obscene publication.

[73] George Ignatieff (1913-1989), Russian-born diplomat. In 1963 he was to be appointed Canada's permanent representative to NATO, in 1966 Canadian ambassador to the UN, and in 1968 president of the UN Security Council. His wife Alison (nee Grant) was a niece of Mrs Vincent Massey. Their son Michael Ignatieff (b. 1947), author, academic, broadcaster and from 2006 Liberal MP, was a godson of CR.

. . . Alison very handsome and amusing; I wish I saw her more often. . . . Towards the end of the evening, dear George returned from New York, looking, I thought, wonderful . . . It was queer to think he had seen you since I had.

Next morning (the nice misty, frosty one) we – girls – went across the street for coffee with Jetty. Judith [Robertson] was there: I was so glad. Then we went for that drive. Then Bunny, Elizabeth and I had lunch in the grill of the Chateau Laurier, a building I'd been dying to get inside since I first saw it – also because you've talked about it. Then we went home; Bunny took a nap in preparation for her party, and Elizabeth and I took the car out and did some shopping; she is looking beautiful; I do love her. We discussed her future, somewhat ineffectually (I can't see why she shouldn't just relax and have a good time for a year or two).

. . . The party, beginning at 6pm, was a great success, I thought. Just the right number of people, and some heavenly judges. At any rate, I had a wonderful time. The Robertsons and George and Alison stayed to dinner. Oh, and Mike Pearson[74] did come. It was so dramatic to be setting eyes on him at last . . .

I did so LOVE being with them. Bunny does really kindle my heart, and I love her slow-motion, fatalistic, almost Deep Southern way of living. As for angelic Roley – oh, he does make me laugh so much. And it means much to me seeing him having the life his stature deserves. He's looking so well – I expect, in consequence – and so handsome. And he is so kind to me.

My last morning, Bunny and I went in and had a drink with Marian Pearson.[75] How her appearance has improved! . . . Now, she looks so creamy-handsome, and digne. Her eyes no longer look hyperthyroid, nor her clothes common.

---

[74] Lester ('Mike') Pearson (1897-1972), then Leader of the Opposition, later, Prime Minister of Canada (1963-1968), had won the Nobel Peace Prize in 1957.

[75] [*sic*] for Maryon Pearson (1901-1989) was known for her wit: 'Behind every successful man, there is a surprised woman.'

. . . It's queer to be writing to you in this room again (the White Lodge drawing-room). A few tattered leaves are still on the trees outside the windows . . . This evening, I'm going to Sunday supper with the Cecils.

My love, my love. Your E.

White Lodge, Tuesday, 21st November 1961

Oh my darling . . . I'm writing (on that folding card-table I use[76]) up in my room at the top. It's a very cold, brilliantly sunny day, rather like a North American one. Quite a lot of light is pouring in at the 3 windows on to the roses on the wallpaper. The time is 5 past one; thinking back (to NY time) 5 hours, I try to imagine what you are doing at this moment. I have not been doing 'writing' writing, this morning, as I had a whole pile of bread-and-butter letters to catch up with.

Oh, this is just the kind of morning when I should be tearing down Madison Avenue to meet you at the dear old Aiglon.

. . . Honours are showered on me: what do you think – I've been elected President of the Old Headington Women's Institute. This may a little interfere with my night life, as the Institute meetings are in the evenings. However, there's only supposed to be one meeting a month.

I was talking to Alistair [*sic*] B on the telephone yesterday evening. He said he supposed you'd be leaving New York soon, and did you yet know where you'd be going next? I said I didn't think anyone had a cat's idea.[77]

. . . Oh my beloved dear love, you dear darling E.

---

[76] This modest folding card-table was inherited by Audrey Fiennes, and passed from her to the antiquarian bookman Colin Franklin, who donated it to the Harry Ransom Humanities Research Center, the University of Texas at Austin, which holds many of EB's letters and papers.

[77] Alastair Buchan was Director of the Canadian Institute of Strategic Studies. His wife Hope was Canadian.

28 November

It's really rather sad that the writer of this diary should have degenerated in his middle fifties into an elderly sex-maniac, but what else can it mean? My fixation on that window opposite, my lack of real interest in anything else. What do I care that the new sitting-room rug is the wrong colour? . . . I am waiting for D [girlfriend] to rescue me from this humiliation. The things that should amuse me do not. Nor can I amuse anyone. I know this sort of thing happens to elderly men; it's what makes them unattractive. . . . Eight days till Dec 6th and if anything goes wrong in the interval and she [D] doesn't come . . . Meanwhile I force my pace through the days towards that destination.

I wonder if E knew whether she would help me to someone else – find me a girl? Do you know I believe if she knew, she would. Provided it was the girl of her choice.

White Lodge, Monday, 11th December 1961

My darling. . . .

How is that fiendish United Nations? Is the Katanga issue as tortuous as it sounds at this distance? It's making me quite frenzied. I'm a Conservative back-bencher for the duration (of this). We should never have given these bombs. It's awful to feel so liée with Lord Beaverbrook and Sir Roy W, but I do. Oh dear darling, more and more I'm beginning to feel (in view of the fact that you yourself could always get nice work elsewhere) that it's high time that insane UN was terminated. All but the New Statesman-y kind of British are getting so bored with it that it's nobody's business; one meets more and more people in streets and shops saying, 'We do hope Katanga wins!' (not that that unfortunate country possibly can, I suppose).[78]

---

[78] After Belgium granted independence to the Congo in 1960, the province of Katanga – the copper belt – seceded from Lumumba's government and violence.

Well, the Connolly weekend [at White Lodge] was great fun. I enjoyed it (always an important point) and from every sign they also did, thoroughly. Cyril was gratified by the affection and fuss with which he was received on all sides, and he had a long run of good eating too – at Maurice's, at the Berlins', and even I must say for myself, on Sunday here. On Saturday we had lunch out at the Bear, Woodstock, joined by Iris Murdoch and her husband John Bayley; afterwards, as it was a beautiful mild sunny afternoon, we went for a walk in Blenheim Park; which I must say this time of year suits; the yellowish stone of the palace shed a pleasing glow, and the silvery reedy lake was dotted with swans. (How beautiful it was too, wasn't it, on our April evening, when all the trees looked so embroidered and silky. That Blenheim view is a born needlework picture. And the place also is haunted for me by you and me; when ever I go there I have a fresh wave of thinking, when will Charles be back?)

Deirdre, Cyril's third and I do hope permanent wife[79] (I must say, she promises to be so; I think their having had the child is a great factor) is a very young, pleasant, tall-slender, gazelle-eyed, generally sympathetic blonde. They were both very nice and cosy to have in the house. Beloved Cyril's shadow hasn't grown less; he has practically given up drinking (except wine) as he says liquor's bad for his waistline. Eating he's simply not prepared to give up. Funny, I'd so much rather give that up, wouldn't you?

Alistair B and Hope came . . . to lunch on Sunday. Alistair in very good form, and enjoyable – he's on the wagon, strictly nothing but water. The great non-click of the ages was, I fear, Cyril and Hopie. (I had to put them next each other at lunch, there was no

ensued, the UN sending in soldiers to restore order. There was controversy about whether arms should or should not be shipped to the Congolese government. The Beaverbrook press in Britain was against, as was Sir Roy Welensky, prime minister of the Federation of Rhodesia and Nyasaland, who was hostile to the UN. CR was heavily involved in UN discussions and negotiations about the Congo crisis.

79 Cyril Connolly married his third and last wife Deirdre Craven in 1959.

other way of arranging the table.) I'm very fond of Hopie, genuinely. But her clothes are no help. She wore a hat like one of the Queen Mother's. However, she had David [Cecil] on the other side of her, and you know what a dependable mopper-up and genuinely enthusiastic and affectionate talker he is; so I don't think she had a bad time. David brought, instead of Rachel [his wife], a charming and intelligent woman who is staying with them called Frances Partridge;[80] and the other guest was a very young fellow of All Souls called Francis Hope,[81] who seemed rather to hit it off with Alistair.

I had lunch in Oxford, last week with Susan T[82] and the daughter Alice (Fairfax-Lucy) who I must say I thought was looking charming; I've always found her an attractive creature.[83] (Has she ever played any part in your life, considering how well you know all the other Buchans?) Alice seemed gay, in spite of the fact that her husband Brian F-L was in the Radcliffe hospital having an operation on his head. Poor Susan looked <u>very</u> drawn and worried; partly I think about Brian's head-operation, partly because poor dear William has got himself thoroughly into the soup – partly sex, partly money. (This <u>very</u> private, of course.) Susan had to leave early to go to a committee, Alice and I sat on to have a gossip, and she told me the whole sad story of William. He has now apparently

---

[80] Frances Partridge (1900-2004), née Marshall, had the previous year lost her husband Ralph Partridge, whose first wife was Dora Carrington, who loved Lytton Strachey, who loved Ralph Partridge. After Strachey died in 1932, Ralph and Frances married. She published five volumes of diaries, and became the last survivor of the Bloomsbury Group.

[81] Francis Hope, critic, editor and journalist, died in 1974 when a DC-10 Turkish Airlines flight from Paris to London crashed near Senlis killing all 364 people on board. He was European correspondent of the *Observer* at the time.

[82] The Lady Tweedsmuir, widow of John Buchan and mother of Alice, Johnnie, William (Billy) and Alastair.

[83] Alice Fairfax-Lucy, née Buchan, was the author of *Charlecote and the Lucys* (1958). Brian Fairfax-Lucy, who lived until 1974, also drew on his family home, Charlecote in Warwickshire, for *The Children of the House* (1968), co-authored with Philippa Pearce.

got 2 illegitimate children, each by a different mistress, apart from the 6 he had by his second wife (that fertile Barbara) and Perdita. Perdita is the only one he doesn't have to pay for.[84] He has just legitimized the second of the illegitimates by marrying its mother; the tormented Buchan family have clubbed up (financially) and packed the trio off to the South of France, telling William he has to write a book. The S of F doesn't sound a very good place to economise.[85]

. . . Dear dear love, take care of yourself. Your E.

White Lodge, Monday, 27 November 1961
My darling . . .

The Old Headington Women's Institute is being rather fun. I get on so much better with women if I have work to do with them – I mean, work along with them (eg Vassar). It's only in vacuo that women rather paralyse me, unless they're my favourite ones.

My 2 days in London were quite fun. I spent one weird, very cold afternoon wandering around the interior of the former Oscar Wilde home in Tite St, Chelsea. It is proposed that this be redeemed from its present state (a tenement) and turned into a small museum.[86] At the moment it was full of workmen; one of whom told one of my companions that the place was haunted. 'We none of us care for working here after dusk,' he said. Poor O. Wilde himself wouldn't make a very imposing ghost, but I suppose the

---

[84] It was at Perdita's christening that EB and CR had first met, in 1941.
[85] William Buchan (1916-2008) was married from 1939-1946 to Nesta Crozier, with whom he had Perdita. His second marriage (1946-1960) was to Barbara Ensor, and his third (1960) to Sauré Tatchell. He had nine children in all. He was the author of a memoir of his father, an autobiography, and three novels. In 1996 he succeeded his elder brother as the 3rd Lord Tweedsmuir.
[86] Oscar Wilde lived at 34 Tite Street, London SW3, from his marriage in 1884 until his trial and imprisonment in 1895. The house was not turned into a museum.

agonies of mind and nerves he must have gone through, when he realized everything was closing in on him, might well leave a (psychic) mark.

. . . Tomorrow I'm going with David to *Romeo and Juliet* – a play which, I realise, I've never yet seen . . .

But my chief news is, I am writing Chapter 1 of my new novel.[87]

. . . Oh Charles, my beloved lovely Charles. Ring me up before I go to Ireland (Dec. 13th) if you can? Your E.

---

87 *The Little Girls,* published by Jonathan Cape, 1964.

1962

White Lodge, 5th January 1962

Dearest love . . .

In Ireland, not much snow but dead white frosts and everything especially the roads glazed with ice. A queer feeling of tension and drama in the air; on the whole, this was enjoyable, only somehow it took up a lot of time; nobody much seemed able to settle to anything – not anyhow that they much do around Christmas and New Year, I suppose. Much time seemed to be spent in emergency conferences over social plans. At Kinsale, everything further complicated by all the roads being so steep up-and-down hilly that if in the least frozen they're impassable for cars. So we spent much time over the fire playing cards and drinking.[88] And we took one wonderful picnic, during which nobody emerged an inch from the Jaguar with the heater on, to a remarkably beautiful semi-frozen bay on the Atlantic.

I did, in spite of the weather, get to the Blacks' for New Year, and had a v cheerful 24 hours there. Round Doneraile, it was a still more spectacular wintry scene; icicles hanging from almost everything . . .

[88] EB had spent Christmas with the Vernons at Fairyfield, Kinsale, Co Cork.

While I was at Kinsale, I was reading the *Letters of George Wyndham.* They are I think fascinating. And he as a man has always interested me so much. I'll write more about these letters in my next letter. I do wish I could get hold of the 2 vols, to send you. They were privately printed for family circulation – lovingly but woozily edited by his brother Guy. I wish, now, they could be re-published, properly edited and with I suppose a biographical preface. The political part is absorbing, I need not say. And to me, the Ireland part. This edition was published early in 1914, just less than a year after his death. (I had not realized he was only 50 when he died.) The political parts – or rather the personal-political parts, have been a good [deal] cut, I suppose inevitably, 'for discretional reasons'. But now, almost fifty years later, with so much water since then under the bridges, and almost everybody concerned dead, [a] good deal (I should think?) could go back again. One longs to know more about his relations with Balfour; none of what must have been his many letters to Balfour are in the book. And the background of the 1906 election . . .[89] I think now would be a smashing good time for a Wyndham book. I need not say that I would not dream of trying to; I am in no possible way equipped to. But some young Fellow of All Souls.

He would of course be the perfect subject for you. In ways, I thought, not totally unlike you.

Urssie has the book because G. Wyndham was her step-grandfather. He married the Lady Grosvenor who was Bendor's mother.[90]

---

[89] George Wyndham (1863-1913), man of letters and politician, Conservative MP from 1889 until his death. He was Private Secretary to Arthur Balfour when Balfour was Chief Secretary for Ireland, and Chief Secretary for Ireland himself from 1900-1905. Balfour was Prime Minister (Conservative) 1902-5. In the Jan 1906 General election the Liberals had a majority, and Balfour temporarily lost his seat in Parliament while remaining party leader.

[90] Wyndham's wife was Sibell, the widow of Earl Grosvenor, mother of the first Duke of Westminster, known as 'Bendor' because of his famous Derby-winning racehorse Bend Or. Urssie (nee Lady Ursula Grosvenor) was the daughter of the second Duke of Westminster.

. . . I suddenly feel, this moment as though you were in the room. It's 4.30 in the afternoon. 11.30 a.m. in New York? I'm writing in my room up at the top with the rose wallpaper. One lamp is on my table. Through the open slats of Venetian blinds I can see the last daylight expiring behind the tree-tops. I do love you. Your E.

White Lodge, Friday, 19th January 1962
My darling . . .

I do wish I could be in Halifax at the same time as you, some time? Will that forever be impossible?

And then this morning I got your letter posted on Jan 16th. It was the letter written the day after the White Russian ball, to which you'd been with Princess di S Miniato. Tell me, I must know at once, DO you dance the Twist? I feel very pessimistic about it. I suppose I really never shall disengage myself from the 1920-ish idea of dancing I grew up to: impassive, impersonal (almost), rather on the snooty side. I can't imagine taking to any form of dancing which involves hopping about and looking enthusiastic, getting hot. But do all the same tell me, answer this question: have you danced this thing? Is it pleasurable?

. . . I wish it were 6 weeks hence. Oh dear one, it seems as though my missing of you increased; I mean, with each month and year it gets worse and worse, as a pain, as something sticking into one like a needle. It's a sort of irritant, and it's accompanied by this awful feeling of boredom (mental) and inanition. How lucky I am to have you to miss (if you know what I mean): that I do realise. To have you to think about, to 'see', with such a rush of love. I can't think what people must feel like who are not in love (and this slightly separates me from quite a lot of my contemporaries: their lives – or so it seems to me – have a quite different balance and focus from mine).

Oh but I can't help it, I do MISS you.

I have long imaginary conversations with you; do you with me?

I am having a whale of a time with The Little Girls, so far. To be enjoying writing anything so much makes me slightly suspicious. The thing is, I really do most enjoy writing comedy, and this has begun as one and I think will remain one – or at least, comic in general tone. By this I don't want to give the impression that I am 'trying to be funny'. But I know you won't misunderstand me and think that.

What I'll do is, I'll have as much of the book as has become readable (or at any rate, readable as a first draft) typed, with carbons, before I leave for New York, and bring over a chapter or two with me, to give to you . . .

Goodbye for now, dearest love. Your E.

White Lodge, Sunday, 28th January 1962

My darling – I now know that Tuesday Feb 6th is the day I go to Seville; I shall be returning here on Monday Feb. 12th. I hope I am letting you know this in time so's I don't miss any letter of yours. I have not yet elicited from Horizon Pictures Ltd (who are making all these for-free travel arrangements) what is the name of the hotel in Seville where I am to be; as soon as they do tell me, I'll cable you . . . I understand the place is extremely beautiful, so I'm lucky to be having this free trip. Also, *Show* magazine are to pay me $1000 for my article about this film – which I do hope (I mean, the article) will be what they hope. They want it in by March 1st. I feel it may be nice to have the money while I'm in NY in March[91] . . .

I keep rushing along with my novel in an obsessive manner, writing even at nights when I am at home. What I like about it is that I do think it is overtly and unguardedly silly. I realise that why I have from time to time tied myself up into knots over my writing, is, because of efforts to conceal how silly I am, and what a predilection for silliness I have. Now I am casting off the mask.

---

[91] EB's commission from *Show* magazine was to write about the filming in Seville of part of David Lean's *Lawrence of Arabia*, starring Peter O'Toole.

. . . I must stop and post this letter, then pack my overnight bag and catch the train to London. My dear love, so short a time now! Your E.

Charles was appointed Canadian Ambassador to the United States, with effect from May 1962.

27 March [New York]

Back again, with hols over, to the apartment stripped of all humanizing adornment and ready for our permanent departure for Washington. . . . What of the hols? I mean the three weeks just concluded in England. All went well till the end, my return visit to E in Oxford. I was visited by the suspicion that E herself was beginning to be bored, that she was quite reconciled to my departure, that there had been a falling-off of tension and illusion, that we were just two old friends, and that is a prospect I cannot face. It is also something I don't really believe. But she moves me. I was not sorry to go, but now I miss her. It's such a tangled feeling and I am not the one who can disentangle it. Mostly when I think of her I feel an immense sadness – the sadness before the sell-out? – and love mingled with irritation, a sure sign with me that my feeling is love.

March 28

That last drive with E from Oxford to Salisbury on the cold, overcast Sunday a.m., and our arrival in Salisbury, and my really idiotic inability to retain the directions given me by successive policemen and bystanders as to how to get to the station. Turn left, then twice right, and up under the railway arch, and each time I got it wrong. We circled round and round Salisbury, the car stalling at each traffic light, and poor E punting it round the roundabouts in the wrong direction. Then the finish-up of smoked salmon sandwiches and gin in the car drawn up in front of the station five minutes before my train departure-time. Was she relieved momentarily to see the last of me? Had we talked ourselves out? Was she, dire thought, bored with me? If I had at the last moment decided to stay another day and thus made her miss her weekend at the Cecils, would she have been precisely pleased?

Bruree House, Thursday, 3rd May 1962

My darling . . .

I am glad you have got, or are going to have, that Scotch butler you told me about. Next, a cook, I suppose. I long to know whether you're enjoying living in the house now you are in it. Though the fact is I should think that arriving in the middle of such pressure you'll hardly have had any time to be conscious of where you are living – yet.[92]

Oh, it must be exciting. I wish there were such a thing as 'the cloak of invisibility', and that I could don it and be your invisible companion. You would then go around rather like the child Maud and her unseen familiar Gay David, in *A World of Love.*

Well, Urssie and I left Kinsale yesterday, motoring back to here, Bruree, after lunch. She had to get back, as she had 2 horse characters [visitors] . . . Bruree is I must say looking very pretty, embowered in flowering cherry trees in all shades of pink. Stephen still away in England.

But I was sorry to leave Kinsale, which was drenched in wonderful illusory spring light, particularly in the late afternoons and evenings. As soon as Stephen leaves, a whole lot of heavenly men emerge from the woods and surround Urssie. I fear the fact that little is seen of them at other times is due to the fact that they can't stand Stephen. Anyway we had a nice gay time, drinking and driving around the country, to various houses. I think the pleasure of going out for drinks is that it causes one to be out and about at the time of the evening when the light is prettiest . . .

---

[92] The residence of the Canadian Ambassador in Washington was 2825 Rockcreek Drive.

I've had a very gratifying offer from my old friend at the University of Wisconsin, at Madison, Wis, to go there for 3 months in the autumn of 1963. They offer me $10,000 for this. I would not be teaching, I'd be an 'author in residence', giving 3 or 4 lectures during my stay. As I am bound, unless anything should go very wrong, to have finished 'The Little Girls' by then (in fact, I hope some time before then), I think 3 months 'off' writing would do me no harm. I must say the vast sum of money offered flatters me, no less than it tempts me. I do seriously feel touched that when they could (or so I'd imagine) get practically anybody short of Shakespeare at that price, they should want me back. Main preoccupation: I should be for 3 months in the same country as you (if by so far ahead we're both still alive) and could, being temporarily so rich, from time to time take trips to New York, and even – should it suit you – to Washington. So I think I'd be a donkey not to accept, don't you? As I say, there does seem to be something a bit phantom about anything so far
[Ends]

White Lodge, Monday, 7th May 1962
Dearest – a lovely letter from you came the morning of the day I left Bruree . . . Interlocking minds . . . I like knowing about your Spanish household (3?) and Italian gardener. And that fearful Popski[93] vomiting on the blonde carpet after a surfeit of magnolia petals. I bet he never has stopped barking since he arrived, that little ray of sunshine. One thing (much as we all love him; I admit I do) you should in a mansion that size be able to get out of earshot of his infernal noise. And it is infernal: a dog keeping on barking is one of the few things that sends me nearly out of my mind . . .

Well here I am, back . . . England looking very pretty (especially the beech woods on the drive home from the airport) though

---

93 The Ritchies' dachshund

I must say not as pretty as Ireland, which was, as I think I told you in my last letter, in one of its glassily-magic moods. But you know, I'm deeply glad I no longer live there. I suppose the only thing I really loved in Ireland was Bowen's Court. And I must say I am very addicted to Kinsale, though I don't wish I lived there, either – it would be nice having it as a place to come and go from if one were VERY RICH . . .

I had a nice 2 days, Friday to Sunday (that is, yesterday) with Edie and the Colley relations – living around the by now rather Italianate-looking yard at Kilmatide (that former dower house of Corkagh). Corkagh has been completely pulled down, razed to the ground, by the people who bought it: the stables and farm buildings they are using as a horse farm. The (physical) disappearance of Corkagh is a shock: in a way, I had known it almost as long as Bowen's Court.[94]

. . . Darling, a copy of a book by me will be reaching you quite shortly, straight from Knopf's. It's that collection of essays, etc., I told you about. It doesn't actually appear (in New York) till 11th June, but Bill Koshland[95] writes that the advance copies are ready, so I've asked him to send one to you. I'm sorry I can't write your name in it, but will do so later. I wonder what you'll think of the book as a whole. The New York edition (which will be the one going to you) is a bit different from the London one, which is simply called AFTERTHOUGHT (not in the plural). The London edition, however, doesn't appear till autumn . . .

I do feel so very, very near you. Am writing this up in my room at the top of the house. It's just beginning to get dusk. Really, I am

---

94 After Aunt Edie's house, Corkagh Park, was demolished, its 300 acres were farmed until 1983. Corkagh Park is now a landscaped public amenity and tourist attraction, with woodlands, water features, and fishing. Corkagh Park is also the home of the Irish National Baseball Facility.

95 William A. Koshland had been with A.A. Knopf, EB's main US publisher, since 1934, and was EB's editor.

living your life more than my own. Yours, and you is the only thing that interests me, rivets me, obsesses me. Every detail of what you tell me is a joy to hear. All my love beloved. Your E.

White Lodge, Tuesday, 15th May 1962

Dearest – our letters again crossed: the last one I had from you (day after I posted mine) was that HEAVENLY account of your becalmed first days in Washington, as an 'untouchable' not yet purified by contact with Mr Kennedy[96] – i.e. not having yet handed in your credentials, or whatever it is, because the President was, so far, out of town. So snoozing away you were, my beautiful love, like an houri, among the magnolias and singing birds. . . .

That you should be hearing birds and I doing so, as I do here at White Lodge, makes a sort of physical-environment tie. Oh dear though, I hope this won't make you less fond of White Lodge when you come back . . . Darling, you won't ever love this (our home) less?

The Scotch butler does sound a bit of a square. Will anything loosen him up, ever? What a bore. One does like a butler to be mellow and in a quiet way slightly cynical. Could you get one of the pretty Spanish maids to seduce him?

What I AM sorry about is that you are – or have been – worried about Elizabeth Ritchie. Did you go to Montreal, I wonder. It's awful a girl should have to go through a crise like that.[97] Damn university education for women, student life, etc: the more I study it – and heaven knows I have an opportunity to do so here – the less good I think it does to women as women. I think it's far better for girls to be given a chance to educate themselves; as I did. This I know sounds smug. But if they have any brains and/or any temperament,

[96] John F. Kennedy (1917-1963), President of the United States since 1961.

[97] As the only child of her generation in the Ritchie family, Elizabeth was conscious of the expectations placed on her, and suffered feelings of inadequacy and guilt.

they'll do it; and if they haven't what does it matter anyhow. (Unless of course they really are going to be, and by nature should be, teachers, doctors, lawyers or even, heaven help them, civil servants.) Do let me know what any further news of Elizabeth is.

. . . All my love – Your E.

Wednesday, 30th May 1962, Chelsea

Dearest – I'm away from White Lodge for the night: left home early yesterday morning, went out to a luncheon where I met various friends including dear mad-looking Henry Green (York) who says he is dying, and looks as though he might: how awful, when so many superfluous people live and Henry writes like such an angel[98] . . .

My mind now (5pm) is a complete BLANK, as I have just returned from the Annual General Meeting of the National Federation of Women's Institutes in the Albert Hall. It was extremely inspirational but very tiring. An even larger gathering, I suppose, than a General Assembly of the United Nations – 6000 and something women, from all over England, Wales, the Channel Islands and the Isle of Man. Only one of the speakers annoyed me: she kept quacking away saying how WI's ought to use our influence to stop fireworks. I've fallen into your way – or a way you had, one summer in New York – of making opprobrious remarks which I believe to be inaudible under my breath, and heard myself muttering 'Go home, you silly cow'. Evidently the woman next door to me did hear, for she jumped violently.

Anyway, though I'm extremely glad I went to the Albert Hall, I feel completely out. I am writing in, or rather on, a very pretty roof garden at the top of Jean Rowntree's house in Glebe Place, surrounded [by] bright pink climbing geraniums, which I love . . .

---

[98] Novelist Henry Green survived until 1973.

Yes, the queer thing is, I've up to now seen more of, in the sense of being with and right among, Americans than you have. America really has come to be a sort of extra, or further dimension to my life. There are times when I think it's become, even, the norm for me. After all, what a non-attached, divided life I've led, since childhood, haven't I? Nothing ever particularly is <u>the</u> norm, which I suppose is why I attach myself to any surroundings of the moment and 'live in the moment' so very nearly completely. I think, a fact I know, that there's not a living soul other than you to whom I'm not 'adjusting' myself, in one or another way, small or greater way, when I'm with them.

It seems odd that what is the most exciting thing in the world, the presence, the company, of the beloved (you) should also be the most natural thing in the world: in fact the only thing in the world that to me <u>is</u> completely natural.

As I was saying, I can't think of anything more important for you to do – and few things, either, more in themselves important than what you will be in a position to do, AND do, in these next years.

This letter reads as though I were drunk; actually I'm cold sober, have so far drunk nothing but tea (though I hear my hostess on the point of bringing the drink tray up on to the roof, and very nice too). I just am as I say blank exhausted after the Albert Hall.

. . . And partly why I sometimes feel so dotty is, that I miss you.
Your E.

5 June [Washington D.C.]
I have a sad letter in wild writing from E. I feel that she is finding these months as hard to get through as I am; but am fixed on not wanting her to come here at this time, although I miss her and want so much to see her. I feel too unstable in these new surroundings to take the added strain, and I remember those ill-fated early visits to Bonn.

White Lodge, Sunday, 10th June 1962
My darling – This has been a week: I don't know why. 2 visitors, who all but sent me off my unloving head . . .

And a week for you, I expect, as you haven't written either. I haven't been able to read the Times, so don't know how the Canadian elections are going.[99] And in Washington what, I wonder.

I have been writing the novel, but it fusses me having women in or anywhere around this house, or rather flat. I've come to a particularly tense passage in The Little Girls.

I am now taking off for 10 days in Order To Get Away from It All. (Taking the novel with me.) Today I'm driving to near Lewes to stay with Cyril Connolly and Deirdre . . . then, on from Lewes to Cranborne – next Tuesday, that is – to David and Rachel;[100] then, back here for Thursday night, then on Friday 15th a plane straight from London to Cork airport (which now exists[101]) to stay with Urssie
[Ends]

12 June
At last a letter from E. She accepts that she doesn't come till September, but can I now accept it? We miss each other equally. But I am the one who is being 'sensible'. Can anyone love such a cold-blooded person? I should like to take a plane and go over for the weekend. Why the Hell not – because, because that's my history.

White Lodge, Tuesday, 26th June 1962
Dearest . . .

Oh I wish, how I wish, you could take a few days' flip over here

---

99 In the election of 18 June 1962, John G. Diefenbaker and the Conservatives won, but with a minority as opposed to their enormous majority of 1958. This constituted a serious personal defeat for Diefenbaker.
100 The Cecils' house in the country was Red Lion House, Cranborne, Wiltshire.
101 Cork Airport opened October 1961.

at the end of July. I do so much, I don't know when so much, want to talk to you, and see you.

Well, Oxford is blazing away with Encaenia Week.[102] I am going through all the works: Maurice [Bowra] is having a dinner party for Charles (we don't call him Charlie any more) Chaplin tonight, which I'm much looking forward to – only what does one say to CC when one meets him? I shall be paralyzed, as fans always are. 'Mr Chaplin, I should like to tell you how very much I have always enjoyed your films!' No, really. But what else does one say? The bien and/or highminded Americans here are fit to be tied over CC's being given an Hon Degree at all. Maurice has finally won a long battle over this – he tried to get an Hon Degree for CC at [Ends]

4 July

E writes that I should take a 'flip over' to England at the end of this month. It is cruel that she should make it sound so easy, when in fact the very idea shows up the state of confinement in which I live and in which anything free is impossible.

White Lodge, Sunday, 8th July 1962

Dearest . . .,

. . . Part of the infuriatingness for the Americans is CC's degree being awarded in the same batch as Dean Rusk's. The two of them apparently have to be kept apart, are reputed to be non-speakers, and have to be segregated in different parts of Oxford.[103] All of

---

[102] The week of ceremonies and celebration at the end of Oxford's academic year, for the awarding of degrees and honorary degrees.

[103] Dean Rusk (1909-1994), US Secretary of State 1961-1969, was a hawkishly active anti-Communist. Charlie Chaplin was under suspicion as a Communist sympathiser during the McCarthy era, and also incurred opprobrium on account of involvements with under-age girls. He left the USA in 1952 to take up residence in Switzerland. Some Oxford academics, now and previously, opposed his being awarded an honorary doctorate.

us who are more chic are going to the Chaplin parties, I need hardly say. Tomorrow I'm going to the Encaenia ceremonies (at Maurice's orders: I think he wants a strong pro-Chaplin representation there). Then to the Encaenia lunch at All Souls, then the Vice-Chancellor's Garden Party, at Trinity. All the works . . . But ungratefully I do find it the most agonizing snatching-away of time.

I went to a large guest-night dinner at Magdalene [*sic*] on Sunday night, asked by Tom Boase.[104] As the President's guest I was guest of honour in those ancient halls, which was very gratifying, except that as we processed about one of my evening shoes (that Italian pair I bought in New York) kept half coming off. Miss Sutherland of LMH[105] was among those there. When we were introduced she said, oh, was I staying in Oxford for the weekend? Hardly, I replied somewhat icily, as I live here – in Old Headington, next door to the Berlins. Really I think these women's colleges (with the exception of St. Anne's) are the limit. I'm quite a credit to my, the female, sex in a small way, but where all these women are concerned I could die and rot. I always have a feeling that they resent, whether consciously or not, anyone doing at all well in a so-called intellectual profession who hasn't 'been to college'.

I feel I am going on in a most ridiculous way about this book, I mean The Little Girls. I mean, I have been writing for 40 years: anybody would think I'd never written a book before, from the fuss I'm making about never being able to be apart for an hour, if possible, from the dear thing. But it has a sort of hallucinatory excitement about it: that, you understand, I know.

Also the fact is, I never work really well unless I over-work. I am over-working, rather; but I don't really think it's doing me any harm.

---

[104] T.S.R. Boase (1898-1974), academic, art historian and administrator, president of Magdalen College, Oxford, 1947-1968.

[105] Lucy Sutherland DBE (1903-1980), historian, principal of Lady Margaret Hall, Oxford, 1945-1971.

. . . Some children acted scenes from *Midsummer Night's Dream* on the lawn here, White Lodge, last week, in the dusk. They were good. We've always said that under-12 children make (in their own way) ideal Shakespeare actors, haven't we. The fact is, I suppose, Shakespeare's characters, if not actually childish, are full of the passions and queernesses children can understand. I maintain, Shakespeare doesn't write well about love in the 'adult' sense – if there is such a thing. His lovers are always such terrific battlers, storming away at each other aren't they.

Dear dear dear love, I must stop. Write soon? And tell me as much as you can. I so long for you, I miss you so very much – I feel like this summer, dry violent winds, too little warmth, no rain. Your E.

151 Old Church St., Chelsea, Thursday, 5th July 1962
Dearest – this is no more than a token letter . . .

I've just come back from a lunch party, rather drunk as you can see. Mrs Bruce[106] was there; what a charmer she is, with her thin form and her morbid haunted great eyes (which probably don't mean that she is either).

What are all the dinner parties like? The Georgetown in-the-garden ones probably charming (and I mean charming, without irony: nothing would I enjoy more). Cecelia Cha[u]ncy Parker,[107] that Washingtonian, who's come very much into (the outer fringe of) my life in these last weeks rather gives me the creeps when she talks about Washington life, in which she, naturally, sees nothing wrong. There's no eating out, she says, because there are no restaurants, and no country inns outside. Everybody 'enturtains' in their own houses. How absolutely anaphrodisiac the verb 'to entertain' is. It's one of the great divides, isn't it, both nationally and socially.

---

[106] Evangeline Bruce (1914-1995) wife of the then US Ambassador to Great Britain, David Bruce.
[107] Cecelia Chauncy Parker was a Washington blueblood by marriage.

Here, 'They entertain a lot, I believe', is the socially slighting thing to say about people known to have a bit of money and be slightly on the move, whom one doesn't know – and imagines one doesn't want to. In more ordinary parlance one would say, 'the X's have masses and masses of people to dinner, almost every night.'

But, 'enturtain' – no!

It does create to my mind the most terrifying picture of no 2 people, of opposite sexes or not, ever being able to go anywhere for a cosy chat. There are so many quite blameless occasions when a man may want to take a woman out for a meal – or know that she would jolly well like him to take her out, so he takes her. A former girl friend, a visiting duchess needing a slight flirtation and much gossip – what is done? What do highly respectable courting couples (young) do? And what – if one may ask quite quietly and firmly – do lovers do? Or aren't there any? No, I suppose not.

Nobody likes going out to a nice dinner party more than I do – as you know – as a matter of fact I do so with the greatest willingness when ever I'm asked, which is quite often. I'm much looking forward to going to Ann Fleming's this evening.

But at the same time, if there were only dinner parties: yak-yak-yak.

It seems to me that all habitable societies – New York, London, Rome, Paris – are organized both for social parties and for occasional chatty (if they aren't romantic) small meals and meetings. And that not only that but that there's something eunuch-y about a society in which there is nothing but entertaining.

Is this so about Washington, or not? Cecelia Chancy P. may be speaking entirely from her own experience (Anyway, why has she fled Washington, as she appears to have done?[108])

---

[108] It may be relevant that the following year Cecelia married, as her second husband, Luis Bolin (1897-1969), a Spanish journalist who had arranged General Francisco Franco's flight from the Canaries to Spain in 1936, became Franco's press director during the Spanish Civil War, and was the author of *Spain: The Vital Years* (1967).

Are you always or often, now being guest of honour? Oh dearest one, how distinguished your life is. I hope you sometimes still think, how tremendously your head would have been turned by all this when you were 20. Though my life is less distinguished, I quite often think of that. What would it be like if oneself at 20 suddenly walked in: would one be able to converse?

Yes, in spite of Friday 13th this has been a nice day. I read, and re-read your letter at the beginning, wrote through the middle of the day, then went out to a drinks (a small, right-sized party) with the Bayleys: Iris Murdoch and her husband. I think I told you before about where they live: a very charming délabrée[110] stone house in the village of Steeple Aston – one turns off the road to Banbury, about 12 miles along out of Oxford. When you're back here next, we must go there: I'm so fond of them both and I love the house. It's the sort of house I'd like you and me to live in – I thought that from the very first glance. Steeple Aston has not that rather glassy chic of the Cotswolds, but is a very charming stone old Oxon village, on a small river which flows at the bottom of the Bayleys' garden. Have you read Iris's *An Unofficial Rose*[111] yet? I find it very enjoyable, though I'm not sure that I don't like her rather more demoniac ones more.

I said in my last letter that I'd write the next one (which would be this) in type, so's to be able to get in more narrative. But now it comes to the point, this evening, I do feel rather physically exhausted by banging away at that little baby-blue machine, and feel more relaxed writing by hand. Talking of writing by hand, I wrote several sentences of the novel on the back of one of your envelopes, the other day – I was waiting for somebody in a car, and a sentence came into my mind so I dived into my handbag to look for something to write [on], and, as I always carry letters of yours

[110] French: dilapidated.

[111] Iris Murdoch's sixth novel, published 1962.

Well, this letter has reeled drunkenly and boringly along, my darling love. It's the way I would give off, in the middle of an afternoon, if I were seeing you.

The fact is, I've never fully let myself realise – daren't yet – what a NIGHTMARE your having left New York is to me. When I wrote 2 lines up, about 'seeing you in the middle of an afternoon', I suddenly had the most awful PAIN at the picture of your just coming into Hampton House,[109] for the odd half hour, when you found you could get out of the office, as you used to do . . .

If only I could see you. If only we could talk. This is said in a small, controlled voice, you'll understand.

Well, we're now in July. Only one whole month till I see you.

I dreamed the other night that I had a telegram from you saying you were coming to England and I was so excited that I woke up.

Oh my love. Goodbye for now. Do you remember this house I'm staying in till tomorrow morning? A rather nice countrified Chelsea house, with a garden. You once came and had a drink here, or came and picked me up here when we were going out.

Your E.

9 July

Funny, rather drunk letter from E about entertaining in Washington. I want to see her, but dread that her visit at this time and when I am in this place may turn sour. What it comes to is that England is the only place left now where I can be free of being 'Ambassador'.

White Lodge, Friday, 13th July 1962

My darling – I remember any Friday 13th day always gives you the creeps, and you say you always feel you should spend it incommunicado, or in a disaster-proof cork-lined room. I wonder how you spent today. . . .

---

[109] Hotel apartments where EB usually stayed in New York

about with me, used the blank side of one of your beloved blue envelopes, with your handwriting on the other side. I must give you back the envelope as a curiosity some time.

The dinner party at Ann Fleming's was great fun – I stayed till all hours, regardless of time, as several others did too. Cecil B, dear Leslie,[112] the inevitable Lady Waverley[113] (who I do find a bit of a bore, but what a tenacious getter-of-herself-around-the-town, in all forms, she is: fortunately she left early), a new rather exotic young man of Ann's, and . . . Debbo [*sic*],[114] who had to go to dinner somewhere else, came in in the course of the evening and was very funny. Yes, it really was most enjoyable. And how I do like her.

Various other dinner parties of all kinds. Oh the people I've met lately. C. Chaplin (who I thought was a darling man); Agatha Christie[115] – whom I never even dared to hope to meet. I wish one could talk about all these people: we will; it seems tedious when it comes to the point, to write about them.

More urgent (and happy) I'll be in New York on Sept. 20th, and oh my darling You'll be there, unless the skies fall, that weekend. It is heaven to have a definite DATE (I mean, in the calendar sense) to look forward to.

I think I'll go to Hampton House again . . .

All my love, my darling – Your E.

White Lodge [end of July 1962, pages 1 and 2 missing]

. . . I'm going back to Ireland – Fairyfield, Kinsale, I need hardly say, on August 3rd (a Friday) for about 3 weeks. Then coming back

---

112 Cecil Beaton, Leslie Hartley.

113 Ava, Viscountess Waverley (1896-1974), was the widow of Sir John Anderson, 1st Viscount Waverley, successively Home Secretary and Chancellor of the Exchequer in the National Government during World War II. He initiated the development of the prefabricated air-raid shelter called, after him, an 'Anderson shelter.'

114 Deborah (Debo), b 1920, the youngest of the six Mitford sisters and wife of Andrew, the 11th Duke of Devonshire.

115 Agatha Christie (1890-1976), best-selling crime fiction writer.

here, on about August 27th or 28th, to get myself organised before America. I'm supposed to be going to other places in Ireland, Eddy's, Derek Hill's in Donegal, the Desmond Guinness's at Leixlip,[116] but really wonder if I shan't try and slither out of those (with the possible exception of Eddy, who would be piqued if I didn't, and also is likely to let me write while I'm with him). I do in many ways like, as you know, flouncing round country-house-visiting, but am now so fanatically unwilling to be separated from my novel. (Which always sounds unconvincing to me, when spoken of as 'my novel'. It's The Little Girls, or nothing.)

I am now right plumb back into the middle of the time when the 3 of them ARE little girls. They are really even more real to me as little girls as they are as women – but I think that's all right, as that really is the Subject of the book, isn't it? – encaged, rather terrible little girls battering about inside grown-up (indeed, almost old) women.

They are all at a wonderful day-school called St. Agatha's, where what doesn't go on is nobody's business.

. . . I've just come back from staying 4 days in Suffolk, a few miles from Long Melford, with Spencer Curtis Brown . . . It's rather fun. He said for me to bring my writing and write (which, as he is my [American] lit agent Collins's opposite number, seemed appropriate), so I jolly well did – never appeared till lunch-time, which consisted of me drinking my Metrecal,[117] out of a beer mug, and him gnawing bones left over from dinner the night before. Then after lunch I firmly went back to my room – in which the table I was typing on wobbled like anything, owing to the rippleness of the floor – and not emerging again till between 5.30 and 6, when

---

[116] Desmond Guinness (1931-), second son of Diana Mitford (later Mosley) and Bryan Guinness (Lord Moyne), writer and connoisseur. Co-founder with his first wife Mariga of the Irish Georgian Society in 1958 and, with her, the restorer of Castletown House and of Leixlip Castle, both in Co Kildare.

[117] A liquid slimming-aid.

we went out in his Jaguar, which was extremely enjoyable, as he also likes trickling about small roads in a car, and looking over walls and houses, and exploring those weird, enormous Suffolk perpendicular churches which are so lavishly scattered, aren't they, like a huge family-party of cathedrals, all over that lush and I must say beautifully [lit *crossed out*], but in many ways, from the point of view of 'progress', obsolete rolling Suffolk landscape . . .

You and I must go there – that part of the world – when you're back here again. I've now learnt quite a lot about it, including the roads hither-and-thither from here. I've also got to be – since you were here – much at once nippier and more calm (TOUCH WOOD!) in the matter of tearing about miles of England in my car. I was a very dim driver last spring, my darling; you deserved better. But really you know the humiliation of those fussy driving lessons, necessary for the tests, and then failing the tests on top of them, did not so much rattle me as undermine – though only, thank God, I find temporarily – my morale.[118] I am now back again (TOUCH WOOD) to my original form – such, I must say, whatever that was.

. . . Oh, dearest love, beautiful Charles, goodbye for now. Your E.

Fairyfield, Kinsale, Friday, 10th August 1962

My darling . . .

Tell Roley, there's a character in The Little Girls called 'Cousin Roland'. I hope he won't mind. As a matter of fact, this character never actually enters the story, but remains on the margin, off-stage, influencing events to a certain degree. I have a very clear idea, though, of Cousin Roland – who could not be less like Roley. As a matter of fact, I've never thought the name 'Roland' suits Roley very well: 'Roley' suits him perfectly. And this cousin Roland could

[118] There were no driving tests at all in Ireland when EB learned to drive. To obtain a British driving licence, as a British resident, she had to take the test.

not have any other name. He has a brother, Cousin Claud, who is a bishop.

I'm reading a novel I never read when it came out – found it in this house; the Enid Bagnold novel with Diana in it, *The Loved and Envied.*[119] Good in parts, I think, very? And wonderful as a portrait of Diana, except that, one can't somehow, separate 'true' characters from the true stories. I mean, people may make their own lives, up to a point, but, far more, I think, their lives make them? A great factor in the life of Diana, I think, is that at no point, since birth, was she quite obscure. I mean, if she'd been nothing more, even, than a duke's daughter (even if the duke wasn't, as said, actually her father[120]) she'd have been that.

. . . It is less than 6 weeks now till I see you. Goodbye for now, beloved. Your E.

Fairyfield, Kinsale, Co.Cork. 22nd August 1962

My darling . . .

Well, I had a whale of a time, those 3 days, staying with Derek [Hill] in Donegal. What a weird atmosphere it is – all those weird, well-appointed, aesthetic though sumptuous homes spaced apart from each other by miles and miles of noble but desolate scenery. 3 charming Italians – a Milanese Count, Enrico Luling, with big business interests, his v talkative but engaging wife Marina and their child, a wonderful little 15 year old decadent called Diamantee, with Alice-in-Wonderland long hair – were staying with Derek at the same time.[121] So we all trooped about the countryside like anything, ending up [at] a barbecue (how does one spell it?) given by rich

---

[119] Enid Bagnold's *The Loved and Envied* was published in 1951.

[120] It is believed that the biological father of Lady Diana Manners, later Lady Diana Cooper, daughter of the Duchess of Rutland, was not the Duke of Rutland but, among other candidates, the handsome MP and writer Henry Cust.

[121] Count Enrico Luling Buschetti and family lived in Italy at the Villa di Maser, Treviso, built by Palladio, which his wife Marina inherited from her father.

Belfast linen manufacturers, in the Donegal Celtic twilight, on an icy headland projecting into the Atlantic, attended by all sorts – the Donegal 'county', beatniks from where I don't know, the Belfast rich set, and 'the military', rather like the darling subalterns of my young days, over the Border from the 6 Counties.[122]

Well, it was quite restful to get back to Kinsale. (I forgot to tell you, Enrico is the Master of the Milan foxhounds – would you ever think?)

. . . Blessed love, goodbye for now. Your E.

8 September

I dare not try to pin this new certitude to paper, in case it may join so many other false starts recorded here. Can an old man have a new insight? And live by it? Or is this only a seasonal awakening after the long summer of discontent? Dare I believe that one day – those few hours – can shake off the shackles? . . . If the miracle has happened, it is the gift of a love which has caused me the most guilt and pain. I cannot – surely? go back now to the womb of self. It seems that I can only at last embark on the voyage out, whatever the risks.

Charles went to New York to see Elizabeth and then returned to Washington.

Hampton House, Wednesday, 20th September 1962

My darling . . .

You've left yourself behind in this apartment, as you used to do at Bowen's Court, as you do at White Lodge. In that sense, I've been happy going on being here, and yet there is this awful jaggingness of missing you. And it's hard not to feel that New York is an empty

[122] Co Donegal, in the Irish Republic, abuts Co Londonderry, one of the Six Counties of Northern Ireland, (part of the United Kingdom), and is a holiday destination for both sides of the divide.

shell – dear New York . . . In a way though – indeed, I think mostly – I'm glad to be going. An at all continuous stay here without you would be pointless (though I can't of course keep being haunted by the thought that if I were here for these next weeks, you might occasionally be able to hop over on the shuttle and we'd have lunch. However, one can't have everything.)

Marshall [Berland] has been very kind. I spent Tuesday evening in his Brooklyn glamourous [*sic*] interior (which is becoming more and more so) first having my photograph taken, in a rather 1920ish manner, then being given a rich dinner. Unfortunately I again went to sleep. What is it about that apartment? I wonder whether he sprays the air with opium, or anything. It's not boredom; the boy isn't boring, to do him justice, and he supplies one with many pretty toys to play with. I think it may possibly be the v rich food, which sends fumes up into the brain. I also doubt whether he ever opens windows in that apartment, owing to fear that a tornado may burst in and upset his bibelots.

He also yesterday morning took me shopping at Ohrbach's

I was interrupted. Thursday morning:

I was going to say he took me shopping Ohrbach's (on 34th St, at Fifth) a place which I must say is all it's cracked up to be. As you've no doubt heard, they copy French and other models, in quite good materials with great skill and finish, at 1/3 the price. For those, you go to the Oval Room, on the 6th floor. All the other floors are a great surging sea of Jewesses, young, old, good, bad or indifferent, beauteous or god-forsaken, dashing about, shopping. Literally millions of them, I thought, whizzing up and down on the escalators, too. I don't think I saw a Gentile in the place, other than myself. I ended by buying, I think, a very delightful Balenciaga, thin brown wool, (the brown of this year). It's by way of being a 6p.m. dress, and looks like that in front, but unfortunately is almost backless (I say 'unfortunately', as it makes it less suitable for University of Wisconsin functions than I'd hoped). One apparently can clip it up at the back, with a brooch. I think it's becoming, anyway; and I do think (which is one of the reasons I went for it) it should be a good set-off for my beloved turquoise beads.

My series of lunches, dinners, etc with that series of magazine (glossy) editresses and editors is rolling along its way. I have not called up any friends . . .

I finished, and have sent to be typed, that long further chapter of The Little Girls . . .

You know what it means to me that you should read that book. It means so much to me that I can't tell you – but you do know, I know.

Beloved love, goodbye for now. Your E.

25 September

No miracle happened. And I am back where I was, becalmed. But last weekend I spent with E in NY and so was alive for forty-eight hours. Now I am back in loathed Washington trying to put the best face I can on it, but so restless, so bored . . . And to think of E sitting in Hampton House, NY, and I am sitting here, and what's all this in aid of, for the Lord's sake. Why didn't I stay there all week at the dear A Hotel?[123]

The voyage out.

The Claridge Apartment Hotel, Apt. 209, Madison, Wis. Monday, 1st October 1962

My darling . . .

Well, here I am, and it is fun being back. Have been received back with the greatest enthusiasm, literally hugged and kissed, which does warm my heart – what heart indeed would it not warm? Madison (city) looking very spectacular and gay. It consists as you know of long wide avenues, raying out and downhill from the uphill Capitol (Washington DC having been the model) and many

---

[123] Probably the Algonquin.

sidestreets of on the whole rather old-fashioned houses: all being heavily tree-planted. The trees are so far just taking a golden tinge, on the point of 'turning'. There have been two very bright, sunny days. It's an oddly <u>cosy</u> place, as I think I told you – cosy in a sense that so many places in the East, for all their prettiness, somehow fail to be.

Have hardly been on the campus, so far: am having lunch with dear Helen C. White[124] (who also met me on Saturday, at the airport) today. This is now only 10.30 on Monday morning – and I started rushing about <u>far</u> earlier than most of the Madison citizens.

The Claridge is up near the Capitol, which is rather fun. I mean, one can enjoy the night-life (or at any rate apparent night-life) of the town, instead of being totally secluded in academic society.

My apartment <u>is</u> odd: rather a shock at first – in that it's one huge room, instead of the 2, plus kitchen, I thought it was going to be. But it's a curiously pretty, airy, sunny room – 3 windows, looking out on gardens and painted wooden houses. Something slightly central-European about it. Distinctly <u>under</u>-furnished and a bit student-y. The only real snag is that the bed is one of those infernal divans with <u>no</u> end, at either end. Which for
[Ends]

1 November
In the a.m. telephoned E. I feel further from her than when she was in England. No, it's not that exactly either, more as if we were on another footing of accustomed friendship – the state which I often looked forward to in the days of our civil war. A state in which there can even be something almost resembling friendliness between her and S.

---

[124] Professor of English at Wisconsin University and chair of English Department 1961-1967.

Elizabeth went to Washington for a weekend and stayed with the Ritchies.

11 November

Going for a walk with E this p.m. I wish it was this beautiful but breezy a.m. I know it will cloud over in the p.m; we'll both have had too much to drink before lunch and be feeling sad and stupid. What I dread most is that I won't be able to think of anything to say to her – a new form of impotence.

16 December

I said to E that the chilly exhilaration of her new book, 'The Little Girls', springs from revenge. 'Oh yes,' she said, meaning, 'You don't know the half of it.' Revenge on love. Revenge on me.

17 December

It's a bit odd this time with E here; not really satisfactory, something leaks away during these friendly social weekend visits. Yet when we were alone in NY everything seemed to be back again. The truth is that she likes to come to stay, and I only care for a 'life apart'. Anyway, let's drop it.

Elizabeth returned home from the United States. She spent Christmas 1962 in Ireland, then went back to Old Headington, Oxford.

1963

White Lodge, Wednesday, 23rd January, 1963
My darling . . .

I have been thinking about you so much, here in this womb-like world of frost, ice, snow. Sno-o-o-w. I haven't felt far away from you, or you from me.

I can't tell you how extraordinary (for England) this complete interminable unbroken whiteness is. Air outdoors, or if one opens a window, like the blade of a knife. I can't tell you how beautiful, either . . . A tremendous rather terrifying dramatic abnormality . . . which I must say I am rather enjoying, but it makes one feel a pig to do so, because really I believe people are dying like flies or feeling so unnerved that they wish they were dead. If there were a complete electric power-cut in White Lodge it really would be rather jolly fun, as you know all my heating's electric. And the device of lighting the kitchen gas-oven door and sitting on top of the oven with the door open might not work either, as we're told there may be going to be a gas-cut too.

However I'm at the moment having such a selfish nice time (secretly) that I can't complain. It's been simply wonderful staying locked up in this spell of snow, all day and most evenings, with The Little Girls.

I've finished that beach picnic chapter I showed you the beginning of in New York: the end of it really is rather heart-breaking.[125] I'll send you a copy as soon as I can get a copy made. I've done quite a lot more, too.

The one to me real horror-horror is that an enormous BAT has got into the house. You do know that I have this absolutely insensate horror and terror of them, an uncontrollable one. First it was whirling round and round the dining-room: that wouldn't have mattered so much as I don't use that room when I'm alone, and this is no weather for having parties, except for the drink being kept in there – the bat used to come whirling at me. (Why I never had the sense to move the bottles out of there, I don't know.) It did that one evening when David [Cecil] was here, and he nobly said he didn't mind bats and thought he could either catch it or drive it out, so I gave him a bath towel to hit at the bat with and left them both shut up in the dining-room. There were tremendous leapings and bangings and poundings: he had very sensibly got the window open, top and bottom, and was persuading the bat towards it, also standing on chairs and hitting at it when it went and sat on the cornice. The room afterwards was a shambles, I need hardly say; but I was so grateful. He must have either got the bat out or given it a nervous shock: nothing more seen or heard of it in the dining-room. But then 3 evenings later, when I was working up here, either that same bat or a friend of its came SWOOPING, without warning, over me and the typewriter. I uttered I think the most ghastly and shameful shriek that I ever have. I was so furious at being interrupted, too. I rushed downstairs, where I sat on the drawing-room sofa, shaking all over. I did manage to steal in here, while the bat was having a rest for a moment, and snatch my typewriter and manuscript out. I slept on the drawing-room sofa that night (the other room, yours, hasn't been slept in for so long that

[125] In *The Little Girls* as published, this is Part II, Chapter 7.

I thought that under present weather-conditions it might not be much of a catch). Next day, Aline B sent in her very kind gardener to make a thorough search for the bat: he practically took the carpets up, up here, but no squeak or sign of it. They are the most sinister horrors, besides being such bores.

In fact the whole thing set me off wondering about HATRED. I really did feel ill with hatred of that bat . . . Is it wrong to hate – even a member of the brute creation? Obviously it's wicked to hate a person (not that I often or at any rate consistently do) but is the sheer sensation of hatred in itself wrong (in the sight of God, I mean?) I think it probably is, because it distorts and darkens one, thereby doing injury – I should think? – to the soul.

I'm sorry to keep on about this bat, but it, the science-fiction weather and The Little Girls have been really the 3 outstanding things in my life since I got home. I've seen, apart from David, friends such as Aline (Shaya's due back from the US today), John Sparrow,[126] James Joll[127] – I think that's all . . .

The tragedy which has coloured all these weird days – as you can imagine – has been Hugh Gaitskell.[128] How he was loved (even I, though I only spent one morning with him, cared about him so much: how one prayed and prayed for him to get well). I think the sheer shock of the whole thing, and the infuriatingness of it, has hit a lot of people to the point of almost dementing them. . . . And of course he had been with the whole pack, the Berlins, Stuart [Hampshire], Maurice, out there at Portofino last August. Went

---

[126] Warden of All Souls, Oxford.

[127] James Joll (1918-1994), political and intellectual historian, Fellow of St Anthony's College, Oxford; later, professor of International History at London School of Economics.

[128] Hugh Gaitskell, b 1906, Leader of the Labour Party from 1955. An able man and a 'moderate' socialist, educated at Winchester and New College, Oxford, he was one of the few Labour politicians with friends and admirers in all walks of society. He died on 18 Jan 1963 from lupus disease, and was succeeded by Harold Wilson.

there chiefly to meet Ann Fleming, who was with them. Mrs G.[129] was there too, of course. Aline says she's sure Mrs G never realized how tremendously and obsessively he was in love with Ann: he was, apparently, when they were both of them in London, seeing her almost everyday. And the awful thing for Ann was, she'd gone to Jamaica (now is there). She went before it had been realized how mortal-serious his illness was. Not I imagine that she was, or claimed to be, more than very very very fond of him – but still it must have been awful to realise he'd died wanting to see her (as he must have longed to see her) and she not there.

Snow makes one think of the dead: since he died I have kept looking out of the window, while I'm working, thinking, I'm sorry <u>he</u> won't see this – I think I told you, he told me and told other people he liked EB books so much, and was always re-reading them.

And of course the whole fundamental thing about this death of his – I mean, the kind and nature and manner of his death – is that it's increased my terror, my terror, my TERROR of something happening to you . . .

By the way, I am going to Lewes this coming week-end . . . Not the ideal time to go away, and I don't really like leaving the house (in case it freezes into a block of ice) but this isn't simply a visit to Bee Horton – such as I could put off – I promised months ago to speak to the Lewes Literary Society (which was started by the Woolfs and is very high class[130]) on the 28th . . .

I love you, my dearest love. Your E.

10 February

I told Diana [Cooper] that I thought I had got to the stage of throwing in my hand and 'settling down'. 'Don't,' she cried immediately,

---

[129] Dora Gaitskell, Hugh's wife.

[130] The Woolfs did not start the Lewes Monday Literary Club, but Leonard Woolf was its president for many years until 1968.

'Don't do that.' She fixed me with her fabulous eyes. 'I thought you might advise it,' I said. 'What me? Never' – said with immense energy.

White Lodge, Wednesday, 13th February 1963
My darling . . .

D'you know, I'm glad I have to come over to the US in the second half of March – 'have to' I mean, because I've promised to be at the University of Pennsylvania, in Philadelphia, from March 18th – 25th. I knew you would otherwise say, 'Don't come just then' – with the Canadian Elections so soon pending, I mean. I know that the chances of seeing you for more than one hour (if that) will be extremely slender. I know there'll be no hope of your getting anywhere near New York, or anything of the sort. But if the worst came to the worst I could even just take a flip to Washington for a 1/2 day. Anything would be better than nothing. And I do want more to see you at this time – in a way – almost more than I ever have.

I shall come over to New York on about the 14th of March, I think, and stay till the 28th. (On March 30th, I am starting off on that Hellenic Cruise, till April 15th.)

Yes, if you could be here . . . If you could just be wafted here for 24 hours . . .

I am glad you saw Diana [Cooper] and that she was looking beautiful and seemed happy. Are you having a party for her? Not easy, I should imagine, to arrange anything immediately now, as I suppose they always may be wanting you back in Ottawa . . .

All my love. Your E.

16 February

Diana was saying how necessary it is for husband and wife to sally separately into the world, so that they each can bring something fresh to put into the vase – so true.

White Lodge, Saturday, 2nd March 1963

My darling . . .

The time I now cannot wait for is March 26th to 28th. Yes, that is a weekend: I finish work at Philadelphia on Friday 25th p.m. I shall have to take off back to England on an overnight plane on the 28th; that would be Monday evening. I shall move in to Hampton House on the evening of Friday 25th. Oh my love . . .

I airmailed off to you yesterday, in a large packet, chapters of The Little Girls. You'll find a rather prim (I mean undemonstrative) note attached to it, with a few remarks – I never feel a letter packed in a parcel is as intact as a letter inside an envelope. Oh I do hope you'll enjoy those chapters: I've now written quite a lot more, beyond them.

I had a lovely time with Elizabeth R.[131] Never have I enjoyed myself more with her, and that's saying a lot. I thought she looked not only handsome but lovely – very glowing. I think short hair really is more of a success on her than long. With this short hair she looks at once younger in the appealing sense, older in the chic sense. I think that in spite of her admirable cynicism about the whole set-up here she is, really is, having a good time and getting quite a lot out of things. I much look forward to seeing her for as much time as she can spare me, and I think it would be fun to make various other plans. What a good brain she quite evidently has, too – in spite of the vague, off-hand modesty of her conversation. I realise that I equally can't bear people (of either sex) not to be clever, and equally can't bear it if they too much 'show' it . . .

Oh my dear angel, good bye for now. Your E.

---

[131] Elizabeth Ritchie went from McGill University, Montreal, to Lady Margaret Hall, Oxford.

30 March

I think of the day before yesterday, sitting in L'Aiglon with E drinking vodka martinis at 11.30am. She is back in England, now at this moment starting on her tour. Why can't I go too?

E says we have 'interlocking minds'. I feel I have no mind at all. I miss her.

S.S. Ankara. Saturday, 6th April 1963

My darling . . . What I was distraught to hear was that you'd arrived back to Washington after our perfect time in New York into yet another US-Canadian crisis, and one which you felt in some way involved you personally. Too complicated, you say, to write about in a letter, and I can well see it could be; I expect by now it's been pushed out of the way by another; as they seem to be proceeding to take form one after another, like ice-bergs in a procession. What a horrible time . . . And now on Monday next the [Canadian] Elections[132] . . .

This is a whole day at sea, making back from N Africa towards Greece, various parts of it, Crete, and so on. I had rather been looking forward to this 'day at sea' as I thought I'd settle down at a table, write comfortably a long and still better legible letter to you. There's rather a nice, unfrequented writing room. But far from it. Today since sunrise there has been the most GHASTLY tempest, which has chosen to crop up just when we are crossing 616 miles of sea. The poor SS Ankara is leaping and banging about, passengers falling in all directions like ninepins, not to speak of being as sick as dogs. This morning the moment I sat down to write the table rose up and hit me WHANG in the face. I haven't actually been seasick but have got a ghastly headache, which for me is most

---

[132] An issue which produced recurring crises and dominated the Canadian election was whether or not to arm Canada's Bomarc Missile with nuclear warheads.

unusual, as you know. It's now 7 p.m. and I have spent most of the day in my cabin, taking dope and sleeping. And look how worse than ever my writing's become, which maddens me when there's so much to say.

This however, has been the one bad patch: this I must hasten to make clear. I only wish we had never left North Africa. Oh Charles it surpasses one's wildest expectations – one's very wildest, you and I must go there . . .

You must have heard so much (I had) about those honey-coloured Roman ruined cities, standing either up over the sea (which looks hyacinth-blue between their columns or through their arches) or else – as the one in Tunisia did – in the middle of an undulating empty sea of land, with shapely small mountains floating round like clouds: and this (now, in April) is a sea of flowers. Tiny orange marigolds and large yellow daisies melt into each other, making the miles they cover seem to be spread with golden shot-silk. Each of these cities is a world in itself; I mean completely a 'pure' ruin, deserted as a ruined city should be, with no shack-settlements or anything around them. Yes, after years of wanting to see them these cities really do exceed imagination, towering over it . . .[133]

The Tunisians are delightful, so elegant to look at and they do have the most beautiful children. Beautiful tall little girls with so far no busts, and faces in which there is a mixture of innocence (whatever that is, but it's quite palpable when one sees it) and mystery and mirth. And the little boys all very slender and grave and courteous – they look high-bred even when it's unlikely (as it is in general) that they actually are . . .

[Ends]

---

[133] In Tunisia her Hellenic Cruise took in the ruins of Thuburbo Majus and, in Tripolitana (Libya), of Leptis Magna.

White Lodge, Monday, 22nd April 1963

My dearest – I didn't write yesterday, Sunday, as I thought I'd wait and see if a letter from you came this morning. And it did. I have been so very happy for you that Mike Pearson is now there.[134] And that it is him you will be working with. And that – though nothing is ever perfect in this imperfect world, where work is concerned, at least (love is perfect) – you are out again at the other side of what I can see was, what I did realise at the time was being, a time of horror . . .

Shall you be going to Ottawa, I wonder? Anyway, he, I see is soon to be going to Washington. Is it true that he and Mr Kennedy[135] are very close and great friends? So the papers here say, at any rate . . .

I DO understand about the postponement of your coming here; I expected nothing else, in a way. I don't see how – as things are – you could come in the middle of May. I couldn't love you as much as I do and not understand this. Oh though how I pray that in June you can come – that is, feel that you can come. I am perfectly free all June; free as air. Nobody is coming here; I have not promised to go anywhere. (So am perfectly free all July, too. But I hope it will be June because June is sooner.) So I will simply wait here, as placidly as possible, like Penelope or Nausicaa or whoever it was, till you can come . . .

The Little Girls will be out by then, I expect,[136] and I shall in a way be feeling lonely. But it will be lovely to have you reading the final chapters here. I've had 3 very trying days 'correcting typescript'. I have to send 3 different copies of the book to different places, unfinished as it is. When I was working away at this niggly

---

[134] Lester (Mike) Pearson and the Liberals won the Canadian election, defeating John Diefenbaker and the Progressive Conservatives. Pearson, as Prime Minister, headed a minority government from April 1963 to April 1968. CR considered himself a Conservative, but the Department of External Affairs had suffered from Diefenbaker's suspicion of its officers as former colleagues of Pearson.

[135] President John F. Kennedy

[136] *The Little Girls* was not published until the following year.

task (which seems quite irrelevant to The Little Girls) very late one night and rather drunk, a vast gale, a real titanic coup de vent hit the top of this house, wrenching the windows of this (my top room) open, and sending the literally hundreds of sheets of typed paper flying like mad white geese into the air and all over the room. In the state of tension I'd got myself into, it was terrifying; in a way, do you know, I nearly did go mad: I first shrieked and shrieked, then sat down in the middle of the room, deep in those innumerable sheets of sheer 'typescript' and wept. As none of the pages had yet been numbered, it took me most of the rest of the night to get them sorted into order again. However, that's now over; and I am back again into writing the rest of the book . . .

I love you so very much. Your E.

[*Fragment, early May 1963, from White Lodge*]
The chief thing is that I shall have *finished* 'The Little Girls' three days hence. You may wonder why it has taken me so long. It's simply that I am ending it with a tremendously ambitious finale; in a way almost a novella in itself, but also like the finale in a musical: almost, one might say, like a comedy version of the mad scene in *The Duchess of Malfi*[137]. . . . Technically the thing is at once very tricky and very fascinating to write.

Bruree, Monday, 13th May 1963
My darling – I loved your letter and finding it at Bruree . . . And, WHAT a lot has happened since (to you, I mean). Because I've since, of course, had your cable saying you were going to Hyannisport with Mike[138] . . . I think it is angelic that in the middle of all this

---

[137] Macabre and melodramatic play by the Jacobean dramatist John Webster.
[138] CR accompanied Mike Pearson on a visit to President John F. Kennedy at the Kennedy Compound on the waterfront at Hyannisport, Cape Cod. CR was put up in Robert Kennedy's house.

tumult that you've written to me – my dear and angelic love; I mean, you are angelic, keeping me in touch with what's happening, not letting me feel out of things . . .

Well, my life here (Ireland) has pursued an even and pleasurable tenor. Urssie very well, except for having given herself a black eye – however, it's slight, so quite becoming, looking more like unusually heavy eye make-up. Stephen very pleased with himself (therefore, particularly nice) and with the Baron Von Wedel.[139] Quite a lot of gay life . . .

I've had a very nice letter about The Little Girls from William Plomer – who, being in Cape's (my London publisher's) office, is literally the first person in England other than the typist who has re-typed it, to read it. He seems to see the point of it. They, Capes, haven't yet, any more than Knopf's have.[140]

. . . I don't want to plague you by questions as to WHEN you can come. I'm simply waiting, as placidly as possible. As I say, from now on my life is an open book.

Oh, but I do love you so much. Your E.

16 June [Oxford]

I have been seeing something of Isaiah, and other philosophers with a taste for scandal.[141] But I have the impression that apart from

---

[139] Count Ernst von Wedel, horse-racing German aristocrat on whom Stephen Vernon doted.

[140] The novelist William Plomer was employed as a reader by EB's new publishers, Jonathan Cape. Knopf found what she described to CR as the 'tremendously ambitious finale' of *The Little Girls* unsatisfactory, and she worked out a new ending with the help of her friend and agent Spencer Curtis Brown.

[141] The scandal was the Profumo Affair: Conservative MP John Profumo (1915-2006) had a brief affair with model Christine Keeler, whom he got to know at Clivedon, the home of Lord Astor. He denied the affair in the House of Commons in March 1963, but confessed to the truth in June, after which he resigned from the cabinet and from Parliament. Keeler had also been sleeping with a Russian naval attaché at the Soviet Embassy in London. In the atmosphere of the Cold War this circumstance, since Profumo was Secretary of State for War, was thought to constitute a threat to

beloved E, no one much wants to see me this time. The pitcher can come too often to the well, and perhaps has also from the pitcher's point of view. E and I went for a drive last night through wooded escarpments and green valleys in the Chilterns to find Norman churches and red manors buried in trees. In a rare interval, a pale sun burned on cottage roses. We had drinks at the Waggoner at Ewe Elm[142] and came back to smoked salmon and claret, followed by the Berlins and Stuart Hampshire here till one in the a.m. drinking on and on and talking of Profumo. This Sunday a.m. I disrupted the household by getting up early. I don't know that E has yet forgiven me.

30 June [Washington D.C.]

I was a fool to come back on a holiday. The beautiful house, full of flowers, is ticking over emptily. S sits on the terrace. Colin [the Scots butler] whistles as he polishes my tooth-pick case in the pantry. The discontinuity after the life with E, the clean break – the amputation – has left me strung up and tautened. I could take on anything, but cannot take on nothing.

E thinks the reason the Duchess of Argyll had to have tape-recorders and photographs of her acts of love was that the act in itself meant little or nothing to her. She could only believe in it with aids. But she puts the case in her new book, E does, that many people's feelings are undifferentiated and have to be forced into some pattern, whether it suits their owners or not; and sexual love is the usual pattern for feeling.[143]

national security. In August 1963 Stephen Ward, a society osteopath who lived on the Clivedon estate, committed suicide after being prosecuted for living on the immoral earnings of prostitution. The British press and public were consumed by the Profumo affair throughout the summer of 1963.

142 [*Sic*] for Ewelme, a village south-east of Oxford.

143 Another sex scandal of 1963 was the divorce of the Duke and Duchess of Argyll. The Duke had found in their Mayfair flat her incriminating diaries, a Polaroid camera, and photos of the Duchess, naked but for her pearls, performing sex acts with a man or men whose heads were not in the frame. The identity of the 'headless

White Lodge, Saturday, 20th July 1963

My darling . . . Oh my heavens yes, are weekends not exhausting! I think it's the concentrated sociability. I'm now in favour of staying with people either for one night or for 5 or 6 days – if one is there for a longer term (longer than a weekend, I mean) one's hosts occasionally allow one to slip through their clutches for an hour or two, if only because they are already becoming slightly bored with one. I know I definitely am becoming less and less sociable; that is less fond of conversing. In fact I really like everything to be highly concentrated: a dinner party is most nearly my cup of tea. Not to speak of the joy of getting home after it: kicking one's shoes off, giving oneself one pre-bed drink which one can relax over . . .

I seem to pass from Jaguar to Jaguar (which illustrates what we were saying, here, one evening, about almost everybody one knows being so rich). Eddy has a Jaguar, Spencer has a Jaguar; the Vernons have, the Blacks (to whom I'm going for a week in August) have. Only my own family have Austens.[144] I had an Austen at B Court, if you remember.

Talking of family, though I suppose it is not sad, under the circumstances, Beatrice McNaughton [*sic*][145] dying, it is sad. I mean, any being gone is. Let me know (and though this sounds heartless I don't think it's heartless) whether she's left Sylvia any money, and how much.

This is to be Girl Friend Week for me . . .

[Ends]

men' was a source of much gossip and speculation, as well as judicial investigation. One rumour suggested the American actor Douglas Fairbanks Jr, and the other the then Minister of Defence, Duncan Sandys, the son-in-law of Winston Churchill. Both denied it. EB expressed her insight about the artifices of feeling in *The Little Girls* through her fictional Dinah (Part III Chapter 3).

144 [*Sic*] for Austin, EB being more accustomed to write about Jane Austen than about motor-cars.

145 Lady Macnaghten, Sylvia's maternal aunt.

28 July

The beautiful, fated and peculiar 'heroine' of Iris Murdoch's latest book *The Unicorn* reminds me of Urssie Grosvenor [Vernon]. It must be a coincidence. It isn't possible that E in talking to Iris about Urssie has started her imagination working in that direction.[146]

President Kennedy was assassinated on 22 November 1963. Nothing that Elizabeth wrote to Charles about this was preserved.

---

[146] Many people who knew Ursula Vernon shared CR's identification of her with Hannah in *The Unicorn* (1963), which is set in a notional Co Clare. Iris Murdoch first met Urssie at Bowen's Court in 1956.

1964

Tayibi, Jordan.[147] *Wednesday, 11th March, 1964*

My darling . . . We have been ceaselessly, ceaselessly, and very enjoyably on the move ever since I got out of the plane from Beirut at Jerusalem airport last Friday morning. (That very same morning, we started off to Petra.) When not in movement we are either looking at maps or sleeping.

Well, first about this house. It is most bizarre, as you may well imagine – but most likeable. Very new built – only (just) finished, I think – and actually it isn't apparently quite finished yet as masons are still energetically at work around it. Built and gorgeously furnished within about 5 weeks by a delightful Arab called Mr Jeriash. . . . The house bristles with balconies and loggias, which overhang a thundering view of the surrounding landscape. It is built of cut stone, the local rock, which is creamy-yellow. The architecture outside and in is modernissimo, 1927. (Not unlike some of those modernissimo not very high-class but agreeable villas one sees built

[147] Jean Black had taken a house in Jordan for three weeks. Eddy S-W, another of her guests, was said in De-la-Noye's biography to have visited Taybah, which exists, though EB wrote 'Tayibi' very clearly at the head of her letter.

by local characters in the South of Italy.) It (this house) is on the edge of a hill village, as it were Kildorrery and of about the same size. We, as the only non-locals, are the objects of ceaseless but I cannot tell you how courteous interest. Everything about Arab manners being impeccably beautiful is true, I must say. Nobody ever stares; they merely turn upon one a reflective gaze.

. . . All the rooms are differently painted in bright colours, on to which streams the very very very bright light from outdoors – the sky, and dazzling reflections from the rocks. This landscape is very rocky, and is also bright with scarlet anemones.

The furniture is partly Jazz, partly Arab-Jacobean, partly Arab-Regency. There was a sofa covered in very bright tight white satin in the living-room, but it rather got on our nerves so we moved it out into one of the upper halls, which I do hope won't hurt Mr Jeriash's feelings. The cook turns out to be Mr Jeriash's sister. There is also a very Biblical-looking but efficient housemaid. The cook does very good Arab cooking, all sort of delicacies wrapped up in cabbage leaves. We are drinking almost nothing but wine (the local) and I must say drinking a lot of that: hard liquor one somehow doesn't seem to want so much – which I have sometimes found to be the case in Italy.

But the key personality of this whole organization and set-up and regime is the famous Joseph – who I may tell you is in many ways very like Francis in The Little G.'s[148] (In fact, I have found myself calling him Francis more than once.) He has got the entire household, Mr Jeriash, Jean and me exactly where he wants us. Jean and he – except that she's in no other way like Dinah – have a very Dinah-Francis relationship. A ceaseless battle for power, and stormy quarrels, punctuated by thunderous sulks on one or the other side or sometimes both. But it is impossible to get the better of Joseph, in the long run, because he always proves to be right.

---

[148] Francis in *The Little Girls* is Dinah's Maltese houseboy.

Officially he is the driver. He lives in the house and is with us constantly, including meals. This I must say I enjoy, because the comedy is ceaseless. If Jean and I start talking between ourselves he either relapses into Hamlet-like gloom or interrupts us by loud, imperious shouts. At the same time, he is fundamentally well-behaved, never impertinent. Myself I don't think he knows whether he's on his head or his heels, so his equilibrium is surprising. At one moment he is addressed as 'My sweet', or 'Duckie', at the next he is being bawled at as an inefficient employee. She calls him 'Zou-zou.' I said, that sounds like Colette, and she said, 'Zou-zou is the Arab for Joseph.' I said, 'I thought Yusef was the Arab for Joseph,' and she said, 'No, Zou-zou is the real Arab for Joseph.' So there you are.

I've never seen Jean happier, handsomer or more thoroughly in her element. I am devoted to her, I must say, and am having a roaring time in her company. She and I are both very childish characters. In a way, this time here is being like an additional chapter to The Little Girls. I mean, our vocabulary and our recreations and our mental level seem to be about the same (as those of the Little G.'s, I mean). And if one likes doing the sort of things we are doing, one could not have a better country to do them in . . .
[Ends]

White Lodge, Friday, 29th May 1964, morning
Dearest – I'm just waiting for your telegram with the Rome address. . . . This time last week we were drifting up and down Hythe High Street, before taking off to Dover. That dear White Cliffs Hotel . . .

Such happiness is impossible to imagine. I mean, nothing one could imagine in one's wildest moments could have been as perfect as this was in reality. The feeling of reality, or of what we both call naturalness, is what beats the band. I mean, that's what happens when we're together, quite together. In places which take on a phantasmagoric beauty when we are there – but also are dear and what one might call comely in themselves. It's as though the soul of a place came to the surface and came to meet us.

I am living in such a suffusion of happiness, still. Are you: I hope you are? It went without saying, so I didn't say it, how I dreaded that drive back from the airport with your side of the car empty beside me, and, still more, coming back at the end of the drive into this house in which you were not.

But you were here. White Lodge was full of that wonderful evening light. I mixed myself a VERY strong drink, settled myself lying on the red sofa and picked up the Leslie Hartley novel.[149] Then, what do you think? In 10 minutes I was fast, dead asleep. Pole-axed. Only woke up again at midnight. I suppose actually it was nothing more mystical than a pass-out; that drink had been so very strong.

I worried as I drove away from the airport in case the bar there wouldn't be open at that early hour? But I think L[ondon] Airport keeps bar hours of its own? You know, I was glad that we so suddenly got there: no time for the feeling of parting to creep over us. Out you had to jump, to look for a porter, and on I had to drive, because of the traffic pressure, and that was that. I do think suddenness is better.

On the return drive, as I passed the place where there'd been that accident, I was passed by an ambulance taking that poor dead man away. (He was dead, I'm sure.) Do you know, the glimpse of him lying there, covered by a sack gave me a feeling that someone else had been paying the price for our perfect happiness. I said a prayer for him, did you. It seemed the least one could do.

. . . But the great thing, my dear love, is, be very happy in Rome. And you will think of me there, won't you. Bless you for your dearness and everything that you are, and everything that we have, you beloved Charles. Your E.

---

[149] Probably L.P. Hartley's *The Brickfield*, just published.

Bruree House, Co Limerick. 6th June 1964
My darling – your letter from Rome which I loved arrived today . . .

Oh but my love, I have felt so low and lonely. So bereft. I am made listless by this longing for you and awful missing of you. It was true what I said in my last letter, that White Lodge remained full of the happiness we had had. But the inverse of that is, that even that tears my heart.

And the moment I emerge from White Lodge into Oxford itself – when you've gone, I mean, I am overcome by a 'weary, flat, stale and unprofitable'[150] feeling. The fact is, I cannot go on living there (Oxford) perpetually. You do agree that?[151] . . .

I'm so glad you had a good time with *The Death of the Heart.* Yes I do really enjoy parts of it, I must say. Though particularly, as you can see, the seaside part. One might think – I was thinking – that Eva Trout[152] was going to be a *D of the H* situation over again. But in a queer way it's the reverse, (or inverse?) Everything turned upside down, so that the weights shift. One might say like a sand-glass reversed, so that the sand is flowing the other way. You'll see what I mean. When not thinking about you, I think about Eva Trout.

What would I do (I mean, under the circumstances) if I were not a writer? I simply can't think. Writing (I hate to say, 'my writing') is more than a compensation for not being with you: it's become an extension of us, a part of us.

While here, I'm going to be working on the new Nativity Play, to be performed in Limerick Cathedral this coming Christmas. In fact I must start that now.

---

[150] From Hamlet's soliloquy 'O that this too too solid flesh would melt . . .' Act I, Scene 2.

[151] EB's old Oxford friends, at the height of their careers, were busy, important and involved in the university world to which she did not belong, nor wish to. She decided to move to Hythe on the Kent coast, where she had taken Charles on his recent visit, where she had lived with her mother as a child, and where part of *The Death of the Heart* was set.

[152] The new novel which she had begun to draft.

I wonder how you feel, back in Washington? All my love. Your E. Oh those days we had, those lovely days. I keep on living in them.

Fairyfield, Kinsale. Tuesday, 12th August 1964
My darling . . .

Oh why is it so long still till November? I am beginning to feel run-down, you know.

I had a good surveyor's report (I mean, a satisfactory one) on the house at Hythe. I can't wait to get back to Hythe (early Sept.) and see my new home again[153] . . . Your E.

Scatorish,[154] Bennettsbridge, Co Kilkenny. Monday, 24th August 1964
Yes, beloved . . . It's nice to be writing to you with your envelope still, as it were, in my hand, freshly opened. Oh I do wonder how your 4-hour, starting at 5.30 a.m. journey with Lady Bird Johnson[155] went, my love. I laughed most heartlessly at the idea because you made it sound so comic – but what an outing, really!! . . .

I was sad to leave Urssie, who was rather distraught: she'd just come back from a 48-hour dash to England, to see dear old Mrs Cooper[156] who, smashed into bits by a traffic accident, is still lying there (nearly 7 weeks after the accident) semi-conscious and doped in a Nottingham hospital. She can only die of this, sooner or later, but there's a hope of bringing her back to Ireland before she does. The unfortunate Urssie then spent the remainder of her time

---

[153] The house EB found in Hythe was a small, modern, red-brick box called Wayside on Church Hill, which is a steep footpath, with some steps. The house faces the church and churchyard and has views from the back over Romney Marsh. The price, £4,700, was more than covered by the sale of some of her papers to the Humanities Research Center at the University of Texas at Austin.

[154] Home of Noreen and Gilbert Butler

[155] Lady Bird Johnson was the 'First Lady,' wife of President Lyndon B. Johnson, who succeeded President Kennedy. The purpose of CR's dawn journey with her is unrecorded.

[156] Possibly an old family retainer [?]

visiting a cousin of hers called Nell who has had most of her limbs broken, and her face smashed up, in a smash in, I think the Cotswolds. And on top of it all, Ursula missed her plane home to Shannon. However, an official at London Airport, overcome by her despair and beauty, managed to squeeze her on to another plane.

While she was away those 2 famous Dublin painters, Patrick Hennessy and H. Robertson Craig[157] came to Bruree to entertain Stephen. (Ernest von W[edel] is away.) I wrote away at the Nativity play, they painted, and we all played cards in the evening . . . [Ends]

Port Hall, [Lifford,] Co.Donegal. Sunday, 30th August 1964
Dearest love . . .

Well it is great fun here, in this noble home, with a wide river[158] flowing blandly and shiningly past the house . . .

Inside, the house is sumptuous and beautiful. All done by Tony Marreco himself, apparently.[159] First he had his Brazilean [*sic*] wife Regina, and now his present one, Anne.[160] And here Loelia[161]

---

157 Patrick Hennessy (1915-1980) and Henry Robertson Craig (1916-1984). Hennessy painted the formal portrait of EB at Bowen's Court previously noted, now in the Crawford Art Gallery, Cork.

158 The river Froyle.

159 Anthony Marreco (1915-2006), barrister and junior counsel at the post-war Nuremberg Trials, co-founder of Amnesty International. He was associated with publishers Weidenfeld & Nicolson, and bankers S.G. Warburg. A colourful figure and a serial heart-breaker, he inherited a small fortune, with which he bought – and embellished – Port Hall from his much older lover, Lali Horstmann.

160 Marreco's first wife was Lady Ursula Manners, a niece of Lady Diana Cooper. He also had a long liaison with the French writer Louise de Vilmorin, a former mistress of Lady Diana's husband Duff Cooper (later Lord Norwich). Marreco's second marriage, from 1955 to 1961, was to the Brazilian Regina de Souza Coelho. Anne, his third wife, whom he married in 1961, had previously been married to Lord Ebury, to Rennie Hoare, and to Lt. Col. Frederick Wignall.

161 Loelia, Duchess of Westminster (1902-1993), another of Marreco's long-term conquests, divorced by the 2nd Duke of Westminster in 1947, was a stepmother of Lady Ursula (Grosvenor) Vernon, though born in the same year.

rather tormentedly comes to stay. I look at this face, Tony's, which launched a thousand ships, with great interest. To me he's so very like a non-crippled, non-homosexual version of Stephen Vernon. In many ways strikingly like, even the voice. And the same strong opinions. He's a very nice creature and easy-to-get-on-with host, very conversible. I can't imagine him starting a fatal passion, but fortunately 'chacun à son goût'. Anne is a great gossip and a friendly and entertaining woman; I like her very much and am enjoying myself. She and Tony are both veterans: he is her 4th husband and as far as I can make out she is his 4th wife.[162] Which is probably why they get on so well.

Do you know I am looking forward to getting home again, because do you realise I've been galumphing about country-house visiting for literally the last two months: first America, then all round Ireland. In a way I am cut out for this sort of thing (it's in the blood, I suppose, as all the Anglo-Irish adore paying 'rounds of visits') but in a way not. It will be quite a peculiar sensation to be once again in my own surroundings. And I am longing to get on with Eva Trout.

And I am longing, as I told you, to dash over for a day or two to Hythe . . .

Goodbye for now, oh my darling; goodbye for now. You will write soon. All my love. Your E.

White Lodge, 15th September 1964
My darling . . .

Hythe was lovely; the weather was golden and the sun blazed. I kept thinking of you at every turn, and thinking, 'Now how soon will Charles and I both be here?' Toddy [woman friend] and I stayed at the White Hart, which is a tremendous home from home. Nice

---

[162] Anne was only Marreco's third (legal) wife. He did marry a fourth time, when in 2004 he re-married his second wife, Regina.

sunny bar, open from 10 a.m, and filled from then on (or at least on a Saturday morning) with happy natives of both sexes boozing away. Oh I do like a town where people enjoy themselves, instead of rushing about with tense faces furrowed by self-importance.

Well I saw again my dear house (for the first time after that one fleeting view on the strength of which I bought it). I like it better than ever; in fact I love it. I think you will. There's a charm to me in its smallness; which isn't claustrophobic smallness, because the rooms – so few – are of pleasing size. And I think you'll like your room, looking out into the distance over the Marsh. It will be able to be a comfortably big room – that is, compared to your little ship's cabin here – with an armchair and a writing table and things; so you'll always feel you can get away from it all. The garden outside the French window of the living room is a mass of flowers. There's something slightly weird about the whole set-up, but weird I do think in an endearing and cosy way. It's a completely new house, did I tell you? Built 1962. But it seems to me to have no vulgarities (or any very slight ones there at present are I shall be able to remove). It's comfortably modern, without straining in any way to be 'contemporary'. Not a bit suggestive of 'gracious living', but lending itself to what I've liked best from childhood: ease and a kind of prettiness and endearingness. At the same time I DON'T really think it's at all gemütlich[163] . . .

Toddy leaves the day after tomorrow, Thursday; and on that same day Marshall arrives . . . I can't quite imagine being under the same roof with him for 10 days or a fortnight. However, I do want him to be happy, the dear boy. But oh how I want you, Charles. I do so painfully miss you. Nothing, without you, seems to have full meaning. All my love Your E.

---

[163] German for cosy, homelike, a word implying, for EB, something twee and claustrophobic.

White Lodge, Tuesday, 29th September 1964

Dearest – I got your letter, about the trip with Mike and the President,[164] yesterday morning. It was fascinating to hear about; you gave the 'feel' of the whole thing, and those two men, completely. I'm so particularly glad you felt so in touch with Mike, so much back into your friendship for each other, as it had been. You know, outside and apart from love (as you and I know it and understand it) how extraordinary one's relations with people (I mean particular individuals, one's friends) are. I mean, I suppose a friendship has something in common with a love affair? What one would describe as the ups and downs – and advancing and receding. Of course that can only be so when there's a professional relationship as well: I mean, when the 2 people concerned are also colleagues

In the 23 years since I've know you (it is 23 years) I've been so fascinated by your relationships with Mike, also with Norman; also, when he was here on earth, with Hume.[165]

I'm miserable that I forgot your birthday. I do remember it about 2 out of every 3 years. (Whereas, I don't think you even know when mine is!) All the early part of September I kept thinking, 'The 23rd is my beloved's birthday.' But ever since Marshall's been in the house I have been absolutely demented . . .

I do think he enjoyed himself and for quite a bit of the time he was very pleasant company; a dear nice affectionate and rather touching creature. He has great powers of appreciation (beauty, etc). And considering he's never stayed with anybody before (as far as I can make out) he did very well. But he also, the poor young creature, [has] a sort of Caliban side which comes up at intervals – brash, smug. The awful thing is, being with him has (sometimes) made me see for the first time how and why people can hate Jews. A sort of crassness? In fact more than that, a sort of hell-bent stupidity.

---

[164] Lyndon B. Johnson

[165] Hume Wrong died in 1954.

God forgive me for saying so, but he's so greedy. Feeding him became a nightmare; it was like entertaining a cormorant. I got so fed up with him perpetually pluming himself on drinking so little. If I had really got to the point of a nervous breakdown, or of psychoanalytical frankness, I'd have cried out, 'For God's sake, can't you realise how much less trouble you would be if you drank more and ate less? and, how much less unattractive?'

Oh I am a pig writing about him like this, particularly this very day when he's just gone. And he can, I repeat, be so quick-witted, so adaptable, so affectionately prévenant and understanding.

. . . I love you so much. Your E.

White Lodge, Thursday, 22nd October 1964
Dearest . . .

Yes, Rome was lovely. It always tears my heart having to leave (we had one more night there after leaving Florence) but I now learn to console myself by the conviction that I'll come back (as far as one can be certain of anything in this life). I think it's one of the few places I am thoroughly happy in for its own sake (Hythe is another, and long may it be so). But also I enjoyed being with Audrey.[166]

She says I am the most energetic person she knows. Am I the most energetic person you know? Hardly I should think . . .

The evening I got back from Rome I went to a large and rather gay dinner party given by the Berlins, at All Souls. I was in high spirits and really rather enjoyed myself. Not having seen any of the people for 3 months (except the Berlins, who were here in September) made it quite nice seeing them again. The Cecils, Iris Murdoch and John Bayley, John Sparrow, Maurice [Bowra] etc.

Next Sunday I'm going out to Ann Fleming's, at her house in

---

[166] EB had been in Rome and Florence with her cousin Audrey Fiennes.

the country, the one we went to. Driving Maurice back into Oxford in the evening and having dinner with him. David's book *Max*[167] comes out here on November 5th, and is having a coming-out party at the Café Royal (a haunt of Max's apparently) on November 4th. David's given me an advance copy of the book and I'm halfway through it: he's done a brilliant job and a fascinating one, I think, on it – considering the unpromisingness of the subject. Not that I don't like Max, but it was hard to see how there could be much to say about him when he'd already said so much about himself.

. . . Also do think Iris's new novel *The Italian Girl*[168] is good: to me, one of her best, luridly improbable though the scenes are. There's a scene where the 'I' of the story makes a pass at his niece.

Talking of nieces, is Elizabeth back at Oxford?

. . . The people move out of my Hythe house at the end of this month, so I shall be going to Hythe as soon as I can in early November to see what's to be done, and who can best do it. I don't think I'll have anything actually put in hand till January, when I get back from Ireland after Christmas. But I do want things put in hand then, as I want the house to be completely 'into existence' when you come in Spring.

I must say I am longing to see it empty, and 'at last my own', with the former people (nice though they were) and their furniture all gone out of it.

. . . My darling, I am definitely coming over to New York on November 18th, a Wednesday. For just over two weeks. Will you in so far as it is possible think out your life during then? I will not – as ever – make a single plan till I've heard from you.

Oh you beloved. Life will begin again. All my love – Your E.

---

[167] Biography of Max Beerbohm by David Cecil.
[168] Iris Murdoch

White Lodge, Sunday, 31st October 1964

My dearest . . .

I seem to have had a very mouvementé week, one way and another, though have also spent hours and hours with Eva Trout . . . I'm now beginning to feel, 'But I can tell Charles all that, when I see him.' . . . My love, there is so much to say. There never seems to have been more to say. Though I must say there is never nothing to say, is there (to use a famous EB double negative). O it has been such a ghastly long time since July.

A dead-still white fog is wrapping up this house. I am writing this up in my top room – can just see some bronzy branches of a tree, like a ghost, appearing through the fog. Some people are supposed to be coming up (from Oxford) for a drink: I wonder whether there is the slightest hope (fog) that they won't come? I feel very torpid, very.

. . . This time tomorrow, I shall be walking about in my Hythe house, looking about. I do hope there won't be a fog at Hythe, so's I can't see anything.

Oh my darling, drink to our little Hythe home!

I love you. I live for two weeks hence. Your E.

Bruree, Friday, 11th December 1964

Dearest . . .

The Nativity play (first performance last night) is most beautifully done, really beautifully. I couldn't be more happy about it. Oh I do WISH you were here – so does everyone else. . . . And the play, besides being I think both a spectacular and poetic and really in a gentle way a quite religious performance, has come into being in an atmosphere of extreme amity, I'm glad to tell you. A succession inevitably of nerve-storms caused by crises and emergencies, but no bad blood. As I told you, I'd been afraid of arriving here and finding the play has occasioned 'feelings'. On the contrary. In fact the breach, or at least non-affection, between Bruree and Creagh Castle seems to have been healed by it; a great relief to me. Jean [Black] and Stephen [Vernon], who once were almost non-speakers, are now au mieux. Acting and/or play-promoting seems to bring out either the best or the worst in people; and thank God in this case it seems to have been the former. God must be with us . . .

Jean is a wonderful 1st Narrator; and her opposite number, Man, 2nd Narrator, a young man called Harry (hitherto unknown) is in his way as good. The BVM[169] is a keen hunting girl called Virginia Goodbody, and we live in terror that she will break her nose. Off a horse, she is very gentle and sweet, anything but tough, with a shy, haunting quality and great dark rather fey eyes – very much my idea of the youthful Mary. The Archangel is being played by Joseph, the Italian chauffeur, a young Roman – Ernst von Wedel said he would rather be stage-manager, and is doing very well as that. I think he felt he has too many enemies in Co Limerick (<u>all</u> of whom are attending the play) to stand up and play the Archangel in front of them.

'Every hunt in Ireland will be among the audience,' I was told. I must say, I think this extremely funny.

What fun doing a play, holy or otherwise, is, isn't it. And what oceans of drink one consumes. The only bother about a cathedral is, one – naturally and properly – can't smoke. I am sleeping, here, in that big room with the triple-sized bed and cherry-and-white striped satin sofa. In the dressing room with the connecting door is sleeping Hedli MacNeice,[170] the poet's widow, that great prima donna, who is leading the [Limerick] cathedral choir, singing descants, etc. and some solos. She has now – just now – come in and is practicing her singing exercises – <u>most</u> weird. I find this a trifle distracting, so think I'll stop and take refuge downstairs . . .

---

[169] Blessed Virgin Mary

[170] Hedli Anderson (1907-1990), singer and actor, married the poet Louis MacNeice in 1942. They separated in 1960. He died in 1963.

(The singing exercises are getting louder and wilder.) Goodbye for now, you dearest Beloved one. Your E.

Fairyfield, Kinsale, Co. Cork. 22nd December 1964

Dearest. . . .

The Nativity Play rolled to its triumphant close, on Saturday 12th evening – everybody in tears, including the bishop and the organist. I can't tell you how beautiful it was, or how I longed for you to be there. It ended (as only possible in Ireland) with a still very holy but thoroughly drunken party, a sort of agape,[171] at the Intercontinental Hotel, Limerick. What was interesting was that a very great number of RC's were among the audience, on those 3 evenings. They crowded in, taking advantage of the Pope's having lifted the ban against going into Protestant churches. There was also, as promised, a large representation from the hack-on-regardless Limerick Hunt, and various other hunts.[172]

You know how I shall be thinking of you at Christmas. I hope the Smellies[173] won't be trying . . .

I'll think about you particularly when I'm in church at Christmas. God bless you, you dearest beautiful dear. All my love. Your E.

---

[171] Love-feast (Greek)

[172] EB's *Nativity Play* was included in the posthumously published volume *Pictures and Conversations: Chapters of an Autobiography* compiled and edited by Spencer Curtis Brown (1975). There was another performance at Christmas 1970 in the Protestant cathedral in Derry, Northern Ireland, with Anglicans, Catholics, and Presbyterians all taking part – probably the first fully ecumenical event in living memory in that fiercely sectarian place.

[173] Sylvia's brother Peter and her sister-in-law Fran.

1965

White Hart, Hythe. Wednesday, 10th February 1965

My darling – a week today since my last sight of you in Washington airport – and so very few days since the last time I heard your voice, in New York on that telephone, Saturday morning. I'm still in a state of suspension, of nowhereness; I suppose a feeling of being nowhere because we're not still together . . .

I cannot forget any moment of that weekend in New York we had, that beautiful spell of the cold, that particularly lovely Plaza room and the outlook, everything that we said and did in our world of nearness-together and stillness and love. It's extraordinary how New York creates itself around us; into cloud-capped palaces, into something which vanishes when you are not there (with me). Only, unlike Prospero's cloud-capped palaces it does leave a wrack behind,[174] something always to be felt, afterwards, when I am in New York alone, and haunts me. Dear dear one, I do love you so much.

---

[174] Prospero in *The Tempest*, Act IV, Scene 1: 'The cloud-capped towers, the gorgeous palaces,/ The solemn temples, the great globe itself,/ Yea, all what it inherit shall dissolve,/ . . . and leave not a rack behind.'

I was opposite the Plaza that last Saturday morning before I left New York, wandering about in that wonderful toyshop looking for a present for a child, Andrea Mezvinsky,[175] she had already given me a handsome valentine card, on her own initiative, apparently. I finally settled for rather a fascinating box of tricks called 'Valentine lively pets' – all sorts of bugs, birds and smaller vermin such as white mice, all of which could be wound up or made to flap or peck or whir or rush madly about 'by friction'. They sat in a sinister group on a heart-shaped lace-frilled tray, which fitted inside a large red-and-white striped Valentine box. I hear the child is crazy about them, as I hoped. She will torture her highly strung parents with them, I'm quite sure.

The days in Washington were very very happy too, weren't they. Our lunches together; and in a different way, our party-evenings. I love being in your home. Thank you.

Hythe is very sweet even in February. I do like all the townspeople, they all seem to become one's friends. And all the ilex trees (there are so many) give the hillside and town a sort of cozy darkness. I arranged today with a Hythe furniture-remover to come and collect my stuff at White Lodge on March 4th, and move it into Carbery,[176] Church Hill, on March 5th. Having fixed a date gives me an excellent stick to beat the builders and decorators with and make them hurry up. I am longing to begin to reside here, and get on with Eva Trout here, in peace and quiet . . .

All my love, dear beloved. Your E.

---

[175] Daughter of Shirley Mezvinsky, whose novel *The Edge* was published that year. Mezvinsky (b. 1936) is also well-known as the award-winning playwright Shirley Lauro. The 'wonderful toyshop' is FAO Schwartz, 767, 5th Ave.

[176] EB changed the name of her house in Hythe from Wayside to Carbery, after Castle Carbery in Co Kildare, Ireland, a long-lost family property on EB's mother's side.

White Hart, Hythe, Saturday, 6th March 1965
Dearest . . .

When I telegraph you my Carbery address, saying also to write there from then on, I shall send you the telephone number also, as it would be lovely to hear your voice in our new home. Not that I don't want always, wherever I am, to hear your voice. It seems now too long since I have. To telephone me at the White Hart wouldn't be much good, as they have only one wee telephone booth down in the hall, which echoes with voices from the bar.

The departure of the furniture (such as I am taking) from White Lodge took place very dramatically last Thursday afternoon in the twilight of a furious, almost North-American blizzard. The Hythe van which came to fetch it had been on the roads since 6 a.m. I thought it very brave of the 2 men of Kent to take off again, that same evening. And I had then to dash over to here on a series of late and belated chaotic snowbound trains in order to meet the furniture at Carbery, here, Hythe, at 9.30 the following morning. It was a quite mediaevally awful night, full of primitive experiences.

So now the furniture and the packing-cases of 'effects', books, etc, are sitting dumped in dear little Carbery, with 5 or 6 workmen, decorators, etc, seething around them. I can't think why Carbery is taking so long – one would think I was totally redecorating and partially re-modelling Chatsworth.[177]

I see this whole place, and the house, in terms of you and me, and our life. Nothing else. I do think, too, that it will be an easier place for me to make out in and be happy (or at any rate not unhappy) in, in small ways, than Oxford was.

I am so glad to be out of Oxford. You know how glad. And yet, why? Look how nice everybody has been . . .

Beloved, your end-of-February letter that I found here, about your feeling of restlessness, and more, exacerbation with the

---

[177] The great house of the Dukes of Devonshire, in Derbyshire.

Washington existence has haunted me very much. As though you were consuming yourself. It has got me into a frenzy about not being with you, a frenzy which is latent in me all the time. I cannot resign myself to this inevitable feeling of wastedness because we are not together . . .

Write again soon, my darling. All my love. Your E.

Carbery, Church Hill, Hythe, Kent. Sunday, 28th March 1965

My darling – I was so happy to have your letter (as my telegram said). I had got into a sort of an out-of-contact 'state' about you. I don't think it really had, probably, been so long since you had written, but my ideas of time lately had been so confused, and I became panic-stricken . . .

I am so glad you are getting these journeys and engagements over to clear May. What are Sylvia's plans (for that month) by the way? You will be sure and see that she has some, won't you.

Oh Charles, what pressure you have been living at. What is going on about Vietnam.[178] Ideas of the subject on this side of the water are most confused: a queer blend of apathy and suspicion – mostly the former, except for the Left of the Labour party. It sounds as if the US were being so idiotic, but I suppose they're not, or not absolutely? Your Government isn't enthusiastic, is it – that must be difficult for you? . . .

Talking of time, it has only just dawned on me that this day week I shall be in the Middle East with Jean Black. The angelic Jean has been making all the arrangements – tickets, reservations, visas etc – so I have been drifting along in a placid dream . . .

---

[178] The US had been vainly trying to build up South Vietnam as a barrier against the spread of Communism in S-E Asia. Heavy US bombing of North Vietnam in February 1965 was followed by the landing of US marines in March, and of 125,000 American servicemen in August. This was the commencement of the 15-year Vietnam War, to which both Canada and the UK refused to send troops in support of the USA.

Lucky as I am to be going, I LONG to stay here. I can't tell you what happiness it is to be in this house at last. To wake up in my room in the mornings and see the sun rising behind the church and long misty shadows cast over the graves. To hear the masses of birds singing. I am writing this letter in YOUR room. Darling love, I think you will be happy here and like it, in this new home of ours. It makes me – and I hope you – feel so unclaustrophobic and free as air. Workmen are still in the downstairs room, pasting on the gold wallpaper with the horses; I haven't yet been able to unpack and arrange all my poor books . . .

I constantly think of you, miss you and imagine us together again. Your E.

St George Hotel, Jerusalem. Sunday, April 11th 1965

My darling . . .

Well, it's exactly a week, this Sunday morning, since Jean and I arrived here, and not yet (you will be surprised to hear) have I had an opportunity to set pen to paper – even a picture postcard. It's been like whirling about with an enormous dynamo, bless her great handsome cheerful heart. We dashed down to Petra for 2 nights and rushed up and down rocks. It is so dreamlike, zooming along that Desert Road, to and from Petra, hour after hour, in the queer glassy haze that the desert light is. We saw all sorts of fauna and flora, including a number of buzzards, a superb golden eagle, which had been having a doze by the side of the road but took off and soared majestically away into the distances of the sky; and a great white eagle. At Petra there was a lizard the size of a small crocodile. And in many parts of the country around here there are great pools of black irises. And there are all sorts of heavenly bright burning-blue flowers. (The scarlet anemones are over.)

Among other things, we are house-hunting, as Jean is set on buying a house in this locality. And we have now tracked down the most enchanting little house in Bethlehem (of all places) which I think she <u>will</u> probably buy . . .

We had a gay journey out; night in Beirut. What a great ostentation-and-squalour city it is, but with a fascination in its own way. This hotel, the St George,[179] is a great success. Very charming and pretty rooms (seldom have I slept in a prettier one than mine, in any hotel) with wide views: it's quite in the middle of (modern) Jerusalem, but surprisingly quiet: nothing but church bells, cocks crowing, and a roar from an occasional donkey . . .

Must stop. Jean sends LOTS of love, and to tell you we are having a spiffing time, and that it's high time you stopped being pompous in Washington and came here too.

Oh, I love you so much. Your E.

NO time to read this through: forgive its nonsense.

Carbery [?June] 1965[180]

Fragment: EB has visited for the first time the house in Broadstairs on the Kent coast not far from Hythe where Charles Dickens wrote Bleak House.

. . . a really very vulgar but enchanting stone house on a low promontory overhanging the sea. . . . As I told you, I am deep in *David Copperfield.* It has given me an almost terrifying illumination about my own writing. Here really are the roots of so many things I have felt, or perhaps my way of feeling things and seeing them.

Bushey Lodge, Firle, Lewes, Sussex. Sunday, 12th July 1965

Dearest love, this is just a line from the Connollys', where, as I told you I would be, I'm staying for the weekend on my way to Ireland . . .

---

179 Now the St George International, it had opened in 1965 as the first five-star hotel in Jerusalem just a month before EB's visit.

180 This is another of the letters which has survived only as an edited typed fragment provided by CR to VG for her biography of EB.

Eddy's sudden death was a shock.[181] I'd been going to stay with him for 2 days, tomorrow, on my way to the Vernons'. A postcard picture, from him, about meeting me at Cork airport on Monday 13th, had just arrived, and was lying on the table by the telephone, at Carbery, when his sister Diana rang up from Sevenoaks to tell me he had died in the middle of the night (at Cooleville) the night before. Asthma. I'd never realized anybody could die of that. He had sounded so cheerful, and, typically, had had a lunch party at Cooleville on what was to turn out to be the Sunday he died. Everybody is, apart from everything else, so surprised; because so often those very delicate people live so long, live to dance on almost all their friends' graves. The poor dear innocent creature; he wanted to live, so much.

A very cosy week-end here, surrounded by howling winds and lashing rain. In a comfortable house, which this is, this kind of day can be v enjoyable. Everybody stayed in bed till nearly lunch-time, we then came down and ate a wonderful lunch, and have all 4 of us now retired again, for the rest of the afternoon. The 4th is dear Maurice B.[182] Duncan Grant[183] came to lunch. Later on we are going out to drinks . . . Your E.

Fairyfield, Kinsale. 18th July 1965
Dearest . . .

Great sadness here (with the exception of the Vernons) about Eddy. I was met at Cork airport by Jean Black, looking most ravaged and distraught. And have had many, many accounts of the funeral

---

[181] Eddy Sackville-West (from 1962 the 5th Lord Sackville) died 4 July 1965.

[182] Maurice Bowra

[183] Duncan Grant (1885-1978), painter. Bisexual, he was the long-time companion of Vanessa Bell at Charleston, near Lewes in East Sussex, and father of her youngest child, Angelica. After Vanessa Bell died in 1961, he stayed on at Charleston until his own death.

at Clogheen. My own feeling is that his death was saddest of all for Eddy, who was having a good time and so much wanted to live. He died – in apparently mercifully few minutes of an extra violent attack of asthma which brought on a heart attack – at the end of a perfectly ordinary social Sunday. It's still quite hard to realise he is no longer there. I'll tell you everything else about this sad happening when I see you[184] . . .

Oh my darling, take care of yourself. I am rather badly suffering from shaken nerves. Suppose the news I had about Eddy had been about you.

I love you so much Your E.

Carbery, Hythe. 9th October 1965

Dearest love – it seems months since I last wrote to you – from Italy. You'll have had my telegram, I hope, explaining all my rushing to and fro. The whole thing – a hellish drive from here to Oxford (Headington) then back the same hellish road the next day, then dashing over to Ireland, then back, then to Oxford again, became too much for me and I packed up with the most revolting attack of flu: real classic flu, aching bones and everything. I am now up and about and quite out of danger (not that I ever was in it) so DO NOT WORRY. I just feel like rather an old fly crawling torpidly about on a hot wall. Point is given to this by the fact that we're having a golden October heat-wave.

Meanwhile, I've had the joy of that letter from you to here.

---

[184] It is unclear whether EB ever knew what there was to tell. According to Eddy S-W's biographer Michael De-la-Noye, Eddy returned from a holiday in the west of Ireland with his friend, Father Christopher Pemberton, on Sunday 3 July, and early the next morning went to Fr. Pemberton's bedroom suffering from an asthma attack and then locked himself in the lavatory. Fr. Pemberton put a ladder up outside, climbed in through the lavatory window, and found Eddy dead. Eddy's discreet and kindly friends in Ireland, according to De-la-Noye, put out 'a concocted version,' about Eddy dying from the asthma attack late the previous evening 'while listening to music.'

And a heavenly thing you sent (in a letter to Italy), that thing of Marguerite Young swooning over the 5-ton completed MS of *Miss MacIntosh My Darling.*[185] I never commented on, I don't think, but was fascinated by – particularly because, DON'T you remember, I became involved with that author M. Young, and 2 1/2 tons of the MS used to be in that small apartment on E16th St NY that I rented for the week-ends . . .

[*page missing*]

. . . I am living for the 30th of October. Oh Charles, I so love you

Your E.

Carbery, Hythe. 13th October 1965

Dearest – just to tell you that the Robertsons, Norman and Jetty, came here last Saturday and we had the most heavenly day: at least, I did, and I think they enjoyed themselves also – I thought it sweet of them to come, when they had so many things to fit in. Norman looks angelic but very changed (doesn't he?) by the illness: the whole proportions of his face seem to have altered – not that he looks shrunken or weazened-up or anything, indeed he is in a sense better-looking and even more distinguished-looking than he was. And he holds himself well. Simply that he's visually, physically a 'changed' man.[186] He seemed in good spirits and was, as ever, heaven to talk to and to hear talk. I love his love for you: he never expresses it, but a special warmth, almost tenderness, breathes from him when you come into the conversation.

And Jetty looking very handsome, and a dear. Thank you v much for giving them my address, which I gather you did.

It is now only 2 weeks and a few days till I see you.

---

[185] *Miss MacIntosh, My Darling,* the 1,198-page first and only novel by the visionary and eccentric poet Marguerite Young (1908-1995), was published in 1965.

[186] Norman Robertson, a heavy smoker, had a lung removed because of cancer.

I'm having a very happy time at Hythe, really appreciating this stretch here on my own, in what has been beautiful weather. I feel I am really settling in. This is how I hoped life at Hythe was going to be, and (touch wood) it's being it. I am making quite a number of fascinating chums, whom I must tell you about – in fact it's hardly worth while to write about them. There is more to Hythe than meets the eye. I am also getting to know some of the curiously fascinating hinterland country, and have been taken to some divine pubs (where one can eat, I mean) which you and I can enjoy, my love, when you come back again . . .

I am over my beastly attack of flu – quite over it. I don't mind telling you now that it is all over that I felt like death for about 2 days. I am now living on all sort of mysterious tonics and capsules to recover my strength. But as I say, I have already recovered it, really. All my love, my love. Your E.

There are no diaries of Charles Ritchie's in existence from December 1963 to October 1967. He wrote in Storm Signals *that he could not remember whether he had not kept any during this period, or whether they had been lost.*

His mother died in September 1965.

In July 1966 he went to Paris as Canadian Ambassador and Permanent Representative to NATO.

In May 1967 he was appointed Canadian High Commissioner to the United Kingdom. He and Sylvia now lived in London, at the High Commissioner's official residence, 12 Upper Brook Street, which required five servants to run; and his official car was, he said, 'the largest, most indecently ostentatious vehicle to be seen in London.'[187]

No letters from Elizabeth to Charles have survived between October 1965 and September 1969. She remained living in Hythe and continued to visit friends and go to Ireland. She would go up by train to meet Charles in London and, when he could, he went down to Hythe to see her.

---

[187] *Storm Signals: More Undiplomatic Diaries, 1962-1971*, Macmillan of Canada, 1983.

1967

29 October [London]

In the rainy morning I had gone into the Griffin [pub] in Villiers St, near to Charing Cross Station to meet E. It is perhaps to become our London equivalent of the Plaza Bar. We sat drinking, talking, and eating cold beef sandwiches. She looked and was extraordinarily young. She began to talk about the figures of Bloomsbury she had known in her youth: Virginia Woolf, the Stracheys, Duncan Grant. It was a sudden outbreak of her odd, brilliant, visual talk which has been muted lately; and it exhilarates. She made me see the ingrowingness of that little Bloomsbury world; their appalling habit of writing endless letters to each other, of analysing, betraying, mocking, envying each other, of the kind of amusement they had, and the kind of pains of jealousy and treachery which they inflicted on each other. She thinks that kind of intellectual, professional upper-middle-class of the Stracheys tends more to corruption than any other . . . She made me see Duncan Grant, his fascination, and said that at one point she could very well have done with him herself. She says that at eighty he is still alive and radiating charm.

E is approaching the last chapter of 'Eva Trout'. God knows how it will be received; her delight in it is catching. The people she now can't bear are those who nostalgically say to her, 'I did so love *The Death of the Heart*'.

2 November

E feels 'in despair because she sees me for such short times'.

Sylvia had broken a hip in a fall and was about to have an operation.

5 November

E struck a wrong note last night when I telephoned to tell her the news. She doubtless wishes that the injury was fatal. She didn't seem to grasp how stricken I was, and worse still began to reproach me for not asking her to the dinner I am having for the Adeanes.[188]

18 November

Drinks with E. She irritated me considerably by saying that I had not been a good relations official between her and Sylvia and should have told each that the other thought her charming. This coming from her was the last straw, but I said nothing with a great effort. But what is the good? Came home feeling that I loved no one, which is as bad or worse than no one loving me. E says that if I turn against her, she can easily stop living by smoking all the time and taking no care of herself. I see that she secretly worries about lungs. Turn against her! How agonising that would be for me.

20 November

I sympathise at the moment with E's anti-queer phase which was one of the precipitants of her new novel 'Eva Trout', now so nearly finished[189] . . . I have known E cross-grained, black-Irish, insolent, but never, never dull.

---

[188] Sir Michael Adeane was private secretary to the Queen.

[189] There are two definitely homosexual men in *Eva Trout*, plus two possibly homosexual men, and a deliberate ambiguity about sexual identity, both in women and men, throughout.

1968

7/8 May

Went down on the a.m. train to Hythe to spend the day with E. . . . We lunched in the hot sun at the hotel White Cliffs at Dover, where the glass-enclosed lounge looks at the esplanade to the equable blue Channel and the boats coming in and out. It has always been warm and sunny when we went together to Dover. We are always happy there, and always have Dover sole and Pouligny Montrachet and walk afterwards under the cliffs . . . We then drove back to Hythe, and I took to my bed in my upstairs room at Carbery and read . . .

I surfaced for drinks, and at once got talking as I only can to E. God knows what about. Youth movements, snobbery, gossip, religion. The time was good, but the fire which E had set herself to making did not come off. I broke down all reserves, which is what she wants so that we can be really together as before. She doesn't mind my silliness – likes it – but is never silly herself, so that one has [would have] a hangover of humiliation if one was small-minded enough; but it was generously enjoyable, like an orgy.

11 July

Dinner with E last night [in London]. An undercurrent of disturbance, an echo of past distress muffled by age and habit. We seem to be clinging frantically to joint happiness. And I talked and talked compulsively. Her stammer was very bad and she looked ill. Yet she is starting a new book and in the interval has two or three stories in mind, including one to be called 'Births, Marriages and Deaths'. Today we meet, or don't meet, strangely as in a dream of two people against an unlikely background – at the Royal Garden Party.

24 July

Dinner at Aperitif with E. The bar-tender remembered me from the days when I used to sit for hours on a high bar stool drinking martinis and waiting for Margery – cursing her for always being three-quarters of an hour late and in an accumulating rage which changed in a jiffy to pleasure and relief when her tall figure came through the door with a rush of modish Mayfairish excuses interlarded with darlings. I wish I could be back waiting for her now with the promise of a night ahead – a promise often unfulfilled.[190]

1 September [Hythe]

E was waiting for me at the station, at Folkestone. I heaved my suitcase, heavy with whisky and shoes, into the back of her car and off we drove to Hythe. I find her subdued in mood, and wonder if she is ill. Exhausted perhaps by her permanent cough. I seem to do all the talking. Do I ever give her a chance? The weather is sunless and cool with a wind that blows all the doors in this house.

[*Later, back in London*]

I was happy being with E, but am nagged by the fear that I bored her. Yet that is not the point. We are not after all social acquaintances. R[oley] sometimes bores me, but that doesn't prevent my loving him.

---

[190] An example of how CR adapted his diaries for publication: In *Storm Signals* this entry is dated 'July 30,' Margery appears (as elsewhere) as 'Margot,' and he supplemented the last half-sentence in the published version with more about Margot's sexual prevarications, and his minor role in her life.

7 December

Saturday, so up late and went to call for E at her flat in Markham Square[191] to take her to lunch. She had on a new olive green dress, which she had just bought at Harvey Nichols. We went to a new restaurant in the King's Road – Alvaro's,[192] was it? Cheerful, crowded and noisy – just the place for a grim December day, and then to the film about the mongoloid killer.[193] E came back and asked Sylvia to lunch at the Berkeley Buttery. The first time she has asked Sylvia to a meal in twenty years – during which I have been pressing her to do so. Finally she has hauled down the flag of defiance, and I am not sure that I am altogether pleased. She once told me that the day she came to like Syl would be the day she ceased to love me. Just as E was leaving, the hall door 'opened to admit' Anne and John Maher. I had not remembered they were coming; but I am sure E thinks that I concealed from her that they had been invited, as she thinks I prevent her from meeting Anne. As it was they met only for a moment. I was so pleased to see Anne.[194]

18 December

Perhaps the great mistake of my life – the Real Divide – was my decision to accept the Bonn Embassy. It did something to me that time in Germany . . . I went there partly, or principally, because of E to be near her, but it was poison to our love – or nearly so. Also it was deadly attrition of my ability. Syl is at this moment 'depressed', a state she rarely admits to. Instead of trying to amuse and distract her, here I am scribbling away self-centredly. The debit

---

[191] In order to have a London base, EB was renting a flat in Markham Square, Chelsea, at the top of the house of Gladys Calthrop, Noel Coward's set and costume designer.

[192] An 'in' place favoured by trendy Sixties youth.

[193] The Boulting Brothers' ill-judged and controversial *Twisted Nerve* (1968) starring Hayley Mills and Hywel Bennett.

[194] The old girlfriend with whom CR never lost touch.

side of my marriage is a heavy one, and almost all the entries[195] put me in the red. What have I had? Complete loyalty, originally love, always affection, endless accommodation to me, congenial understanding, and amusing companionship; and how irreplaceable is this addition. How irreplaceable is she to me. And what has she had in return? Well, quite a lot. But the score won't come out. If I had put more into my marriage – more in every way, including sexually – would that have made it better, I wonder? Isn't this present basis the one which she wants and knows that I want, or was there a time when we were first married in Paris when I could have made a real breakthrough with her? But there was always E and there was always the World of Fashion! I have had years of happiness and affection with her; something beyond that we never quite touched, except as a glimpse . . . But no I never wanted more and neither, I think, did she. Besides, our brand of married happiness doesn't show up in a diary.

24 December

Reading E's letters written to me when we were in love – or should I say it in a different way? When she was different and so I suppose was I. Such letters. They make me awed and sad. I had that and it is gone, but its ghost, thank God, remains to haunt me till I die. If anything lasts till one dies . . .

---

[195] CR was reading through his old diaries

1969

24 January

Went down in the train from Charing Cross to Hythe for the day. There was E waiting at the central station, Folkestone. God, how will it be if I must outlive her? We walked on the leas at Folkestone under the grain of the cliffs and went back to her house, Carbery, for dinner. She showed me the outline of her new book 'Pictures and Conversation'[s].[196] Yesterday was the London birthday of *Eva Trout* and the reviews are just beginning to come out. Already she is at work on the new book. In it she asks the question 'Is writing allied to witchcraft?' I am very happy with her and drink a lot of 1949 Nuits St Georges and wait burgundy-filled in the dark night in little Sandling[197] station for the London train to come in.

---

[196] This was planned as a writer's autobiography – a non-linear, selective one. The title was adapted from the first page of *Alice in Wonderland.* The completed sections, and her notes towards further chapters, were the main content of *Pictures and Conversations: Chapters of an Autobiography,* edited by Spencer Curtis Brown (1975), which also includes other work.

[197] The fast trains to London went from Folkestone. Slow trains called at Sandling, closer to Hythe, which had no station.

23 March

E says, 'He [André Durand[198]] has made you into a pink pig – get him out of the house, him and the portrait.'

18 April

I thought briefly of the day that E and I walked down that road by the park lined with flowering cherry trees. How many years ago was that? It was during the war when I stayed with her in Clarence Terrace. I was recovering from flu and it was my first day out. It must have been the same time in April as today, because the fruit trees lining the road were just in bloom. She will be back tomorrow from Italy, and I will spend next weekend with her in Hythe.

8 May

Dinner with E at the Jardin des Gourmets. We swam on a lake of Burgundy and walked in the first summer night round the flowering trees in the garden at Markham Square. The ghost of our love accompanying us everywhere.

2 June

Tomorrow I dine with E. I see her so sporadically. It's the only way, but aren't we drifting apart more than if the Atlantic separated us? Being in the same country but not together makes the change explicit.

28 June

I went down in the train to Hythe to spend the day with E . . . E is starting her book. Her 'free association' anti-memoirs; but had a

---

[198] André Durand, Canadian artist, graduated from l'École des Beaux Arts in Montreal in 1964. He paints romantic portraits often with mythological or fantastical elements. When he arrived in the UK in 1969, CR fostered his career by introducing him to eminent subjects for portraiture. His portrait of CR was relatively austere, and CR thought it made him look like a banker.

sudden wish to start a novel with the title 'O Richard', the beginning of a quotation from *Richard II.*[199] She starts her anti-memoirs (which sound very much like memoirs to me) with her Anglo-Irish relations who, coming to this country, 'wormed their way into the interstices of English society' and exercised power, as she herself has done.[200]

We had tongue and Cumberland sauce for lunch. She thinks nothing of my being awarded the CC,[201] because it doesn't carry a title. I told her I was too much of a snob to want a knighthood. It categorizes one . . . I told E about the PM[202] lunching here and his appearance. She said that in her childhood there were rubber balls with faces painted on them, and that Harold Wilson's face was like a face painted on a rubber ball. It was a very happy day and it was hard to leave her.

11 July

I had a drink with E at the Ritz. She has been drawn closer into the imbroglio[203] by having her portrait painted by André, and in a breath-taking volte-face finds him no longer repulsive and shows signs of taking a distinct fancy to him.[204]

13 July

E at the Ritz yesterday was talking about 'frenzy', saying that it was a peculiarly male thing; that Alan and I and every other man she

---

199 The Duke of York in Act II, Scene 1: 'O Richard! York is too far gone with grief . . .'

200 *Pictures and Conversations* actually begins with a description of the Kent coast, and with memories of the time she had lived there before, as a child, with her mother.

201 Companion of the Order of Canada

202 Labour Prime Minister Harold Wilson. The lunch was at the Ritchies' house, 12 Upper Brook Street.

203 André Durand was at this time involved with Elizabeth Ritchie.

204 Durand painted EB in the flat in Markham Square (see Note 177 above) wearing a multi-coloured summer dress. The portrait was commissioned by Elizabeth Ritchie, and in 1973 was accepted by the National Portrait Gallery in London, where it was exhibited in 1981 and again in the mid-1990s. It has been in store since 1997.

has known was subject to it. When men roll the whites of their eyes, tremble, and become beside themselves, what is a woman to do? It's frenzy, male frenzy.

14 September

E's departure was quite different from Elizabeth's.[205] A windy gusty day as we shambled up Bond Street through the ugly people crowding the narrow pavement to buy her a cornelian signet ring in a discreet jewelers. 'I want something solid to wear to remember you.' The parting was submerged, no easy – or difficult – tears, but Lord, what a sad, lachrymose entry this.

110 Stanworth Drive, Princeton.[206] *Saturday afternoon, 13th September 1969*

My dearest – well, here I am. A good journey, and I was to my great relief met at the airport: Stuart H[207] was there – fond as I am of him at any time, never have I been gladder to see him, or indeed anybody: the devil himself, even Harold Wilson would have been welcome . . .

Yesterday evening arriving in this house, I felt v like Eva Trout arriving in Cathay. (Could not find switches that turned anything on, for instance.) And like Eva relapsed into infantilism and ate a supper of milk and rusks (not actually Swiss roll)[208] though I must say this simple meal followed on 2 or 3 thundering strong drinks: bourbon on the rocks.

The house has that sort of inherent misused charm so many American houses do have. An L-shaped living-room with a number

---

[205] Elizabeth Ritchie

[206] EB was at Princeton to teach for a term on the Creative Writing Program.

[207] Stuart Hampshire was also teaching at Princeton.

[208] Cathay was the name of the large house on North Foreland in Kent that the eponymous Eva Trout takes to live in, on her own. Her first evening, literally unable to boil a kettle, she contentedly consumes a Swiss roll.

of large lamps. Furniture made of some sort of semi-polished red wood: not bad. 2 enormously long sofas facing each other across a grey-blue drugget; under the drugget a wood block floor – very well polished at the moment, but it soon won't be, unless I can find a slave.

Waking up this morning at 4 a.m., I came down at 5 a.m. and rearranged all the furniture – pulling out armchairs from their coy hiding places and folding up and pushing back against a wall an enormous dining table – the last thing I want! Everything now looks much more human, except for reproachful empty bookcases. Very empty. I only brought 6 books with me (one an Agatha Christie bought at Heathrow; though one of the others, I must say, Maurice Bowra's version of the Odes of Pindar). As time goes on I shall buy a lot of lovely American paperbacks; but even they won't go far towards filling these aching shelves . . .

If you were here . . .

I am fighting off a paralyzing feeling of loneliness for you. Which I suppose is why I write such a prosaic, domesticated letter. Oh my dearest dear one; oh dear Charles.

Your E.

ps. There was quite a lot of food, in fact masses, in this house, installed by kind friends. Also a well-stocked bar, on which I'm trying not to draw too heavily. I do feel what you call discombobulated. Am going out to dinner tonight.

Princeton University, Tuesday, 16th September 1969

Dearest . . .

I am writing this in my impressive office[209] (which is almost like a minor (very minor) imitation of yours). An enormous knee-hole

[209] At 185 Nassau Street

desk, of which I could not get a single one of the drawers to open; I rattled at all the handles and nearly cried, till someone came in and came to the rescue – one touches a sort of secret spring apparently, which operates them all. Apart from that, there are numbers of handsome armchairs, small tables, ashtrays, table-lamps etc. And again, of course, I'm surrounded by bookcases – all but empty.

. . . Yesterday I went to a Faculty meeting, which seemed to be in the nature of a convocation, or something. I could not understand one word that was said – why? – but was much interested studying the types . . .

Last night, at a preliminary meeting, I met the 8 undergraduates who are to be doing 'advanced' work with me. They seemed as mild as gazelles; and long may they remain so. That is, they showed no signs of Student Unrest;[210] indeed, the reverse. Their names (family names) are: Connell, Hyde,[211] Lamp, Monahan, Moore, Nelson, Tuller and Von Schilling.

. . . Dearest – Your E.

185 Nassau St., Princeton. Monday, 22nd September 1969

Beloved . . . You were angelic to write before you left. Today you'll be home again, I suppose. I hope Mr Wilson didn't intervene, that horror, between your Royal Mistress and you. I've been thinking about you so much, up there (Scotland) during this last week-end.[212]

---

[210] On university campuses in the USA and Europe there were demonstrations and protests, sometimes violent, against the Vietnam War and all repressive politics and policies.

[211] Thomas Hyde became her friend and protégé. They kept in touch after she left Princeton, she encouraged him to go on to Oxford (England) and furthered his application to New College; he visited her in Hythe. She also took him to Ireland to stay with the Vernons in Kinsale, and to see the empty site of Bowen's Court.

[212] The Ritchies and the Prime Minister, Harold Wilson, spent the weekend with the Royal family at Balmoral.

. . . Like dear Mrs Dancey,[213] I seem to be 'permanently exhausted'. Don't be alarmed, though, my darling: I feel quite well.

I've been out to some rather nice little dinners. Some of the houses are very 'taking' and agreeable. Princeton has got a curious atmosphere (physical atmosphere, almost) I can't analyse it. Parts of it (Princeton) are, as Stuart Hampshire says 'very Surrey'[214] and then all at once, round a corner, one comes on a foetid area of decay – broken fences, for apparently no reason at all. Much the coziest part is the Coloured quarter, through which I take a zigzag route in the mornings walking to work – heaved-up pavements, heavily tree-shaded, very gaily-painted balconied small houses with trellis arches in the gardens and flowery flower-pots swinging from the porches. Everybody (in that region) seems to be having a good time, brightly-clad, bumping about in bright pastel-coloured motor-cars.

Then (some distance away) there's the tremendously bien portion of Princeton, all sweeps and lawns. Really, individually many of the houses in that are delightful: if one saw just one, one would think, 'Oh, just my dream home!' But unfortunately there's a plethora of them . . . It was just the same in parts of Washington, I expect?

The most amusing couple I've wined-and-dined with so far are a pair of boys: Ed Cone, a composer (v well known, I believe) and his heart's delight a v saturnine philosopher called George.[215] George wears his hair in a bang over his brows and squints at one round it: he only looks about 22, but must I suppose, as he's been a practicing philosopher for some time, be more.

. . . Oh my love, dear love, write again soon – Your E.

---

[213] Mrs Dancey in *Eva Trout.*

[214] i.e., comfortably and prosperously suburban.

[215] Edward Cone (1917-2004) was composer, author, professor of music at Princeton, and a generous benefactor of the university. George Pitcher, the Princeton philosopher, was his partner for nearly half a century.

110 N. Stanworth Drive, Princeton. Sunday, 9th November 1969
My darling . . .

But I realise that all my goings-away, each weekend since I've seen you, have been dodging the blues. Yesterday, Saturday morning, before my guests from NY arrived, was really intolerable. A most beautiful (weather) repetition of the Saturday morning, 3 weeks back, on which I went to NY to meet you. I DARE not ask myself, how am I throwing away all these irrecoverable months. The moment I begin to think, it is unbearable.

The only time I feel all right here is when I am working. I mean, these undergraduates and what they are doing: it really is some good. Their entire egotism and sense of existence is involved in it. That I respect. Somebody during one of my weekends away asked me, perfectly reasonably, 'But don't you feel the generation-gap?' 'No, I don't' (and really cannot be bothered to ask myself whether they do) because – like Cyril C's statement that inside every fat man there is a thin man crying to get out[216] – I think there is a buried 20-year-old in most of us (certainly, you and me) and this operates with me when I look at these strange MSS, and face their authors.

But I tell you what is sending me off my head, and that's this Vietnam to-do. This second one (November) of these I do think hysterical Moratoriums.[217] This sounds a (to me) more or less artificial convulsion through this noble and should-be imperturbable university. Why cannot 'they' let these unfortunate youths alone and let them work? Really I do loathe American intellectuals. The whole place is infected by them, as yet another Moratorium approaches: they are like cockroaches. And the awful thing is, dear Stuart Hampshire, with his friends in the 'new American Left' is,

---

[216] 'Imprisoned in every fat man a thin man is wildly signalling to be let out': Cyril Connolly in *The Unquiet Grave: A Word Cycle by Palinurus* (1944).

[217] 'Moratoriums' were days organized by the peace movement when students and many others took to the streets to demand the withdrawal of US troops from Vietnam.

I know, responsible for bringing them in. Oh the boredom, the boredom, the BOREDOM of these perpetual demonstrations.

Give me Mr N's 'silent majority',[218] at any price. They are silent, at least.

. . . Marshall B came down here for the day, last Tuesday. It was a nice day. He now looks madly distinguished. He ended up by making a wonderful omelette in this house, for supper, before catching the bus back to NY . . .
[Ends]

Hunt's House,[219] *Sunday, 21st December 1969*
Well my dearest . . .

This will reach you too late to say A VERY HAPPY CHRISTMAS, but carry it over to NEW YEAR – and never have I looked forward to any January so much. As you can imagine.

Shall be sending you off a Greetings Telegram, with more in it than that kind are able to say, from Princeton tomorrow. And on that Day, Xmas, shall be thinking particularly of you, having again a London Christmas. Because when I think of that, I remember a particular London Christmas, during the war, you and me wandering into the Ritz, where a solitary child was wandering round and round an electrically-lit Christmas tree in that part of the Ritz where one usually has tea, I think under a dome?

. . . Do you remember Pom[220] as a child? He was my idea of an absolutely repulsive one. He has now grown up into a surprisingly good-looking and pleasing 17-year-old youth. I am surprised at him being so affectionate and kindly to me, because I used to be beastly

---

[218] On 3 November 1969 President Nixon addressed the nation, defending his policy in Vietnam and appealing for support from 'the great silent majority of my fellow Americans.'

[219] EB was spending Christmas with Catherine Collins, the widow of her American literary agent, Alan Collins.

[220] The Collins's younger son.

to him, at one time. I remember once when he was about 5, and I was left for a minute alone in a room [with] him, saying to him: 'Really you are the most horrible child I have ever met.' It's strange that he should bear me (apparently) no malice. Possibly he's forgotten? I have never forgotten anybody who snubbed me or showed me downright enmity in my childhood . . .

I must say some of the parties Catherine goes to, in the guilelessness of her heart, are pretty shocking. Bohemian. At one we went to yesterday evening, there was a lady dressed as a full-rig Toreador. She did not seem to be having a very good time. She was the highly-respected mother of 5 children; so what had got into her, I cannot say.

New York, the week in the Cosmopolitan Club, was funny. I mean, fun. It's a comfortable, old-nannyish atmosphere, as you probably know. Nice to come back into out of the cold; and NY was VERY cold. I saw many old friends, and succeeded in buying a quite nice coat. I also saw that film 'Z':[221] I wonder if it is in London? So many people told me one really had not lived till one had seen 'Z'. I found that a slight exaggeration. Still, very thrilling, all right . . .

. . . Immediately, I go, as I think I said, to Eudora Welty – 1119 Pinehurst St., Jackson, Mississippi, on the 26th Dec; and return here (I mean to my house in Princeton and my office address) on the evening of Sunday Jan. 4th. And there I shall be, till I leave for England.

Can this really be true? Oh dear love, I feel within so few weeks of coming alive again. I don't think I realized, at the time, that time CAN pass. But it has. Your E.

---

[221] The 1969 French-language thriller about the assassination of Greek politician Gregoris Lambrakis in 1963, directed by Constantin Costa-Gavros.

1970

185 Nassau St., Princeton. 5th January 1970

Dearest . . .

It was tremendous fun down there,[222] as ever. I hadn't been there for 10 years, but it was extraordinary how little everybody had changed. They are, of course, having a ghastly time with those do-gooding fiends, the Supreme Court, bullying them about de-segregation. I got the feeling that anything might happen, if the really UGLY element, down there, were to break out. However, Eudora had a wonderful New Year's Eve party, and we drank 1970 in with I cannot tell you how many bottles of Old Crow (that much favoured Tennessee bourbon). I must say those Southerners have got wonderful heads: drink flows down their charming throats in an ever-rolling stream, but one never sees anybody tiresomely drunk.

And now: well here I am back again at Princeton, with – how weird – less than a fortnight more of Princeton ahead of me.

Darling, WILL you – if you are strong enough to do so – give your brain to our plans. I told you mine (for coming back) but no

[222] In Jackson, Mississippi

comment from you, pas de réponse! (I suppose you do want to see me again?)

I shall fly by night, leaving New York in the evening of Thursday 15th Jan, and arriving Markham Square – I hope –
[*page or pages missing*]
All my love – your E. I shall be in P'ton from now on, till I leave on the 15th.

Charles Ritchie did not preserve for the eyes of others any more letters from Elizabeth Bowen after 5 January 1970.

Charles Ritchie's Diary, January 1970–December 1973 London

11 January
E comes back on Thurs from America and my 'double life' begins again.

29 January
Dined with E at the Etoile. She speaks of the 'Arctic circle' of all old age. She is fighting with 'unresigned despair' to escape it. When she says to me 'Are you still in love with me?' does she mean 'Am I still in love with you?' She says she has turned against her aesthetic and literary contemporaries – hates their physical flabbiness, their pot bellies and loose wrists and their sensitivities; feels 'ruthless' and wants ruthlessness.

7 February
Lunch with E on her return from Ireland[223] and felt sadly at a distance, although we talked and seemed as ever.

---

[223] This was the visit during which her Nativity Play was performed in the Protestant cathedral in Derry, Northern Ireland.

15 February

Spent the weekend with E at Hythe. Cold sunny weather, quite warm when you had been walking briskly up and down the sea front past the early Victorian seaside lodgings, past the 1920 bungalows (one of which, but which one I can never remember, is the seaside house in *The Death of the Heart*) . . . Then walking back past the now leafless trees of Ladies Walk (which are in dripping leaf when Karen and her lover walk there in *The House in Paris*) and so on up the hill to Carbery. E is everywhere. Never come back to Hythe when she is gone from there. She herself, however, does not join me in my walks. She says that neither of us ever stop talking and that when she talks as she walks the cold air catches in her throat and makes her cough. Now her mind is fixed on Ireland and going to live there. She will prowl round a little Regency terrace in Clontarf[224] and choose a house there, or somewhere like it, not too far from Dublin. She will stay in Hythe only so long as I stay in London. I say to her, 'I wonder if I am as indispensable to you as you are to me.' I come away disturbed by the happiness of being with her, but when we meet in London it is not the same.

25 February

Dined with E at Daphne's.[225] I talked in what I now feel was a tiresome way about death (my own) and she talked about going to Ireland to settle, which is now the project which most interests her. But I sense an underlying sadness or perhaps illness. I don't like that permanent cough.

14/15 March [Hythe]

E and I had lunch as usual in Folkestone, and then my after-lunch nap in the bedroom overlooking the church, and then rushing

---

[224] EB was probably talking about Marino Crescent. Clontarf is an inner suburb of Dublin, bordering Dublin Bay on the north side.

[225] Fashionable restaurant in Chelsea.

down to the sea for my solitary recce along the front. Back again along L[adies] Walk, over the bridge, up the hill to the church, and so right and left to Carbery's white gate and the key under the rock. Drinks and talks and dinner. Nothing ever goes wrong between us when I am on her ground in Hythe. All is natural. Different from our dinners in London restaurants. She has won the [James] Tait Black Memorial Prize for *Eva Trout* and is very pleased. She is starting on her new book 'Anti-Memoirs'. She says it must be done by 'free association' at a tremendous clip and with the aid of much drink. I came home from Sandling station completely happy and full of red wine.

At Easter 1970 Elizabeth went to the Vernons in Kinsale, where she had a severe bout of the bronchitis which was recurring at shorter and shorter intervals.

23 April

Lunch with E at Scott's[226] – smoked salmon and Puligny Montrachet. She says she is going to found an institution called Lovers Incorporated to provide lovers or platonic or romantic admirers for middle-aged wives. They will be disturbed or delighted to receive burning epistles of admiration from chaps who claim to have fallen in love with them at first sight.

10 May

I am off to Hythe with an uneasy heart. I shrink from leaving Syl now even for a day. And yet – I go – oh yes, I go.

At Hythe with E. She says she is happier in a different way now, than ever. The happiness of old age.[227] The day-to-day kind of sensuous pleasure in the visible world. She wants to go on living;

---

[226] Fish restaurant in Mount Street.

[227] EB was two months short of her seventy-first birthday.

and so do I, if I could be guilt-free, fear-free, and pain-free. Not much to ask!

21 May

Lunch with E, gorging at Tiberio's[228] and mulling over yesterday's party.[229] Walked back with her through St James's Park. It is a long time since I have walked in the park with her, as she says walking brings on her cough. We watched the pelicans and stood before that blazing forest of tulips and wallflowers of yellows and tawny reds and purples, pinks, mauves, all moving in the light wind. I fancied I saw word-pictures forming in her mind to describe these flowers as in her book 'Look, all those Roses'.[230]

E arrived [at the party] in an uncertain mood and took a violent hatred to her own portrait which hung upon the wall. She said that if I liked that portrait I could not like her. I can hardly quarrel with her as that is just how I felt about André's portrait of me.

20 October

Went to see E in her London eyrie above Gladys Calthrop [Markham Square]. She was wearing her new aubergine suit and was rightly pleased with it. Just back from Ireland where she had revisited B Court in a bus-load of Catholic nuns, priests and acolytes. The house she says is gone without a trace. The ground where it stood so smooth that she could only trace where the library was by the prunus tree that used to obscure the light in one of the windows. She says it's better gone than having it degraded.

---

228 Restaurant in Queen Street, Mayfair.

229 The party was for exhibition of André Durand's paintings hosted by CR in Durand's studio.

230 EB's short story 'Look at All Those Roses' was the title story of a volume published in 1941.

13 January [1971]

Had a drink at the Charing Cross Hotel with E. She worries me; there is a frailness about her appearance which is new to me and I can't think it is just my imagination. Do I have to live through her death. (How drear and sad my outlook is.)

Shortly after this, Elizabeth was in a nursing-home with pneumonia, and on her release stabbed her foot with a pruning-tool. The wound went septic and never healed properly.

In September 1971 Charles retired, and he and Sylvia returned to live in Ottawa, at 216 Metcalfe Street. He was appointed special adviser to the Privy Council of Canada on security matters.

In early 1972 Elizabeth stayed at the Bear Hotel in Woodstock for a couple of months to escape the damp sea-fogs of Hythe in winter. By the summer she had lost her voice. Telephoning became impossible. Charles came over and made her see a specialist, and lung cancer was diagnosed.

Elizabeth had a course of radium treatment at University College Hospital, and insisted she was getting better. She went up to London from Hythe from time to time, even though the train journey exhausted her.

For Christmas 1972, she went to the Vernons in Kinsale, but spent her days there in bed. On her return in the New Year of 1973 she went straight into University College Hospital in London. Her constant visitors were her cousin Audrey Fiennes, and Charles. He had come to England to be with Elizabeth for the last weeks of her life and visited her almost daily, bringing champagne.

She wrote a poem, which she gave to Charles:

I have forebodings of Thee. Time is going –
I fear for all that in Thy face I see.

The sky's aflame, intolerably glowing;
Silent I wait in love and agony

And in me thou dost awake a bold suspicion, –
Thy face will change from what it used to be.

How shall I fall! How sorrowful and lowly,
Unmastered all my mortal fantasy!

The sky's aflame. Draws near thy splendour holy,
But it is strange. Thy look will change on Thee.

Elizabeth Bowen died early in the morning of 22 February 1973.[231]

[231] Audrey Fiennes, the same day, registered the death of Elizabeth Dorothea Cole Cameron, maiden surname 'Bowen.' Under the heading 'Occupation,' Audrey had the Registrar enter 'Widow of Alan Charles Cameron' – and nothing at all about EB being a writer. EB might have understood and condoned Audrey's sense of priority.

CODA

On 28 February 1973, Charles Ritchie wrote, on a sheet of the headed writing-paper of the Travellers' Club in Pall Mall, London:

Now Prose endless prosey Prose to the last of my life – the Poetry gone. I am getting each day more and more letters about her. How wide she cast the net of her fascination. She is still about in the air around me and the fact that so many of her friends believe in the after-life combined with her own belief adds a new uncertain dimension to my own state. At the funeral, as they lowered her coffin into the grave under the dripping sky in the small churchyard at Farahy my face worked with choked sobs and I felt her calming hand on my shoulder and contained myself. The trouble is that I never know when one of these attacks of grief is coming on or what will trigger them off. For the rest it is an endless flat plain stretching ahead so far as I can see until the day I too die. I am bone-tired and bone-indifferent to my future. Of course I suppose the mechanics of living will take over. And it is less than a week since she died. What a subject for her pen the disturbance, the fissures when – the emotion released – by her death. All the attempts in letters and press notices to describe her do not improve on R[oley]'s description –

'She was a witch but a good witch.' There was some kind of witchcraft at work – and it's still operating. For how long?

8 May [London][232]

My longest get-together was with Ann Fleming. We talked about E. I only remember what I said, and that under her modish cleverness I caught a trace of human affection and regret for E. More than I can say for Diana [Cooper] who was jealous of her and who will say that I am becoming a bore on the subject. She had got it wrong and insisted that Alan died before I was married. The implication being that I had been free to marry E but had not done so. This is psychologically true. I doubt if I should have married her then, if she had been free; but it is chronologically false, as Alan died two to three years after my marriage.[233] I think however that Diana will hold to her version of events and may think I was lying to put a romantic gloss of lifelong devotion on the story.

24 May

Dinner with Curtis Brown. He talked about E all the time and thoroughly upset me. The more they talk about her, or I talk about her, the remoter she seems. I shall never mention her name again. I hate hearing about how he and the Butlers spent that weekend in OUR house in Hythe clearing things and boozing on the wine supplies. They found my letters to her and Noreen recognized my writing and said she would put them in a package and send them to me. This she has not done, perhaps she burned them. I hope so – and read them? What does it matter now?[234] She had left me five

---

[232] Written after a party.

[233] CR and Sylvia were married on 16 January 1948. Alan Cameron died on 26 August 1952.

[234] Noreen Butler did send his letters to EB back to him. It seems that he then destroyed them.

hundred pounds. Curtis Brown asked me if I would like anything from the house as a 'memento'. As if the house and everything in it has not been part of our two lives and many things I gave her, but that is not the point. It is the painful realization of how many lives she led and how many now claim her intimacy. Spencer CB was obviously enamoured of her – or to put it differently, under her spell. Now all her contrivances are revealed. She told him that she knew she was dying and yet till the end she pretended to me that she did not know. It was I now believe to spare my feelings. I do believe in her love for me. I do believe it and in mine for her.

31 May

Is Audrey right that E is 'undiscussable'? At the time I read her letter I thought that she was right – that talking about E in an intimate, gossipy, even critical way cheapened us and was a denigration of E. But I wonder. If she is never to be mentioned except in terms of an obituary tribute, then there is little more to be said; the tributes have been paid. On the other hand if she were alive, would I be talking about her in the free way I did to Audrey? Hardly.

E kept many of her friendships in 'watertight compartments'; now that she is dead, they are emerging from the compartments and the result is somehow disquieting. There is a sort of 'one-upmanship' among those who loved her to prove, if not how much they meant to her, at least how much she meant to them. This would be a good subject for her pen . . . Underlying all this is some jealousy. I do not for one moment doubt that E loved me more than any living creature. She talked to me freely about her other friends and brought most of them into my life. But she is not here to talk to me now and the others are. There is something slightly chilling about their knowingness. If I had had the title of 'Husband'.

11/12/13 June

Then on Tuesday I went down to stay with Spencer Curtis Brown in Suffolk. Between us we finished off a bottle of whisky after dinner and talked endlessly about E – endlessly, on my part foolishly. Our talk of her left me with the desolating feeling that she was a stranger to me. It had the same effect as when I try to talk about religion; I am left with the total lack of belief.

14 June

Syl and I walked and sat in Regent's Park. Just too early for the full explosion of the roses. Being there made it very simple. Whatever thought I have about E, whatever I say or write about her, I shall never see her again in this world or the next. Never, never, never. And she will never see the roses again, and she knew this when she wrote to me about 'the heart-breaking beauty of the roses at Kinsale'. She will never advance to me across the grass of Regent's Park at any time of day. She is gone from me forever.

4 July [Ottawa]

What should I do that I have done on arrival in every transatlantic migration for thirty years or more, send a cable to E, 'Arrived safely missing you terribly, love C.' And in a few days time there would be the airmail letter on the hall table with her writing on the envelope, already talking of plans for our next being together.

14 July

Things are no better because it is Saturday. In a drawer in a cupboard[235] are her letters. I am tempted, but I dare not read one. I am half-weeping walking in the streets. Is this delayed shock, or boredom, or despair?

---

[235] In the Ritchies' house in Ottawa.

Charles was reading his old diaries with a view to publishing a selection, with the editorial assistance of Ramsay Derry.

30 July

All this culminating in the cold-blooded mechanical way in which I sorted and read my diaries of E's death,[236] thinking, or not thinking, just acting as if they could be handled safely and filed away. But their impact was stunning. I am never to recover or cease to feel the absence and the pain till I cease feeling anything.

11 August [Chester, Nova Scotia]

A thunderstorm last night and cracking lightning bolts have done nothing to dispel the brooding swamp-like weather in which I walked the steaming empty streets to early church today. The Holy Communion service meant to me the last communion which E received in hospital and seemed to join us.

13 August

Reading old diaries and writing new ones in the same day is death on one's sense of equilibrium. Are today's Chester fir trees against an anxious mackerel sky any more the present than the roses in Regent's Park which drew E and me together there that fine day in 1941, which I smelled again in the pages of my war diary?

15 August

It is odd – 'an odd coincidence' – that the only book of E's in the Chester Library should be *The Heat of the Day* and that as I re-read my diaries of 1940-42, I should be re-reading her novel of those same years in wartime London – dedicated to me. The first, most obvious, surface conviction from reading this book is to be reminded with full force of the power and quality of her writing.

---

[236] These diaries are missing.

18 August

For me it[237] is filled with echoes, reflections (as from a mirror, or a mirror-lined room). Also of premonitions, backward questionings, unanswered, and now unanswerable guesses. It is the story of our love, with a flaw in it, or did she feel a flaw in me? This renewed communication with her through her books and letters is almost unbearable. She has been dead – how many months? – six. Not that it matters how many the months are. The loss has plenty of time to last and never heal while I have feeling left. She should have become old before she died (that would have made it easier), but she never did. Changed she was by illness, but old – no. This has been a slumberous Sunday of pale glare . . . I thought of Hythe, of walking beside the shingle there, and going back to our house where she was, and my heart jumped with pain like a hooked fish.

19 September [Ottawa]

E has provided an escape route for me from beyond the grave, as she did when she was alive. Spencer Brown has cabled asking me urgently (a cri de coeur) to come over to England to help with the preface he is writing to E's unpublished work.[238] Of course I shall go, and Syl says I should. I don't think it is really necessary, or that I can contribute anything of value. It is rather to hold his hand, as he feels so humble and insecure about doing the job. Also it is something, perhaps the last thing, that I can do for E. I am sure she would have done the same for me if the case had been altered.

25 September

I am rudderless without E.

---

[237] *The Heat of the Day.* Both it and *Eva Trout,* are dedicated 'To Charles Ritchie.'

[238] *Pictures and Conversations,* with a foreword by Spencer Curtis Brown. Published by Allen Lane, 1975.

28 October

It gave me a shock when Roger handed me a copy of *The Heat of the Day* with E's writing on the fly-leaf sending it to me with her love. I suppose I must have lent it to Elsie[239] all those years ago, and now it has come back. It seemed almost like a message from her. I see now how it is that people seek messages from their departed loved ones. A word reaching me from her today would mean more to me than anything in this world. But she didn't believe in such nonsense and neither do I.

11 November

It is the house in Hythe which appears with such desolating clearness to me. 'Our home', she always said, and so I felt. Are 'our' things still in it? Has it been emptied of the furniture and china and pictures? Has it reverted to what it was originally, a small red brick villa like a thousand others? Is the key still kept under the stone in the aperture of the front garden wall? How are her roses? Who will be driving their car in and out of the impossible angle of the garage entrance? Is her spirit still alive, or gone with her body and her voice?

15 December

In the course of describing the visit to the ranch hotel in California, I invented an episode. True it has a foundation in fact, but all the same it was fiction[240] . . . Oh why did I wait till I am nearly seventy to understand that fiction could be like telling an anecdote with exaggeration, 'embroidering' a tale based on something seen, heard, or experienced. Whereas when I sat myself down to write

---

[239] Roger Rowley was a younger cousin of both Charles and Sylvia. Elsie, Roger's mother, was Sylvia's aunt.

[240] See entry for 15 June 1945 in CR's *The Siren Years: Undiplomatic Diaries 1937-1945* (1974).

those unutterably feeble attempts at a novel or a short story, I thought I had to invent, to imagine, to construct something out of my head.

Each night for the last three nights I have dreamed of E. Each dream has been a variation of the same theme, alienation. Either in my dream I have in some way neglected or angered her or she has retreated from me, so that last [night] I dreamt that I stood facing a row of her books saying, 'Perhaps I can find her here since she eludes me and I elude her.'

19 December [New York]

Awoke in our old apartment in New York to a backwash of self-disgust that nearly knocked me out. I had . . . dined with Bill Koshland[241] to push my book. What it came to, as he knew even more clearly than I did, was that I was attempting to cash in on his affection and admiration for E to hook him on Knopf's publishing it, and he didn't play. He may be sentimental, but he is not silly. We talked about E and this I think is what disturbed me and what I cannot look in the face. These admirers of her give me this photograph of her like a photograph on a blurb of her book. They come between me and her.

I need to know again from her that I was her life. I would give anything I have to give to talk to her again, just for an hour. If she ever thought that she loved me more than I did her, she is revenged.

The End

[241] William A. Koshland, EB's editor and then chairman of Knopf, did not offer for *The Siren Years*. It was published by Macmillan, Canada, and then Macmillan in the UK.

INDEX

Note: Mentions of countries such as Canada, Ireland, England, Italy, Germany, and the United States, and of cities such as London, Dublin, Cork, Ottawa, Bonn, Paris, Rome, and New York, recurred so regularly in what EB and CR wrote that they have been omitted from the index. The same is true of small towns such as Hythe in Kent. Nor is there a specific entry for Bowen's Court. To note every reference to these and some other places would have overloaded the index with meaningless lists.

The lower case letter "n" following a page number indicates that the topic can be found in a footnote on that page. The number following "n" indicates the footnote number.